®

MW01102216

1979
Cars

CONSUMER GUIDE

Contents

Big Changes for '79

We've made a few changes in our *1979 Cars* issue this year, as you've probably already noticed if you're a regular reader of CONSUMER GUIDE Magazine's automotive reports.

A significant addition to our coverage this year is a special report on station wagons. As sedans and coupes continue to shrink, wagons are becoming the last resort of car buyers who have a lot of cargo to carry, large families to transport, or trailers to pull. Our detailed examination of wagons provides all the information you'll need about wagons of all sizes, from the smallest economy models to some of the largest cars on the road.

Another change in *1979 Cars* for 1979 is our arrangement of articles about the cars. Our table of

contents lists the cars in alphabetical order by make and model—not by size. The reason: the editors of CONSUMER GUIDE Magazine decided a while back that the traditional size categories —subcompact, compact, intermediate, full-size and others—used by the auto makers to position their products in the marketplace lost their value as a means of comparison when the industry-wide downsizing program began. Prior to downsizing, a car that was called a compact was recognizable as a compact because it was of a particular size and was priced to compete with other cars of similar dimensions. Now, however, some "compacts" are as large as "full-size" cars; others are as small as "subcompacts." The size classifications have pretty much lost their meaning.

For *1979 Cars*, we've abandoned the auto companies' size designations. To replace them, we have developed what we believe to be a much more useful method of determining a car's market niche and value.

The term used by an auto manufacturer to describe a car's size is no longer used by our test staff as the most important criterion in judging the car's value relative to other cars. Oh, we do occasionally refer to these terms in our articles simply because there is sometimes no better way to compare one car with others; however, in every test report we rate each car on its own merits first and foremost, and only once we've done that do we mention other cars we feel are comparable. And the cars we compare in a story do not always occupy what the car makers would call the same class. So, rather than making a statement such as, "This model is the best of the compacts in ride," we might say something like, "The ride of this car is comfortably soft and smooth."

We believe that the latter system of describing a car's test results is more applicable than the old system to the method buyers use in making a decision.

Another change has been made—this one in our Road Test Ratings Charts. These charts look like charts we've used in the past to summarize the results of our test drives. But this year, instead of rating all the cars of one size group together in a single chart, we have arranged the cars in alphabetical order.

The numbers a car was given in each test—from one to five points, five being the highest possible score—are totaled in the last column. You'll notice as you read down the last column that cars priced thousands of dollars apart can obtain an identical point total. This, of course, does not mean that we believe a tiny economy car as good a value in every way as a large luxury car simply because they both obtained a total score of, say, 30 points. The economy car may deliver top mileage; the luxury car may be best of all models tested in comfort. The totals are significant, however, in helping us to explain how we select a Best Buy car in each of the price ranges. Clearly, the CONSUMER GUIDE Magazine Best Buy is the car that obtained the highest total number of points in its price class—the best comparative dollar-for-dollar value.

Now that we've told you about the changes we've made, we want to assure you that the most important part of *1979 Cars* has not been altered. The unbiased, no-holds-barred kind of reporting you've come to expect from CONSUMER GUIDE Magazine is still very much in evidence. Our test staff continues to drive every car and rate them with your needs and your pocketbook in mind. Our exclusive price listings at the back of this year's *1979 Cars*, as in years past, provides you with an excellent bargaining tool when it comes time to dicker with the dealer.

Here then, are the cars of 1979—the good and the not-so-good.

Domestic Models

AMC Concord

The newest model in the Concord line is the richly appointed Limited. It is available in two-door and four-door sedans, and in station wagon styles.

We believe that this version of the Concord is a first-class job, equal in appearance and quality to any other compact car. AMC may have discovered a niche in the small-car market that the Big Three are unable to reach. GM, Ford and Chrysler put their high-line trim packages on large cars, and build the smaller models with less luxury. But AMC builds no big models, and that's why it can afford to upgrade the Concord's interior.

Concord is built on the same body as the old AMC Hornet. The name was changed in 1978, along with some exterior and interior styling, but the present body structure is the same one that AMC has had in production for a decade. The advantages and disadvantages of the old Hornet have been carried over into Concord.

Inside, woodgrain trim dominates the instrument panel, steering wheel and door panels. It is attractive. Controls and gauges are grouped well, and are easy to use.

Passenger accommodations in Concord, however, are not very good. The interior is far too small for three passengers to sit side by side. Rear headroom is tight too, more so in the two-door than in the four-door. Compared with the newer models in this class—Fairmont/Zephyr and the Aspen/Volare —Concord's interior room is below average. Furthermore, Concord's doors are comparatively small and the severe inward slant of the top of the body makes the process of getting in and out feel like an acrobatic exercise.

During our tests, we found interior sound levels of the Concord to be a bit higher than those of its competitors. At low and high speeds, the Concord interior is noisy. This is traceable mainly to the window seals and engine roar.

For all its problems, AMC does put excellent engines in its cars. We found that the 258 cubic-inch Six is the best compromise engine you can get in Concord. Its performance is adequate—no head-snapper off the line, but no slouch in highway driving—and it is almost as smooth and quiet in operation as a V8. It will go from 0 to 60 miles an hour in just about 15 seconds. That's about the best you can expect in a car of Concord's weight.

City driving conditions will result in mileage of about 16 mpg when Concord is equipped with the six-cylinder engine and automatic transmission. On the highway, the same engine will deliver about 21 mpg. The optional V8 engine substantially lowers mileage. For that reason, we do not recommend the bigger engine. For best economy, the 232 Six is recommended. It gets up to 26 mpg when used with manual transmission. However, the performance of this small Six is poor.

Concord is a proven design. It offers a power train that is reliable and durable. Yet, it looks to our test staff as though AMC's competition has passed it by. The Fairmont and Zephyr from Ford are better values than Concord. The car's claim of a high level of luxury trim is valid, but we think most buyers in the compact class are looking for practicality foremost. Concord's pleasing looks cannot hide its shortcomings.

AMC CONCORD
Test Model Specifications

Body type 4-door	Rear hiproom . . . . 53.6 in.
Overall length . . . . 186 in.	Engine type . . . . 6 in-line
Overall width . . . . 71 in.	Net hp @ rpm . . . . 120 @ 3600
Overall height . . . . 51.1 in.	Net torque @ rpm . . . . 210 @ 1800
Wheelbase . . . . 108 in.	Displacement . . . . 258 cu. in.
Turn diameter . . . . 34.9 ft.	Compression ratio 8.3:1
Tire size . . . . DR 78x14	Carburetion 2V
Curb weight . . . . 3015 lbs.	Transmission . . . . Automatic
Cargo space . . . . 11.4 cu. ft.	Axle ratio 2.53:1
Front headroom . . . . 38.1 in.	Acceleration 0-60 mph . . 15.0 sec.
Front legroom . . . . 40.8 in.	Brake stop 60-0 mph . . . . . 156 ft.
Front hiproom . . . . 54.4 in.	Fuel tank capacity . . . . 22 gal.
Rear headroom . . . . 37.5 in.	EPA city economy rating . . 17 mpg.
Rear legroom . . . . 36.1 in.	

AMC Pacer

Pacer is too heavy for its class, delivers relatively low fuel economy, and has a reputation for heating up inside like a hothouse when the outside temperature is high.

These problems are inherent in the car's unique styling. The use of extra-large windows gives Pacer a one-of-a-kind look, but also means that the car has a higher curb weight than its major competitors. It weighs in at 3000 pounds or more. That's a couple of hundred pounds more than imports in the compact class weight, and more than the Fairmont and Zephyr series. Generally, the heavier a car, the lower its fuel economy, the poorer its performance, or both. In Pacer's case, it's both. Pacer has never been known for performance. Equipped with the base six-cylinder engine, the two-door crawls from 0 to 60 miles an hour in over 21 seconds. With the bigger Six, which delivers about the same fuel economy and is now standard on the 1979 models, performance is a few seconds quicker. But even when equipped with the gas-guzzling 304 cubic-inch V8, which delivers only 14 to 16 mpg in city and highway driving, Pacer's acceleration is slower than that of most or all other cars of its size and type.

Of the two Pacer models, the base two-door and the station wagon, the wagon seems to be the better car. It offers added space. Furthermore, its less radical styling makes it a better used-car value than the two-door.

CONSUMER GUIDE Magazine's test staff drove a two-door, which was equipped with the six-cylinder engine and automatic transmission. The problems of poor fuel economy and substandard performance that plagued earlier Pacers are still part of the package. However, Pacer handles well and rides smoothly, thanks mostly to its very wide track. Front and rear axles have a track that is up to five inches wider than that of many of Pacer's competitors. As a result, Pacer is controllable in tight turns.

Visibility is excellent. Not only is there an extra expanse of glass all around, but the hood and body sides are low in relation to the passenger's position. That makes it easy to see straight ahead and to the sides. In addition, the low, short hood, a carry-over from the days when the car was slated to be equipped with a rotary engine, makes Pacer one of the best cars in the business in terms of forward visibility.

Pacer has a hatchback body that provides a great deal of cargo volume once the rear seat is folded down into the floor. Two catches hold the seat in place. They are sometimes balky, making it difficult to convert the rear section quickly.

Seating in the rear of the car is poor. The rear wheel wells intrude on hip room; the seat cushion is thin and offers little side support. Front room is more acceptable, thanks to the swept-back shape of the instrument panel.

AMC's Spirit is new for 1979, and Concord is marketed in Pacer's class. A company as small as AMC cannot afford to have two cars compete for the same buyers. Both Spirit and Concord appear to have much more sales potential than Pacer. So, if AMC begins importing the Renault 18 to this country, and that looks likely to happen by the end of this year, Pacer's place in the lineup will be precarious. AMC would be offering too many cars in an already crowded section of the market. The weakest, Pacer, would be the most likely to be dropped.

The competition from GM, Ford and Chrysler in the compact market will intensify in the next 18 months. Pacer will be a liability to AMC. Right now, the car is outclassed by Concord, Fairmont and Zephyr. We believe that fans of Pacer's unique looks should not allow styling to keep them from considering other cars in this size class. AMC's competitors are offering better fuel economy and better performance than Pacer can deliver.

AMC PACER
Test Model Specifications

Body type	2-door	Rear hiproom	42.2 in.
Overall length	172.7 in.	Engine type	6 in-line
Overall width	77 in.	Net hp @ rpm	120 @ 3600
Overall height	52.8 in.	Net torque @ rpm	210 @ 1800
Wheelbase	100 in.	Displacement	258 cu. in.
Turn diameter	37 ft.	Compression ratio	8.3:1
Tire size	DR 78x14	Carburetion	2 bbl.
Curb weight	3204 lbs.	Transmission	Automatic
Cargo space	32.2 cu. ft.	Axle ratio	2.53:1
Front headroom	38.4 in.	Acceleration 0-60 mph	17 sec.
Front legroom	40.7 in.	Brake stop 60-0 mph	172 ft.
Front hiproom	56 in.	Fuel tank capacity	21 gal.
Rear headroom	36.9 in.	EPA city economy rating	17 mpg.
Rear legroom	35 in.		

AMC Spirit

Spirit is AMC's newest line, but it is based on an old car, the Gremlin. That is good and bad. It's good because all of Spirit's basic functional parts have a proven history in the Gremlin, a car that had been in continuous production, with few major changes, for eight years. It's bad because many of the features that we found deficient on Gremlins are carried over into Spirit.

There are two Spirit bodies: a sedan that looks like the old Gremlin, and a fastback. The fastback is clearly the best-looking car in AMC's lineup. In addition to a fresh new look, the fastback has a hatch opening at the rear that solves one of Gremlin's biggest problems: poor cargo capacity. The hatch allows you to easily store more than 24 cubic feet of cargo. That's more volume than is offered by the big Lincolns and Cadillacs. The sedan model also has a large luggage area, but its high liftover makes loading difficult. All loads must be lifted high up over the rear panel, then dropped more than a foot to the load floor. Removal of loads is also awkward.

CONSUMER GUIDE Magazine selected the new

hatchback body style for test this year. The new car looks as good inside as it does outside. Bucket seats are standard. They are fairly comfortable, but offer little side support. We rate them slightly above the seats of the GM and Ford small cars in shape and support.

The rear seat of our test car was the optional split-bucket type. Half of it can be used as a seat while the other section is folded down to form an extra load floor. This is not an innovation: European cars and some recent domestic models have offered a similar layout. AMC's layout works very well. Skiers may find the system excellent. The only shortcoming is that two seats instead of just one must be lowered and raised each time the entire rear area is switched from passenger to cargo capacity and back again.

Our engine recommendation for Spirit is the optional 258 cubic-inch in-line Six that comes with a two-barrel carburetor. It offers the punch that most drivers need in traffic, and it is smoother and quieter than the base four-cylinder engine. AMC offers five engines for Spirit, including a big 304 V8. The 258 looks best to us for all-around driving. This engine, combined with automatic transmission, will deliver about 17 miles per gallon in city driving and as much as 23 mpg on the highway. That is poor for a car of Spirit's size—a car that must compete with Chevrolet's Chevette. For buyers interested in Spirit and who are willing to give up some performance to maximize economy, the Volkswagen-based 121 cubic-inch Four can be acceptable. It can deliver 20 mpg in city driving when used with automatic transmission, and about two more miles per gallon when used with the manual four-speed.

The styling of Spirit demonstrates AMC's desire to set the car apart from other subcompacts. The modern front styling features dual headlights. You can outfit the car with leather upholstery, and many of the convenience and comfort options that are found on high-priced cars. Spirit's interior is the dressiest of any car in its class.

AMC has improved the ride of the old Gremlin suspension. The choppiness has been smoothed out. As a result, Spirit's ride is one of the better ones of all small cars. The change is striking, because the old Gremlin was substandard in ride and inside comfort.

AMC has done an excellent job of upgrading its small-car line for 1979. We do not recommend it over the Horizon and Omni, or Chevette.

Another new model in the AMC line this year is the downsized AMX. This car is essentially the same as the Spirit hatchback. It comes equipped with the performance engine, and special exterior and interior trim to give the impression of performance. But this year's AMX is not in the same league with the performance-model Mustangs and Camaros. It should be considered no more than a dressed-up pretender.

AMC SPIRIT
Test Model Specifications

Body type	2-door	Rear hiproom	40.3 in.
Overall length	168.5 in.	Engine type	6 in-line
Overall width	71.1 in.	Net hp @ rpm	120 @ 3600
Overall height	51.6 in.	Net torque @ rpm	210 @ 1800
Wheelbase	96 in.	Displacement	258 cu. in.
Turn diameter	31.5 ft.	Compression ratio	8.3:1
Tire size	DR 70x14	Carburetion	2 bbl.
Curb weight	2850 lbs.	Transmission	Automatic
Cargo space	24.8 cu. ft.	Axle ratio	2.53:1
Front headroom	37.8 in.	Acceleration 0-60 mph	16.8 sec.
Front legroom	40.8 in.	Brake stop 60-0 mph	150 ft.
Front hiproom	54.3 in.	Fuel tank capacity	21 gal.
Rear headroom	33.5 in.	EPA city economy rating	17 mpg.
Rear legroom	27.7 in.		

Buick Century

Century was downsized dramatically for the 1978 model year. The automotive press gave Century high marks in everything from performance to handling to styling; yet the car-buying public shunned the smaller Century and sales lagged. Buick officials are hoping that resistance to the car's smaller dimensions is over and sales will once again climb.

The Century series comprises a four-door sedan, four-door wagon and a two-door coupe. The underpowered 196 cubic-inch V6 engine is still standard for all models except the wagon. Optional power plants are a 231 cubic-inch V6, 301 V8 and 305 V8.

Buick once again offers a Century Sport Turbo Coupe, which comes standard with the 231 cubic-inch turbocharged V6 power plant. This vehicle was CONSUMER GUIDE Magazine's test model this year. As a result of Buick's "free-breathing" refinements, horsepower of the turbo Six has jumped from 165 to 175. Equipped with the standard automatic transmission, our Turbo Coupe accelerated from 0 to 60 in under 12 seconds.

(When running for maximum acceleration, the transmission in our test car produced a loud thump as it shifted gears. We don't believe this interfered with performance, but it was annoying.)

Overall handling of the Turbo Coupe is exceptional, thanks to the use of an extra-firm suspension system. High-rated front and rear springs helped make our Turbo nimble. It passed all cornering tests with flying colors. Wide radial tires and front and rear stabilizer bars also seemed to help glue the car to the roadway.

Last year, we tested a four-door Century sedan and found the brakes to lock the rear wheels very quickly and thus reduce directional control during braking. This year, we found that the coupe version suffers the same affliction, especially when the brake pedal is depressed hard. Controlled stops from 60 miles an hour can be obtained in about 170 feet, but the driver has to be careful not to exert too much pedal pressure. Otherwise, the lock-up occurs and traction almost disappears.

Buick Century

Exterior modifications to this year's Century series are few. The Turbo Coupe, however, has been freshened up a bit by the addition of a front air dam and a rear spoiler. The front air dam enhances the car's look of performance. The rear spoiler, though, does little. It seems to us to be a carry-over from the '60s, when it was chic for performance cars to have a rear spoiler.

The spoiler seems unlikely to have any noticeable effect on the car's performance or handling. What it does is interfere with the already-limited visibility to the rear. Up front and to the sides, however, Century's visibility remains above average.

Even though the car has been downsized from what traditional Buick owners are accustomed to, the Century offers room enough for six adults in relative comfort.

Buick has shown in its Turbo Coupe that a turbo-charged engine can provide good performance and deliver good mileage. Not all turbos we've tested work this well.

BUICK CENTURY
Test Model Specifications

Body type 2-door	Rear hiproom . . . . 52.6 in.
Overall length . . . . 195.6 in.	Engine type . . . . . . 6-cylinder turbo
Overall width . . . . 72.2 in.	Net hp @ rpm . . . . . . 175 @ 4000
Overall height . . . . 53.3 in.	Net torque @ rpm . . . . 225 @ 2000
Wheelbase . . . . 108.1 in.	Displacement . . . . 231 cu. in.
Turn diameter . . . . 37.5 ft.	Compression ratio 8.0:1
Tire size P195/75R14	Carburetion . . . . 4 bbl.
Curb weight . . . . 3160 lbs.	Transmission . . . . Automatic
Cargo space . . . . 18.1 cu. ft.	Axle ratio 3.08:1
Front headroom . . . . 37.9 in.	Acceleration 0-60 mph . . 11.6 sec.
Front legroom . . . . 42.6 in.	Brake stop 60-0 mph . . . . . . 170 ft.
Front hiproom . . . . 51.2 in.	Fuel tank capacity . . . . . 17.5 gal.
Rear headroom . . . . 38.2 in.	EPA city economy rating . . 17 mpg.
Rear legroom . . . . 35.2 in.	

Buick LeSabre/ Electra

Buick's LeSabre was one of the first full-sized automobiles to be put through the General Motors downsizing process that first occurred back in 1977. All information points to the fact that 1979 is probably the last year that LeSabre and Electra will be offered in their current size. Since these two models are the largest offered by Buick, we think it reasonable to assume that the next step, possibly for 1980, will be a further reduction in size and a lightening of body and drive train components. This assumption seems to go hand in hand with the news that Buick probably will unveil its 350 cubic-inch V8 diesel power plant for 1980. The introduction of such an engine in the LeSabre and Electra line would certainly help to increase corporate fuel economy averages.

Both the Electra lineup and LeSabre lineup share a wheelbase of 118.9 inches. Both include two-door and four-door models. In addition, a station wagon is available in the LeSabre line.

There is little to distinguish the 1979 LeSabre from last year's model, besides trim, a new grille, and new taillights.

Our four-door test vehicle came with the top-of-the-line 350 cubic-inch V8 power plant that is rated to deliver 155 horsepower. Standard for all LeSabre models is a 231 cubic-inch V6. The other optional engine is a 301 V8. Overall performance of our 350 engine was not spectacular, and that's understandable when you consider the fact that the curb weight of our test car was almost 3600 pounds. In acceleration tests, the LeSabre moved from 0 to 60 miles an hour in about 13.5 seconds. We've tested a LeSabre equipped with the standard V6, and its 0 to 60 time was in excess of 20 seconds. The V6 is more economical, but is not a wise choice for buyers seeking any sort of performance. An optional turbo charging unit will once again be offered for the LeSabre Coupe.

CONSUMER GUIDE Magazine's test car averaged about 20.5 miles per gallon in combined city and highway driving.

Even though LeSabre is one of the largest cars in Buick's lineup, it is still a neat and trim automobile that handles well. During our tests, accelerated cornering was flat and true, and there was very little side-to-side sway when tight steering maneuvers were initiated. During braking tests, our car exhib-

Buick LeSabre

ited a tendency to dip radically in panic stops. Our LeSabre stopped safely from 60 mph in about 180 feet, which is well within acceptable limits.

Driver visibility is good. The nose of the car is not long enough to block the view of the roadway ahead or reduce the driver's feeling of control. The roofline is relatively flat all the way back to the rear window, so side vision is good. Pillars are angled in the rear corners and are thin enough to minimize blind spots. LeSabre's high roofline also provides plenty of headroom for front and rear passengers. Legroom is excellent for all occupants; seating is plush and tasteful. As plain as the basic car may look on the outside, the interior is plush, and is one of the strong selling points throughout the LeSabre line. So many comfort features are included as standard equipment that few are left to purchase as extras.

The LeSabre line will again include a "limited-edition" series of dress-up packages.

BUICK LESABRE
Test Model Specifications

Body type	4-door	Rear hiproom	55.2 in.
Overall length	218.2 in.	Engine type	V8
Overall width	77.2 in.	Net hp @ rpm	155 @ 3400
Overall height	55.7 in.	Net torque @ rpm	280 @ 1800
Wheelbase	118.9 in.	Displacement	350 cu. in.
Turn diameter	38.9 ft.	Compression ratio	8.0:1
Tire size	HR 78-15	Carburetion	4 bbl.
Curb weight	3592 lbs.	Transmission	Automatic
Cargo space	21.2 cu. ft.	Axle ratio	2.41:1
Front headroom	39.1 in.	Acceleration 0-60 mph	13.5 sec.
Front legroom	42.2 in.	Brake stop 60-0 mph	180 ft.
Front hiproom	55 in.	Fuel tank capacity	21 gal.
Rear headroom	39.5 in.	EPA city economy rating	15 mpg.
Rear legroom	39.5 in.		

Buick Regal

Available only as a two-door coupe, the 1979 Buick Regal comes standard with a 196 cubic-inch V6 engine. Optional power plants are a 231 V6, 301 V8, and a 305 V8 for California. The Regal Sport Coupe comes with the turbocharged 231 V6, which has a four-barrel carburetor.

In our tests last year, the turbo V6 performed like an eight-cylinder engine. Unfortunately, the similarities between the turbo and a V8 did not stop there: the turbo V6 slurped up gasoline like an Eight. Net savings in fuel when the turbo is chosen instead of a V8 are minimal. And when you consider the price premium you'd have to pay for the turbo, you may decide to opt for any one of the unturbo-charged power plants. CONSUMER GUIDE Magazine's test model this year was a Regal equipped with the unturbocharged 231 cubic-inch V6. What is newsworthy about this small power plant is the fact that this year it incorporates some technical modifications that Buick calls the "free-breathing" treatment. The engine has been given a new inlet manifold, cylinder head, exhaust manifolds, camshaft and two-barrel carburetor. The new carburetor is of the same design that was used on the turbo engines in 1978 Regals.

Free-breathing results in improved acceleration. Probably the biggest contributor to the overall improved efficiency is the redesigned cylinder head. The head uses enlarged inlet and exhaust ports that increase the flow of air and gases. And a new camshaft has been developed to work more efficiently with the new cylinder head. We found that all the new components work well together: the net gain is almost 15 horsepower.

Last year, the turbo Regal we tested accelerated from 0 to 60 miles an hour in 11.8 seconds. Our 1979 Regal equipped with the "free-breathing" refinements accelerated from 0 to 60 mph in 11.9 seconds. Considering all of the extra money you'd have to spend for the turbo version, we recommend the 231 V6 instead. The redesigned V6 provides plenty of power for almost every driving situation. And fuel economy is good. Our average of 22 miles per gallon this year is one mpg better than the mileage that the 1978 turbo delivered.

Our Regal's handling and ride were sure and smooth. Even though Regal is a large car, having a curb weight of 3100 pounds, its steering is agile enough to negotiate city traffic and tight parking spaces. The car's brakes worked well in our tests, bringing us from 60 mph to a stop in about 163 feet. Brake fade was minimal, even after six panic stops caused the brakes to become excessively hot.

The Regal for 1979 has a new interior design that looks luxurious. Seats are large and comfortable.

Legroom in front is good, and headroom in front and rear is more than adequate.

The new interior design may be more sporty-looking, but shortcuts seem to have been taken in sound-deadening insulation. The Regal we tested this year was noisier than our test car of 1978. We heard what we considered excessive noise for a car so luxurious: the sounds of the engine winding up to speed, shifting into the next lower gear and winding out again. We also heard wind whistle from two small openings under the dashboard. (We put an end to this noise by stuffing paper towels into the holes.)

Few options are available on the Regal series, since most appointments are standard. The Regal buyer does have many options when it comes to power plants, however. Now that we have tested the turbo V6 and the 231 V6 without turbocharger, we can advise buyers to select the non-turbo 231.

BUICK REGAL
Test Model Specifications

Body type	2-door	Rear hiproom	54.5 in.
Overall length	199.6 in.	Engine type	OHV V6
Overall width	72.2 in.	Net hp @ rpm	115 @ 3800
Overall height	53.4 in.	Net torque @ rpm	190 @ 2000
Wheelbase	108.1 in.	Displacement	231 cu. in.
Turn diameter	38.3 ft.	Compression ratio	8.2:1
Tire size	P205-70R14	Carburetion	2 bbl.
Curb weight	3100 lbs.	Transmission	Automatic
Cargo space	16.5 cu. ft.	Axle ratio	2.93:1
Front headroom	37.9 in.	Acceleration 0-60 mph	14 sec.
Front legroom	42.6 in.	Brake stop 60-0 mph	163 ft.
Front hiproom	51.6 in.	Fuel tank capacity	17.5 gal.
Rear headroom	38.1 in.	EPA city economy rating	19 mpg.
Rear legroom	36.4 in.		

Buick Riviera

First introduced back in 1963, Buick's Riviera took buyers of stylish performance cars by storm. Over the course of the past 16 years, Buick has tried to broaden the car's market. As a result, Riviera's original beauty and integrity were compromised. Riviera continued to sell well, but its popularity continually decreased.

Now it seems Riviera is poised to regain that lost popularity. The car is back in the spotlight, having been completely redesigned. The 1979 Riviera sports an entirely new body, and an entirely new front-wheel-drive chassis.

The Riviera Luxury Coupe is equipped with a 350-cubic-inch V8 engine; the sportier S-Type comes standard with a new four-barrel, turbo-charged 231 cubic-inch V6. The 350 will out-accelerate the turbo V6, but it uses more fuel. Also, the heavy V8 has a noticeable effect on the car's handling. The Riviera we tested this year was the sporty S-Type, equipped with the turbo. In our acceleration tests, the car ran from 0 to 60 miles an hour in under 12 seconds. Our car delivered 21mpg in combined city and highway driving.

This year, Riviera also has four-wheel independent suspension. This setup on the S-Type incorporates the use of stiffer shocks and springs along with large-diameter stabilizer bars front and rear. The results are impressive: Riviera corners flat and its ride is smooth. There is absolutely nothing harsh or abrupt about the suspension of the Riviera. An automatic leveling system adjusts the suspension to compensate for changes in the car's load.

The handling characteristics of the new Riviera are excellent. The front-wheel drive smoothly pulls the car through all maneuvers. In adverse weather—snow, ice, or rain—the Riviera remains stable and true. Torque steer is held to a minimum, even during quick acceleration from a stop. In addition, the car's power steering enables fast cornering with little loss of road feel. Even as the tires begin to squeal and break traction with the road surface, the driver remains in control and can easily straighten the vehicle out.

The power-assisted brakes enabled our test car to stop from 60 mph in approximately 175 feet, without locking up. In a panic-stop maneuver, the Riviera tracked straight.

Riviera and Buick's Regal share the turbo engine but it is mounted differently in each car. If the turbo unit were mounted high and to the side of the engine in the Riviera as it is in the Regal, the hood could not be closed. So Buick engineers decided to mount the turbo unit behind the engine in the Riviera and modify the exhaust system. The change was to the benefit of the Riviera: the engine now runs cool and has had a net gain of 15 horsepower. The Riviera turbo is rated to deliver 185 hp; the Regal puts out only 170.

Riviera's interior appointments are luxurious. Six-way power-adjustable seats allow for a comfortable driving position, and enables the driver to maximize visibility to the front and sides. Overall visibility has been greatly improved as a result of Riviera's new styling, but the large and obtrusive rear roof pillars create blind spots that become noticeable when changing lanes in traffic. Standard interior equipment in the Luxury Coupe and S-Type includes air conditioning, stereo radio, power antenna, electric door locks and side window defrosters.

Well insulated against road noise, Riviera is one of the quietest automobiles we have tested. The turbocharged models are noisier than those equipped with the standard engine, but the insulation throughout the car is so good that even this noise is hardly noticeable—even at high speeds.

Driver and passenger comfort are two of Riviera's best features. Rear legroom is 39.4 inches. This enables passengers of nearly any size to stretch out with comfort and ease.

Revamped, restyled and redesigned, Riviera for 1979 is a most enjoyable automobile.

BUICK RIVIERA
Test Model Specifications

Body type	2-door	Rear hiproom	55.9 in.
Overall length	206.2 in.	Engine type	Turbo V6
Overall width	70.4 in.	Net hp @ rpm	185 @ 4000
Overall height	54.3 in.	Net torque @ rpm	275 @ 2000
Wheelbase	114.0 in.	Displacement	231 cu. in.
Turn diameter	36.5 ft.	Compression ratio	8.0:1
Tire size	GR70-15 W/S	Carburetion	4 bbl.
Curb weight	3762 lbs.	Transmission	Automatic
Cargo space	17 cu. ft.	Axle ratio	2.93:1
Front headroom	37.9 in.	Acceleration 0-60 mph	11.8 sec.
Front legroom	42.8 in.	Brake stop 60-0 mph	174 ft.
Front hiproom	56.5 in.	Fuel tank capacity	20 gal.
Rear headroom	37.9 in.	EPA city economy rating	16 mpg.
Rear legroom	39.4 in.		

Buick Skyhawk

Buick's Skyhawk, like its cousins—Pontiac Sunbird, Chevrolet Monza and Oldsmobile Starfire—is going to have a rough year in competing against the brand-new Ford Mustang and Mercury Capri. Unlike the others, Skyhawk suffers further because it is available in only one body style, and only one engine is available to put into it. This "what you see is what you get" problem is hurting Skyhawk's sales.

However, what you get is a well-performing 231 cubic-inch V6 and a sporty 2+2 hatchback body. A choice of transmissions is available: Skyhawk comes standard with a four-speed manual; a five-speed manual and a three-speed automatic are offered as options. Our test Skyhawk was equipped with the automatic, which we feel complements the V6 nicely. In comparison to the four-speed, the automatic eats up a bit of low-end speed. However, the automatic compensates for this by squeezing three to four more miles out of a gallon of gas than the manuals do. Our test car accelerated from 0 to 60 in 15 seconds and delivered an average 22 miles per gallon. We consider the 231 an excellent choice for a car of this size and type. The four-cylinder engines available in Sunbird, Monza and Starfire tend to be too slow, and their V8s are gas hogs. The 231 provided us with an economical ride and plenty of power when needed.

On the road, Skyhawk handles itself respectably, more so than Monza; less so than Sunbird. Skyhawk's steering is quick, and its cornering abilities are above average. Our test drivers say they could easily maintain control in panic maneuvers, even at high speeds as the steering wheel was suddenly jerked. Our Skyhawk's brakes seemed to lose some of their grip, though, after a series of emergency stops. And because of the car's short wheelbase, road bumps come through to the passenger compartment, sometimes with real bone-jarring force.

Rear seating is substandard. The front seats provide adequate legroom, but they are placed deep in the car. Entering and exiting the Skyhawk is awkward. Cargo space is ample with the rear seat folded down: almost 28 cubic feet of volume. Since the rear seats are almost useless anyway, Skyhawk is best viewed as a two-seater with plenty of space behind the seats.

We found rearward visibility to be poor. The thick side posts and sloping roof create potentially dangerous blind spots. Passenger compartment noise in our Skyhawk was rated equal to that of the other GM makes in its class. Extreme noise problems became apparent only at higher speeds.

Styling changes in Skyhawk for 1979 consist of alterations in grille, taillights and trim. A new carburetor has given the 231 engine a slight increase in horsepower. Two new sporty packages are available as options this year. They include special paint, decals and mag-style wheels.

Skyhawk is a nice-looking car. Its power plant is a good one and can be serviced with ease. Skyhawk's fuel economy is acceptable, and the car's price is right. This otherwise-pleasing package is hurt, however, by an interior that is uncomfortable for all but the most limber individuals.

Mustang and Capri, two completely new designs, have been attracting a great deal of attention from automotive experts and car buyers alike. These two cars, which offer better interior accommodations than the Skyhawk and its cousins, are available in two body configurations, and can be equipped with a wide range of suspension and power train components, pose a very serious threat to Skyhawk.

BUICK SKYHAWK
Test Model Specifications

Body type	2-door	Rear hiproom	42.0 in.
Overall length	179.3 in.	Engine type	OHV V6
Overall width	65.4 in.	Net hp @ rpm	105 @ 3200
Overall height	50.2 in.	Net torque @ rpm	185 @ 2000
Wheelbase	97.0 in.	Displacement	231 cu. in.
Turn diameter	35.8 ft.	Compression ratio	8:1
Tire size	BR70-13	Carburetion	2 bbl.
Curb weight	2835 lbs.	Transmission	Automatic
Cargo space	27.8 cu. ft.*	Axle ratio	2.93:1
Front headroom	37.7 in.	Acceleration 0-60 mph	15 sec.
Front legroom	43.0 in.	Brake stop 60-0 mph	178 ft.
Front hiproom	47.5 in.	Fuel tank capacity	18.5 gal.
Rear headroom	35.3 in.	EPA city economy rating	19 mpg.
Rear legroom	29.6 in.		

*with seats folded down

Buick Skylark

It was a short year for the 1979 Buick Skylark. Buick dropped its compact line from production last November to start the changeover to the 1980 model, which will be introduced in April. The unusual timing results from the development of an unusual car, one that could set the standard for compacts of the future.

This report is unusual for CONSUMER GUIDE Magazine's *1979 Cars,* because our staff will not be able to test the new car until later this year; therefore, all the following comments are based on a very brief look at the new model and what few details we have been able to obtain. (For a fuller description of technical details, see the Chevrolet Nova article. Under the sheet metal, the two cars are identical.)

Buick will offer two body styles in the 1980 Skylark: a two-door and a four-door sedan. Both will have notchback styling, the same as the Oldsmobile compact. The Chevy and Pontiac versions will have a fastback body profile and hatch openings at the rear. The new Skylark will be 20 inches shorter than the 1979 models on the outside. However, General Motors officials say the new model will provide about the same amount of room for passengers and luggage as the '79 Skylark. The front-wheel-drive system can be credited with the feeling of interior roominess, since the car will not have a transmission hump or drive shaft tunnel.

The new car, weighing in at about 2400 pounds, will be much lighter than the '79 Skylark. That means there should be a big jump in fuel economy—five miles per gallon or more.

Cadillac
DeVille/Fleetwood

According to Cadillac spokesmen, the large, full-sized Cadillacs are the division's bread-and-butter models.

Riding a wheelbase of 121.5 inches and having an overall length of 221.2 inches, the De Villes and the Fleetwood Brougham are indeed among the last of the full-size luxury cars. They look over-weight and clumsy in a world of downsized automobiles.

The CONSUMER GUIDE Magazine test car was a Coupe de Ville equipped with the 425 cubic-inch V8 engine. The engine in our test car had electronic fuel injection. The standard power plant for the De Ville series is a 425 cubic-inch V8 without the fuel-injection system. (The standard engines feature an intake manifold with new exhaust gas recirculation riser tubes that is said to provide an improved mixing and therefore increase fuel economy.) The fuel-injection system in our test car worked well, making the engine very responsive.

Our Coupe de Ville, loaded with much equipment, weighed in at 4275 pounds. In our estimation, that is a lot of steel to haul around town. Yet the large engine was able to move the car from 0 to 60 miles an hour in approximately 14 seconds.

The feel of the car is smooth; handling is true and stable. But the Coupe de Ville's bulk is a handicap, especially in heavy traffic and on narrow city streets. Anyone who is accustomed to driving anything but a full-sized Cadillac would find a transition to a Coupe de Ville difficult.

That great bulk, as could be expected, holds fuel economy down. Last year, the De Ville series suffered from extremely low fuel economy. In combined city and highway test, the figure was as low as 12 miles per gallon. The new De Villes have undergone some minor modifications that have boosted the car's mileage. The results are not spectacular, but we averaged 16 mpg in combined city and highway driving this year. This increase is a direct result of a sophisticated tightening-up of the

Cadillac Coupe de Ville

car's structure, including modification of sheet metal and body, body mount rates, shock absorber valving and tire pressure.

Interior appointments of the Coupe de Ville are exactly what buyers of this kind of car would expect. Attention to detail is superb; layout and design are practical, eye appealing and comfortable.

The Coupe offers luxury-car buyers everything they are looking for in comfort. The d'Elegance and Phaeton packages enable buyers to outfit the car with an array of tasteful extras. By the middle of this year, Cadillac is expected to unveil a diesel engine for both the Coupe and Sedan de Ville. It probably will be the same engine that is currently used in Seville. We suggest that potential buyers of this engine read the story on the Seville and make note of the diesel's shortcomings. Cadillac's plan to equip the heavier De Villes with Seville's power plant is a mistake in our opinion. For we believe Seville's diesel engine will be a sluggish nonperformer in De Ville.

CADILLAC COUPE DE VILLE
Test Model Specifications

Body type 2-door	Rear hiproom ....57.1 in.
Overall length ....221.2 in.	Engine type ....OHV V8
Overall width ....76.4 in.	Net hp @ rpm ....180 @ 4000
Overall height ....54.4 in.	Net torque @ rpm ....320 @ 2000
Wheelbase ....121.5 in.	Displacement ....425 cu. in.
Turn diameter ....44 ft.	Compression ratio 8.2:1
Tire size ....GR 78-15B	Carburetion ....Fuel injected
Curb weight ....4275 lbs.	Transmission ....Automatic
Cargo space ....25.0 cu. ft.	Axle ratio 2.28.1
Front headroom ....38.0 in.	Acceleration 0-60 mph ..13.9 sec.
Front legroom ....42.1 in.	Brake stop 60-0 mph ......172 ft.
Front hiproom ....55.3 in.	Fuel tank capacity ....25 gal.
Rear headroom ....37.9 in.	EPA city economy rating ..12 mpg.
Rear legroom ....39.7 in.	

Cadillac Eldorado

So often when a car is being downsized, the procedure is to chop a little off here, shorten a little there, remove this and replace that with a lighter one of these. This, however, is not the case with the new Cadillac Eldorado, which is truly a new car from the ground up. Its overall length shortened by almost two feet to 204 inches, the new Eldorado is 1200 pounds lighter than the 1978 model. The car's curb weight is less than 3900 pounds.

CONSUMER GUIDE Magazine's test car came equipped with the new 350 cubic-inch V8 engine. The reduction of the car's weight has enabled Cadillac to get by with a small power plant. Gone from the Eldorado line is the 425 cubic-inch V8, but not at the expense of performance. The acceleration of the new Eldorado, a car that can still be termed a large luxury model, is surprising. From a standing start, our Eldorado ran to 60 miles an hour in about 12 seconds.

Our only concern about the engine is its tendency to heat up at low speeds. The temperature seemed to increased dramatically in stop-and-go freeway traffic. While never entering the red zone, signifying a possible boil-over, we came close. It is our guess that the radiator cooling fan is adequate for normal city and freeway conditions, but a bit too small to handle the load of low-speed running in traffic.

The Eldorado's redesigned front-wheel-drive system pulls the automobile around with excellent straight-line stability that seems to get better the faster you go. Cornering maneuvers are also extremely flat and controlled. Last year a major complaint was the Eldorado's sluggish steering when quick maneuvers were required. The new version is extremely well balanced, front to back as well as side to side. The result is the ride of a big car combined with the handling capabilities of higher-priced European compacts. Through all phases of testing, our Eldorado's ride was quiet and very smooth. The car's four-wheel independent suspension transmitted no bumps or thumps whatsoever to the passenger compartment.

Eldorado's new suspension system and short wheelbase has enabled Cadillac engineers to move the rear wheels forward almost 10 inches from where they were last year. Despite that, usable trunk space actually was increased 75 percent, and interior room differs so little from 1978 that it isn't noticeable.

Interior comforts are plush. Great attention to comfort and detail are clearly evident. Improved lower back supports in the front seats makes long rides more comfortable than before. Headroom and legroom for front and rear passengers is excellent.

Even when the front seat is moved all the way back on its tracks, there is plenty of legroom in the rear.

The new Eldorado has a long hood and what is for Cadillac a radically slanted windshield. We believe forward visibility has been increased. Visibility to the rear and off to the sides of the car is not good. The nearly vertical rear window seems small for the car. Although stylish and attractive, the large rear pillars at each corner quite noticeably interfere with the driver's view.

Most Eldorados come complete with numerous comfort items as standard equipment, so there is little the buyer can order as extras. One option is Cadillac's diesel V8, the same as offered in the Seville line. Available soon will be the Eldorado Biarritz package, which will feature leather-trimmed steering wheel, a brushed stainless steel roof, and tufted seats.

The new Cadillac introduction is a real winner for the buyer seeking comfort, performance, good handling and roominess in a luxury car.

CADILLAC ELDORADO
Test Model Specifications

Body type 2-door	Rear hiproom . . . . 48.8 in.
Overall length . . . . 204 in.	Engine type . . . . OHV V8
Overall width . . . . 71.4 in.	Net hp @ rpm . . . . 170 @ 4200
Overall height . . . . 54.2 in.	Net torque @ rpm . . . . 270 @ 2000
Wheelbase . . . . 113.9 in.	Displacement . . . . 350 cu. in.
Turn diameter . . . . 38.7 ft.	Compression ratio 8.0:1
Tire size L78-15B	Carburetion . . . . Fuel injected
Curb weight . . . . 3897 lbs.	Transmission . . . . Automatic
Cargo space . . . . 19.6 cu. ft.	Axle ratio 8.0:1
Front headroom . . . . 37.9 in.	Acceleration 0-60 mph . . . . 12 sec.
Front legroom . . . . 42.8 in.	Brake stop 60-0 mph . . . . . . 176 ft.
Front hiproom . . . . 51.8 in.	Fuel tank capacity . . . 19.6 gal.
Rear headroom . . . . 37.9 in.	EPA city economy rating . . 14 mpg.
Rear legroom . . . . 39.4 in.	

Cadillac
Seville

L ast year, Seville made up about 16 percent of
Cadillac's total sales. If Seville merely match-
es that figure or takes a nosedive this year, the

blame will be placed on the remarkable new Eldorado. Seville is a carry over; Eldorado is all-new, and praiseworthy. Despite last year's rumors that a front-wheel-drive version of Seville would be introduced for 1979, it looks like Cadillac has opted to hold this new design back until sales data are in on the Eldorado.

CONSUMER GUIDE Magazine evaluated a Seville equipped with a conventional gasoline engine last year. For *1979 Cars*, we tested the diesel version. Under the hood of our test car was a 350 cubic-inch V8 diesel power plant.

Once we started the engine, it became all too apparent that we were diesel powered. The engine clanked and rattled so much that an unknowing passerby told us he thought we either had a diesel engine under the hood or were sorely in need of a complete overhaul. The diesel did, however, quiet down considerably after attaining a little speed. Yet acceleration was slow. In typical diesel fashion, the engine in our Seville required a lot of running room to wind up to speed. The best acceleration time we obtained from 0 to 60 miles an hour was 18.5 seconds. When entering freeway traffic, we looked for long entry ramps that would enable us to get a running start and be up to speed before entering traffic. Any attempt at passing was a challenge.

On the plus side, our diesel-powered Seville averaged 23 miles per gallon in combined city and highway driving. One engineering change in the diesel is worth mentioning: a modification of the glow plugs that shortens the wait for the plugs to heat the combustion chamber. Traditionally, especially in cold weather, the wait before starting a diesel could be as long as two minutes. The new system cuts the time to approximately six seconds—even at zero degrees.

The ride of our Seville was good on everything

from a special handling course to bumpy gravel roads. The car remained flat in sharp corners.

Braking, even in controlled panic situations, was straight. The disc brakes can bring the 4300-pound car down to a stop from 60 mph in less than 145 feet. That we consider excellent for an automobile of Seville's size.

Sound-deadening insulation seemed to be insufficient in our diesel Seville, and does not seem to be much better in gasoline versions. Controls and gauges are positioned well for easy use. Visibility is good. Despite the large corner pillars, visibility to the rear is fine.

Overall, the diesel Seville is a car not made for everyone. Diesels are a world apart from traditional gasoline engines in performance and economy. Using a diesel, you would attain better mileage than a gasoline engine of comparable size could deliver, but you'd have to trade off a great deal of performance—the kind of performance normally associated with cars in the Cadillac Seville's price range.

CADILLAC SEVILLE
Test Model Specifications

Body type	4-door	Rear hiproom	50.7 in.
Overall length	204 in.	Engine type	Diesel OHV V8
Overall width	71.8 in.	Net hp @ rpm	120 @ 3000
Overall height	54.6 in.	Net torque @ rpm	220 @ 1600
Wheelbase	114.3 in.	Displacement	350 cu. in.
Turn diameter	42.3 ft.	Compression ratio	22.5:1
Tire size	GR 78-15	Carburetion	Fuel injected
Curb weight	4360 lbs.	Transmission	Automatic
Cargo space	12.8 cu. ft.	Axle ratio	2.56:1
Front headroom	38.6 in.	Acceleration 0-60 mph	18.5 sec.
Front legroom	41.7 in.	Brake stop 60-0 mph	145 ft.
Front hiproom	51.4 in.	Fuel tank capacity	21 gal.
Rear headroom	36.8 in.	EPA city economy rating	21 mpg.
Rear legroom	38.2 in.		

Chevrolet Camaro

The basic design of the Chevrolet Camaro has not changed noticeably since 1970. The 1979 Camaro is basically the same car it has been for the past nine years, although a luxury model, the Berlinetta, has been added to the line this year. The Berlinetta is the only new model that Chevy has to compete with Pontiac's redesigned Firebird.

The Berlinetta Camaro we tested was equipped with the 305 cubic-inch V8 (5.0 liter) engine. Considering that the curb weight of the Berlinetta is close to 3500 pounds, the 305 V8 did an adequate job. Acceleration from 0 to 60 miles an hour took 9.4 seconds, which we consider very good.

Camaro's overall ride has traditionally been stiff. This year, however, the Berlinetta package has a few minor changes that did indeed soften the harsh

Chevrolet Camaro

ride. Little things like a softer shock valving and larger body mounts all add up to a greatly improved ride. In fact, it is surprising how little had to be altered on the basic suspension system to result in such a difference.

Equipped with power recirculating-ball steering, the Camaro held tight in the turns with a little understeer noticeable when the car was pushed extremely hard into a corner. However, that is a traditional trait of the Camaro and nothing serious enough to cause the driver to lose confidence in the automobile.

The basic styling of the Berlinetta package is, in our estimation, an attempt to tone down the sports car image of the basic Camaro. Included in the treatment is a bright grille, limited striping, sport mirrors, black rocker panels, side-angled taillights, a rear spoiler and color-coordinated wheels.

The interior, even with the Berlinetta option, is still Camaro. The only real change made for 1979 has been in the dash panel. The instrumentation is the same, but the dashboard panel no longer curves around the driver. In addition, the Berlinetta package features a brushed-aluminum face panel. Comfort controls still seem cramped and somewhat awkward to reach, but the custom bucket seats were very comfortable. Rear seat passenger comfort is still poor for anybody over five feet tall, and driver visibility is as poor as ever.

Camaro's interior noise level is very low this year. A lot of sound deadening work has been put into the ceiling, where a thick foam roof liner extends to each corner. In addition, special seals have been used around the doors, and extra padding has been placed between the instrument panel and windshield cowling.

Camaro's base price has gone up. With the Berlinetta treatment, the price is even higher. But Camaro has never tried to appeal to anyone's practicality.

CHEVROLET CAMARO
Test Model Specifications

Body type	2-door	Rear hiproom	46.3 in.
Overall length	197.6 in.	Engine type	V8
Overall width	74.5 in.	Net hp @ rpm	130 @ 3200
Overall height	49.2 in.	Net torque @ rpm	245 @ 2000
Wheelbase	108 in.	Displacement	305 cu. in.
Turn diameter	38.5 ft.	Compression ratio	8.4:1
Tire size	FR 78-14B	Carburetion	2 bbl.
Curb weight	3410 lbs.	Transmission	Automatic
Cargo space	7.1 cu. ft.	Axle ratio	3.42.1
Front headroom	37.2 in.	Acceleration 0-60 mph	9.4 sec.
Front legroom	43.9 in.	Brake stop 60-0 mph	196 ft.
Front hiproom	55.3 in.	Fuel tank capacity	21 gal.
Rear headroom	36 in.	EPA city economy rating	16 mpg.
Rear legroom	28.4 in.		

Chevrolet Caprice/Impala

Caprice Classic won raves from the car-buying public in 1977 and 1978. For 1979, Chevrolet has made only minor changes in Caprice, so the car's popularity will no doubt remain high. But this year Caprice faces some truly fierce competition from outside General Motors with the introduction of the new downsized Mercury Marquis, the Chrysler New Yorker/Newport, and the Dodge St. Regis.

However, this new wave of competitors in the standard-sized class cannot take away from the fact that Caprice Classic is an excellent automobile, offering the consumer good performance, luxury and economy at a reasonable price.

Except for trim and option packages, the Caprice and Impala are identical. They share a wheelbase of 116 inches. The lineup for '79 comprises two-door and four-door models in both series. Both the Caprice and Impala series also include station wagons.

Chevrolet offers three engines for the 1979 Caprice: a 250 cubic-inch V6, a 305 V8 and 350 V8. The 305 combined with a three-speed automatic transmission is the base power train. Its Environmental Protection Agency mileage rating is 18 mpg. Our test car, with the same power train, delivered a slightly lower figure: overall average fuel consumption of 16 miles per gallon. Under normal driving conditions, the 305 provides sufficient muscle. The Caprice ran from 0 to 60 mph in a respectable 13.6 seconds during our tests. From a stop, our Caprice accelerated slowly, but it had all the extra power needed for passing.

When equipped with the available F-41 special handling suspension, Caprice can come close in handling ability to some sports cars. It is a remarkably stable car. During high-speed highway driving, you won't find Caprice sloshing about in its lane. It responds quickly to steering commands and hugs the roadway in curves. At the same time, it remains relatively flat. However, when forced into a series of emergency maneuvers, our test Caprice faltered slightly in responding to sudden jerks of the steering wheel. The brakes—power discs in front, drums in the rear—handled all test situations efficiently.

A high roofline and doors that are lighter and thinner than most allow for easy passenger access into the Caprice's luxurious interior. The car offers optimum headroom and comfortable hip room in front and back. Legroom forward is excellent because of the flat instrument panel. This is unusual compared to the deeply curved panels found on most cars in Caprice's class. Although the downsizing of 1977 thinned and lightened much of the car's body. Caprice is still quiet and comfortable. The special acoustical headliner and solid construction shuts out all but the faintest of engine and wind noises.

The six-way adjustable seats put the driver in a good position to view the roadway. Caprice's large windows offer good visibility, though when looking over your left shoulder, vision is somewhat obstructed by the roofline.

The 1979 Caprice has a 20.2 cubic-foot trunk, which sounds like more than enough for any cargo-carrying situation. Unfortunately, the spare tire is positioned so that it sits partly on the trunk shelf and partly down in the center of the cargo area, making it difficult to jocky baggage around.

Like most standard-sized automobiles loaded with air conditioners and power options, Caprice can be a difficult car to service yourself. But Chevrolet dealerships and garages able to service GM cars are not hard to find, parts are plentiful, and there is no shortage of qualified GM mechanics around. So if you have no qualms about letting someone else work on your car, servicing the Caprice is no problem.

Offering acceptable fuel economy, excellent ride and handling abilities, and a reasonable price, Caprice stands as the major threat to its competitors from within GM as well as the new downsized models from Ford and Chrysler.

CHEVROLET CAPRICE
Test Model Specifications

Body type	4-door	Rear hiproom	55.3 in.
Overall length	212.1 in.	Engine type	V8
Overall width	76 in.	Net hp @ rpm	145 @ 3800
Overall height	56 in.	Net torque @ rpm	245 @ 2400
Wheelbase	116 in.	Displacement	305 cu. in.
Turn diameter	38.8 ft.	Compression ratio	8.5:1
Tire size	GR 70-15	Carburetion	2 bbl.
Curb weight	3640 lbs.	Transmission	Automatic
Cargo space	20.2 cu. ft.	Axle ratio	2.41:1
Front headroom	39.4 in.	Acceleration 0-60 mph	13.6 sec.
Front legroom	42.4 in.	Brake stop 60-0 mph	144 ft.
Front hiproom	55.0 in.	Fuel tank capacity	21 gal.
Rear headroom	38.2 in.	EPA city economy rating	18 mpg.
Rear legroom	39.0 in.		

Chevrolet Chevette

Compared with most low-priced economy cars, Chevette's interior is very well designed. The instruments are thoughtfully laid out; all gauges are well-defined and placed in easy-to-see positions, and a multifunction control switch is conveniently situated on the steering column. The seats are stiff but comfortable, and reclining front buckets are available as optional equipment. The four-door hatchback we tested provided ample legroom and hip room up front, good hip room and adequate legroom in back, and excellent headroom throughout. A high roof with narrow side posts, combined with a shorter hood for 1979, allow exceptional visibility. In fact, we found Chevette to be completely free of blind spots, even in the rear deck area, where visibility is a problem in most hatchbacks. Wind-whistle and engine noise are distracting at high speeds, but under normal driving conditions the noise level in the passenger compartment is reasonably low. Considering Chevette's size, we were surprised by the amount of cargo

Chevrolet Chevette

space offered. Our test model had a full 27 cubic feet of unobstructed cargo space when the rear seats were down—plenty of room for most cargo needs.

We found Chevette's performance much improved over the 1978 model, due to some needed changes under the hood. A two-stage, two-barrel carburetor has replaced the tiny one-barrel carburetor of last year, producing a noticeable increase in horsepower and a slight improvement in fuel economy. Our test car accelerated from 0 to 60 miles an hour in a respectable 17 seconds, which is peppy enough to enter freeway traffic and perform most passing maneuvers without inducing heart failure in the driver. Our Chevette seemed unsuited for very high speeds, though—a noisy engine and a tendency to wander in its lane convinced us that Chevette is happier at speeds under 60 mph.

The 1979 Chevette offers as optional equipment a new sport suspension system. The ride is a little stiffer with this option, but the improvement in handling is well worth it. We were able to take tight corners and make sudden emergency maneuvers with a feeling of full control. And with the standard brake system we could detect no brake fade during a series of panic stops.

One area in which Chevette has not been improved for 1979 is the location of its engine components. It is still difficult to perform a simple tune-up. The spark plugs are easy enough to get to, but the distributor and oil filter are placed in awkward areas that become even harder to reach when the Chevette is equipped with the optional air conditioning unit.

Other changes in the 1979 Chevette are minor body improvements. A bright aluminum stamped grille, accented by single rectangular headlights, has replaced the painted front of the 1978 Chevette.

Overall, the Chevette for 1979 is a comfortable, sturdy little car that offers increased performance and fuel economy, and an improved ride. There is talk that a front-wheel drive model might be introduced before 1980. If that happens, Chevrolet will have a mini-compact that will rival the best of its imported competitors.

CHEVROLET CHEVETTE
Test Model Specifications

Body type 4-door	Rear hiproom .... 48.8 in.
Overall length .... 162.6 in.	Engine type .... OHV 4 in-line
Overall width .... 61.8 in.	Net hp @ rpm .... 70 @ 4800
Overall height .... 52.3 in.	Net torque @ rpm ..... 86 @ 3200
Wheelbase .... 97.3 in.	Displacement .... 98 cu. in.
Turn diameter .... 30.9 ft.	Compression ratio 8.6:1
Tire size P155/80D-13	Carburetion .... 2 bbl.
Curb weight .... 2096 lbs.	Transmission .... Automatic
Cargo space .... 27.8 cu. ft.	Axle ratio 3.70:1
Front headroom .... 38.1 in.	Acceleration 0-60 mph .. 17.0 sec.
Front legroom .... 41.5 in.	Brake stop 60-0 mph ...... 195 ft.
Front hiproom .... 49.9 in.	Fuel tank capacity .... 13 gal.
Rear headroom .... 37.3 in.	EPA city economy rating .. 25 mpg.
Rear legroom .... 33.1 in.	

Chevrolet Corvette

For a quarter century, Corvette has been one of America's automotive favorites. Its sleek body and high performance have kept it popular despite its high price and impracticality.

Changes are few and small for 1979 and mostly under the hood. Modifications have been made to increase horsepower and torque, and cold-engine performance has been improved. Suspension changes are apparent, and some previously optional interior outfits are now standard.

The 350 cubic-inch engine with four-barrel carburetion is still Corvette's standard power plant—

and it's still a firebreather. A choice of automatic or four-speed manual transmissions is available. Our test car had the standard engine and automatic transmission.

The transmission was extremely responsive; the rear end ratio has been increased from 3.08:1 to 3.55:1 this year, which makes an impressive difference. Our acceleration test was exhilarating—0 to 60 miles an hour in nine seconds. As for power, Corvette has it to spare; not once did we reach for a power burst without getting more than we needed. With that kind of power, gas mileage is predictably low. In combined city-highway driving we averaged only about 15 miles per gallon. But gas economy is not what most Corvette buyers are looking for.

Corvette's handling is superb. The low-slung body and wide tires easily took the tightest turns we encountered. Its steering system responded instantly to the slightest commands. In a succession of emergency maneuvers, we had no trouble maintaining full control. Our car tested fair in braking, losing traction in only a few hard stops. Nor could we detect any brake fade after numerous controlled panic moves.

The 1979 Corvette has a quiet, smooth, ride. Even the T-top roof is effectively sealed against wind noise. This year, Corvettes with manual transmission are equipped with the type of shock absorbers previously used only on Corvettes having automatic transmission. These shocks give a smoother ride.

Inside, the changes are few. Safety locks have been incorporated into the backrests of the seats; during sudden braking, the locks automatically set to keep the backrests from flopping forward. High-back seats, once available only on limited-edition Corvettes, are now standard equipment. Cargo room has been slightly improved by an ingenious seat design that allows part of the backrest to fold back flush with the cargo bed.

Corvette's interior is comfortably snug. Legroom is ample, and headroom is more than adequate. All controls are within easy reach of the driver, and the gauge clusters on the well-designed instrument panel are easy to see. The wraparound rear window, when it was introduced in 1978, greatly improved rearward visibility. Forward visibility can still be a problem, though, until you get used to the low driver's position and the car's dimensions.

Cargo capacity was slightly improved by the introduction of the wrap-around rear window, but storage space never has been one of Corvette's assets. In fact, the tiny deck behind the seats has enough room for a jacket or handbag but not much else.

Corvette is America's only true sports car; it's also an image car. This combination of high performance and sex appeal is what keeps people lining up, often for months, to buy one at full list price (and often more).

CHEVROLET CORVETTE
Test Model Specifications

Body type	2-seater	Rear hiproom	—
Overall length	185.2 in.	Engine type	OHV V8
Overall width	69.0 in.	Net hp @ rpm	185 @ 4000
Overall height	48.0 in.	Net torque @ rpm	280 @ 2400
Wheelbase	98.0 in.	Displacement	350 cu. in.
Turn diameter	37.0 ft.	Compression ratio	8.2:1
Tire size	P225/70R-15	Carburetion	4 bbl.
Curb weight	3530 lbs.	Transmission	Automatic
Cargo space	—	Axle ratio	3.55:1
Front headroom	36.2 in.	Acceleration 0-60 mph	9.0 sec.
Front legroom	42.1 in.	Brake stop 60-0 mph	167 ft.
Front hiproom	49.9 in.	Fuel tank capacity	24 gal.
Rear headroom	—	EPA city economy rating	16 mpg.
Rear legroom	—		

Chevrolet Malibu

The Chevrolet Malibu has been somewhat of a disappointment since its major design changes of 1978. For 1979, it has some slight exterior improvements, and a few new engineering features have been built into it. All the models have a new grille and taillights, and woodgrain side panels are available on the wagon.

Malibu's downsizing in 1978 made it a car that was extremely easy to drive. This still holds true in 1979. The steering system on the two-door coupe that we tested provided very good control and responded quickly to panic maneuvers. We consider Malibu's brake system to be average, offering controlled brake patterns, although we detected slight brake fade after a series of power stops.

Although shortening Malibu's wheelbase affected its ride characteristics, the car certainly is not any worse in that department than its competitors. Road bumps were regularly felt, but overall we did not consider the ride uncomfortable.

Choices of power plants have been increased this year with the introduction of a 267 cubic-inch V8. This mid-size V8 joins a lineup that includes the base 200 cubic-inch V6, the 231 cubic-inch V6 and the 305 cubic-inch V8. Our test Malibu was equipped with the standard 200 V6 and an automatic transmission. Judging by the sluggish response we received from this engine, we feel that any of the other available engines would be a better choice. From a dead stop our test car accelerated extremely slowly and was sluggish when forced into passing situations. In a pinch the power just wasn't there, and although the 200 has been given an 18 miles per gallon rating by the Environmental Protection Agency, we feel that the saving in gas mileage is not worth the loss in horsepower. From reports we have received, the new 267 V8 offers a much needed power boost and still maintains respectable fuel mileage.

Where Malibu has really slipped behind its Pontiac, Oldsmobile and Buick competitors is in its almost Spartan interior design. Instrumentation is well laid out and easy to see, but the whole setup looks like something you'd find in a stripped-down mini-car. Headroom and legroom were good both in the front and in the rear seats, but hip room seemed cramped in the rear. The upholstery and inside door trim had an overall cheap appearance. And the rear side windows don't roll down. Even in the four-door and station wagon models the windows are stationary. We feel that there is no reason for this in a car of Malibu's size and price. This poor design is sure to affect Malibu's sales.

Malibu does have some strong points, however. The high-set roof, the narrow side pillars and the clear rear deck allow an almost totally unobstructed view for the driver. Interior noise levels are not the best, but are reasonably low, with engine and wind noise usually apparent only at high speeds. And Malibu's trunk provides a full 16 cubic feet of cargo space.

Malibu is relatively easy to service when not equipped with many extras. Accessory motors and pumps do present problems for the do-it-yourselfers, but with patience such problems can be overcome. With Chevrolet's extensive service network, dealer maintenance is usually readily available.

Overall, Malibu's interior is its greatest drawback. For just a few hundred dollars more, you can buy a car that equals Malibu's good points while also offering superior comfort, convenience, and appearance inside.

CHEVROLET MALIBU
Test Model Specifications

Body type 2-door	Rear hiproom .... 54.5 in.
Overall length .... 192.7 in.	Engine type .... OHV V6
Overall width .... 71.5 in.	Net hp @ rpm .... 95 @ 3800
Overall height .... 53.3 in.	Net torque @ rpm .... 160 @ 2000
Wheelbase .... 108.1 in.	Displacement .... 200 cu. in.
Turn diameter .... 37.2 ft.	Compression ratio 8.2:1
Tire size P195/75R-14	Carburetion .... 2 bbl.
Curb weight .... 3091 lbs.	Transmission .... Automatic
Cargo space .... 16.1 cu. ft.	Axle ratio 2.73.1
Front headroom .... 37.9 in.	Acceleration 0-60 mph .. 18.6 sec.
Front legroom .... 42.8 in.	Brake stop 60-0 mph ..... 170 ft.
Front hiproom .... 51.7 in.	Fuel tank capacity ..... 17.5 gal.
Rear headroom .... 37.8 in.	EPA city economy rating .. 18 mpg.
Rear legroom .... 35.1 in.	

Chevrolet Monte Carlo

Since its introduction into GM's personal luxury car line in 1970, Chevrolet Monte Carlo has been the most popular car of its class. Monte Carlo for 1979 has minor exterior improvements and offers a wider selection of engines but otherwise remains the same as it was in 1978.

Monte Carlo comes with a choice of four engines in 1979, from the standard 200 cubic-inch V6 to a 305 cubic-inch V8, with a 231 V6 and a 267 V8 to fill the space in between. A four-speed manual transmission is optional. The 305 cubic-inch engine is equipped with a four-barrel carburetor instead of the two-barrel offered last year. With the new 305 and an automatic transmission, our test Monte Carlo delivered slightly more horsepower and better acceleration from 0 to 60 miles an hour than last year's model, but it did so at the expense of gas mileage. The Environmental Protection Agency gave the 305 four-barrel a city rating of 17 miles per gallon, but we averaged only 17 mpg. This isn't a bad fuel average compared to Monte Carlo's competitors, but it's not very good compared to the 22 mpg average of Monte Carlo's own optional 200 V6.

What the 305 V8 lacks in fuel economy it makes up in power. In a series of 0 to 60 mph acceleration tests, our test Monte Carlo averaged just over 13 seconds. The automatic transmission responded extremely well; we could detect no lag between gears as the automatic shifted. And when the two additional carburetor barrels kicked in, there was more than enough power to complete any high-speed maneuver.

Monte Carlo's ride is that of a true luxury car. Its suspension compensates for all but the roughest of road conditions. The interior seals very tightly against outside noises. Wind whistle does not exist in the Monte Carlo, and the engine can be heard only at high speeds or when the four-barrel opens

Chevrolet Monte Carlo

up fully. At idle and at low speeds the engine literally cannot be heard from inside the car.

The luxury of Monte Carlo's ride has a slightly negative effect on the car's handling. Our test car tended to lean in tight corners and completed some emergency maneuvers a little more slowly than we would have liked. But the steering response was good, and we could detect no brake fade even after repeated hard stops.

The interior of the Monte Carlo is not as plush as those of other cars in its class. The instrument panel is plain, but functional. All gauges are easy to see, and controls are within easy reach. Its simplicity, however, gives the entire dashboard layout a rather cheap appearance. But Monte Carlo's overall roominess is above average. The trunk has a wide, flat bed and 16.5 cubic feet of usable cargo space. If Chevrolet designers could take one more step and brighten the interior appearance a little, the Monte Carlo would be an even more appealing automobile than it already is.

CHEVROLET MONTE CARLO
Test Model Specifications

Body type 2-door	Rear hiproom .... 54.5 in.
Overall length .... 200.4 in.	Engine type .... OHV V8
Overall width .... 71.5 in.	Net hp @ rpm .... 155 @ 3800
Overall height .... 53.9 in.	Net torque @ rpm .... 250 @ 2400
Wheelbase .... 97.0 in.	Displacement .... 305 cu. in.
Turn diameter .... 37.2 ft.	Compression ratio 8.4:1
Tire size P205/70R-14	Carburetion .... 4 bbl.
Curb weight .... 3129 lbs.	Transmission .... Automatic
Cargo space .... 16.5 cu. ft.	Axle ratio 2.29:1
Front headroom .... 37.3 in.	Acceleration 0-60 mph .. 13.3 sec.
Front legroom .... 42.9 in.	Brake stop 60-0 mph ..... 170 ft.
Front hiproom .... 51.7 in.	Fuel tank capacity ..... 17.5 gal.
Rear headroom .... 37.6 in.	EPA city economy rating .. 17 mpg.
Rear legroom .... 36.5 in.	

Chevrolet Monza

The 1979 Monza is essentially the same car that was produced in 1978. Minor cosmetic changes have been made on the interior, and the engine design has been modified slightly.

Our major complaint against the Monza has always been its inadequate interior space, and it is no different this year. No matter where you sit, you're going to be cramped. We tested the coupe model and found front seat room to be tight and awkward. To allow adequate headroom, the bucket seats have been set so low between the door and the huge transmission hump that the driver sits with his legs stretched out straight in front of him. It's an uncomfortable arrangement, one in which you can't help but feel you don't have complete control of the car. In the rear seats there is only enough legroom for small children. Rear headroom is adequate in the coupe model, but in the fastback it's almost impossible to find a comfortable position. Cargo space in the coupe consists of a tiny 6.6 cubic-foot trunk.

As a result of the low driving seat, forward visibility doesn't seem to be as good as it should be. The coupe's wide rear roof pillars create blind spots.

On the road, the Monza doesn't have a solid feel. This impression gets stronger at higher speeds, when wind whistle and engine noise are extremely noticeable.

Monza performs relatively well on the road. Equipped with an optional suspension system, our test coupe remained stable during fast freeway driving and braked from 60 miles an hour to a stop in approximately 180 feet. We noticed, however, considerable sway in sharp turns.

The 1979 Monza again comes with a choice of four power plants: the standard four-cylinder, a 196 and a 231 cubic-inch V6, and a powerful 305 cubic-inch V8. Our test Monza was equipped with the larger of the V6s and an automatic transmission. Acceleration from 0 to 60 miles an hour took 18 seconds, which we felt was a fair time considering the car's weight and axle ratio. In extensive city and freeway driving we averaged 22 miles per gallon.

In some ways, Monza is equal to most of its competition. But we feel that Monza's interior layout definitely puts Monza behind the likes of the completely redesigned Mustang and Capri.

CHEVROLET MONZA
Test Model Specifications

Body type 2-door	Rear hiproom .... 41.2 in.
Overall length .... 178.6 in.	Engine type V6
Overall width .... 65.4 in.	Net hp @ rpm .... 105 @ 3800
Overall height .... 49.8 in.	Net torque @ rpm .... 205 @ 2400
Wheelbase .... 97.0 in.	Displacement .... 231 cu. in.
Turn diameter .... 35.8 ft.	Compression ratio .... N/A
Tire size .... BR 78-13	Carburetion .... 2 bbl.
Curb weight .... 2712 lbs.	Transmission .... Automatic
Cargo space .... 6.6 cu. ft.	Axle ratio 2.29:1
Front headroom .... 37.6 in.	Acceleration 0-60 mph .... 18 sec.
Front legroom .... 43.0 in.	Brake stop 60-0 mph ..... 180 ft.
Front hiproom .... 46.7 in.	Fuel tank capacity ...... 18.5 gal.
Rear headroom .... 37.2 in.	EPA city economy rating .. 16 mpg.
Rear legroom .... 28.2 in.	

Chevrolet Nova

Chevrolet took the 1979 Nova out of production in November as the first step of a 1980 design change that should set the standard for small cars for the next decade. However, except for minor styling differences, the 1979 Novas that were produced are identical with the '78s.

Nova has always been a solidly built, dependable car that has served its owners well and offered unusually low maintenance costs. It has been a car that could stand up to abuse over a long lifetime. The 1980 Nova will be entirely different in concept from Novas built until now; we hope it will live up to the reputation of its predecessors.

A major difference in 1980 will be size. The 1980 will have a 104.5-inch wheelbase, compared with the 111-inch base of the 1978-79. Overall length will be chopped to 176.7 inches, a loss of 20 inches, which will make the new Nova the smallest of the domestic compacts. Curb weight will be cut almost 30 percent, from 3250 to 2385 pounds.

Another big difference in 1980 will be Nova's chassis design. The car will offer a front-wheel-drive system that is all-new to GM. Four-cylinder and V6 power plants will be installed crosswise in the engine compartment. Independent suspension will be provided on all four wheels through coil springs. The buyer will still have a choice of a large list of options, including automatic transmission, air conditioning, and handling packages.

Three body styles will be offered in the Nova line: a two-door and a four-door fastback sedan, both with a rear hatch opening; and a sporty semi-fastback coupe. The other GM compact lines from Pontiac, Oldsmobile and Buick will offer other combinations of body styles that will also include notchback two-door and four-door sedans.

The staff of CONSUMER GUIDE Magazine will not have a chance to examine the car before next March, but from the written descriptions that are available, we have formed some opinions about its design detail and value.

The big change that GM seems to be looking for in the new cars is a boost in fuel economy. The base engine used by all divisions—Chevy, Olds, Pontiac and Buick—will be a 151 cubic-inch in-line Four that is now standard on a number of GM subcompacts, including Sunbird and Monza. We look for this engine to deliver good performance in the new compact, while delivering combined city-highway mileage in the range of 24 to 27 mpg.

Because the curb weight will have been slashed, performance with the smaller engine should be as good as or better than that with the 250 cubic-inch Six in the present Nova.

For even better performance, Chevy is developing and will have ready a 173 cubic-inch V6 engine that should be able to give V8-like performance and smoothness. This engine is an entirely new design, not based on any other present power plant. Look for fuel economy with this engine also to be in the mid-20 mpg range for combined city-highway driving.

While Nova for 1980 will be decidedly smaller than the present Nova, interior room will be about the same. Chevy will do this by the same means it used when downsizing its full-size and intermediate cars. Door panels will be flatter and narrower, with less curvature; the roofline will be two inches higher, providing adequate headroom for both front- and rear-seat passengers; and the front-wheel-drive system will provide a flat floor in both the front and rear, which will open up the passenger space even more.

Chrysler Cordoba

Cordoba is a personal luxury car in the old sense of the term: large on the outside and luxurious on the inside, with a dash of sportiness thrown in. The Chrysler name still means a lot to many buyers. On this model it apparently makes a world of difference, since the Dodge Magnum, which is the same car with a different name, is not nearly so popular with buyers.

Cordoba is a curiosity. Its oversize body, low fuel economy, and clumsy handling are passé. When compared with the newest competition, especially new cars from General Motors, the present Cordoba is clearly outclassed. Chrysler officials know this, and that's why they plan to replace the present car just as soon as changeover schedules can be worked out. This could very well happen as soon as next year. Then Cordoba will shrink and lose more than 500 pounds in weight. Perhaps it will then be able to compete with Thunderbird, Grand Prix and other personal luxury cars on an equal basis.

Chrysler Cordoba

Cordoba nonetheless offers a few desirable features in its present form. The interior is almost too roomy. The seats are extra wide and legroom is excellent. The quality of the trim inside is first-class. The upholstery fabrics, chrome trim, and woodgrain appliqué are of high quality. They combine to make the Cordoba interior the equal of anything in its class. Headroom, however, is just adequate. And the trunk will fool you: it looks big enough on the outside, but inside the compartment is shallow, and not as well laid out as the trunks offered by Chrysler's competitors.

Because its base price is about $6000, Cordoba is considered a competitor for the mid-size personal luxury cars from GM and Ford, but below the luxury class of the Buick Riviera, Oldsmobile Toronado, Cadillac Eldorado and Lincoln Mark V. That means Cordoba has some tough competition, cars that offer many superior features. Typically, the GM personal luxury cars are smaller on the outside than Cordoba, but offer greater interior room. They're better than Cordoba in fuel economy, and they are more agile. Cordoba has a built-in tendency toward understeer that becomes more apparent the faster the car is driven. In emergency turns at speed, the car tends to continue on in the direction it was going, rather than swinging out to one side or the other. This reaction may not be important at lower speeds, but it can be felt by the driver, who gets a sense of lagging response in all types of driving. In tight traffic, where the car is expected to weave in and out of a straight path, the handling lag means a lack of control.

If you want excellent performance, the 360 cubic-inch V8 is the best choice for Cordoba. Our test crew averaged about 13.5 seconds in 0 to 60 miles an hour acceleration runs with the 360. Average fuel economy with the 360 is in the range of 17 mpg—about a mile per gallon less than when the car is equipped with the much slower 318 V8.

Because the quality of its competition is so high, and since Chrysler plans to make a substantial change in the Cordoba next year, we cannot recommend the car to personal luxury shoppers in 1979. Grand Prix, Regal, Monte Carlo and Cutlass Supreme offer superior value.

CHRYSLER CORDOBA
Test Model Specifications

Body type	2-door	Rear hiproom	57 in.
Overall length	215.8 in.	Engine type	V8
Overall width	77.1 in.	Net hp @ rpm	190 @ 3600
Overall height	53.1 in.	Net torque @ rpm	275 @ 2000
Wheelbase	115 in.	Displacement	360 cu. in.
Turn diameter	41.2 ft.	Compression ratio	8.4:1
Tire size	GR 78-15	Carburetion	2 bbl.
Curb weight	3827 lbs.	Transmission	Automatic
Cargo space	16.3 cu. ft.	Axle ratio	2.45:1
Front headroom	37.7 in.	Acceleration 0-60 mph	13.5 sec.
Front legroom	42.6 in.	Brake stop 60-0 mph	165 ft.
Front hiproom	55.8 in.	Fuel tank capacity	25.5 gal.
Rear headroom	36.6 in.	EPA city economy rating	14 mpg.
Rear legroom	32.1 in.		

Chrysler LeBaron

LeBaron is almost a duplicate of the Plymouth Volare and all its relatives at Chrysler Corporation. It shares its body, drive train, suspension and dimensions with the Volare, Aspen and Diplomat. However, LeBaron offers more luxury, higher-quality trim inside and out, and a quieter ride than the Plymouth and Dodge compacts.

Chrysler now considers LeBaron a mid-sized car. It will remain in that position even after Volare and Aspen are downsized in 1981. Originally, LeBaron was slated to be Chrysler's answer to the Cadillac Seville and Lincoln Versailles. But that role never developed. LeBaron costs $5000 to $7000 less than those models, and does not approach either in luxury, ride or quietness. LeBaron's ride and handling are very much like the Volare's. Road vibrations and gaps in the pavement are easily felt through the steering wheel. Noise levels inside the car are relatively high in comparison with Versailles and Seville. By driving LeBaron and other cars of its price and class in quick succession, it becomes clear that the Chrysler has a loose feel. LeBaron's brakes must be depressed a fraction more than those of the other cars, its rear end breaks loose sooner, and its steering seems less precise.

LeBaron's instrument panel has a busy appearance, but the number of functional gauges in the panel is surprisingly low: alternator, temperature, gasoline, speedometer and trip odometer.

Three LeBaron models are offered: the four-door sedan, a personal luxury two-door hardtop, and the Town & Country station wagon. Changes in the cars for 1979 are strictly superficial—a new grille, and minor changes in the quarter windows of the two-door.

The engine lineup remains the same as last year. The 225 cubic-inch Slant Six is the standard engine; options are a two-barrel-carburetor version of that engine, a 318 V8, and a 360 V8. Our experience has shown that the 318 is best suited to the LeBaron. It provides good performance and fuel economy of 16 miles per gallon in city driving. The two-barrel 225 delivers one more mile per gallon than the V8, but offers lower performance. We recommend the 360 V8 only for the station wagon or for other heavy-duty uses like trailer towing.

CHRYSLER LEBARON
Test Model Specifications

Body type	4-door	Rear hiproom	56.6 in.
Overall length	206.1 in.	Engine type	V8
Overall width	73.3 in.	Net hp @ rpm	140 @ 4000
Overall height	55.3 in.	Net torque @ rpm	245 @ 1600
Wheelbase	112.7 in.	Displacement	318 cu. in.
Turn diameter	40.7 ft.	Compression ratio	8.5:1
Tire size	FR 78-15	Carburetion	2 bbl.
Curb weight	3430 lbs.	Transmission	Automatic
Cargo space	16.2 cu. ft.	Axle ratio	2.94:1
Front headroom	39.2 in.	Acceleration 0-60 mph	13.1 sec.
Front legroom	42.5 in.	Brake stop 60-0 mph	148 ft.
Front hiproom	56.8 in.	Fuel tank capacity	19.5 gal.
Rear headroom	37.5 in.	EPA city economy rating	16 mpg.
Rear legroom	36.6 in.		

Chrysler Newport/ New Yorker

This year's Newport is a downsized version of the 1978. However, Chrysler used what was once the company's intermediate chassis as the platform for the downsized Newport, so the car is not completely new. Only its body panels and windows were changed as the intermediate chassis was adapted to reduce Newport's size. Our tests of Newport show that its smaller size and lighter weight hold many advantages. But the new car also has its shortcomings. They will surely influence the way buyers react to the changes.

The Newport is noisier than its competitors by a wide margin. In fact, many compacts and intermediates are quieter than the Newport. Most of the noise is wind whistle. Our test car's front door windows bulged out from air pressure when the car was driven at freeway speeds, and that created wind roar and whistle. At high speeds, the noise levels in the Newport's passenger compartment were several decibels higher than those in the comparably priced Chevy Caprice and Ford LTD.

The car feels much lighter than it looks, especially when extended in turning maneuvers. The rear end tends to break loose from traction quickly. This has been a Chrysler trademark for the past decade, but one that was usually found only in mid-size and compact models.

The design of the Newport's instrument panel is a mistake. It is set down low, well below the driver's line of sight. That means the driver must move his head every time he wants to check the instruments. The dials are set in deep recesses, and are poorly lighted. They are especially difficult to read in the daytime. Furthermore, the colors of the dials and background are too similar, and that makes reading them even more difficult. In the Newport we tested, the dials were light gray, and the faces of the instruments were medium gray.

The positive features of the Newport are mostly the result of the downsizing that Chrysler undertook in its full-size car lines this year. The Newport for 1979 is 800 pounds lighter than the '78, and almost a foot shorter. The new package is easier to drive in traffic, easier to park, and more economical.

There has been little loss of performance, even though the 440 cubic-inch engine previously available for Newport has been discontinued. The 360 cubic-inch V8 is now the top power plant. Chrysler also has retained in the Newport the passenger space and luggage room that big cars are noted for. The quality of the car's ride has remained about the same as it was last year. Actually, if you prefer a controlled, flat ride, you may find the new model to be an improvement over the 1978.

Fuel economy advances are impressive. Equipped with the 360 V8, the 1979 Newport can deliver 14 miles per gallon in city driving and over 20 mpg on the highway. The 1978 Newport, equipped with the 440 engine delivered only 10 mpg in the city and 16 on the highway. The acceleration and performance of the new Newport are equal to or better than those of the big-engine 1978s. The key here is the 800-pound weight loss. The car needs less power now than it used to.

Newport and New Yorker, which is basically a Newport with additional luxury items, are available in one body style—a four-door hardtop sedan. The two-door model has been discontinued. A 318 cubic-inch V8 is standard for Newport. The 360 V8 offered as an option for Newport is standard for New Yorker.

CHRYSLER NEWPORT
Test Model Specifications

Body type	4-door	Rear hiproom	57.4 in.
Overall length	220.2 in.	Engine type	V8
Overall width	77.1 in.	Net hp @ rpm	150 @ 3600
Overall height	54.5 in.	Net torque @ rpm	265 @ 2400
Wheelbase	118.5 in.	Displacement	360 cu. in.
Turn diameter	42.4 ft.	Compression ratio	8.4:1
Tire size	P195 75R	Carburetion	2 bbl.
Curb weight	3640 lbs.	Transmission	Automatic
Cargo space	21.3 cu. ft.	Axle ratio	2.71:1
Front headroom	38.6 in.	Acceleration 0-60 mph	13.9 sec.
Front legroom	42.3 in.	Brake stop 60-0 mph	154 ft.
Front hiproom	57.6 in.	Fuel tank capacity	21 gal.
Rear headroom	37.4 in.	EPA city economy rating	14 mpg.
Rear legroom	38.2 in.		

Dodge Aspen

A Dodge Aspen can be a bargain this year because of a change in pricing policy at Chrysler Corporation. Right now Aspen sells for less than the Dodge Omni. Traditionally, bigger cars carry higher prices. But now Aspen starts at about $3900; Omni is in the $4100 bracket.

So to car buyers who weigh value in the traditional manner — the bigger the car, the more it should cost — this turnabout presents an opportunity to get a lot of value at a low price. Yet Aspen suffers from a few old-fashioned designs.

Its fuel economy is no better than average. With the 225 cubic-inch Slant Six engine and automatic transmission, Aspen will deliver only about 18 miles per gallon in city driving and about 23 mpg on the highway. An Omni equipped with a four-cylinder engine and automatic transmission is rated at a believable 24 mpg in the city and 32 on the highway. If you select the optional 318 V8 engine for the Aspen, economy will drop by a couple of miles per gallon.

Dodge Aspen

We recommend the six-cylinder engine for Aspen because it is economical to buy and maintain, and is a proven design that will deliver smooth performance and perky acceleration in moderate-duty service. We believe the V8 is needed only for heavy-duty driving or for trailer towing.

If you like a big-car ride, Aspen will not disappoint you. It is smooth and relatively quiet. It gives the impression of a car half-again its size. Aspen's front suspension is soft enough to match those of the Caprice and LTD.

Aspen's acceleration is not of the head-snapping type, but it will keep you out of trouble in tight places where a little extra speed is needed. In handling tests, our staff noted that the car tends to understeer (go straight ahead in turns) to a point, then oversteer as the rear wheels break loose from the pavement during high speed turns. This is a typical Chrysler reaction, and is predictable; not anything that would throw the driver into an unexpected situation.

The Aspen's instrument panel is clean, simple, and neatly laid out. The radio and heater controls on the right side, and the lights and wiper-washer controls on the left are all in easy reach of the driver. Interior room is good. The two-door is rated as a five-passenger model: three in the front and two in the rear. Three passengers in the back seat of either the four-door sedan or the two-door can feel squeezed.

Aspen is nearly identical with the Plymouth Volare in design and model lineup. Also, the Chrysler LeBaron and Dodge Diplomat share the Aspen four-door and station wagon body, but their trim levels are a step above the Aspen's, and that is reflected in their higher prices.

Its size, carrying capacity, simplicity of design, and big-car features have made Aspen Dodge's biggest-selling model. But the car has a history of poor durability and numerous recalls. That's why we cannot give Aspen a top rating among mid-size cars, even though its low price weighs heavily in its favor.

Aspen is Dodge's second-best model, next to Omni. Aspen must be compared with Ford's Fairmont and Mercury's Zephyr, cars that are similar to Aspen in size and price. In such a comparison, the Ford Motor Company products show themselves superior to the Dodge.

DODGE ASPEN
Test Model Specifications

Body type	4-door	Rear hiproom	57 in.
Overall length	201.2 in.	Engine type	6 in-line
Overall width	72.8 in.	Net hp @ rpm	110 @ 3600
Overall height	55.3 in.	Net torque @ rpm	180 @ 2000
Wheelbase	112.7 in.	Displacement	225 cu. in.
Turn diameter	40.7 ft.	Compression ratio	8.4:1
Tire size	DR 78-14	Carburetion	2 bbl.
Curb weight	3206 lbs.	Transmission	Automatic
Cargo space	16.2 cu. ft.	Axle ratio	2.76:1
Front headroom	39.2 in.	Acceleration 0-60 mph	16.9 sec.
Front legroom	42.5 in.	Brake stop 60-0 mph	146 ft.
Front hiproom	57.2 in.	Fuel tank capacity	18 gal.
Rear headroom	37.5 in.	EPA city economy rating	18 mpg.
Rear legroom	36.6 in.		

Dodge Diplomat

Feature for feature, Diplomat can't compete with the likes of the Buick Regal and Pontiac Grand Prix, but its relatively low price and simplicity of design are worth considering.

The differences between Diplomat and the Dodge Aspen are almost entirely superficial: Diplomat's seats and upholstery are a grade above the Aspen's; its exterior trim is more extensive and of a higher quality than the Dodge compact's. Engines, transmissions, suspensions and other functional parts of the one car are identical with those of the other.

Three body types are offered: a two-door coupe

based on the Aspen four-door chassis, a four-door, and a station wagon. Dodge now refers to these Diplomat models as mid-size cars, though they are the same size as the compacts sold under Volare and Aspen names. Of the three models, the four-door and wagon offer the most competitive value. The two-door does not measure up to its major competition, especially the Oldsmobile Cutlass Supreme and the Regal, mostly because Diplomat's rear seat room is tight and its fuel economy is comparatively low.

Thanks to a relatively low beltline and cowl, the visibility for front and rear passengers is good to excellent. You have no closed-in feeling when riding in the Diplomat's rear seat. The car's instrument panel is straightforward for an American car, though some drivers might feel that the bright trim on the instruments is excessive. The instruments are placed well for easy reading, but the controls are scattered and somewhat less easy to locate quickly.

The Chrysler 318 cubic-inch V8 is smooth running, and its noise levels are among the lowest of any Chrysler engine. The 318 is the best choice for Diplomat even though the 225 Slant Six runs with nearly the same fuel economy, and just a bit less power and smoothness. CONSUMER GUIDE Magazine's test staff says the optional 360 V8 engine is recommended only for station wagon use or for those drivers who need the extra lugging power that only big engines deliver.

No matter which engine is selected, Diplomat's fuel economy is less than spectacular. The 318 is rated at 16 miles per gallon in city driving. That is below the fuel economy of similar vehicles from General Motors.

In tests of performance the 318 V8 accelerates from 0 to 60 miles an hour in about 14 seconds. That's relatively slow for a V8 in a car of this size. A

Pontiac Grand Prix equipped with a 301 V8 will accelerate to the same speed in about 12 seconds. For normal city and highway driving, though, the Chrysler 318 is acceptable.

Two other factors set Diplomat apart from the more expensive personal luxury cars: a light chassis, and a looseness in the handling that is typical of Chrysler mid-size sedans. Compared to the isolation built into the suspension and steering of the Oldsmobile Toronado, Buick Riviera, and Lincoln Versailles, the Diplomat chassis transfers more noise and vibration to the driver through the steering wheel. The difference is striking.

Diplomat has the same big-car feel that is found in all its related models—Volaré, LeBaron, Aspen—as a result of its long, level hoodline and high, level front fender lines. This is another reason why Diplomat remains slightly out of step with its competitors.

DODGE DIPLOMAT
Test Model Specifications

Body type	2-door	Rear hiproom	52.8 in.
Overall length	204 in.	Engine type	V8
Overall width	73.5 in.	Net hp @ rpm	140 @ 4000
Overall height	53.3 in.	Net torque @ rpm	245 @ 1600
Wheelbase	112.7 in.	Displacement	318 cu. in.
Turn diameter	40.7 ft.	Compression ratio	8.5:1
Tire size	FR 78-15	Carburetion	2 bbl.
Curb weight	3525 lbs.	Transmission	Automatic
Cargo space	16.1 cu. ft.	Axle ratio	2.94:1
Front headroom	37.5 in.	Acceleration 0-60 mph	13.8 sec.
Front legroom	42.5 in.	Brake stop 60-0 mph	155 ft.
Front hiproom	55.6 in.	Fuel tank capacity	19.5 gal.
Rear headroom	36.2 in.	EPA city economy rating	16 mpg.
Rear legroom	34 in.		

Dodge Magnum XE

Magnum XE is designed to cover Dodge's interests in the two-door luxury coupe market. At the same time, because it offers some sporty features, Magnum XE is also marketed as a personal luxury model.

Our own examination of an XE shows that it is not significantly different from Chrysler's Cordoba. The two cars share all the important features: chassis, power train, interior layout, and many body panels. Shoppers who like the shape of Cordoba and who want a little extra sports styling in their car should take a look at the Magnum XE. The two cars operate identically. Only the sporty touches, like the slanted front end, make Magnum different from Cordoba.

Sporty styling is one thing; sporty performance is another. In the Magnum we tested this year, the 360 cubic-inch V8 engine was a disappointment on a couple of counts. Its performance is no better than average. Our tests show that it will go from 0 to 60 miles an hour in about 14 seconds. That's slightly slower than average for a V8-equipped full-size

Dodge Magnum

sedan. With the smaller 318 V8, the standard power plant, acceleration times are in the 16-second range. That is not what most buyers would expect from such a car.

Careful driving will result in fuel economy of about 17 mpg in combined city-highway driving with the 360 engine. In city driving, the average drops to 14 mpg or less. The base 318 V8 can better that city average by two miles per gallon. On the highway, the 318 is only about one mpg better than the 360.

Dodge offers a four-barrel version of the 360 that provides enough power to satisfy just about any personal luxury car buyer. This engine is not recommended except for heavy-duty service like trailer towing, however, since its fuel economy is unacceptable.

Despite the full-size exterior, the inside of the Magnum is disappointingly small, especially in the rear seat. Passengers there must put up with less knee room and headroom than is offered by just about any other car in Magnum's class. Rear headroom is minimal for people of average height. Up front, there is plenty of room for the driver and passenger in the bucket seats. However, the seats are set low on the floor—in the sporty manner—and do not offer the comfort of chair-height types. The driver's position is generally comfortable. Controls and gauges are located in predictable positions. Yet the instrument panel has a swept-back design that makes the controls difficult to reach.

Magnum's trunk is spacious, but it has a high liftover, which makes loading and unloading heavy cargo quite difficult. The spare tire, located in the center front of the trunk, takes up much of the load space.

Dodge is said to be planning to build a smaller Magnum next year as part of its downsizing plans. That car probably will offer an improvement in passenger room, smaller outside dimensions than today's Magnum, and an improvement of up to four mpg in fuel economy.

For now, though, the automotive staff of CONSUMER GUIDE Magazine point to the GM models—especially Regal, Monte Carlo and Cutlass Supreme—as superior values in Magnum's class. Buyers interested in a bigger package have the Toronado and Riviera to consider, though their prices are considerably higher than Magnum's.

DODGE MAGNUM XE
Test Model Specifications

Body type	2-door	Rear hiproom	57 in.
Overall length	215.8 in.	Engine type	V8
Overall width	77.1 in.	Net hp @ rpm	155 @ 3600
Overall height	53.1 in.	Net torque @ rpm	270 @ 2400
Wheelbase	114.9 in.	Displacement	360 cu. in.
Turn diameter	41.2 ft.	Compression ratio	8.4:1
Tire size	HR 78-15	Carburetion	2 bbl.
Curb weight	3785 lbs.	Transmission	Automatic
Cargo space	16.3 cu. ft.	Axle ratio	2.45:1
Front headroom	37.7 in.	Acceleration 0-60 mph	14.2 sec.
Front legroom	42.4 in.	Brake stop 60-0 mph	178 ft.
Front hiproom	55.8 in.	Fuel tank capacity	25.5 gal.
Rear headroom	36.6 in.	EPA city economy rating	14 mpg.
Rear legroom	32.4 in.		

Dodge Omni

Omni is more than just an Americanized Rabbit with a Dodge nameplate: it's Dodge's best vehicle, considering fuel economy, handling and ease of driving. Omni also offers an acceptable ride, and very good room for four passengers. Dodge obviously copied the Volkswagen Rabbit when it designed the Omni, but made improvements.

The most noticeable feature is the ride. Omni's ride is distinctly different from that of all other small cars. The car feels like a bigger, heavier model—more like an intermediate than a subcompact. This is the result of a combination of front-wheel drive and a successful effort on the part of Dodge engineers to give Omni the softness of the big American cars. There is a lot of soft rubber in the front suspension, and that's the key. The rubber inserts between suspension members soak up road shocks before they get to the body.

As a tradeoff, the reaction of the Omni to steering imput is slower than a Rabbit's. But this is not a serious drawback. Despite all the bad publicity the Omni (and its companion car from Plymouth, the Horizon) got recently in regards to its handling,

80   CONSUMER GUIDE

Omni is safe to drive and will actually outperform most U.S. cars in standard handling tests.

Our test staff examined a four-door Omni this year. (Our comments on the two-door Plymouth Horizon apply to the Omni two-door, the 024.) We found a lot to like. The car deserves high marks for its down-the-road stability. This is especially commendable considering the car's 2200-pound weight. Front-wheel drive turns small, light automobiles into stable cars that feel much like full-size, two-ton models. The four-door hatchback body offers outstanding luggage space, and comfort for four passengers.

Some small items inside the car miss the mark, however. The seats are set low to the floor, and this reduces forward vision. The position of the accelerator pedal is also a problem. It is positioned too high off the floor for comfort.

Our test car was equipped with the only engine available—a four cylinder power plant—and a four-speed manual transmission. This combination delivers about 30 miles per gallon in average driving. That does not make Omni a super-economy car, but 30 mpg is a respectable figure in comparison

Dodge Omni

with the mileage of other U.S. subcompacts. The beauty of Omni is that little performance is sacrificed for economy. The car will go from 0 to 60 miles an hour in about 16 seconds. That's more than adequate for all types of American roadways.

It should be noted that the engine and four-speed transmission are Volkswagen products. The power train is imported from Germany and installed in Omnis in Dodge's plant. Noise levels in the passenger compartment are exceptionally low for a small car.

Omni is a best buy in the subcompact class, along with the VW Rabbit. You can't ask for a better ride in a car that lists for less than $5000. And Omni provides all the handling and comfort features of the best cars in its class. Dodge is selling the Omni four-door at a higher price than it asks for the four-door Aspen, even though the Aspen is a bigger car. We believe that Omni is the more modern car, offering all the advantages of hatchback construction and four-cylinder economy.

DODGE OMNI
Test Model Specifications

Body type	4-door	Rear hiproom	52.4 in.
Overall length	164.8 in.	Engine type	OHC in-line 4
Overall width	66.2 in.	Net hp @ rpm	55 @ 5600
Overall height	53.4 in.	Net torque @ rpm	120 @ 3200
Wheelbase	99.2 in.	Displacement	104.7 cu. in.
Turn diameter	34 ft.	Compression ratio	8.2:1
Tire size	P165x75 R 13	Carburetion	2 bbl.
Curb weight	2200 lbs.	Transmission	4-speed Manual
Cargo space	10.2 cu. ft.	Axle ratio	3.37:1
Front headroom	38.3 in.	Acceleration 0-60 mph	16 sec.
Front legroom	41.8 in.	Brake stop 60-0 mph	140 ft.
Front hiproom	52.6 in.	Fuel tank capacity	13 gal.
Rear headroom	37.4 in.	EPA city economy rating	25 mpg.
Rear legroom	33 in.		

Dodge
St. Regis

St. Regis is a new model from Dodge this year. Its introduction marks the first time in two years that Dodge has offered a full-size car. St. Regis replaces Monaco as Dodge's biggest sedan. Only one body style is available, the four-door. Surprisingly few upgrading options are offered.

The interior seems to be of a middle luxury grade. You can buy a Chevrolet or Ford and get more luxurious trim throughout than is found in St. Regis. Traditionally, Dodge has been a more expensive make than those competitors. However, times have changed. You now must pay $10,000 to $11,000 for a top-line Caprice or LTD; St. Regis sells for a few thousand less. Chevy sells a base Impala and Ford offers a base LTD at low prices. But once you get into the higher-priced models from Chevy and Ford, and add the cost of options, their prices zoom past the Dodge's.

Dodge has positioned St. Regis a notch above the Newport, its twin from Chrysler Division. St. Regis has more luxurious trim than Newport and costs about $200 more, even though both cars use the same body.

CONSUMER GUIDE Magazine tested a St. Regis equipped with the 360 cubic-inch V8 and automatic transmission. The car was noisy. Most of the noise resulted from poorly fitted seals around the front windows. However, the whole chassis and drive train of the St. Regis was substantially noisier than that of the top-line Ford and Chevy models.

Dodge uses a frameless design for its door glass that relies on the glass to seal directly to the door frame to keep the interior quiet. It is a difficult design to work with. The glass, under pressure from the air conditioning system inside the car, is pushed away from the seal. Wind whistle and roar are the results. Dodge's unit body construction also creates problems. There is no separation between the chassis and body, so road noises are transferred to the interior of the car more directly than is the case with separate body-and-frame cars like Fords and Chevrolets. The combination of noises in our St. Regis was among the highest we've experienced in full-size cars.

Fuel economy is about average for a big V8 in a big car. The 360 V8 with two-barrel carburetor averaged 17 miles per gallon in combined city and highway driving. You can expect 14 mpg or less in the city. You can purchase a St. Regis with a 225 cubic-inch Six or a 318 V8, but these engines are too small for the car and do not provide the kind of performance big-car buyers have come to expect. Furthermore, fuel economy with the smaller engines is not as good as you might expect. Highway fuel economy among the three is nearly a draw.

Although heavily disguised, St. Regis is an updated version of last year's Dodge Monaco. The new model uses many of Monaco's chassis and body parts. One carry-over design is the sweptback shape of the instrument panel. Our test staff cited this as the least appealing feature of the interior. The instruments are recessed deep into the panel where they are difficult to read, and all controls mounted on the bottom third of the panel are difficult to reach.

The interior is comfortable, and offers good room for four or five passengers. For six, the accommodations are tight.

Our overall impression of St. Regis is that it barely misses being a good value. Some of the problems that were present in Monaco have not been ironed out in the new car. St. Regis's biggest attractions are its size, which is among the biggest in its class, and its fair price. However, the top-line Chevys and Fords offer more luxury and a quieter ride than the new Dodge.

DODGE ST. REGIS
Test Model Specifications

Body type	4-door	Rear hiproom	55.3 in.
Overall length	220.2 in.	Engine type	V8
Overall width	77.1 in.	Net hp @ rpm	150 @ 3600
Overall height	54.5 in.	Net torque @ rpm	265 @ 2400
Wheelbase	118.5 in.	Displacement	360 cu. in.
Turn diameter	42.4 ft.	Compression ratio	8.4:1
Tire size	75 R 15	Carburetion	2 bbl.
Curb weight	3640 lbs.	Transmission	Automatic
Cargo space	21.3 cu. ft.	Axle ratio	2.71:1
Front headroom	39.4 in.	Acceleration 0-60 mph	13.9 sec.
Front legroom	42.4 in.	Brake stop 60-0 mph	156 ft.
Front hiproom	55 in.	Fuel tank capacity	21 gal.
Rear headroom	38.2 in.	EPA city economy rating	14 mpg.
Rear legroom	39 in.		

Ford Fairmont

Fairmont for 1979 is virtually unchanged from 1978, so we give it the same evaluation this year as we did in the car's debut year. It's an outstanding design, more economical than its closest competitors, and provides comfort for five people.

There is no scrimping on interior room. The thin door panels open up the interior significantly, and the boxy roofline is a tipoff to the extra headroom that rear passengers enjoy in a Fairmont. However, seats are softly padded and offer little side support. We would like to see Ford and other domestic manufacturers put the same kind of firmness in their seats that we find in the imports, especially those from Europe. Fairmont's lack of support can be especially tiring on long trips: the passengers' muscles have to take up the slack in the seats.

Visibility, though, is excellent. Ford starts off with a low cowl height which lowers the windshield, and that gives the driver an excellent view forward. The low beltline increases the driver's view of the roadway to the sides, too. Visibility is one feature that must be experienced to be appreciated. Fairmont is among the best of the American cars in this respect.

However, Ford made a mistake in positioning the front seat cushions too close to the floor. We think that all the revisions the designers made to improve driver visibility were nearly negated by the low placement of the seat cushions. Apparently, Ford designers think low-slung seats are sportier than the chair-height type, and that's why they came up with the current shape. The top-priced optional Fairmont seats have a higher cushion level than the two lower-cost seat types, and thus offer better visibility. However, all three seats should be redesigned.

The problem of selecting an engine for Fairmont is complicated by the wide range of offerings and each buyer's intended use of the car. The smallest engine is the 140 cubic-inch Four—the same one used in the subcompact Pinto and Mustang. It is too small. We're certain that most buyers will find its poor performance and high noise levels inconsistent with the high comfort levels of Fairmont's body and chassis. The 200 cubic-inch Six offered as the first option seems well suited to Fairmont. It can deliver acceptable performance. It's our choice as the best compromise engine here, though its 18 mpg city driving fuel economy is a trifle low even for cars in Fairmont's class. The top engine is Ford's 302 V8, which we recommend only for heavy-duty driving or trailer towing. It offers good performance, and its noise levels are slightly lower than those of the six-cylinder engine, but city fuel economy with this engine is a mediocre 16 mpg.

(The 140 Four has a higher horsepower rating than the 200 Six, but we consider this a mere technicality. The bigger engine offers more power in actual driving situations than the Four.)

We still object to the layout of Fairmont's instrument panel. At best it is unimaginative; at worst it is something pulled from Ford's archives. It is designed to be simple, but the layout is unbalanced, uncoordinated and unfocused. We especially object to the offset position of the speedometer and gauges. The shift quadrant indicator, strangely, is placed in a more prominent position—directly in front of the driver.

Considering all the criticisms we've listed, can we rate Fairmont the best car in the compact class? Right now, we can. Its combination of economy, passenger room and performance are unmatched. But soon the picture may change. General Motors is preparing its new X-body cars—replacements for Nova, Phoenix, Skylark, Omega—for introduction next spring. Their design suggests a completely new level of quality for compact cars. Our opinion of Fairmont's value may change greatly once we've been able to compare it alongside the new GM cars.

FORD FAIRMONT
Test Model Specifications

Body type	4-door	Rear hiproom	53.7 in.
Overall length	193.9 in.	Engine type	6 in-line
Overall width	70.2 in.	Net hp @ rpm	85 @ 3600
Overall height	53.5 in.	Net torque @ rpm	154 @ 1600
Wheelbase	105.5 in.	Displacement	200 cu. in.
Turn diameter	39 ft.	Compression ratio	8.5:1
Tire size	DR 78-14	Carburetion	1 bbl.
Curb weight	2668 lbs.	Transmission	Automatic
Cargo space	16.8 cu. ft.	Axle ratio	2.73:1
Front headroom	38.5 in.	Acceleration 0-60 mph	16.1 sec.
Front legroom	41.8 in.	Brake stop 60-0 mph	155 ft.
Front hiproom	56.2 in.	Fuel tank capacity	16 gal.
Rear headroom	37.7 in.	EPA city economy rating	18 mpg.
Rear legroom	35.4 in.		

Ford Granada

Priced at $400 above Fairmont, Granada is the second half of Ford's one-two punch in the compact-intermediate car market. We've concluded that Granada is the second-best compact-intermediate from Ford. In direct comparison with Fairmont, it loses almost every time. But when compared with outside competition, Granada fares a little better. We rate it equal to the Chrysler compacts, and slightly higher in value than the AMC Concord.

Granada offers an acceptable ride, a quiet passenger compartment, and trim that is superior in quality to that of just about every other car of Granada's size and price. Those are the traditional features that Detroit emphasized before the fuel crunch hit.

Ford Granada

Fairmont (and the Mercury version, Zephyr) is lighter, more fuel efficient, provides more room inside and handles better than Granada. It is built in the modern mold. Granada's instrument panel is set high up on a high, level cowl. This, combined with a low seat position, gives the driver the impression that he or she is peeking up over the panel to see the roadway ahead. By contrast, Fairmont has a low cowl, instrument panel and hoodline; the driver has a clear view of the road.

Granada's reaction to steering changes is stiff. The car has a strong tendency to plow straight ahead in severe turns at speed. It is one of the widest and longest cars in its class, and this bulk adds to its clumsiness in traffic.

Our test Granada was equipped with a 250 cubic-inch six-cylinder engine that seems to be just right for this model. It delivers about one more mile per gallon than the optional 302 V8, and runs with the same smoothness. The performance of the V8 is well above that of the Six, however, so to buyers interested in a quick car, or one that will see heavy-duty service, we recommend the V8.

Fuel economy, even with the Six, is disappointing. We averaged less than 20 mpg for combined city and highway driving—just about what Environmental Protection Agency results show. Fuel economy averages in the low 20s are possible with competitive compacts, but these cars are usually equipped with four-cylinder engines that deliver unacceptable performance.

The layout of Granada's trunk is odd. There are two wells outboard of the main center section. Use of a small, compact spare, which can be tucked into one of the side wells, reserves a great amount of room for luggage. But if a standard spare is used, it must be mounted atop the axle hump, and takes up about one third of the best storage space.

Our test model was the Ghia, which is more luxuriously trimmed than the base model. Soft cloth trim, extra pull handles for the doors, a center arm rest in the rear and woodgrain trim are some of the Ghia's attractive appearance features.

If you want luxury in the compact class, Granada may be a good choice. But it is outvalued by Fairmont and Zephyr in fuel economy, handling and passenger room.

FORD GRANADA
Test Model Specifications

Body type 4-door	Rear hiproom .... 51.2 in.
Overall length .... 197.8 in.	Engine type .... 6 in-line
Overall width .... 74 in.	Net hp @ rpm .... 97 @ 3200
Overall height .... 53.3 in.	Net torque @ rpm .... 210 @ 1400
Wheelbase .... 109.9 in.	Displacement .... 250 cu. in.
Turn diameter .... 39.7 ft.	Compression ratio 8.6:1
Tire size .... ER 78-14	Carburetion .... 1 bbl.
Curb weight .... 3249 lbs.	Transmission .... Automatic
Cargo space .... 15.4 cu. ft.	Axle ratio 2.79:1
Front headroom ...... 38.2 in.	Acceleration 0-60 mph . 16.6 sec.
Front legroom .... 40.6 in.	Brake stop 60-0 mph ..... 168 ft.
Front hiproom .... 55.9 in.	Fuel tank capacity .... 18 gal.
Rear headroom .... 37.6 in.	EPA city economy rating .. 17 mpg.
Rear legroom .... 35.6 in.	

Ford LTD

Ford's full-size LTD has undergone an extensive change. The '79 version is smaller outside, lighter, and is powered by smaller engines than previous models, but offers just as much carrying capacity as in the past. We believe the changes were all for the good.

The new LTD—offered in two- and four-door sedans, and a station wagon—is more than a foot shorter in length than the LTD was last year. The 1979 body is about five inches narrower than the 1978. As such, it is easier to drive in tight places and easier to park. Handling has been tidied up considerably.

As big as the changes were, there is little feeling that LTD is anything but a full-size car. LTD's passenger room is better than before in most respects, and about the same as you get in Ford's major competition. The trunk is larger, and is deep enough to make bulky packages a cinch to load.

The first thing we noticed in driving the new LTD was the difference in ride and handling between it and the earlier LTD. The ride is flat and controlled. The heave and lurch felt in previous LTDs as they traveled over rises in the roadway have been reduced. Agility like that of a small car is highly evident in the new LTD. This makes the Ford a worthy competitor to the Chevrolet Caprice for the first time in three years.

Ford developed a new steering system and new suspension for the 1979 LTD. The LTD still lacks the feeling of complete integration between suspension and body that Chevrolet offers, but the Ford is nearly as controllable as the Chevy in emergency handling maneuvers. Our tests of 1978 and 1979 LTDs over the same handling course indicate that the new model has been improved about 10 percent in high-speed control and about 8 percent in low-speed agility. These improvements make the 1979 LTD a pleasurable car to live with.

The biggest engine available in the LTD for 1979 is the 351 cubic-inch V8; the only other engine is the 302. The wasteful 400 and 460 V8s are no longer available. Despite the decrease in horsepower, the light new LTD accelerates and performs as well as the big-engine 1978s. More important, our tests of an LTD equipped with the 351 show that the car will deliver about 19 miles per gallon at freeway speeds; in city driving, economy drops to about 14 mpg. Last year, an LTD equipped with the 460 engine delivered about 17 mpg on the highway and 12 in the city.

The styling changes in the LTD for '79 have resulted in improved visibility also. The glass area is either bigger this year or appears so; the car's hood has been shortened by at least eight inches; the driver's position is high in relation to the cowl.

Front visibility is substantially better this year than before. Vision to the right rear is not good, though, because the panel at the C post is wide.

The LTD instrument panel is new. The horn button is now located at the end of the turn-signal stalk, where it's difficult to find when needed in a hurry. However, the control for the windshield wiper and washer, mounted on the steering column, is easy to reach. For the most part, control levers and knobs are placed conveniently, but the low position of the instruments causes some problems: our drivers had to lower their line of sight considerably as they switched from the roadway to the instruments. The gauges should be mounted higher up, closer to the straight-ahead view of the driver.

Overall, the new Ford LTD ranks right up there with the Chevrolet Caprice as an outstanding value in the full-size market. CONSUMER GUIDE Magazine's test staff still rates the Chevy higher than the LTD, but the new Ford doesn't miss the bull's-eye by much.

FORD LTD
Test Model Specifications

Body type	4-door	Rear hiproom	58 in.
Overall length	209 in.	Engine type	V8
Overall width	77.5 in.	Net hp @ rpm	132 @ 3200
Overall height	54.5 in.	Net torque @ rpm	268 @ 1400
Wheelbase	114.4 in.	Displacement	351 cu. in.
Turn diameter	39.4 ft.	Compression ratio	8.3:1
Tire size	FR 78-14	Carburetion	2V
Curb weight	3920 lbs.	Transmission	Automatic
Cargo space	23.3 cu. ft.	Axle ratio	2.26:1
Front headroom	38 in.	Acceleration 0-60 mph	13.9 sec.
Front legroom	42 in.	Brake stop 60-0 mph	148 ft.
Front hiproom	61.2 in.	Fuel tank capacity	19 gal.
Rear headroom	37.4 in.	EPA city economy rating	14 mpg.
Rear legroom	40.5 in.		

Ford LTD II

A lame duck—that's the 1979 version of the Ford LTD II. This "mid-size" car, which is bigger and heavier than many full-size cars, has one more year to go. Ford plans to drop this car and nameplate from its lineup for 1980. The LTD II is a leftover from the days of the gas-guzzling behemoths; only a quirk in Ford's downsizing program has kept it in the lineup to this point.

In our estimate of value for a mid-size car, the LTD II ranks dead last. The same can be said for duplicate models at Lincoln-Mercury, the Cougar sedans. They're all too big and wasteful, and their handling is poor. They look very bad in comparison with other cars in their class.

Ford has a problem in marketing the LTD II against the mid-size models from General Motors and Chrysler—cars that are smaller than the LTD II —deliver much better fuel economy, and are easier to drive and park than the Ford. The LTD II also must compete against the all-new Ford LTD. The two Fords are about the same size outside but the

Ford LTD II

LTD offers a number of advantages inside and in its drive train and chassis.

The LTD can deliver 14 to 15 miles per gallon in city driving when equipped with either the 302 or 351 cubic-inch V8 engine; using those power plants, the LTD II is rated at only 14 and 13 mpg. LTD offers more interior room than the LTD II, and a quieter, more controlled ride. The only advantage offered by the LTD II in this comparison with the LTD is price. But the couple of hundred dollars difference is insignificant when resale value and operating costs of the new design and the old-fashioned one are compared.

Ford will carry the LTD II for one more year; then Granada will become the division's mid-size car and the LTD II will be dropped from production.

The 1979 version of the LTD II is unchanged from the 1978. Two body styles are offered—two-door and four-door sedans (the station wagon was discontinued last year). They are designed and styled in the old manner: bloated bodies; adequate but not spacious accommodations inside for six passengers.

Our main objection to this type of car is the handling. In tight turns, the front end of the LTD II is slow to respond to movement of the steering wheel. On uneven pavement, the body lurches and heaves. The steering is too light, and leaves no room for road feel. This is a car that is driven almost by sight only, not by feel.

The LTD II drive train has a loose feel too. The engine typically speeds up well ahead of the transmission — something like winding up a rubber band — before the rear wheels take hold. A feeling of inefficiency reminds the driver that the LTD II has the lowest fuel economy ratings of any car in the mid-size class.

In terms of trim, the LTD II looks good alongside intermediates from GM. The GM cars have a Spartan appearance; three LTD II trim levels are offered, and the top-of-the-line Brougham is the equal of many full-size luxury models inside and out.

Nonetheless, buyers of intermediates would do well to look to the GM lineup for two- and four-door sedans this year. They offer efficiency and ride that are better in most ways to the LTD II's. The Chrysler mid-size cars, LeBaron and Diplomat, also look like better values than the LTD II, especially in light of Ford's plans to drop the car at the end of this year.

FORD LTD II
Test Model Specifications

Body type 4-door	Rear hiproom . . . . 57 in.
Overall length . . . . 219.5 in.	Engine type V8
Overall width . . . . 78.6 in.	Net hp @ rpm . . . . 140 @ 3800
Overall height . . . . 53.3 in.	Net torque @ rpm . . . . 255 @ 2000
Wheelbase . . . . 118 in.	Displacement . . . . 351 cu. in.
Turn diameter . . . . 41.3 ft.	Compression ratio 8.0:1
Tire size . . . . HR 78-15	Carburetion . . . . 2 bbl.
Curb weight . . . . 3979 lbs.	Transmission . . . . Automatic
Cargo space . . . . 15.8 cu. ft.	Axle ratio 2.47:1
Front headroom . . . . 37.3 in.	Acceleration 0-60 mph . . . . 13 sec.
Front legroom . . . . 42.3 in.	Brake stop 60-0 mph . . . . . . 163 ft.
Front hiproom . . . . 59.2 in.	Fuel tank capacity . . . . 21 gal.
Rear headroom . . . . 36.3 in.	EPA city economy rating . . 13 mpg.
Rear legroom . . . . 32.8 in.	

Ford Mustang

A fresh European-like look and a new turbo-charged engine are not all that is new about Mustang for 1979. The new car is completely unlike the 1978 model from the ground up. A number of improvements have been made in interior room, instrument layout, performance and handling.

Aside from its new exterior appearance, Mustang's most interesting feature is the new turbo-charged four-cylinder engine. The test staff of CONSUMER GUIDE Magazine had a chance to examine this engine, but we decided to test the 302 cubic-inch V8 optional engine for the purposes of this review. For performance drivers, the V8 is the most logical choice in Mustang's engine lineup. It is powerful at all speeds, especially at start-up.

In acceleration tests with the V8, the Mustang with manual four-speed transmission can move from 0 to 60 miles an hour in just over nine seconds. That puts the Ford on a par with the best of the Camaros and Firebirds. The V8 does not give the car the front-heavy feel that was evident in previous Mustangs. Instead, it makes a balanced contribution to performance and handling. Acceleration at all speeds is excellent, as you might expect when a V8 is installed in a car of the Mustang's weight: 3000 pounds.

Compared with the turbocharged engine, the V8 is quicker at most speeds, and certainly more responsive at low speeds where performance is most important.

The turbo is a boosted version of the four-cylinder, 140 cubic-inch power plant that Mustang offered last year. It has been equipped with stronger parts, especially pistons, plus the turbocharging mechanism.

The Mustang Four can deliver about 21 mpg in city driving; the V8 delivers only about 16. Ford's V6 is rated at about 18 mpg in city driving.

One of the most impressive features of Mustang for '79 is the improvement in handling over that of previous versions. The car rides flat, stays in control, and gives the driver a feeling of security never before offered in a Mustang. Part of the reason for the improvement can be found in the chassis. Mustang now uses a modified Fairmont chassis, including its excellent suspension structure. That, combined with the small size and light weight of the new Mustang, make handling predictable and agile. Add to these factors the optional wheels, tires and handling suspension components that compose the TRX package, and you have a sporty handling car unlike any other that Ford has ever offered.

In handling tests, CONSUMER GUIDE Magazine's test staff found that the Mustang is the equal of the Camaro and Firebird, and only slightly less agile than Corvette. Furthermore, the control and predictability of Mustang's handling are much better suited to the average driver.

The appearance of the interior has been upgraded too. The instrument panel face is new, flatter and more expensive looking than the 1978 version. However, the "luxury" appearance of the standard panel is better suited to the Mustang Ghia trim than to the sportier packages. A sportier instrument panel is available as part of an option group.

Ford is trying to cover two distinctly different groups of competitors with Mustang: the lightweight sporty cars in the Monza group, and the heavyweight muscle cars in the Camaro group. One of the results is a split personality in the features of the car.

Ford has been mostly successful in designing a modern sporty car that can compete with Camaro and Firebird. Equipped with the V8 engine, the Mustang can keep up with both of them.

Mercury's Capri is almost a twin of the Mustang. So what is true about Mustang also holds true for Capri. However, Mustang is available in two body styles, the notchback coupe and the hatchback model; Capri is offered only as a hatchback. Otherwise, all systems, including the handling packages and turbocharged engine, are interchangeable.

FORD MUSTANG
Test Model Specifications

Body type	2-door
Overall length	179.1 in.
Overall width	69.1 in.
Overall height	51.8 in.
Wheelbase	100.4 in.
Turn diameter	N/A
Tire size	TRX/R/14
Curb weight	2516 lbs.
Cargo space	10 cu. ft.
Front headroom	37.2in.
Front legroom	40.9 in.
Front hiproom	54 in.
Rear headroom	36.3 in.
Rear legroom	29.8 in.
Rear hiproom	47.1 in.
Engine type	V8
Net hp @ rpm	140 @ 3600
Net torque @ rpm	243 @ 2000
Displacement	302 cu. in.
Compression ratio	8.4:1
Carburetion	2 bbl.
Transmission	Automatic
Axle ratio	3.08:1
Acceleration 0-60 mph	11.0 sec.
Brake stop 60-0 mph	140 ft.
Fuel tank capacity	12.5 gal.
EPA city economy rating	16 mpg.

Ford Pinto

Ford's domestic subcompact enters its 10th year on the road with new front styling, but it will take much more than that to polish up the car's tarnished reputation. Recent reports of fire hazards in crashes involving Pintos have resulted in Ford's recall of whole years' production. The 1978 and 1979 Pintos are designed to eliminate this hazard.

Why Pinto should be plagued with these problems is a puzzle, since the car is a simple design that does not involve complicated techniques in manufacture or assembly. The engine is up front; the rear wheels do the driving. It's a traditional design—one that Ford is planning to replace with a front-drive subcompact of about the same size in 1981. Until then, Ford will continue to offer the line in three body styles: the two-door sedan, two-door hatchback, and the station wagon. The engine line-up includes the same 140 cubic-inch Four and 171 cubic-inch V6 that were available in 1978.

Changes in the front styling for 1979 are matched inside by changes in the instrument panel layout. The gauges and warning lights are housed in two separate, square pods that look more modern than the old design. No additional information is pro-

Ford Pinto

vided by the new instruments; however, the altera-
tion is needed to bring Pinto up even with Chevette,
Horizon and the imports in instrument panel layout.

We rank Pinto behind Horizon, Omni and Chevette in handling, but on a par with most of the
small Japanese sedans. The main problem with
Pinto's handling is that the car is built on a wide
body. That makes it clumsy in comparison with the
best of its competition. Body roll in tight turns is
our main objection. Pinto's ride has been improved
several times since the car first hit the showrooms
in 1970, but even now it lacks the solid feel of the
front-drive cars. Ford has not yet found the ideal
balance between firm ride and comfort—something that becomes more difficult to attain as cars
get smaller.

On balance, we believe the Horizon, Omni and
Chevette among domestic cars offer better value
for subcompact-car buyers. A number of imports,
including Rabbit and Honda, are also superior.
Most of Pinto's competitors offer front-wheel drive,
a design that makes a great deal of sense in a car of
Pinto's size.

Pinto's resale value has been hurt by the bad
reports about hazards in accidents. Ford makes

recall kits available for Pintos that have been found defective, and owners can have the new plastic fuel tank shields installed free. But the damage has already been done as far as public opinion is measured. We expect Pintos to offer less value as used cars than any of its competitors.

Ford continues to boost Pinto as its most economical domestically built car. This year a Pinto equipped with a four-cylinder engine can average about 22 miles per gallon in city driving, and about 32 mpg on the highway. We think these figures are acceptable for a car of Pinto's size. However, economy with the optional V6 engine is much lower—18 mpg in city driving—so the Six is not recommended, except for the station wagon. Subcompact shoppers will note that these figures can be surpassed easily by many imports.

Comparison shoppers will also note that the Mercury Bobcat is virtually identical to the Pinto, except that the Bobcat is not available in the two-door sedan body style.

FORD PINTO
Test Model Specifications

Body type	2-door	Rear hiproom	41.3 in.
Overall length	168.8 in.	Engine type	4 in-line
Overall width	69.4 in.	Net hp @ rpm	88 @ 4800
Overall height	50.6 in.	Net torque @ rpm	118 @ 2800
Wheelbase	94.5 in.	Displacement	140 cu. in.
Turn diameter	30.7 ft.	Compression ratio	9.0:1
Tire size	A 78-13	Carburetion	2 bbl.
Curb weight	2472 lbs.	Transmission	4-speed
Cargo space	8.2 cu. ft.		Manual
Front headroom	37.3 in.	Axle ratio	3.08:1
Front legroom	40.2 in.	Acceleration 0-60 mph	15.8 sec.
Front hiproom	51.6 in.	Brake stop 60-0 mph	147 ft.
Rear headroom	35.7 in.	Fuel tank capacity	13 gal.
Rear legroom	30.3 in.	EPA city economy rating	22 mpg.

Ford Thunderbird

Thunderbird's downsizing is overdue. This year is the last for the present T-Bird body. The new car, set for introduction as a 1980 model, is expected to be lighter, more economical to drive, smaller on the outside, and easier to handle than the present Thunderbird. Ford will finally make the same changes in its personal luxury car that General Motors has already made in its similar models.

The present Thunderbird is a thinly disguised LTD II coupe. They have different rooflines and windows, and some trim differences inside, but the two cars are identical in most other ways. They share engines, transmissions, suspensions and frames. So buyers interested in a Thunderbird-type car might do well to select the LTD II as an alternative. The savings in price can be significant. However, we can't say we like either car.

Our advice to Thunderbird shoppers is to wait. Next year, there will be a new T-Bird (and a new LTD II) that may be able to compete more equally with GM's solid lineup of personal luxury models.

Although Thunderbird was downsized three years ago, it is still too big, too heavy, and too clumsy. The ride is typical of Ford: soft and floating on smooth roadways; apt to rock and sway on uneven pavement. Even the famed quiet ride of Ford products has deteriorated in the current Thunderbird to a point where the competition has equaled or surpassed its interior noise levels. Thunderbird's rear seat layout also is a sore point. It's short on headroom and legroom. In addition, the support of the soft seats is poor, and results in an uncomfortable ride.

Worst of all is the car's fuel economy, whether you choose the 302 or the 351 cubic-inch V8. City mileage is about 14 and 13 miles per gallon with these engines—significantly less than the mileage of comparable cars from GM.

Three Thunderbird series are offered this year: the base car, the Town Landau and the Heritage. They are essentially the same, two-door coupe, having only trim levels to differentiate them. The Town Landau that we tested this year offers the best-looking and richest interior of all the personal luxury cars, and sells in the $10,000 price range. The instrument panel, seats, and door trim all say "expensive" in an emphatic way. By comparison,

Ford Thunderbird

the GM personal luxury cars look unfinished.

Thunderbird still offers some standard Ford components that owners of old Mustangs and even Pintos will find disconcertingly familiar. One of them is the bent-bar steering wheel with the overdesigned speed control system built in. The horn bar on this steering wheel has sharp edges, and is not easy to find in an emergency.

The T-Bird's automatic transmission is still sloppy, permitting excessive engine overrun between shifts and some lag in acceleration from a stop. We suspect the basic problem with Ford's fuel economy in big cars is traceable to their transmission. And there is no way a Thunderbird buyer can get around that.

Summing up, 1979 is a poor year for Thunderbird fans. The car is scheduled to be replaced with a completely new design in 1980. The competition from GM is new, and changes made in those cars have put Ford years behind in the personal luxury class. A wait until 1980 is strongly recommended.

FORD THUNDERBIRD
Test Model Specifications

Body type	2-door	Rear hiproom	57.2 in.
Overall length	215.5 in.	Engine type	V8
Overall width	78.5 in.	Net hp @ rpm	135 @ 3200
Overall height	53 in.	Net torque @ rpm	268 @ 1400
Wheelbase	114 in.	Displacement	351 cu. in.
Turn diameter	43.1 ft.	Compression ratio	8.3:1
Tire size	HR 78-15	Carburetion	2 bbl.
Curb weight	4028 lbs.	Transmission	Automatic
Cargo space	15.6 cu. ft.	Axle ratio	2.47:1
Front headroom	37.3 in.	Acceleration 0-60 mph	11.3 sec.
Front legroom	42.1 in.	Brake stop 60-0 mph	148 ft.
Front hiproom	55.6 in.	Fuel tank capacity	21 gal.
Rear headroom	36.2 in.	EPA city economy rating	13 mpg.
Rear legroom	32.6 in.		

Lincoln Continental

There is only one really big luxury car left: it is the huge Lincoln Continental. Lincoln produces the Continental in two sedan models—a two-door and a four-door. They are offered in three series: the base car; the Town series, which offers a step up in luxury; and the top-of-the-line Collector's series, which features all the equipment offered on the other models plus a few extra touches to make it even more luxurious.

The 1979 Continental is little different from the 1978 model, though a change has been made in the engine lineup. This year the 400 cubic-inch engine is the only one offered. (It comes in three versions—for the 49 states, for California, and for high altitude areas.) The 460 V8 has been dropped from production because it was too wasteful. That's not to say the 400 is an economy power plant. It has been rated by the Environmental Protection Agency at no more than 12 miles per gallon in city driving and 17 on the highway. We think the EPA

Lincoln Continental

figures are optimistic. Our experience with Continental indicates that its fuel economy can be a couple of miles per gallon less than that in city and highway driving.

The Continental sedan is more than a foot longer, at 233 inches, than the Cadillac Sedan de Ville. Its curb weight of two and a half tons puts it in the heavyweight class, and helps to explain the poor fuel economy. Despite the size difference, Continental is not far behind the gasoline-powered Cadillacs in fuel economy. One model of De Ville is also rated at 12 mpg in city driving. Fuel economy as low as this doesn't seem to matter to big-car buyers. In fact, Lincoln Continentals are hot items on the new-car market now, and could end up with back-to-back sales records for 1977 and 1978. It appears that if you can afford the price of a Continental, the prospect of higher gas prices means little.

Continental's being the last of the big cars is mostly a matter of timing. Ford Motor Company plans to introduce a Continental of a smaller size in the 1980 model year. The biggest Ford Motor Company car has had to wait while the smaller Fords have been downsized.

Continental offers many of the big-car features that have made American cars the smoothest riding and quietest on the road. It glides over smooth pavement. Continental's interior is the quietest in the industry. Luxury is everywhere. The seats and upholstery invite relaxation. Continental truly is a comfortable car.

But what do you give up for the sake of quietness and comfort? Plenty, in addition to the average parking spot when you cruise around in this barge. Continental lurches and heaves when riding over uneven roadways. Also annoying is the overrun of the engine as it winds up the transmission when starting from a stop.

Rating Continental on luxury value is easy. If you equate bigness with luxury and prestige, Continental is the top choice of the expensive sedan lines. But if your tastes are less flamboyant, then Cadillac, with its smaller dimensions and better workmanship record, is your wisest choice. De Ville and Fleetwood are superior values; Chrysler's new New Yorker is a poor third choice among the big luxury cars.

LINCOLN CONTINENTAL
Test Model Specifications

Body type	4-door	Rear hiproom	60.6 in.
Overall length	233.0 in.	Engine type	V8
Overall width	79.9 in.	Net hp @ rpm	159 @ 3400
Overall height	55.4 in.	Net torque @ rpm	315 @ 1800
Wheelbase	127.2 in.	Displacement	400 cu. in.
Turn diameter	N/A	Compression ratio	8.0:1
Tire size	225 R-15	Carburetion	2 bbl.
Curb weight	4843 lbs.	Transmission	Automatic
Cargo space	21.2 cu. ft.	Axle ratio	2.75:1
Front headroom	38.1 in.	Acceleration 0-60 mph	14 sec.
Front legroom	42 in.	Brake stop 60-0 mph	180 ft.
Front hiproom	56.0 in.	Fuel tank capacity	24.2 gal.
Rear headroom	38.6 in.	EPA city economy rating	12 mpg.
Rear legroom	42 in.		

Lincoln Mark V

The Lincoln Mark V is entering its final year in production in its present form. The oversize luxury car is the last of a breed. Its 400 cubic-inch engine will barely deliver 12 miles per gallon fuel economy in city driving, and is unlikely to top 17 mpg on the highway. The Mark V looks big enough from the outside to hold an infantry squad, but inside dimensions are barely adequate for four persons. Its handling is ponderous. Its ride on rough roadways is similar to a tanker's in a typhoon.

Compared to some of the newer, downsized cars on the road, guiding the Mark V through traffic is like taking the helm of an ocean liner. The long hood, laid-back seating position, soft suspension and relatively slow response of the car to turns of the steering wheel create a feeling of delayed reaction. There is no chance of the driver's getting a feel of the road surface through the steering wheel: it's all filtered out by the super-soft suspension and power steering unit.

The power train produces a similar isolated and slow feeling. You depress the accelerator, hear the engine rev up, and then float away. The quick response enjoyed by drivers of downsized luxury cars is not available to drivers of the Mark V.

But Mark V sells well. It does have its virtues, though they do not appeal to all buyers. The Mark V is an unabashed prestige car. One look at the heaviness of exterior trim, long hood, and oversize body confirms that. It is a symbol of the traditional, now old-fashioned, definition of American automotive luxury: the bigger the car, and thus the more expensive it is, the better. Recent downsizing efforts by GM, Chrysler, and Ford have redefined the term "luxury car" but some buyers cannot accept the small models. Therein lies the reason for the Mark V's continued success.

The car is impressive, in more ways than size. Its body—dripping with bright moldings, affixed with a Rolls-Royce look-alike grille, and topped with a padded vinyl roof—shouts "expensive!" Interiors are equipped with thick carpeting, velour or leather seats and soft padding on just about every surface. The list of convenience and comfort options would fill a page of this book.

Two coupe models are available: the base Mark V; and the Designer Series that incorporates styling touches by Bill Blass, Emilio Pucci, Givenchy or Cartier.

Lincoln-Mercury's frame-and-body construction,

Lincoln Continental Mark V

the type that enhances noise control, is the basis for the Mark V's chassis. The suspension system that makes the driver feel isolated from the road also makes the interior of the Mark V one of the quietest of any car on the road. The Mark's floating ride signals opulence to most big-car buyers.

Buyers of personal luxury cars should note that Lincoln has a brand-new Mark planned for introduction next fall. It will be smaller and probably more efficient, but no less luxurious, than the present car. The biggest engine for the 1980 car is expected to be the 351 V8.

From what we've heard of the 1980 Mark V, it sounds like a much better value than the current model. If you can't wait until '80 to inspect the downsized Mark before making your personal luxury car purchase, we recommend a drive in the Cadillac Eldorado as well as a drive in the '79 Mark V. The test staff of CONSUMER GUIDE Magazine is thoroughly convinced that the Eldorado is the better of the two cars, by a long shot.

LINCOLN MARK V
Test Model Specifications

Body type	2-door	Rear hiproom	54.3 in.
Overall length	230.3 in.	Engine type	V8
Overall width	79.9 in.	Net hp @ rpm	159 @ 3400
Overall height	52.9 in.	Net torque @ rpm	315 @ 1800
Wheelbase	120.4 in.	Displacement	400 cu. in.
Turn diameter	45.1 ft.	Compression ratio	8.0:1
Tire size	225/15	Carburetion	2V
Curb weight	4779 lbs.	Transmission	Automatic
Cargo space	18.1 cu. ft.	Axle ratio	2.47:1
Front headroom	37.5 in.	Acceleration 0-60 mph	14.8 sec.
Front legroom	42.3 in.	Brake stop 60-0 mph	168 ft.
Front hiproom	55.4 in.	Fuel tank capacity	25 gal.
Rear headroom	37.1 in.	EPA city economy rating	12 mpg.
Rear legroom	34 in.		

Lincoln Versailles

The squared-off roofline of the 1979 Versailles is the first major styling change that has been made in the compact Lincoln since the car was introduced in early 1977. Other changes for '79 involve radios, headlamps, special vinyl treatment for the rear deck lid, door locks and voltage regulators. In all other respects, the 1979 model is nearly a duplicate of the 1978. It is still produced in one body style—the four-door sedan, which is based on the Granada body—and is available with one engine only, Ford's 302 cubic-inch V8.

Versailles is being marketed as Lincoln-Mercury's answer to the Cadillac Seville in the luxury compact class. The GM model is superior to Versailles in ride, handling and performance. And the diesel Seville can exceed Versailles in fuel economy.

The Lincoln's fuel economy is a big disappointment. It can deliver about 14 miles per gallon in city driving—the same as a Seville equipped with

Lincoln Versailles

a 350 cubic-inch V8—and only 19 mpg on the highway.

Although Versailles is based on the Granada, there is no doubt that the Lincoln version is a true luxury car. The paint job is special: clear coats of paint over color coats. This is a technique that provides an unusually deep shine that lasts for years; however, repair costs of such a paint job are high.

Driving the Versailles is just about what you would expect from a refined Granada chassis. Handling is nothing special—a little on the slow side, thanks to the relatively soft suspension and to the rubber parts inserted in the suspension to block off noise and vibration. The ride is soft and surprisingly quiet, even for a luxury car.

In the chassis, special attention has been paid to limiting vibration and muting noises both from the roadway and the machinery. Wheels, tires, and even the disc brakes are specially balanced. The drive shaft has a number of additional anchor points and other parts to cut vibration. The steering system also is special, designed to minimize vibrations from the wheels. And Versailles' list of standard equipment will match just about any other car's convenience and comfort features. It includes power windows, air conditioning, electronic engine control, speed control, halogen headlamps and four-wheel disc brakes.

The new roofline is almost all for show, though it does provide some small functional benefits. The interior dimensions of the 1979 model's rear seat area are identical with those of the 1978 model, even though the squared-off design gives the '79 a look of added headroom. Versailles has never been what we would call roomy. However, the new rear doors are slightly more square in shape, and this opens up the rear seat entry space so that it is easier to get in and out of Versailles this year.

Reports from inside Ford Motor Company indicate that the roof costs Lincoln an additional $1100 to fabricate. It is built by a customizer outside the assembly plant. This seems to us to be an excessive price to pay for so little advantage. It seems that Lincoln-Mercury managers wanted to make Versailles look less like Granada this year than it did before, and this change in the roof appealed to them most of all.

LINCOLN VERSAILLES
Test Model Specifications

Body type	4-door	Rear hiproom	51.2 in.
Overall length	200.9 in.	Engine type	V8
Overall width	74.5 in.	Net hp @ rpm	129 @ 3600
Overall height	54.1 in.	Net torque @ rpm	223 @ 2600
Wheelbase	109.9 in.	Displacement	302 cu. in.
Turn diameter	39.7 ft.	Compression ratio	8.4:1
Tire size	FR 78.14	Carburetion	Variable Venturi
Curb weight	3848 lbs.	Transmission	Automatic
Cargo space	14.1 cu. ft.	Axle ratio	2.75:1
Front headroom	38.2 in.	Acceleration 0-60 mph	15.2 sec.
Front legroom	40.6 in.	Brake stop 60-0 mph	170 ft.
Front hiproom	53.4 in.	Fuel tank capacity	19.2 gal.
Rear headroom	37.6 in.	EPA city economy rating	14 mpg.
Rear legroom	35.6 in.		

Mercury Bobcat

Lincoln-Mercury's version of the Ford Pinto, Bobcat, is available in two-door hatchback and station wagon models, and is available with the same engines as the subcompact Ford—a 140 cubic-inch in-line Four and 171 cubic-inch V6. We examined the hatchback equipped with the four-cylinder engine for this report. We found that the car performs adequately, but is in need of updating in several areas.

Don't be fooled by the new front appearance and the revised styling of the instrument panel on the 1979 model: the car is still basically the same as the import-beater Ford introduced as the original Pinto back in 1970. Refinements have been made in the ride and some serious safety hazards have been eliminated, but Bobcat's body panels and chassis have remained unchanged. Even the current 140 four-cylinder engine is little different from the original.

So the criticisms we've stated in the past continue to be valid. Bobcat's body is too big and heavy for the amount of passenger space it provides, and the car's fuel economy is lower than that of many cars having similar exterior dimensions.

Equipped with the four-cylinder engine and automatic transmission, Bobcat will not top 30 miles per gallon, even in highway driving. That's barely good enough to compete with the high-economy cars in Bobcat's class—especially Rabbit, Chevette and Omni/Horizon.

The interior layout of the Bobcat has never been one of our favorites, and since nothing has been done to the 1979 to improve the seating area, the problems remain. Bobcat's seats are of a low-quality construction. They offer little support in turns. The position of the seats is wrong, too. They are built close to the floor. This makes for an uncomfortable riding position, and makes getting into and out of the car more difficult than it should be. The shortage of interior room is not a question of seat design and quality only: the barrel shape of Bobcat's body is roomy in the wrong places; it feels tight in the areas where a few fractions of an inch really have an effect on comfort.

Performance of the automatic transmission and four-cylinder engine is poor: acceleration times from 0 to 60 miles an hour are in the high teens. However, this engine-transmission combination is superior in terms of fuel economy to the V6 option. The V6 is rated at 23 mpg highway and 18 in city driving, well below the average for a subcompact car. The performance of the Six is nothing to brag about either, though Bobcat can accelerate to 60 mph in less than 15 seconds with this engine. Our advice is: stick with the four-cylinder engine in the hatchback model, choosing either the manual or automatic transmission; order the V6 with automatic for the station wagon.

How does Bobcat stack up against the competition? Poorly. The Chrysler Horizon/Omni and Chevrolet Chevette are true economy cars that offer better interior layouts, fuel economy and handling than Bobcat. In addition, Lincoln-Mercury has already committed itself to replacing Bobcat with a front-drive model in a year and a half. This news, combined with Bobcat's tarnished safety reputation, will no doubt keep the car's resale value low.

Bobcat is well past its prime, and is showing its age. Newer designs, especially those offering front-wheel drive, surpass Bobcat in economy, ride, room and handling. Bobcat and Pinto occupy spots at the low end of CONSUMER GUIDE Magazine's subcompact-car ratings.

MERCURY BOBCAT
Test Model Specifications

Body type	2-door	Rear hiproom	39.4 in.
Overall length	169.3 in.	Engine type	in-line 4
Overall width	69.4 in.	Net hp @ rpm	88 @ 4800
Overall height	50.6 in.	Net torque @ rpm	118 @ 2800
Wheelbase	94.5 in.	Displacement	140 cu. in.
Turn diameter	30.7 ft.	Compression ratio	9.0:1
Tire size	A78-13	Carburetion	2V
Curb weight	2492 lbs.	Transmission	4-speed
Cargo space	29.0 cu. ft.*		Manual
Front headroom	37.3 in.	Axle ratio	2.73:1
Front legroom	40.8 in.	Acceleration 0-60 mph	15.8 sec.
Front hiproom	51.6 in.	Brake stop 60-0 mph	155 ft.
Rear headroom	35.8 in.	Fuel tank capacity	11.7 gal.
Rear legroom	29.6 in.	EPA city economy rating	22 mpg.

*with rear seat folded down

Mercury Capri

Capri puts Mercury up among the leaders in the sporty compact class. From what our test staff can determine, Capri is fully competitive with the top-selling General Motors sportsters, Firebird and Camaro.

We selected the brand-new turbocharged four-cylinder engine for examination in this year's test. Its 140 cubic-inch displacement is exactly the same as that of Capri's base four-cylinder engine, but the addition of the turbocharger has improved its acceleration to a level near that of a V8. Acceleration runs from 0 to 60 average 11.6 seconds in the turbo Capri—about a second slower than the V8-equipped Camaro and Firebird, and about a second slower than a V8-equipped Capri.

The Turbo is said to increase horsepower by 50 percent in the four-cylinder engine. A driver can feel the turbo cut in while accelerating, though there is no kick-in-the-pants effect. Instead, the turbo comes on gently and gets stronger as the speed of the engine increases. At 1500 rpm, the turbo boost begins. At peak engine output—about 3500 rpm—the engine acts just like a V8. The surge of power does not let up as long as the accelerator is depressed past cruise speed.

The turbocharger itself is not noisy. In fact, turbos are noted for their suppression of noise, since they add a muting section to the exhaust system. (Some drivers, though, say they can detect the whine of the turbo shaft, which turns as fast as 100,000 rpm.)

Our test staff did, however, object to the inherent noise and shake of the four-cylinder engine. This has nothing to do with the turbo, but is a result of the design of the base engine. Compared with V8s in the same body, the Four is shaky and noisy.

The beauty of turbocharging is that engine power is not wasted to turn the air-fuel booster pump. Instead, the force of the exhaust stream does all the work. Since this energy would be wasted otherwise, its use does not lower performance or fuel economy.

Driven carefully, a Capri equipped with the turbo can duplicate the economy of the base four-cylinder engine in the Capri, averaging about 23 miles per gallon in combined city and highway driving. (The turbo comes with a performance axle ratio that brings fuel economy down a notch from the standard Four—a 3.45:1 ratio for the turbo rather than a 3.08:1 ratio for the regular engine.)

The turbo is available only with a four-speed manual transmission. This seems appropriate, since the engine is designed for performance-minded drivers who probably prefer a manual transmission over an automatic.

Our road tests show that Capri handles exceptionally well, especially when equipped with the optional TRX tires and wheels. These not only enhance Capri's sporty look, but are first-class tires and wheels that improve handling considerably. In handling comparisons with the best of the Firebirds and Camaros, Capri can hold its own. Its light weight makes it fun to drive because a good feel of the road comes through to the driver.

Capri is a completely new car for 1979, no longer imported from Europe. It is lighter by 400 pounds than the 1978 Mustang, though it is virtually identical with the 1979 Mustang. Capri is available only in a hatchback model; Mustang offers a notchback body as well.

A 1979 Capri equipped with the turbocharged four-cylinder engine, the TRX tires and wheels, and other performance features can be purchased for less than $7000 list. That makes it one of the better values in the sporty-car field. Although it is not exactly a sports car in the European sense, the turbo Capri will outperform and outhandle most of the competition.

MERCURY CAPRI
Test Model Specifications

Body type	2-door	Engine type	in-line 4
Overall length	179.1 in.		(turbocharged)
Overall width	69.1 in.	Net hp @ rpm	133 @ 0000
Overall height	51.8 in.	Net torque @ rpm	N/A
Wheelbase	100.4 in.	Displacement	140 cu. in.
Turn diameter	N/A	Compression ratio	9.0:1
Tire size	190 65R 390	Carburetion	2 bbl.
Curb weight	2517 lbs.	Transmission	4-speed
Cargo space	32.4 cu. ft.		Manual
Front headroom	37.2 in.	Axle ratio	3.45:1
Front legroom	40.9 in.	Acceleration 0-60 mph	11.2 sec.
Front hiproom	54 in.	Brake stop 60-0 mph	170 ft.
Rear headroom	35.9 in.	Fuel tank capacity	12.5 gal.
Rear legroom	29.9 in.	EPA city economy rating	23 mpg.
Rear hiproom	47.1 in.		

Mercury Cougar

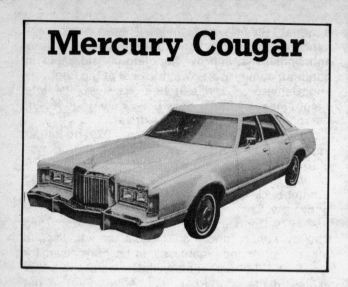

Lincoln-Mercury plans to discontinue production of the two- and four-door Cougar sedans at the end of the 1979 model run. Only the Cougar XR-7 personal luxury model, which we discuss elsewhere in this issue, will continue.

In its last year Cougar has been relegated to a small role. Cougar cannot compete well with the big Mercury Marquis, though Cougar is bigger on the outside and heavier than Marquis and offers a Marquis-type interior layout. In fact, of all the cars in the current Mercury lineup, our test staff believes Cougar represents the least value. It is inferior in many ways to the General Motors intermediates. Chrysler also offers some cars that are better buys, LeBaron and Diplomat among them.

From the outside, Cougar gives the impression of a very expensive car; yet its list price starts at a relatively low $5400. Our experience with past Cougars and the current test shows that the car rides with luxury, but handles poorly. In fact, the understeer of this chassis is about the worst in the intermediate class. That's part of the price you must pay for a car that has a high curb weight and boasts of an ultra-soft ride.

Visibility is relatively poor. The long hood looks good from outside, but interferes with the driver's view of the roadway from the inside. In the two-door model, the wide C post reduces the view to the right rear, and this can be a problem when changing lanes. Other features that contribute to poor visibility are the high beltline, high cowl, and low seating position for the driver.

Cougar's fuel economy is our biggest complaint. Although smaller than the full-size Marquis, a Cougar equipped with a 351 cubic-inch V8 actually delivers fewer miles per gallon than a comparably equipped Marquis: 15 mpg for Cougar; 17 for Marquis in combined city-highway driving. You can select the 302 V8 that is standard for Cougar, but the economy improvement amounts to only one mile per gallon. So, despite its poor showing in our economy tests, the 351 engine is the recommended size for Cougar. It has the power to provide adequate performance and fuel economy.

The finish of the Cougar interior is a cut above the competition, and is one of Cougar's biggest attractions. Mercury went overboard in giving Cougar all the features of a luxury model, including

Mercury Cougar

woodgrain inserts, extensive chrome trim and heavy padding on the soft trim. Cougar has the amenities, including rear windows that roll down, and a full complement of optional accessories that traditional car buyers look for.

The two-door model is different from the four-door in a number of ways. The two-door's wheelbase, at 113.9 inches, is four inches shorter than that of the four-door. Overall length differs too. Of the two, the four-door is the body we prefer, since it offers better room inside; easier entry and exit for passengers; and smaller, lighter, more manageable doors.

However, our recommendation to buyers of cars like Cougar this year is to skip the Cougar sedans altogether and select the Marquis. In addition to providing better fuel economy, Marquis handles better, offers greater interior and luggage space, and is a more modern design that will be around for many more years. By contrast, the Cougar sedan ranks among the worst of the intermediates.

MERCURY COUGAR
Test Model Specifications

Body type	4-door	Rear hiproom	57 in.
Overall length	219.5 in.	Engine type	V8
Overall width	78.6 in.	Net hp @ rpm	140 @ 3800
Overall height	53.3 in.	Net torque @ rpm	255 @ 2000
Wheelbase	118 in.	Displacement	351 cu. in.
Turn diameter	41.3 ft.	Compression ratio	8.0:1
Tire size	HR 78-14	Carburetion	2 bbl.
Curb weight	4115 lbs.	Transmission	Automatic
Cargo space	15.7 cu. ft.	Axle ratio	2.47:1
Front headroom	37.3 in.	Acceleration 0-60 mph	15.8 sec.
Front legroom	42.1 in.	Brake stop 60-0 mph	168 ft.
Front hiproom	55.6 in.	Fuel tank capacity	21 gal.
Rear headroom	36.1 in.	EPA city economy rating	13 mpg.
Rear legroom	32.7 in.		

Mercury Cougar XR-7

If Lincoln-Mercury's Cougar XR-7 personal luxury car handled and performed in accordance with its styling, it would be a big winner. However, the XR-7 has too much of the regular passenger sedan in its makeup, and not enough sportiness. Don't be deceived by appearances: the XR-7 is little more than a dress-up Cougar two-door.

Its chassis, body and drive train are identical with the intermediate Mercury's. Differences show up only in superficial features like front styling and trim. The XR-7 is more luxurious than Cougar, but where performance and handling are measured, the cars are twins.

The XR-7 we tested was equipped with the Ford 351 cubic-inch V8 engine that is also used in the standard Cougar sedan. Its acceleration in the XR-7 is slightly better than average for a full-size car equipped with a V8: we clocked 13.7 seconds for the acceleration run from 0 to 60 miles an hour. By comparison, most sporty cars like Firebird Trans Am, Mustang and Camaro will average 10 seconds or less in the same run. It's easy to see that the XR-7 is no sports car. But then Lincoln-Mercury sells the XR-7 in the personal luxury class, where luxury is emphasized.

The large dimensions of the XR-7's body, the soft springing that allows for a very smooth ride on paved roadways, and the use of overpowered assist systems rob the driver of all feel of the roadway. The car is slow in responding to turns of the steering wheel—heavy understeer in the traditional American manner. The front end plows straight ahead when excessive speed is used in turns. The natural reaction of the driver, more turns of the steering wheel, brings the car into control.

One body style, a two-door coupe, is offered. Buyers can dress up the XR-7 with a long list of options, especially for the interior. A number of front seat styles are also available.

Next year, Lincoln-Mercury plans to introduce an all-new XR-7, and in doing so will clear up a lot of confusion among models in its lineup. The Cougar line has not undergone a downsizing change, and is rated as an intermediate by Mercury. However, the Marquis line, the full-size entry, is smaller and lighter in weight than the Cougar. And Marquis is more costly than Cougar. This is a result of the timing of Lincoln-Mercury's downsizing program. The confusion will last only through the 1979 model year. Next year, the XR-7 nameplate will be affixed to an enlarged version of the Fairmont body. The new model will be smaller on the outside than today's XR-7, but probably will provide more room inside for passengers and luggage. At the same time, fuel economy probably will increase. This year's XR-7 delivers fuel economy in the range of 15 to 16 miles per gallon in combined city and highway driving. Next year, using the smaller body and a smaller engine, average mileage could top 20 mpg.

The changes in store for the XR-7 will give the car a more acceptable ratio of interior space to exterior bulk. Among the biggest problems of the 1979 body is the lack of real room in the passenger compartment, especially for rear passengers. Rear occupants are cramped for space, and ride in a very uncomfortable environment.

The competition in the XR-7's class has already made its downsizing moves, and offers many of the features that the XR-7 Mercury lacks. All of the GM personal luxury cars, including the Pontiac Grand Prix and Buick Riviera, offer superior handling, passenger space and equal or better fuel economy. We also consider Chrysler's LeBaron and Diplomat good alternatives to the XR-7.

MERCURY COUGAR XR-7
Test Model Specifications

Body type 2-door	Rear hiproom . . . . 57 in.
Overall length . . . . 215.4 in.	Engine type V8
Overall width . . . . 78.6 in.	Net hp @ rpm . . . . 135 @ 3200
Overall height . . . . . : . . . . . 53 in.	Net torque @ rpm . . . . 276 @ 1400
Wheelbase . . . . 114 in.	Displacement . . . . 351 cu. in.
Turn diameter . . . . 41.25 ft.	Compression ratio 8.3:1
Tire size . . . . HR 78-15	Carburetion 2V
Curb weight . . . . 4050 lbs.	Transmission . . . . Automatic
Cargo space . . . . 15.7 cu. ft.	Axle ratio 2.47:1
Front headroom . . . . 37.3 in.	Acceleration 0-60 mph . . 13.7 sec.
Front legroom . . . . 42.1 in.	Brake stop 60-0 mph . . . . . . 170 ft.
Front hiproom . . . . 55.6 in.	Fuel tank capacity . . . . 21 gal.
Rear headroom . . . . 36.1 in.	EPA city economy rating . . 13 mpg.
Rear legroom . . . . 32.7 in.	

Mercury Marquis

This year's Marquis is the best full-size Mercury model we've seen, a car with the potential to change the image of the entire line. After putting the all-new model through its paces in standard tests, we have to say that great improvements over the 1978 model are evident in handling, fuel economy, visibility, and ease of parking. Yet there is little or no deterioration in Mercury's traditional strengths: a pleasing ride and a quiet interior.

Our test car was a four-door sedan. It offered all the luxury in function and appearance of the older Mercurys. Interior trim and finish are particularly impressive, until you consider the price Mercury is asking for this car. Ordered with all the convenience and comfort equipment, the car's delivered price easily tops $10,000. That price puts the Mercury in the luxury class. But you don't have to look at the pricetag to know that: the car is outfitted to match all but the super-luxurious models, and does indeed match the Oldsmobile, Buick, Chrysler and Dodge luxury models in opulence. During the downsizing that resulted in smaller dimensions for Marquis, Lincoln-Mercury solved some of the car's biggest problems: those of handling and fuel economy. Marquis now is able to challenge the GM full-size cars for value leadership.

Three body styles are offered: two-door and four-door sedans, and a station wagon. The car we tested was a four-door sedan, lavishly equipped. (Its list price topped $10,000.) It was powered by a 351 cubic-inch V8, which is now the only optional power plant. A 302 is standard.

Performance of our Marquis was good. We averaged just under 14 seconds for our standard runs from 0 to 60 miles an hour. We think it remarkable that the Mercury can perform this way with a 351 — matching the acceleration times of the 460 V8 in earlier models. This is proof that a lighter car can use a smaller engine and deliver equal performance. The 1979 Mercury is an average 750 pounds lighter than the 1978. We found the performance of the 351 equal to that of the 460 in all driving conditions except one: trailer towing. The bigger engine had the reserve power to haul big trailers with ease.

Fuel economy is much improved over 1978, though still not outstanding. Our te ' staff averaged just under 15 miles per gallon in city driving, but topped 20 mpg on the highway. The smaller 302 cubic-inch V8 adds very little to fuel economy, and its performance is below that of the 351.

Mercury Marquis

The biggest improvement over the 1978 Marquis is in handling. The new car rides flatter, exhibiting little of the heave and roll of the 1978 and earlier Mercurys. In turns, it's highly responsive to input from the driver. Understeer has been cut to a minimum, and for the first time a Mercury can keep up with a Chevy and Pontiac in high-speed turns.

Noise levels inside the passenger compartment are just about what Mercurys have offered in the past, and that's a compliment. However, the Marquis' noise levels are still slightly higher than those of the GM full-size cars, which evidently have benefited from refinements made over the past two years.

Summing up, our test staff was impressed with the new design of the 1979 Marquis. We rank it near the top in value among full-size sedans. GM has the advantage of a two-year head start on Mercury as far as chassis and luxury refinements go, but the difference is smaller now than it has been in the past decade.

MERCURY MARQUIS
Test Model Specifications

Body type	4-door	Rear hiproom	58 in.
Overall length	212 in.	Engine type	V8
Overall width	77.5 in.	Net hp @ rpm	132 @ 3200
Overall height	54.5 in.	Net torque @ rpm	268 @ 1400
Wheelbase	114.4 in.	Displacement	351 cu. in.
Turn diameter	39.4 ft.	Compression ratio	8.3:1
Tire size	FR 78-14	Carburetion	2V
Curb weight	3691 lbs.	Transmission	Automatic
Cargo space	19 cu. ft.	Axle ratio	2.26:1
Front headroom	38 in.	Acceleration 0-60 mph	13.9 sec.
Front legroom	42 in.	Brake stop 60-0 mph	173 ft.
Front hiproom	61.2 in.	Fuel tank capacity	19 gal.
Rear headroom	37.3 in.	EPA city economy rating	15 mpg.
Rear legroom	40.5 in.		

Mercury Monarch

Monarch has taken a back seat to the more modern Zephyr in recent Lincoln-Mercury promotions, but the division still plans to market the car as its top intermediate for the next couple of years at least. Our belief is that Monarch is not as good a car as Zephyr.

Priced about $500 higher than Zephyr, Monarch is offered as Lincoln-Mercury's luxury model in the small-car class. The two cars are of just about the same size. But Zephyr's is the more modern design, offering better fuel economy, more interior room, better visibility, superior handling and a number of other features that outshine Monarch.

Monarch's handling is a big drawback. There's a "tall" feel to the body, the result of severe lean on curves when taken at high speeds. In contrast, Zephyr is quick to react to turns of the steering wheel and rides fairly flat in turns. Zephyr's ride is more controlled than Monarch's.

Ford Motor Company has plans for the Monarch. That's why the line is being kept in production. Next year, when Cougar is dropped from Lin-

Mercury Monarch

coln-Mercury's lineup (only the Cougar XR-7 will remain), Monarch will take over as the inter-mediate-class sedan for the division, and Zephyr will be marketed as a compact-intermediate or compact.

Our test Monarch this year was a four-door se-dan, equipped with a 302 cubic-inch V8 engine and automatic transmission. This is the power train we recommend in this model, though the 250 in-line Six that is offered as standard delivers performance nearly as good as the 302's and one or two more miles per gallon of gas than the larger engine. Our own tests show that the V8 will deliver only 16 mpg in city driving and 22 on the highway. Despite this disappointment, we recommend the V8 over the Six, primarily because the V8 can provide the pow-er needed to run the usual accessories on the Monarch, including air conditioning and power as-sist systems.

The ride of the car is about average for a sedan of Monarch's size, but interior noise levels are very low when compared with the car's competition. In fact, the quiet ride is the biggest positive feature of the Monarch in comparison to Zephyr.

Visibility for the driver and passengers in Monarch is hampered by a relatively high cowl and beltline, though only the best of the new cars offer a superior view to the front and sides. One major problem here is that the driver sits low and must look up over the instruments. The instrument panel face is flat and laid out with little imagination. The reach to lights and heater controls is long.

Although Monarch has the look of a modern sedan on the outside, the shape of the passenger compartment is a throwback to the days when the full-size car was king. Rear seat room in both four-door and two-door Monarchs is tight, especially where legroom and knee room are measured. The big doors of the two-door need lots of room to swing open; the rear doors on the four-door model are small, and thus make getting in and out difficult. Trunk space is good: 15.8 cubic feet.

In the Mercury lineup, Zephyr is better than Monarch for a number of reasons. Monarch has the look of a more expensive car, and it does cost a bit more than Zephyr. But looks are not everything. Zephyr offers greater value than Monarch, at a lower price.

MERCURY MONARCH
Test Model Specifications

Body type	4-door	Rear hiproom	51.2 in.
Overall length	197.7 in.	Engine type	6 in-line
Overall width	74.5 in.	Net hp @ rpm	97 @ 3200
Overall height	53.3 in.	Net torque @ rpm	210 @ 1400
Wheelbase	109.9 in.	Displacement	250 cu. in.
Turn diameter	39.7 ft.	Compression ratio	8.6:1
Tire size	DR 78-14	Carburetion	1 bbl.
Curb weight	3246 lbs.	Transmission	Automatic
Cargo space	15.8 cu. ft.	Axle ratio	2.79:1
Front headroom	38.2 in.	Acceleration 0-60 mph	17.9 sec.
Front legroom	40.3 in.	Brake stop 60-0 mph	146 ft.
Front hiproom	55.9 in.	Fuel tank capacity	18 gal.
Rear headroom	37.6 in.	EPA city economy rating	17 mpg.
Rear legroom	36.1 in.		

Mercury Zephyr

Zephyr (along with Fairmont, its twin at Ford Division) is the hottest-selling new car of recent times. In all of its body styles, Zephyr offers the buyer the best of the old and the new schools of car design: a roomy interior and good ride for passenger comfort, tidy outside dimensions, and respectable fuel economy. For 1979, unchanged in appearance and function from '78, Zephyr remains one of the top values in the compact-intermediate class.

The car's clean, is up-to-date, and Zephyr is as modern under the sheet metal as it appears outside. The four-door model we tested this year can hold five people in acceptable comfort, though four adults should be considered its top capacity. Drivers of big cars will note that Zephyr feels light and its suspension feels firm.

Visibility is excellent. The glass is carefully laid out to improve the driver's view of the roadway ahead and to the sides. A low beltline, a relatively low cowl height and a short hood also contribute to the outstanding visibility. Compare Zephyr with the older Mercury Cougar, and the contrast is great:

Zephyr is clearly the better design.

For our test this year, we selected a Zephyr sedan equipped with the 200 cubic-inch Six. This engine is quieter and smoother in operation than the standard Four, and delivers better fuel economy than the 302 V8. Fuel economy of the six-cylinder power plant works out to about 20 miles per gallon in combined city and highway driving, which is just about what we expect from a mid-size economy sedan.

The in-line Six is easy to maintain. Spark plugs are out in the open and easy to change, as is the oil filter. The Six is almost as smooth in operation as the V8.

Its performance, though not sparkling, is adequate for most U.S. roads. In our performance tests, the six-cylinder engine coupled to automatic transmission rolled from 0 to 60 miles an hour in about 16 seconds. That is mediocre, but what you might expect from a mid-size sedan that can attain 20-mpg economy. For heavy-duty driving or for trailer towing, we recommend the V8. The four-cylinder engine is the same one used in the Pinto, and is a trifle small, resulting in higher noise levels from an overrevved engine and some additional engine shake that can be felt in the passenger compartment.

Mercury Zephyr

The Zephyr interior is unimaginative. It looks much like that used on European Capris of 1978 and before. Its flat face offers little aesthetic appeal, and the location of the shift quadrant directly in front of the driver is a mistake. In addition, the instruments and gauges are positioned well below the driver's line of down-the-road sight instead of up high where they can be read or seen at a glance.

Zephyrs come in four body styles: two-door and four-door sedans, a two-door coupe called the Z-7, and a station wagon. They match, model for model, the cars built under the Ford Fairmont name. Buyers should consider both lines as one, and compare prices between them for the best possible deal.

When you add up all the positive features of the Zephyr models and subtract the negative ones, it becomes evident that these cars are the choice models in the "compact" market right now. However, GM will have brand-new designs ready for introduction this spring. Fairmont's relative value might change once the GM cars make their debut.

MERCURY ZEPHYR
Test Model Specifications

Body type	4-door	Rear hiproom	53.7 in.
Overall length	193.8 in.	Engine type	6 in-line
Overall width	70.2 in.	Net hp @ rpm	85 @ 3600
Overall height	53.5 in.	Net torque @ rpm	154 @ 1600
Wheelbase	105.5 in.	Displacement	200 cu. in.
Turn diameter	39 ft.	Compression ratio	8.5:1
Tire size	DR 78-14	Carburetion	1V
Curb weight	2761 lbs.	Transmission	Automatic
Cargo space	16.8 cu. ft.	Axle ratio	2.73:1
Front headroom	38.5 in.	Acceleration 0-60 mph	15.7 sec.
Front legroom	41.8 in.	Brake stop 60-0 mph	148 ft.
Front hiproom	56.2 in.	Fuel tank capacity	16 gal.
Rear headroom	37.7 in.	EPA city economy rating	18 mpg.
Rear legroom	35.4 in.		

Oldsmobile Cutlass

Overall sales of Cutlass were down last year. The buying public apparently was not ready to accept the downsized model. The poor sales record of '78 contrasts sharply with the record-breaking sales year Cutlass enjoyed back in 1977.

As last year, the Cutlass series for '79 comprises the Salon and Salon Brougham coupes and sedans. The lower-priced Salon and the higher-priced Salon Brougham differ only in trim style.

Both models come standard with the 231 cubic-inch V6. Optional engines are a 260 V8, a 305 V8, and a 260 cubic-inch V8 diesel. CONSUMER GUIDE Magazine's test Cutlass was equipped with this new diesel power plant, which is rated at 95 horsepower.

The overall length of the Cutlass Salon is 197.7 inches, and the car weighs 3180 pounds. Although downsized from 1978 proportions, the new Cutlass coupe still rates as a big car. It is difficult for us to

Oldsmobile Cutlass

understand why Oldsmobile offers a small diesel for a car of this size. The conventional gasoline-fueled 260 V8 is barely adequate to get the car moving and keep it moving. The diesel version of the 260 is unacceptable for use in the Cutlass. Our test car, equipped with automatic transmission, took almost 25 seconds to accelerate from 0 to 60 miles an hour. Why doesn't Oldsmobile take the larger 350 cubic-inch diesel V8 that is available for the Cutlass wagons and expand this option to the sedans and coupes? The larger diesel would give the cars a little more power than the small one can provide. In our mileage tests, we could barely obtain 21 miles per gallon in city-highway driving, so economy should not be considered one of the diesel's strong points either.

The design of the small diesel includes a pre-combustion chamber that Oldsmobile officials say has helped to reduce the characteristic diesel noise and smoke. We think the engine is very loud, but its emissions are acceptably low. Diesel engines often spew thick clouds of smoke when the accelerator is firmly depressed. Oldsmobile has indeed found a way to cut down on this smelly smoke.

Our handling maneuvers were somewhat impaired by the diesel engine's low performance. It was difficult for our test staff to evaluate the car in high-speed cornering and panic-type maneuvers, because the engine lumbered along like an old truck.

The ride of the Cutlass is very smooth. Road bumps are absorbed in the car's suspension system.

Visibility to the front of the vehicle is good, but the car's long, sloping roofline can make backing up very difficult. The ability to judge the exact location of the rear bumper is a skill that comes with time and patience. The Cutlass' side pillars, though, are thin and do not interfere with the view needed for safe lane changing.

We think Olds made a mistake in marketing a Cutlass with the small diesel. Many buyers who are seeking the good economy and ease of maintenance of a diesel engine and who choose the 260 cubic-inch Olds diesel may come away from the experience with negative feelings about diesels in general. In other ways, the Cutlass is a pleasurable automobile.

OLDS CUTLASS
Test Model Specifications

Body type	2-door	Rear hiproom	51.6 in.
Overall length	197.7 in.	Engine type	V8 diesel
Overall width	71.9 in.	Net hp @ rpm	95 @ 3600
Overall height	54.2 in.	Net torque @ rpm	150 @ 2000
Wheelbase	108.1 in.	Displacement	260 cu. in.
Turn diameter	38.2 ft.	Compression ratio	8.3:1
Tire size	P197/75R14	Carburetion	Fuel injected
Curb weight	3180 lbs.	Transmission	Automatic
Cargo space	16.1 cu. ft.	Axle ratio	2.39:1
Front headroom	37.9 in.	Acceleration 0-60 mph	25.3 sec.
Front legroom	42.8 in.	Brake stop 60-0 mph	170 ft.
Front hiproom	52.2 in.	Fuel tank capacity	17.5 gal.
Rear headroom	38.2 in.	EPA city economy rating	24 mpg.
Rear legroom	35.1 in.		

Oldsmobile Cutlass Supreme

The Oldsmobile Cutlass Supreme series shares its chassis, driveline components and basic body shell with three other GM cars—Chevrolet Monte Carlo, Pontiac Grand Prix and Buick Regal. But what separates Cutlass Supreme from the competition is its styling.

With the exception of a new front end treatment and redesigned taillights, the Cutlass Supreme, Supreme Brougham and Calais remain pretty much unchanged from 1978. They have the same common 108.1-inch wheelbase as last year and the same 200.1-inch overall length. All three models are available only as two-door coupes.

The standard engine for all Cutlass Supreme models is a 231 cubic-inch V6. Optional engines are a 260 cubic-inch V8 and a 305 cubic-inch V8, as well as a 260 cubic-inch diesel. The CONSUMER GUIDE Magazine test car was a Cutlass Supreme Brougham equipped with the standard 231 V6 power plant. Overall, we don't think that the standard V6 is a good engine choice. Our combined city-highway driving averaged a respectable 22 miles per gallon. But in the acceleration and performance tests, the V6 was substandard and sluggish. It just was not powerful enough to move a 1½-ton car around easily. Straining on the steep grades, the automatic transmission is kept busy as the car lurches back and forth from overdrive to cruising gear and back again. Flat-out acceleration tests were not much more inspiring, and our time for 0 to 60 miles an hour was almost 17 seconds. We strongly recommend that the buyer opt for the top-of-the-line 305 cubic-inch V8 and sacrifice a little fuel economy to boost the car's performance.

Handling is one area in which the Supreme Brougham shines. In addition to being agile, the car gives the driver the confidence of knowing that he is in control of the car at all times. The power-assisted steering makes maneuvering easy and at the same time gives the driver just enough road feel to let him know exactly what the tires are doing. Our test car took sharp corners easily, with neither sway nor loss of traction.

The Supreme also had good directional stability in our braking tests. Not once did the wheels lock up and break traction with the pavement. From 60 mph, the car came to a halt in just over 165 feet. Our drivers noticed that the suspension system seemed to compensate for hard braking, eliminating nose dips. We detected no fade in the pow-

Oldsmobile Cutlass Supreme

er-assisted front disc and rear drum brakes even after repeated tests.

The Cutlass Supreme Brougham comes with a luxury interior, which is about the only way you can tell the regular Supreme and Supreme Brougham apart. The plush interior of the Brougham features simulated loose-cushion seatbacks for both the divided front and rear seats. All the seats are well padded and comfortable, a plus on long trips. The front seat is wide enough to accommodate three people in reasonable comfort, and the driver's seat features a six-way power adjust system. Visibility is only fair, though, because the Supreme models all have long hoods and trunks. Visibility is cut further by the very wide roof pillar at each corner. Entering and exiting the vehicle's front seats pose no problems, and legroom is sufficient for long-legged drivers. Getting into and out of the rear seats is tight, and further problems arise because the passenger has to duck his head under the shoulder strap.

OLDSMOBILE CUTLASS SUPREME
Test Model Specifications

Body type	2-door	Rear hiproom	54.9 in.
Overall length	200.1 in.	Engine type	V6
Overall width	71.3 in.	Net hp @ rpm	115 @ 3800
Overall height	53.4 in.	Net torque @ rpm	190 @ 2000
Wheelbase	108.1 in.	Displacement	231 cu. in.
Turn diameter	38 ft.	Compression ratio	8.0:1
Tire size	P195/75R14	Carburetion	2 bbl.
Curb weight	3200 lbs.	Transmission	Automatic
Cargo space	16.3 cu. ft.	Axle ratio	2.93:1
Front headroom	37.9 in.	Acceleration 0-60 mph	16.8 sec.
Front legroom	42.8 in.	Brake stop 60-0 mph	166 ft.
Front hiproom	51.7 in.	Fuel tank capacity	17.5 gal.
Rear headroom	38.1 in.	EPA city economy rating	19 mpg.
Rear legroom	36.3 in.		

Oldsmobile 88/98

We tested a Delta 88 equipped with the optional 350 cubic-inch diesel engine, and it was a surprising experience. It far outperformed any other diesel-powered car we have tested. Acceleration from 0 to 60 miles an hour took only 16 seconds.

If that kind of performance had been engineered at the expense of fuel economy, there would be little reason for selecting the diesel option. But our diesel 88 averaged 26 miles per gallon in combined city-highway driving. When you consider that diesel fuel is now from one cent to 16 cents a gallon cheaper than gasoline, the higher purchase price of a diesel begins to seem more worthwhile. The diesel engine adds about $800 to the base price of the Delta 88. But taking into account the diesel's lifetime fuel savings, low maintenance and relatively high resale value, we feel that it is an option very much worth considering.

The diesel-equipped 88 comes with a 27-gallon fuel tank, instead of the 21-gallon tank that is standard on the gasoline version. That capacity allows a 600-mile driving range between fill-ups.

As you stand beside the car, there can be no doubt that the car is equipped with a diesel engine. It is noisy and to the untrained ear sounds like it is just about ready for the scrap heap. But once you are inside, the noise becomes much less audible, due to the car's special sound insulation. Once the car smooths out to a comfortable cruising speed, either in city or open highway driving, it becomes impossible to tell what kind of engine is sitting under the hood.

Both the ride and the steering of the 88 are typical of a large luxury car, and the general road feel is above average. Tight, quick turns seem to cause the car to sway and tip a little more than we would have liked, but tracking remained tight as the car hugged the road securely.

Interior appointments are practical, eye appealing and luxurious throughout. Deep-pile carpets, comfortable seats, and plenty of leg- and headroom for all occupants are only a few of the pluses. Driver visibility is good out of the left side of the car but is limited out of the right side by the door pillar and the slanted roofline.

A diesel engine does not require nearly the

Oldsmobile Delta 88

amount of regular tune-up maintenance that a standard gasoline engine does. Oil changes, however, are required more frequently — every 3000 miles for the diesel in the Delta 88. Tuning a diesel engine is best left to an experienced diesel mechanic. Virtually everything from a diesel's carburetion process to its lack of spark plugs would be confusing to most do-it-yourselfers. As for minor service, we found that the battery, radiator and fluid check points were easily accessible.

Few modifications mark the introduction of the Delta 88 and 98 series for 1979. Both of these luxury models are available in two-door and four-door versions. Exterior modifications are limited to a new grille. The cars are often thought of as identical except for trim and option packages, but the Delta 98 series is actually a little larger than the 88: the 98 has an overall length of 220.5 inches, three inches longer than the Delta 88.

OLDSMOBILE DELTA 88
Test Model Specifications

Body type 2-door	Rear hiproom .... 55.3 in.
Overall length .... 217.5 in.	Engine type .. 350 cu. in. V8 diesel
Overall width .... 76.8 in.	Net hp @ rpm .... 120 @ 3600
Overall height .... 54.5 in.	Net torque @ rpm .... 220 @ 1600
Wheelbase .... 116.0 in.	Displacement .... 350 cu. in.
Turn diameter .... 39.5 ft.	Compression ratio 22.5:1
Tire size GR78-15	Carburetion .... Fuel injected
Curb weight .... 4070 lbs.	Transmission .... Automatic
Cargo space .... 20.3 cu. ft.	Axle ratio 2.73:1
Front headroom .... 39.5 in.	Acceleration 0-60 mph ... 16 sec.
Front legroom .... 42.4 in.	Brake stop 60-0 mph ..... 136 ft.
Front hiproom .... 55 in.	Fuel tank capacity .... 27 gal.
Rear headroom .... 38.3 in.	EPA city economy rating .. 21 mpg.
Rear legroom .... 39 in.	

Oldsmobile Omega

Our test results for the 1979 Omega are out of date, since Oldsmobile has already ceased production of Omega in preparation for production of an entirely new compact line for 1980. The new cars, revolutionary in design among U.S. compacts, will debut in April and will offer worth-waiting-for improvements over the current Omegas. Details of the new Omega are virtually the same as those of the Chevrolet Nova. (Check our writeup on Nova for more information.)

While CONSUMER GUIDE Magazine has not had a chance to test the new models, the general specifications are known. The new Omega will be smaller on the outside, just as roomy on the inside and weigh significantly less than its predecessor. Reduced length will mean niftier handling. Lighter weight (down 850 pounds) should result in an increase of at least five miles per gallon in fuel economy, fewer power options for steering, and smaller braking systems. Interior roominess will be maintained by raising the roof about two inches and building the doors thinner and with less curvature.

Oldsmobile Starfire

Starfire for 1979 is a sporty compact car that is available only as a two-door hatchback model. It has a new grille that is color-coordinated with the body, and a fiberglass-reinforced front replaces the softer plastic panel of last year. Other front refinements include single rectangular headlamps and parking lamps that are neatly hidden behind the grille.

Engine choices remain unchanged for the 1979 Starfire. The tiny 151 cubic-inch four-cylinder power plant is still the standard engine. Optional engines include a 231 cubic-inch V6, and a 305 cubic-inch V8. Our test car was equipped with the 305 and a four-speed manual transmission, which made quite a performance package. The little Starfire accelerated from 0 to 60 miles an hour in 10.1

Oldsmobile Starfire

seconds. Last year, our Starfire equipped with the same engine and an automatic transmission needed 13.4 seconds to run the same test. During all phases of the power performance testing, the Starfire V8 and four-speed transmission behaved with excellence. Combined city-highway fuel economy averaged about 19 miles per gallon.

Starfire's superior performance is matched by its driving comfort and handling ease—but only if you stay on a smooth roadway. The fully independent front suspension system easily handles fast pavement, while the rear construction keeps the car laterally stable via a torque arm network. A low center of gravity further adds to the car's excellent tracking capabilities when accelerating around corners or on twisting and winding roads. But on gravel or washboard roads, the Starfire acts like a fish out of water. Set up for a stiff, responsive ride, the suspension system tends to buck and fight against rough surfaces. As speed increases over a rough surface, the tires begin to skid and loose the traction needed to maintain control.

Starfire's interior room is about the same as that of other cars of comparable size. There is adequate front-seat legroom, but the seats have an awkward angle, so the occupants' legs are almost horizontal. In the back seats, room is inadequate for anyone larger than a toddler. Leather-like vinyl upholstery gives the interior a racy look. Thick carpeting and sound-deadening insulation help keep outside noises and engine vibrations low. Front and side visibility are good, but the rear area is rather poor in that respect. This is due to the rather wide door pillars and the slope of the roof.

Our test car had the top-of-the-line option and dress-up package, which allowed it to wear the name Firenza Starfire. First introduced back in late 1978, the Firenza option package is a super deluxe outfit. Included on our car was a special front air dam, a rear spoiler, flared front and rear wheel openings for better cooling, sport mirrors, wide oval tires, a sport steering wheel and the upgraded Rallye suspension. In addition, a special paint scheme is standard, with the Firenza ID painted across the car's lower body paint stripe.

OLDSMOBILE STARFIRE
Test Model Specifications

Body type	2-door	Rear hiproom	42 in.
Overall length	179.3 in.	Engine type	OHV V8
Overall width	65.4 in.	Net hp @ rpm	145 @ 3800
Overall height	50.2 in.	Net torque @ rpm	250 @ 2400
Wheelbase	97 in.	Displacement	305 cu. in.
Turn diameter	38.7 ft.	Compression ratio	8.0:1
Tire size	BR 70-13	Carburetion	2 bbl.
Curb weight	2825 lbs.	Transmission	4-speed
Cargo space	23.4 cu. ft.		Manual
Front headroom	37.7 in.	Axle ratio	2.93:1
Front legroom	43 in.	Acceleration 0-60 mph	10.1 sec.
Front hiproom	47.5 in.	Brake stop 60-0 mph	174 ft.
Rear headroom	35.3 in.	Fuel tank capacity	18.5 gal.
Rear legroom	29.5 in.	EPA city economy rating	15 mpg.

Oldsmobile Toronado

Introduced in 1966, Toronado was the first General Motors car to have front wheel drive. The basic advantages of a front-wheel-drive car are its superior traction in snow and rain and its lack of a floor hump dividing the passenger compartment. But the newly designed Toronado for 1979 offers much more than those basics. It gives good fuel economy without the slightest compromise in ride, comfort and performance.

Toronado is trimmer this year. It is 22 inches shorter than last year, with a wheelbase of just 114 inches. At 71.3 inches wide, it is also more than eight inches narrower than last year's Toronado. Hip room has suffered a little from the downsizing, but headroom and legroom for front and rear passengers have improved. For this year, Oldsmobile has dropped the large 403 cubic inch V8. The new standard 350 cubic-inch engine delivers better gas mileage and still has plenty of power. A 350 cubic-inch diesel engine is optional.

The Toronado we tested was equipped with the standard gasoline engine. The Environmental Protection Agency rates the 1979 Toronado at 18 miles per gallon in combined city-highway driving, and that's what our test car delivered.

Toronado's ride and handling are excellent. A new independent rear suspension system and a new automatic load leveling system have greatly improved the ride. Our test car rode smoothly and quietly over rough road surfaces that normally would have set up excessive vibration. The tendency for the rear end to hop and lose traction, especially during accelerated turns, has also been designed out of the car this year. In city traffic, Toronado handled nimbly. While it is no European sports car, its reduced size and lighter weight (down almost 900 pounds this year) enabled it to slip easily through traffic. Toronado's turning radius is three feet shorter now than it was last year, which has made the car much more maneuverable and easy to squeeze into tight parking spots. On steep winding roads, our Toronado took the curves like a snake, and stayed flat both while climbing

Oldsmobile Toronado

and while descending. Toronado's overall ride is softer than it was last year, due to an improved suspension system.

The 1979 Toronado has a flush-mounted windshield for smoother air flow and less drag. The rear window is appreciably smaller this year and mounted almost vertically. Combined with the relatively wide pillars, the design presents a visibility problem.

Virtually all the appointments and comforts you could want are included on Toronado's long list of standard equipment. Luxury touches include air conditioning, six-way power seats, power steering, side window defogger, power brakes, digital clock, AM/FM stereo and illuminated exterior door locks.

The new Toronado is nearly identical with the Buick Riviera and Cadillac Eldorado, cars with which it shares its chassis and drive system. The most significant differences among the three cars are small styling features and prices.

OLDSMOBILE TORONADO
Test Model Specifications

Body type 2-door	Rear hiproom .... 49 in.
Overall length .... 205.6 in.	Engine type .... OHV V8
Overall width .... 71.3 in.	Net hp @ rpm .... 165 @ 3600
Overall height .... 54.2 in.	Net torque @ rpm .... 275 @ 2000
Wheelbase .... 114.0 in.	Displacement .... 350 cu. in.
Turn diameter .... 40.5 ft.	Compression ratio 8.1:1
Tire size P205/75R15	Carburetion .... 4 bbl.
Curb weight .... 3851 lbs.	Transmission .... Automatic
Cargo space .... 16.5 cu. ft.	Axle ratio 2.41:1
Front headroom .... 37.9 in.	Acceleration 0-60 mph .. 12.0 sec.
Front legroom .... 42.8 in.	Brake stop 60-0 mph ..... 180 ft.
Front hiproom .... 50.5 in.	Fuel tank capacity .... 26 gal.
Rear headroom .... 37.9 in.	EPA city economy rating .. 16 mpg.
Rear legroom .... 39.4 in.	

Plymouth Horizon TC3

The differences between the four-door Horizon and the two-door are extensive. We selected the TC3 two-door for examination here because it is the newest Horizon, and because the four-door is covered in the Dodge Omni test writeup.

The TC3 we tested was equipped with the standard four-speed manual transmission, and the 104 cubic-inch four-cylinder engine that Chrysler imports from Volkswagen of Germany. The drive train of the two-door is identical to that of the four-door, but the bodies are dissimilar. The two-door's wheelbase is 2.5 inches shorter than the sedan's; yet the TC3's body is half a foot longer. The four-door is almost 2.5 inches taller than the TC3. These dimensions give the two-door a sleek, sporty appearance, and, unfortunately, make the two-door less comfortable than the four-door to ride in.

Rear seat legroom in the TC3 is minimal—actually about four inches less than in the four-door Horizon. The TC3's rear seat headroom is almost three inches less. That makes the TC3 unacceptable for carrying adults in the rear seat for any distance. However, front seat accommodations of the two body styles are about equal: there's just a fraction of an inch less headroom in the coupe than in the four-door sedan.

Both models are hatchbacks. Luggage space is a comparatively small 10.7 cubic feet when the rear seat is upright, but with the rear seat folded forward, the cargo capacity is 33.8 cubic feet—an unusually large volume for a coupe of the TC3's size.

The TC3's instruments and instrument panel are laid out with imagination, and with the convenience of the driver in mind. We particularly like the stalk-mounted windshield wiper and washer control. It is

Plymouth Horizon TC3

as handy as the turn signal lever on which it's mounted, and works with ease. The same lever controls the light dimmer, and that function also is convenient.

The VW-based engine has been reworked a bit by Chrysler. Alterations include electronic ignition, two-barrel carburetor, and a number of other accessories that are added at Chrysler's U.S. assembly plant. High ratios in first, second and third gears keep the engine from racing. One result is that noise levels at 30 miles an hour are exceptionally low. However, at 60 mph, the TC3's noise levels are no better than the average for small cars in its price class,

That Chrysler adopted the Rabbit body for the Horizon four-door model is clear. However, the TC3's long, low body lines and plastic bumper covers give the two-door a look all its own.

Despite the differences between the four-door sedan and two-door TC3 in styling and wheelbase, our test staff could not detect a significant difference in handling between the two models. We found both the sedan and the two-door to handle very well. When we first heard about the TC3's short wheelbase, we wondered whether the sporty version would be more agile than the sedan. As it turns out, any extra nimbleness that might have been built into the car as a result of the shortening of its wheelbase is offset by the TC3's longer body.

Fuel economy of the TC3 is the same as the Horizon sedan's: 25 miles per gallon in city driving. You can squeeze out as much as 35 mpg at highway speeds. Performance, as you might expect from a four-cylinder engine, is not exciting. Our test staff recorded a 16-second time for acceleration from 0 to 60 mph. That is slow.

It is difficult to compare the TC3 with its top competitors, since it's difficult to identify the competition. The small Toyotas and Datsuns sell in the

TC3's price range, but they don't have the same sporty style.

Other small cars that offer styling this sleek, the new Ford Mustang and the Chevrolet Monza among them, can be equipped with large engines and beat the TC3 in performance. However, the TC3 offers something that neither the Mustang nor the Monza have: front-wheel drive. If you are interested in the advantages of front drive, don't consider yourself a performance-car buyer, don't want to spend more than the price of the TC3, and want a car that looks flashy, the two-door Horizon is the car for you.

However, if you're a bit less interested in flashy styling and a bit more interested in comfort and convenience, we recommend the Horizon or Omni sedan. The sedan handles as well as the two-door, delivers the same mileage, and can haul at least as much cargo. What makes the sedan a better value than the two-door is the sedan's boxy shape—a design that maximizes passenger comfort.

PLYMOUTH HORIZON
Test Model Specifications

Body type	2-door	Rear hiproom	46.1 in.
Overall length	172.7 in.	Engine type	4 in-line
Overall width	66 in.	Net hp @ rpm	55 @ 5600
Overall height	51.4 in.	Net torque @ rpm	120 @ 3200
Wheelbase	96.7 in.	Displacement	104.7 cu. in.
Turn diameter	33.4 ft.	Compression ratio	8.2:1
Tire size	P165/75R13	Carburetion	2 bbl.
Curb weight	2256 lbs.	Transmission	4-speed
Cargo space	10.7 cu. ft.		Manual
Front headroom	37.5 in.	Axle ratio	3.37:1
Front legroom	42.5 in.	Acceleration 0-60 mph	16 sec.
Front hiproom	52.6 in.	Brake stop 60-0 mph	137 ft.
Rear headroom	34.7 in.	Fuel tank capacity	13 gal.
Rear legroom	28.6 in.	EPA city economy rating	25 mpg.

Plymouth Volaré

Volaré is selling at a lower suggested price than the Plymouth Horizon, despite the fact that the Volaré is larger, heavier, and has a bigger load capacity and power train. This is an abrupt turnabout for Volaré, and is a hint of what Chrysler plans to do in the future with the two smallest cars in its lineup.

As a rule, the smaller cars carry lower prices. This rule has been broken in the past, but usually only when the smaller car is a specialty model, like the Thunderbird or Corvette. Detroit has built its marketing structure on the fact that buyers will willingly pay more for bigger cars than for smaller ones, other things being equal.

Volaré is a straightforward car that will carry five passengers in reasonable comfort. Its large trunk will easily carry a family's luggage. As the successor to the highly successful and practical Valiant, Volaré offers a lot of car for the money. It should be one of Chrysler's biggest-selling models, and it is.

But there are flaws in the Volaré, the kind that were not present in Valiant. Quality problems have been apparent right from the start of production, and recalls for safety defects have hurt too. So instead of being a strong entry for Chrysler in the small-car market, Volaré has fallen short of Valiant's record.

Behind the wheel, Volaré gives the impression of great size, a compact that rivals the full-size models in interior room, ride and comfort. It is bigger than Fairmont and Concord, and the difference is impressive. For buyers who want a big car, Volaré is an outstanding compact.

Equipped with the 225 cubic-inch Super Six engine, which our test staff recommends for average driving, the car will deliver up to 18 mpg in the city. On the highway, fuel economy is in the mid-20s. Volaré is not as efficient as Fairmont, but the figures are not bad for a car of Volaré's size.

Three body styles are available: the four-door sedan that we tested this year, a two-door coupe that is built on a smaller wheelbase, and a station wagon. The Volaré body is shared by three other cars: the Dodge Aspen, the Dodge Diplomat, and the Chrysler LeBaron. To keep the models in perspective, think of Volaré and Aspen as the low-line cars in the same model lineup with Diplomat and LeBaron. They all offer the same basic features, but Volaré and Aspen sell at a lower price than the other two, and are not as dressed up inside or outside. In addition, Diplomat and LeBaron use a slightly larger body for the two-door model, offering more rear seat room than Volaré and Aspen.

Volaré's interior is simple; its instrument panel is practical, having instruments that are easy to read and controls that are easy to reach.

The trunk is large and has an excellent shape for hauling bulky packages. The sides of the trunk are broken down into small storage bins that are perfect for small items. The center section of the trunk rivals most intermediate-size cars in ease of loading and carrying capacity.

Plymouth offers a variety of models in the Volaré

lineup, including a Road Runner package in the two-door coupe body and a Sport option for the station wagon. Its model offerings have been reduced this year, and such a cut is usually an indication that a car's manufacturer expects the car to be replaced in its market segment in the near future. Add that to the price of Volaré in relation to Horizon and it is easy to see why insiders expect Plymouth to drop Volaré within the next two years and bring out a front-drive replacement that will be better suited to compete with the newer models from the competition.

Volaré has bigger carrying capacity than Horizon, can tow a trailer, and can be equipped to provide the performance American drivers are used to. However, Volaré's fuel economy is not as good as Horizon's. Also, Volaré has acquired a record for poor durability and reliability.

Volaré is not in the same league with most of its competition, especially the Ford Fairmont/Mercury Zephyr.

PLYMOUTH VOLARÉ
Test Model Specifications

Body type	4-door	Rear hiproom	57 in.
Overall length	201.2 in.	Engine type	6 in-line
Overall width	72.8 in.	Net hp @ rpm	110 @ 3600
Overall height	55.3 in.	Net torque @ rpm	180 @ 2000
Wheelbase	112.7 in.	Displacement	225 cu. in.
Turn diameter	40.7 ft.	Compression ratio	8.4:1
Tire size	DR 78-14	Carburetion	2 bbl.
Curb weight	3206 lbs.	Transmission	Automatic
Cargo space	16.2 cu. ft.	Axle ratio	2.76:1
Front headroom	39.2 in.	Acceleration 0-60 mph	16.9 sec.
Front legroom	42.5 in.	Brake stop 60-0 mph	148 ft.
Front hiproom	57.2 in.	Fuel tank capacity	18 gal.
Rear headroom	37.5 in.	EPA city economy rating	18 mpg.
Rear legroom	36.6 in.		

Pontiac Bonneville/ Catalina

The Pontiac Bonneville/Catalina series of cars enters the 1979 automotive scene virtually unchanged from last year. Minor improvements such as a new grille treatment, a series of exterior lamps, new wheel covers and minor interior trim offerings are the only fresh ammunition Pontiac has to throw at the new downsized models from Chrysler, Dodge and Mercury.

Yet Catalina and Bonneville are still very good values in their class. Offered as two-door, four-door and station wagon models, the Bonneville and Catalina share a 115.9-inch wheelbase. The biggest difference between the two models is the base engine: Catalina comes standard with a 231 cubic-inch V6.

The base power train for the 1979 Bonneville is a 301 cubic-inch V8 with a three-speed automatic transmission; two larger engines are available. However, the 301 is sufficiently powerful for a fully equipped Bonneville. The 301 powering our test car

160   CONSUMER GUIDE

provided more than enough muscle to pull the automobile through every situation and maneuver we could find. Acceleration is excellent considering the Bonneville's weight: 0 to 60 mph in just over 12 seconds. Fuel economy is not outstanding. That's understandable. Bonneville tips the scales at close to 4000 pounds. However, equipped with the 301 two-barrel and automatic transmission, our test car delivered a respectable 19 miles per gallon in combined city and highway driving.

Bonneville's radial-tuned suspension produces an extremely comfortable ride and offers excellent control. The car responds very well to steering commands and corners with an agility that is surprising for a car of this size and weight. Our test car was put into some very sharp turns at high speeds. It reacted predictably, and well. When taken through emergency maneuvers, our Bonneville was quick to respond. It held a straight course during hard braking.

The 1979 Bonneville offers an interior design comparable to automobiles having sticker prices much higher than the Pontiac's. The new Bonneville delivers optimum comfort. There is plenty of headroom in the front and rear. The legroom allows plenty of freedom of movement, even for passengers sitting in the rear seat behind a long-legged driver. The soft, loose-cushion-look velour seats can handle six large adults with room to spare. The large windows provide excellent visibility. The rear roof posts are wide, but not enough so to be considered obstructive. Utilizing Bonneville's electric six-way seat adjustment controls, the driver has a wide range of seat positions to insure a comfortable and controlled drive. The Bonneville's ride is smooth and quiet. When the windows are up, wind whistle is nonexistent—even at high speeds—and engine noise is at a minimum.

Bonneville is an automobile not easily serviced

by do-it-yourselfers. The engine compartment is cluttered with an assortment of pumps and motors and belts positioned that make spark plug removal virtually impossible for the shade tree mechanic. The distributor is placed against the firewall on the rear-center of the engine, and is partially covered by the large air filter casing. To reach it a person would need the arms of an octopus, and to work on it he would almost have to climb up into the engine compartment.

At the other end of the Bonneville, Pontiac offers more than 20 cubic feet of cargo space. A deflated spare tire sits back on a shelf and out of the way to provide a large, unobstructed cargo area that is fully carpeted and equipped with a trunk lamp.

The 1979 Bonneville can be considered one of the top buys in the low-price, full-size market. Although this year will put Bonneville into some fierce competition, Pontiac's entry should be able to hold its own. It is an extremely comfortable and good-handling automobile that is priced right for its class.

PONTIAC BONNEVILLE
Test Model Specifications

Body type	4-door	Rear hiproom	55.3 in.
Overall length	214.3 in.	Engine type	V8
Overall width	76.4 in.	Net hp @ rpm	160 @ 3600
Overall height	54.9 in.	Net torque @ rpm	320 @ 1600
Wheelbase	116.0 in.	Displacement	301 cu. in.
Turn diameter	41.5 ft.	Compression ratio	8.2:1
Tire size	GR 78-15	Carburetion	2 bbl.
Curb weight	3769 lbs.	Transmission	Automatic
Cargo space	20.3 cu. ft.	Axle ratio	2.41:1
Front headroom	39.4 in.	Acceleration 0-60 mph	12.3 sec.
Front legroom	42.4 in.	Brake stop 60-0 mph	177 ft.
Front hiproom	55.0 in.	Fuel tank capacity	21 gal.
Rear headroom	38.2 in.	EPA city economy rating	17 mpg.
Rear legroom	39.0 in.		

Pontiac Firebird

Superb performance and sleek styling have made the Firebird one of the top-selling lines in the Pontiac series. Offered in four models—a base Firebird, the Esprit, the high-performance Formula, and Trans Am—Firebird roars into 1979 just as gutsy as ever, in spite of the trend toward small economy cars.

Of the four Firebird models, Trans Am is the undisputed favorite, accounting for more than 50 percent of all Firebird sales and offering the most muscle under the hood. Trans Am comes standard with a 403 cubic-inch V8 and a three-speed automatic transmission. Performance options include a

400 V8 with a four-speed manual transmission. Both engines are equipped only with four-barrel carburetors.

Our test Trans Am was equipped with the 400 V8 and four-speed. This power combination can be described as nothing less than thrilling. Our Trans Am proved to us that its power plant could handle its relatively heavy weight by accelerating from 0 to 60 miles an hour in just over eight seconds. And the extra weight proved beneficial at high speeds—we detected no floating.

In any dynamic power package fuel economy suffers, and the Trans Am is no exception. In a combination of city and highway driving, our test car delivered a meager fuel economy average of about 14 miles per gallon. This is no economy car.

The handling abilities of the 1979 Trans Am are truly amazing. The heavy engine set forward, and the rigid front axle give the impression that the car would ride rough and be hard to steer. But this is a false impression. Turns and road curves are a joy to encounter, and the seemingly stiff suspension handles most road conditions with high marks. The Trans Am does suffer from slight understeer, but this is a common complaint with most domestically built cars. A pleasant surprise for 1979 is the availability of four-wheel disc brakes on the Trans Am and Formula models. Long overdue, they respond with excellence to all emergency braking situations. Unlike the brake system of 1978, the new disc brakes show no tendency to fade after a series of repeated hard stops.

Unfortunately, Trans Am's overall value in performance and style is offset by an inferior interior design. The seating position is one of the worst we have seen. The almost bolt-upright driver's seatback cannot be adjusted for rake. Also, an average-sized person has to move the seat too close to the steering wheel to handle the long clutch throw of the manual transmission. Headroom is lacking throughout; hip room and legroom is adequate up front, but the rear seat is cramped and legroom is almost nonexistent. Due to the deep-set seat positions, visibility is poor over the long hood and obstructed to the rear. The roof slopes low, and the wide side pillars create blind spots. Trans Am does, however offer an extremely snug, quiet ride.

Anyone familiar with the Firebird line knows that trunk space is not one of its major selling points. Our test Trans Am was equipped with the hatch roof. When we placed the roof plates in the trunk along with the spare tire, we found there was not room enough left in the trunk to store anything larger than a briefcase.

The 1979 Firebird line has a nicely redesigned front end and such minor improvements as new bumpers, lamps, and front and rear end panels. The Trans Am and Formula models offer new black-out taillights that remain hidden until activated.

PONTIAC FIREBIRD TRANS AM
Test Model Specifications

Body type 2-door	Rear hiproom . . . . 46.3 in.
Overall length . . . . 198.1 in.	Engine type . . . . OHV V8
Overall width . . . . 73.0 in.	Net hp @ rpm . . . . 220 @ 4000
Overall height . . . . 49.1 in.	Net torque @ rpm . . . . 320 @ 2800
Wheelbase . . . . 108.2 in.	Displacement . . . . 400 cu. in.
Turn diameter . . . . 38.9 ft.	Compression ratio 8.1:1
Tire size 225/70R-15	Carburetion . . . . 4 bbl.
Curb weight . . . . 3601 lbs.	Transmission 4-speed
Cargo space . . . . 7.1 cu. ft.	Manual
Front headroom . . . . 37.2 in.	Axle ratio 3.42:1
Front legroom . . . . 43.9 in.	Acceleration 0-60 mph . . . 8.1 sec.
Front hiproom . . . . 52.4 in.	Brake stop 60-0 mph . . . . . . 189 ft.
Rear headroom . . . . 36.0 in.	Fuel tank capacity . . . . 21 gal.
Rear legroom . . . . 28.4 in.	EPA city economy rating . . 12 mpg.

Pontiac Grand Am

The Pontiac Grand Am is a sporty version of the Pontiac LeMans. And it's virtually unmatched in special features by any other General Motors intermediate-class car—including the Chevy Malibu.

Comfort and high style were featured throughout our test Grand Am, which had sporty white-on-black gauge clusters and firm vinyl bucket seats. Ample legroom in the front is offered along with plenty of hip room and shoulder room, although in some seat positions headroom feels a little tight. The rear seats are somewhat cramped for legroom, and you can get the feeling that you're going to bump your head on the ceiling.

Trunk space is adequate. There's over 16½ cubic feet of almost unobstructed space. The space-saver deflatable sits over in a corner and out of the way.

Driver visibility is excellent to the front and sides. To the rear, the sloping deck makes it a little difficult to see over your left shoulder, but not enough to be considered a blind spot. With the windows up, engine noise heard in the interior is low, and wind whistle is apparent only at high speeds.

Handling has always been one excellent feature of Grand Am. This year, Pontiac has taken steps to improve it further. For 1979, Grand Am comes standard with a new suspension system developed for better handling. The suspension includes a redesigned rear stabilizer bar, new higher-rate front and rear springs, new shock absorber valving, and urethane stabilizer grommets. Our test Grand Am surprised everyone, maneuvering like a sports car while handling the roughest road conditions exceptionally well. The car responded quickly to the slightest steering wheel command and cornered

Pontiac Grand Am

flat, while maintaining real road-hugging traction.

The standard manual front disc and rear drum brakes stopped the 3500-pound car adequately, although in some panic braking maneuvers the rear brakes had a tendency to lock up quickly.

A 231 cubic-inch V6 is standard in the 1979 Grand Am; a 301 cubic-inch V8 and a 305 cubic-inch V8 are available as options. The 231 is stingy with gas but is sluggish. Our test car was equipped with the 301 and three-speed automatic transmission. This power train enabled our test model to run from 0 to 60 miles an hour in just over 12 seconds. Throughout our tests, we maintained a fuel average of just under 19 miles per gallon.

Under the hood, Grand Am is crowded. Removal of the spark plugs is a major project. A Pontiac garage would be the least aggravating solution to servicing problems.

The 1979 Grand Am offers the space and comfort of an intermediate-size automobile plus stylish lines, performance and good handling.

PONTIAC GRAND AM
Test Model Specifications

Body type	2-door	Rear hiproom	54.5 in.
Overall length	198.6 in.	Engine type	V8
Overall width	72.4 in.	Net hp @ rpm	150 @ 4000
Overall height	53.5 in.	Net torque @ rpm	240 @ 2000
Wheelbase	108.1 in.	Displacement	301 cu. in.
Turn diameter	38.0 ft.	Compression ratio	8.2:1
Tire size	GR 60-14	Carburetion	4 bbl.
Curb weight	3541 lbs.	Transmission	Automatic
Cargo space	16.6 cu. ft.	Axle ratio	2.73:1
Front headroom	37.9 in.	Acceleration 0-60 mph	12.3 sec.
Front legroom	42.8 in.	Brake stop 60-0 mph	170 ft.
Front hiproom	51.7 in.	Fuel tank capacity	18.1 gal.
Rear headroom	37.8 in.	EPA city economy rating	17 mpg.
Rear legroom	35.1 in.		

Pontiac Grand Prix

No radical changes have been made in Grand Prix for 1979, but some small alterations are apparent. The grille and taillights have been redesigned, and new two-tone paint options are available to give Grand Prix a longer, lower look. Also new for 1979 is an optional four-speed manual transmission, offered in cars equipped with the 301 cubic-inch V8.

Equipped with the 301 and the four-speed manual, our test car seemed to chomp at the bit. It leaped from 0 to 60 miles an hour in 10 seconds, overtook other cars at expressway speeds with merely a touch on the gas pedal, and delivered an honest 18 miles per gallon over various road conditions. The stickshift was fun and efficient, but seemed out of place in the Grand Prix.

Grand Prix handles well, responding to the slightest steering command quickly, while maintaining a controlled ride. We found it to lean more

Pontiac Grand Prix

than a little in sharp turns; but otherwise, it offered a comfortable, stable ride under all road conditions. The optional power brakes of our test car performed excellently.

The interior of the Grand Prix is somewhat of a disappointment. The crushed-velvet look of the upholstery in our test car was pleasing to the eye, but the seats were stiff. Long periods of time behind the wheel became quite an ordeal. Legroom and headroom is ample in the front bucket seats, but the back seats are no more than barely adequate. The center hump destroys any hope of seating three adults comfortably, and legroom for two is cramped when the front seats are run all the way back. The center console, which contains a change and key tray and an enclosed storage box, is made of thin plastic. It looks cheap.

The rear roofline of the Grand Prix is wide, creating quite a blind spot for the driver. (This can be compensated for somewhat by the use of the adjustable mirrors on each side of the car.) With the windows up, the interior seals tightly for a relatively quiet ride, one that equals that of the Buick Regal and Oldsmobile Cutlass. Little engine hum and wind noise can be heard inside.

A new instrument panel—black background with white indicators—improves the car's gauge visibility. However, the cluster of four gauges off to the right side of the panel is partially obstructed by the padded steering wheel, making it necessary for the driver to lean a bit for an accurate oil pressure and temperature reading.

Cargo space in the Grand Prix is exceptional when you consider the size of the car. Slightly over 16 cubic feet of open luggage volume is available. The space-saving spare tire sits deep in the trunk over to one side, allowing for a nearly level cargo bed.

Pontiac had hoped that the restyled 1978 Grand Prix would hold its following among personal-luxury-car buyers. This turned out not to be the case. Buyers like the larger 1977 model, and showed their dissatisfaction in the new design: sales dropped by more than 20 percent. However, the days of the large cars are gone, and Grand Prix's competitors have downsized their comparable models. Its good performance and handling, and its respectable fuel economy make Grand Prix a strong entry.

PONTIAC GRAND PRIX
Test Model Specifications

Body type	2-door	Rear hiproom	54.9 in.
Overall length	201.4 in.	Engine type	OHV V8
Overall width	72.7 in.	Net hp @ rpm	145 @ 4000
Overall height	53.3 in.	Net torque @ rpm	325 @ 2000
Wheelbase	108.1 in.	Displacement	301 cu. in.
Turn diameter	38.0 ft.	Compression ratio	8.2:1
Tire size	P205/75R14	Carburetion	4 bbl.
Curb weight	3250 lbs.	Transmission	4-speed
Cargo space	16.1 cu. ft.		Manual
Front headroom	37.6 in.	Axle ratio	2.73:1
Front legroom	42.8 in.	Acceleration 0-60 mph	10 sec.
Front hiproom	51.6 in.	Brake stop 60-0 mph	169 ft.
Rear headroom	37.8 in.	Fuel tank capacity	15.0 gal.
Rear legroom	36.3 in.	EPA city economy rating	16 mpg.

Pontiac Phoenix

Pontiac dropped the 1979 Phoenix from production last November as the first step in introducing the 1980 model, which will be radically different in size and mechanical features. The new car, which will feature front-wheel drive, a new V6 engine, and smaller outside dimensions, is set for introduction in April.

It will share most of its body and power train parts with Chevrolet's Nova replacement. Our Nova article contains a more detailed description of what is being prepared.

Pontiac will share two body styles with the new Chevrolet: a two-door and a four-door fastback sedan with hatch opening in the rear. The base engine will be Pontiac's 151 cubic-inch in-line Four that is used now in Sunbird and Monza. This engine will be set transversely under the hood.

Buick and Olds will also introduce new compacts in April. They will have notchback styling. Mechanically, however, they'll be nearly identical with Phoenix and the new Chevy.

CONSUMER GUIDE Magazine has not tested any of the new GM compacts. However, a number of their features appear outstanding. The 1980 model probably will be much easier to drive in tight traffic than the present car, and the 850-pound weight reduction should add at least five miles per gallon to fuel economy. Also, front-wheel drive will allow the cars to retain big-car handling and ride characteristics and open up the interior for more passenger room.

Pontiac Sunbird

One of the major complaints about last year's Sunbird was the lack of power from the standard L-4 engine. So, this year Pontiac has introduced a "crossflow" 2500cc L-4 engine that increases power and torque while maintaining respectable fuel economy. The engine is approximately 35 pounds lighter and uses a new Rochester Varajet carburetor.

Equipped with the "crossflow" L-4 and a four-speed manual transmission, our test Sunbird sport hatchback showed only a slight increase in performance over last year's model. The engine sounds powerful at idle, but moving from a dead stop to 60 mph still took 17 seconds. In our gas mileage tests, Sunbird averaged only about 26 miles per gallon. Also, the L-4 is not an engine that can be easily tackled by the amateur mechanic.

Inside is where the 1979 Sunbird overtakes its sporty economy car competitors. Interior detail is

Pontiac Sunbird

superb for a car in Sunbird's price range. Soft, contoured bucket seats, and padded dash and center console create a rich, comfortable feeling usually found in more expensive cars. The front bucket seats are comfortable and provide ample legroom and headroom. However, the rear bucket seats can just barely accommodate even an average-size adult. Legroom in the rear is cramped, and in the hatchback model, the roofline is so low that it is difficult for anyone except a child to sit upright. Sunbird's hatchback roof design, however, creates no rear blind spots, and overall driver visibility is good. The cab is sealed tightly against wind whistle, and only a very small amount of engine noise gets into the passenger compartment.

Cargo space in the Sunbird coupe is poor. Our test hatchback, however, provided a full 27 cubic feet of cargo space with the rear seats folded down. The deflated space-saving spare tire sits in a compartment beneath the hatchback bed, and there is room around it to store small items.

With its 97-inch wheelbase and a length just short of 180 inches, the Sunbird's ride is rough, but stable. Dips and railroad tracks produce quite a jarring effect, but maintaining control is no problem. The power steering is extremely responsive, and side-sway in tight turns is virtually non-existent. We had the opportunity to run our test car through some emergency maneuvers in heavy rain. Traction was maintained in all but the most extreme moves, and the optional power disc brakes gave above-average performance.

Pontiac offers the Sunbird in a coupe, sport coupe, sport hatchback and sport Safari wagon, with power train combinations including a Four, V6 or V8 engine teamed with a four-speed manual, five-speed manual, or automatic transmission.

Sunbird will probably have a tough time of it in 1979. Changes in its exterior styling have been minor, in contrast to the redesigned Mustang and Capri. The potential Sunbird buyer should take into consideration that the Sunbird is still relatively unknown as a sporty economy automobile. And when a car fails to win acceptance after a few years on the market, it's likely that its resale value will suffer.

PONTIAC SUNBIRD
Test Model Specifications

Body type	2-door	Rear hiproom	42.0 in.
Overall length	179.3 in.	Engine type	L4
Overall width	65.4 in.	Net hp @ rpm	90 @ 4400
Overall height	50.2 in.	Net torque @ rpm	128 @ 2400
Wheelbase	97.0 in.	Displacement	151 cu. in.
Turn diameter	35.8 ft.	Compression ratio	8.3:1
Tire size	BR/70-13	Carburetion	2 bbl.
Curb weight	2806 lbs.	Transmission	4-speed
Cargo space	27.8 cu. ft.*		Manual
Front headroom	37.7 in.	Axle ratio	2.93.1
Front legroom	43.0 in.	Acceleration 0-60 mph	17 sec.
Front hiproom	47.5 in.	Brake stop 60-0 mph	182 ft.
Rear headroom	35.3 in.	Fuel tank capacity	18.5 gal.
Rear legroom	29.6 in.	EPA city economy rating	24 mpg.

*with rear seat folded down

Special Report: Domestic Wagons

AMC Concord

AMC has added a new model, the Limited, to its Concord wagon line. The Limited is part of AMC's attempt to find areas of the wagon market not covered by the larger manufacturers. It comes equipped with most of the convenience and comfort items usually carried only on luxury cars. Among the Limited's standard features are leather seats, air conditioning, automatic transmission, and power assists for steering and brakes.

Except for the introduction of the Limited, though, the Concord wagon has been changed very little for 1979. In fact, it is virtually the same car that AMC sold for most of the 1970s under the name Hornet Sportabout. The name change last year was also part of AMC's plan to upgrade the line.

Concord is a small wagon—smaller than most other compacts. It doesn't offer the passenger space or cargo capacity of wagons in the Ford Fairmont's size class, and although seating is reasonably comfortable for four passengers, the design of the doors creates a feeling of being closed in. In addition, the comparatively small doors hinder entry to and exit from the passenger compartment.

The DL model we examined was equipped with the 258 cubic-inch Six (the two-barrel-carburetor version). It's not a performance engine, but it provides sufficient power in all traffic conditions. AMC excels in one area—power train design. The 258 in-line Six combined with the three-speed Chrysler automatic transmission is one of the smoothest running power trains of its type.

If you use the amount of quality trim as a basis of comparison among cars, Concord gets top honors. Seats and door panels on our DL wagon were covered with soft, chamois-like material. The DL's

AMC Concord

carpet is also a grade above that of the competition.

There are some problems with the interior, though. One is the unattractive tray below the instrument panel; it looks like it belongs on a low-cost car like Concord's predecessor, not on a high-quality automobile. And the door-mounted radio speakers interfere with the window cranks.

Our acceleration runs with the Six proved that the engine is adequate for this car; it posted a 16-second time from 0 to 60 miles an hour. Fuel economy is mediocre. We recorded an average 18 miles per gallon in combined city-highway driving, one mile per gallon less than the Environmental Protection Agency's estimate.

In direct comparisons with Concord's top competitors, Fairmont and Volaré, Concord's lack of room—vital in a wagon—is a big handicap. We feel that the AMC wagon does not provide the dollar-for-dollar value of the Ford and Chrysler compact wagons.

AMC CONCORD
Test Model Specifications

Body type	4-door	Rear hiproom	53.6 in.
Overall length	186 in.	Engine type	6 in-line
Overall width	71 in.	Net hp @ rpm	120 @ 3600
Overall height	51.3 in.	Net torque @ rpm	210 @ 1800
Wheelbase	108 in.	Displacement	258 cu. in.
Turn diameter	34.9 ft.	Compression ratio	8.3:1
Tire size	D78x14	Carburetion	2 bbl.
Curb weight	3044 lbs.	Transmission	Automatic
Cargo space	57 cu. ft.*	Axle ratio	2.53:1
Front headroom	38.1 in.	Acceleration 0-60 mph	15.0 sec.
Front legroom	40.8 in.	Brake stop 60-0 mph	163 ft.
Front hiproom	54.4 in.	Fuel tank capacity	22 gal.
Rear headroom	37.9 in.	EPA city economy rating	17 mpg.
Rear legroom	36.1 in.		

*with rear seat folded down

AMC Pacer

If AMC had it all to do over, it probably would not offer the Pacer sedan at all. The idea seems to work better as a wagon. Pacer's unusually large expanse of glass certainly looks more fitting on the wagon than on the sedan. In fact, Pacer's styling in general looks more conservative on the wagon than on the sedan. Had the wagon been introduced as the first Pacer, it might have brought in many more buyers.

CONSUMER GUIDE Magazine's staff tested the Pacer DL wagon equipped with the 258 cubic-inch six-cylinder engine. The 258 now has a two-barrel carburetor, which gives it added punch. This com-

AMC Pacer

bination makes the 258 the best engine for this car from the standpoint of fuel economy and performance.

In addition to the DL, AMC offers a Limited model. Included in the base price of the Limited are such luxury features as leather-covered seats, thick carpeting, air conditioning, reclining seats and center armrests.

Pacer is one of the smaller wagons on the market. Its total length is about 178 inches—about 15 inches shorter than the Fairmont. Because of its length, Pacer can slip in and out of heavy traffic and is a cinch to park in tight spaces.

Handling is excellent, thanks to the car's extra wide stance. This should not be overlooked when comparing Pacer to other small wagons. The wide stance means greater stability and control.

Performance with the six-cylinder engine is acceptable. Our test staff averaged just over 15 seconds in the standard acceleration run from 0 to 60 miles an hour, which is a fairly good time for a Six. Fuel economy of the Six is the kind you find in big cars. The power plant averages 19 miles per gallon in combined city-highway driving, which is poor for a wagon of Pacer's size. The V8 is worse. Its combined city-highway rating is only 16 mpg. Fuel economy is the primary reason we recommend the Six.

Rear seat hip room is unusually tight because the rear wheel wells intrude into the seating area. Also, the rear load floor is unusually high because the spare wheel is stowed under the floor.

Visibility is excellent to the front and rear. To the side, however, visibility is only so-so because the side post is so wide.

The Pacer wagon is pleasant—even fun—to drive. Its power train is excellent. But poor fuel economy and a relatively small load space are drawbacks.

AMC PACER
Test Model Specifications

Body type 2-door	Rear hiproom ....42.3 in.
Overall length ....177.7 in.	Engine type ....6 in-line
Overall width.............77 in.	Net hp @ rpm ....120 @ 3600
Overall height ....53.1 in.	Net torque @ rpm ....210 @ 1800
Wheelbase ....100 in.	Displacement ....258 cu. in.
Turn diameter ....37 ft.	Compression ratio 8.3:1
Tire size...........P195/75R14	Carburetion..............2 bbl.
Curb weight ....3250 lbs.	Transmission ....Automatic
Cargo space ....52.5 cu. ft.*	Axle ratio 2.53:1
Front headroom ....38.5 in.	Acceleration 0-60 mph ..15.1 sec.
Front legroom ....40.7 in.	Brake stop 60-0 mph ......175 ft.
Front hiproom ....56 in.	Fuel tank capacity ....21 gal.
Rear headroom ....38.0 in.	EPA city economy rating ..17 mpg.
Rear legroom ....35 in.	

*with rear seat folded down

Chevrolet Caprice

Full-size station wagons offer the luxury, size, power and carrying capacity that smaller wagons cannot. Of all the 1979 models offered by the car manufacturers, there are basically only two full-size wagons, one built by Ford and another by GM. Ford makes a big wagon for the LTD and Marquis lines. Chevrolet, Pontiac, Buick and Oldsmobile share GM's big wagon body.

Chevy offers four full-size wagons: a two-seat and a three-seat Caprice; and a two-seat and a four-seat Impala. CONSUMER GUIDE Magazine selected the Caprice Classic four-door, three-seat wagon for its representative test of the GM design. It's Chevy's most prestigious wagon model, incorporating many of the luxury and convenience features that are offered in the Caprice Classic sedans.

The general layout of the Caprice is conventional. The rear-facing third seat is an alternative to Ford's two face-to-face rear seats, although neither arrangement is inherently better than the other. Caprice's second and third seats fold down easily. You need only release one latch for each. When folded, the seats form a relatively flat surface that is ideally laid out for carrying bulky items. The three-way tailgate provides instant access to the rear seat for passengers, with no waiting for the window to be lowered before the door can be opened.

The load area is 90 inches from the closed tailgate to the back of the front seat and 48.2 inches between the wheel wells, which is big enough (with the tailgate down) to carry a 4x8 sheet of plywood laid flat.

Caprice's total cargo volume is 87.9 cubic feet, which is about 10 cubic feet less than that of Ford's Country Squire. However, the Ford's extra capacity is due mostly to its higher roof and is not significant for most cargo-carrying purposes.

We strongly recommend that the Caprice be equipped with the electric rear window option. It is a convenience when loading, and allows the driver to control the window for ventilation.

The big change in station wagons in the past few years has been that of handling. The automakers are now building wagons with just about the same ride and handling as sedans. That means wagons are less tail-heavy, more nimble, and easier to drive than their predecessors. The Caprice wagon still cannot equal the sedan model in extreme handling maneuvers, but its tendency to oversteer has been reduced, and the wagon handles predictably in most driving situations.

Chevy's sedan is top rated this year and a lot of its features appear on the wagon. In fact, driving the Caprice wagon is similar in almost every way to driving a comparable Chevy sedan. In acceleration and braking, the wagon is identical with the sedan. The instrument panel has the same expensive appearance as the sedan and is loaded with controls that make the car seem more a luxury vehicle than a workhorse. Noise levels inside the wagon are slightly higher than those in a sedan, mostly because the rear area is open and transmits noise from the rear axle, wheels and rear door.

Performance of our test wagon with the optional 350 cubic-inch V8 engine was outstanding. The staff of CONSUMER GUIDE Magazine recorded acceleration times of more than 12 seconds for 0 to 60 miles an hour, which puts Caprice at the top of the performance scale.

Which is the better full-size wagon to buy— Chevy or Ford? It's almost a toss-up, though we like the face-to-face rear seats in the Ford better than the single rear-facing third seat in the Chevy. Buyers will find the two wagons so closely matched in a variety of features that the third seat layout may be the deciding factor.

CHEVROLET CAPRICE
Test Model Specifications

Body type	4-door	Rear hiproom	55 in.
Overall length	214.7 in.	Engine type	V8
Overall width	79.1 in.	Net hp @ rpm	N/A
Overall height	58 in.	Net torque @ rpm	N/A
Wheelbase	116 in.	Displacement	350 cu. in.
Turn diameter	39.6 ft.	Compression ratio	8.2:1
Tire size	HR78-15	Carburetion	4 bbl.
Curb weight	4172 lbs.	Transmission	Automatic
Cargo space	87.9 cu. ft.	Axle ratio	2.41:1
Front headroom	39.4 in.	Acceleration 0-60 mph	12.3 sec.
Front legroom	42.4 in.	Brake stop 60-0 mph	161 ft.
Front hiproom	55 in.	Fuel tank capacity	22 gal.
Rear headroom	39.1 in.	EPA city economy rating	14 mpg.
Rear legroom	37.7 in.		

*with rear seat folded down

Chevrolet Malibu

The most striking feature of the GM mid-size wagon body is its tailgate design. It's a two-piece gate that is split horizontally in the middle. The top half is glass and swings upward; the bottom half is a typical fold-down gate. GM is using this tailgate design on four models: Chevrolet Malibu, Pontiac LeMans, Buick Century and Oldsmobile Cutlass Cruiser. What is said about one applies to the others.

The test staff of CONSUMER GUIDE Magazine examined the Malibu Classic four-door, two-seat wagon as representative of the GM mid-size line. Our Malibu was equipped with a 305 cubic-inch V8 engine, the minimum size we recommend for a station wagon of this size.

Performance, ride and handling were excellent. In acceleration runs from 0 to 60 miles an hour, the

Chevrolet Malibu

Malibu wagon averaged just under 13 seconds — about the same as the best of the V8-equipped sedans. Although fuel economy with this engine was not very good, it was better than what we'd expected, considering Malibu's overall high performance. In combined city-highway driving, our Malibu V8 averaged about 17 miles per gallon, which is only about one mpg less than the Fairmont and Volare wagons equipped with similar V8 engines.

If you are interested in better fuel economy than the 305 cubic-inch engine provides, the new Chevy 267 cubic-inch V8 is also available. However, we feel that the smaller engine is not really adequate. Its economy — about two more miles per gallon than the 305 — doesn't offset the decreased performance.

The interior of the Malibu is not unusual. The second seat folds easily, and the load floor is relatively flat. An advantage of the two-piece tailgate is that the top half can remain closed while the bottom half is left open for carrying long loads.

Two bins are built into the side panels at the rear of the cargo area for additional storage space.

However, these are open at the top and do not offer the security of covered bins. What they contain is clearly visible from outside the car—an invitation to thieves.

Like the Malibu sedan, the instrument panel of the Malibu wagon is extremely simple. The instruments are conveniently placed and easy to read and operate.

One of the biggest problems with the four-door Malibu wagon is that the rear door windows are fixed in place—they don't roll down. For ventilation, rear passengers must depend on tiny vent windows mounted behind the rear doors. Chevy has received many complaints about this arrangement.

Malibu costs about $1000 more than either of its principal competitors, Fairmont and Volare. Is the higher price worth it? In our opinion, it isn't, unless you have a special need for Malibu's greater weight or split tailgate. In other respects, Malibu offers no advantage over the Ford or Plymouth wagons.

CHEVROLET MALIBU
Test Model Specifications

Body type 4-door	Rear hiproom ....55.6 in.
Overall length ....193.4 in.	Engine type V8
Overall width ....71.2 in.	Net hp @ rpm ....N/A
Overall height ....54.5 in.	Net torque @ rpm ....N/A
Wheelbase............108.1 in.	Displacement ....305 cu. in.
Turn diameter ....37.19 ft.	Compression ratio 8.4:1
Tire size...........P195/75R14	Carburetion .... 4 bbl.
Curb weight ....3276 lbs.	Transmission ....Automatic
Cargo space ....72.4 cu. ft.	Axle ratio 2.41:1
Front headroom ....38.5 in.	Acceleration 0-60 mph ..12.2 sec.
Front legroom ....42.8 in.	Brake stop 60-0 mph ......162 ft.
Front hiproom ....52.2 in.	Fuel tank capacity .....17.7 gal.
Rear headroom ....38.8 in.	EPA city economy rating ..15 mpg.
Rear legroom ....35.9 in.	

Chevrolet Monza

The Monza wagon is basically the old Chevrolet Vega wagon body, powered by a couple of new engines. When Chevy dropped the Vega two years ago, most of Vega's components, including its aluminum engine, were dropped from production. The station wagon body, however, survived. By adding a Monza front to the Vega body, Chevy has now created a "new" car. Pontiac offers an identical model in its Sunbird line.

Monza's engine lineup is a definite improvement over Vega's. The standard engine is a 151 cubic-inch Four, which has been refined for 1979.

The CONSUMER GUIDE Magazine staff tested a Monza wagon powered by the 151 engine and equipped with a four-speed manual transmission. We found its fuel economy was satisfactory for a wagon body. Our Monza averaged nearly 28 miles per gallon in combined city-highway driving. In straight city driving, it averaged about 23 mpg—a figure few other U.S.-built wagons can duplicate.

Monza's optional engine this year is a new 196 cubic-inch V6. The performance of this engine is only marginally better than the standard Four's and its economy averages from two to four miles per gallon less. We recommend the V6 only for heavy-duty use.

Performance with the Four is good, though not sparkling. Acceleration from 0 to 60 miles an hour averaged 16 seconds, about two seconds slower than a larger car powered by a small V8. Overall, the 151 Four is ideally suited to the Monza line.

Inside, Monza has the same problems that occurred in the Vega. The low front seats are awkward to get into and out of, and they are tiring on long trips. The transmission hump and drive shaft tunnel are unusually large, robbing passengers of space. Getting into and out of the rear seat is a hassle.

The large hatch door allows full access to the rear, and the second seat folds down with a minimum of trouble. The load compartment is small.

Which is the better buy—a small wagon such as Monza, or a hatchback sedan such as Rabbit, Horizon or Omni? We strongly prefer the hatchbacks.

CHEVROLET MONZA
Test Model Specifications

Body type	2-door	Rear hip room	49.2 in.
Overall length	178 in.	Engine type	4 in-line
Overall width	65.4 in.	Net hp @ rpm	85 @ 4400
Overall height	51 in.	Net torque @ rpm	123 @ 2800
Wheelbase	97 in.	Displacement	151 cu. in.
Turn diameter	35.8 ft.	Compression ratio	8.3:1
Tire size	B78-13	Carburetion	2 bbl.
Curb weight	2709 lbs.	Transmission	4-speed
Cargo space	46.6 cu. ft.		Manual
Front headroom	38.5 in.	Axle ratio	2.73:1
Front legroom	43 in.	Acceleration 0-60 mph	17 sec.
Front hip room	46.9 in.	Brake stop 60-0 mph	160 ft.
Rear headroom	40.1 in.	Fuel tank capacity	15 gal.
Rear legroom	30.2 in.	EPA city economy rating	24 mpg.

Chrysler LeBaron Town & Country

Chrysler's LeBaron Town & Country wagon is functionally identical with the Diplomat, Aspen and Volare wagons. In fact, all four models have the same chassis, body and power trains. What distinguishes LeBaron Town & Country is its dressy appearance—and, of course, the added cost of the appearance features.

The staff of CONSUMER GUIDE Magazine tested a LeBaron Town & Country wagon that was equipped with a 318 cubic-inch V8. A middle-range engine, the 318 is probably the all-around best for this car. Its fuel economy, averaging about 18 miles per gallon, was fairly good for a medium-duty wagon. Performance, however, was slightly below average for a V8 wagon: acceleration from 0 to 60 miles an hour took about 14.5 seconds. The optional 360 cubic-inch V8 should improve 0 to 60 acceleration by about two seconds but also decrease fuel mileage by about two miles per gallon.

The standard power plant in the Town & Country wagon is a 225 cubic-inch slant-six engine. It is a superior Six, but we feel that it is too small for a station wagon. Besides, the slant-six engine with automatic transmission will deliver only about one mpg more than the 318; in our judgement, that is not sufficient to warrant choosing the smaller engine.

The level of road noise inside LeBaron Town & Country is relatively low for a wagon. Wagons, however, are typically noisier than sedans, and this wagon is no exception. A wagon's open rear compartment admits noise from the rear axle and wheels that would be absorbed by the rear seat and shelf of a sedan.

On the road, LeBaron Town & Country has the feel of a larger wagon. Its ride is smooth and even. Its comparatively long hood and front fenders add to the full-size feeling.

The interior has the same full-size feel. You can order a 60-40 front seat with center armrest, pull straps on all four doors and carpeting that covers the lower six inches of the soft trim on the doors. The instrument panel is clean, simple and neatly laid out — it's made for easy use.

Front seat room is excellent for a compact wagon. Room in the rear seat is also good, thanks mostly to the high roofline that is found in most wagons. A big plus is the firm, deeply cushioned rear seat, which is of much higher quality than the rear seats of most compacts having the fold-down feature. A single push button atop the rear seat releases the seat back so that you can fold it from either rear door. In the rear load compartment, carpeting covers the lower eight inches of the side panels, thus protecting the soft finish from nicks and scratches.

Optional on the Town & Country wagon are lockable storage compartments in each side of the rear cargo area. This feature provides protection for small valuables that would otherwise be left in plain view on the back floor.

The spare tire stows under the rear floor so that there is plenty of open floor space for carrying bulky loads. With the rear seat folded down, the floor is relatively flat along its entire length.

If you want a wagon with sedan-like elegance, LeBaron Town & Country may be what you are looking for. However, we feel that Volare and Aspen wagons, which cost a couple of hundred dollars less than the Town & Country, give greater dollar-for-dollar value.

CHRYSLER LEBARON TOWN & COUNTRY
Test Model Specifications

Body type	4-door	Rear hiproom	57 in.
Overall length	202.8 in.	Engine type	V8
Overall width	72.8 in.	Net hp @ rpm	140 @ 4000
Overall height	55.7 in.	Net torque @ rpm	245 @ 1600
Wheelbase	112.7 in.	Displacement	318 cu. in.
Turn diameter	40.7 ft.	Compression ratio	8.5:1
Tire size	FR78-15	Carburetion	2 bbl.
Curb weight	3684 lbs.	Transmission	Automatic
Cargo space	73.1 cu. ft.	Axle ratio	2.71:1
Front headroom	39.2 in.	Acceleration 0-60 mph	14.5 sec.
Front legroom	42.5 in.	Brake stop 60-0 mph	173 ft.
Front hiproom	57.2 in.	Fuel tank capacity	19.5 gal.
Rear headroom	38.7 in.	EPA city economy rating	16 mpg.
Rear legroom	36.6 in.		

Ford Fairmont

The Fairmont wagon is one of the newest wagon designs on the market, and it has all the best features of the Fairmont sedan: excellent visibility, responsive handling, good fuel economy and comfort.

Fairmont's closest competitors in terms of over-all value are the mid-size GM cars, which also are relatively new designs. But Fairmont has the edge. Fairmont's hatch-type rear door is more convenient to use and more durable than GM's split door.

Ford offers several engine options for Fairmont. The wagon we tested was equipped with the largest power plant, the 302 cubic-inch V8, and automatic transmission. Acceleration from 0 to 60 miles an hour was about 14 seconds, which is excellent for a small V8 in a station wagon body. We recommend this engine for the Fairmont wagon. We feel that the 305 has the power to meet the demands ordinarily put on a wagon. Of course, to get this power you have to give up some fuel economy. For greater fuel economy, the 200 cubic-inch Six is adequate, but powerful enough for only light-duty use.

Also available is a 140 cubic-inch Four. It is much too small for a wagon of Fairmont's size. In fact, by using the Four for load hauling, you could end up with worse mileage than you might get from the V8.

Fairmont has a standard rear compartment layout with a folding second seat. Third seats are not available in Fairmont's class; they are offered only in full-size wagons. Fairmont's second seat release is simple and straightforward. The seat can be folded with one hand from either side of the car. With the seat folded, the rear cargo area has a capacity of about 80 cubic feet.

The outside dimensions of the Fairmont wagon are identical with those of the sedan, except that the wagon is more than an inch higher. The extra height is necessary to accommodate the hatch door in the rear. It also means that rear seat headroom is better in the wagon than in the sedan.

Driving the wagon is much like driving the sedan. We have the same complaints about seat construction and placement, and the same praise for ride and handling for both Fairmont models. Overall, we rank the Fairmont V8 wagon at the top of the compact-intermediate class. The Mercury Zephyr is the same car, with slightly different trim styling.

FORD FAIRMONT
Test Model Specifications

Body type	4-door	Rear hiproom	48.7 in.
Overall length	193.8 in.	Engine type	V8
Overall width	71 in.	Net hp @ rpm	104 @ 3600
Overall height	54.8 in.	Net torque @ rpm	250 @ 1800
Wheelbase	105.5 in.	Displacement	302 cu. in.
Turn diameter	39 ft.	Compression ratio	8.4:1
Tire size	CR78-14 B	Carburetion	2 bbl.
Curb weight	2795 lbs.	Transmission	Automatic
Cargo space	79.5 cu. ft.	Axle ratio	2.73:1
Front headroom	39 in.	Acceleration 0-60 mph	17.4 sec.
Front legroom	41.8 in.	Brake stop 60-0 mph	142 ft.
Front hiproom	56.2 in.	Fuel tank capacity	16 gal.
Rear headroom	39 in.	EPA city economy rating	16 mpg.
Rear legroom	35.4 in.		

Ford LTD
Country Squire

Ford offers two station wagons in the full-size LTD line: the LTD base wagon and the highly visible LTD Country Squire. The wagon models were downsized for 1979, a move that resulted in a number of improvements.

We tested a fully-equipped LTD Country Squire powered by a 351 cubic-inch V8 engine. This is the engine option we recommend for the LTD wagon. Fuel economy with the 351 averages about 17 miles per gallon, with highway mileage near 20 mpg. The standard engine on the LTD wagon is a 302 cubic-inch V8. We recommend against the 302, however. Its power is not adequate for the wagon body. As a result, its gas mileage is not even as good as that of the 351. The 351 offers both better performance and better fuel economy.

Ford LTD

Although the 1979 LTD wagon is about a foot shorter than the 1978 model, its carrying capacity is about the same. This year the capacity, with both rear seats folded into the floor, is 91.7 cubic feet — just 2.8 cubic feet less than last year. The shorter, narrower body makes the 1979 wagon much easier to handle in tight traffic, and much simpler to park in crowded parking lots. Overall, it's an impressive improvement over the 1978 model.

Other carry-over features include the ability to carry a 4x8 sheet of plywood flat on the floor, and the three-way tailgate that Ford pioneered. The gate can be operated as a door with the window in up or down position, or it can be pulled down as a tailgate. Although it's been on the market for over a decade, it's still the best rear door design there is.

The second seat has been made even wider in the 1979 LTD wagon, making the interior exceptionally roomy. The second seat still releases and folds very easily. The two center-facing rear seats have been carried over on the 1979 model. This arrangement, unique to Ford, gives the LTD wagon special place in station wagon ratings. The removable cushions in the rear seats are also a carry-over feature. This gives additional room under the floor for more secure storage of valuables. The facing rear seats can hold four small children in reasonable comfort, but only a couple of adults.

Security is always a problem with station wagon models because of the lack of a covered trunk. Ford has solved that problem to some degree this year with a lockable stowage compartment that is standard on all LTD wagons. It's built into the side as part of the quarter panel opposite the spare tire, where it is convenient to reach from the rear door opening. Though its capacity is relatively small, the compartment will hold a number of small items that drivers want to keep out of sight of passersby.

Evaluating the 1979 LTD wagon against the 1978 model and all its current competitors is easy. The Ford design continues to impress our test staff with its innovation, carrying capacity and reputation for durability in the toughest service. It's our choice as the best of the full-size wagons for 1979.

FORD LTD COUNTRY SQUIRE
Test Model Specifications

Body type	4-door	Rear hiproom	54.2 in.
Overall length	212.9 in.	Engine type (see carb.)	V8
Overall width	73.9 in.	Net hp @ rpm	132 @ 3200
Overall height	56.7 in.	Net torque @ rpm	268 @ 1400
Wheelbase	114.4 in.	Displacement	351 cu. in.
Turn diameter	39.4 ft.	Compression ratio	8.3:1
Tire size	GR78-14B	Carburetion (Cal. only)	Variable
Curb weight	3845 lbs.		Venturi
Cargo space	91.7 cu. ft.	Transmission	Automatic
Front headroom	38.9 in.	Axle ratio	3.08:1
Front legroom	42 in.	Acceleration 0-60 mph	13.5 sec.
Front hiproom	61.2 in.	Brake stop 60-0 mph	158 ft.
Rear headroom	39.1 in.	Fuel tank capacity	20 gal.
Rear legroom	39.3 in.	EPA city economy rating	15 mpg.

Ford Pinto

Pinto is Ford Motor Company's smallest wagon and it's a car that has a decidedly fresh look for 1979, with new front styling and an all-new instrument panel. Pinto offers only one wagon model, but buyers can dress it up with a number of options, including the traditional woodgrain side panel veneer. Basically, though, Pinto for 1979 is the same Pinto that Ford has offered for the past six years. Only a couple important changes have been made for 1979. These changes have been made to rectify some mistakes in gas tank placement and in the suspension system.

Nominally an economy car, we have found that Pinto offers good fuel economy when equipped with the standard four-cylinder engine. However, we feel that the standard 140 cubic-inch Four is not powerful enough for a station wagon—even for a wagon of Pinto's small size. Pinto's standard Four averages well over 20 miles per gallon of gas. However, with the optional six-cylinder engine, which is big enough to provide the power needed in a wagon, mileage drops to just below 20 mpg.

In most cases you can't get both fuel economy

and adequate performance—and certainly not in the current Pinto. The reason lies in the weight of the wagon. At over 2600 pounds, stripped, Pinto is no longer in the economy car weight class. And that means that it must move up in engine size to maintain performance.

In contrast, the VW Rabbit and the Plymouth Horizon, both four-door hatchbacks, weigh 400 to 500 pounds apiece less than the Pinto wagon; yet they offer outstanding fuel economy and have almost as much cargo capacity as Pinto. We recommend Rabbit and Horizon as alternatives to the Pinto wagon.

Other alternatives are Chevrolet Monza and Pontiac Sunbird wagons. These are built on the old Vega body, so their basic design has been proven over 10 years of service. And, when equipped with the new 196 cubic-inch V6 engine, Monza and Sunbird fuel economy is better than that of Pinto. Both the V6 and the standard 151 cubic-inch Four of Monza and Sunbird are superior in performance and economy to the comparable power plants in the Pinto.

Comparison shoppers should note that for a few hundred dollars extra, the Ford Fairmont wagon is also a very attractive alternative to the Pinto. The

Ford Pinto

Fairmont wagon can handle larger cargoes, offers the convenience of a four-door body, and still has fuel economy that will match or better that of Pinto. In our opinion, Fairmont is clearly the better wagon value.

Pinto's rear door is the standard hatch type that is perfectly suited to a small wagon. But don't expect to get any big loads into the car. The 58 cubic-foot cargo space is just over half of what is available in a full-size wagon and about two-thirds of that available in the Fairmont.

The second seat folds forward easily when the space is needed for extra large loads. A single latch releases the seat back, and it can be reached from either door. The seat can be repositioned with a similar motion.

Overall, we feel that Pinto has neither fuel economy nor cargo capacity going for it. Our advice is to either look to a bigger wagon or opt for one of the roomier four-door hatchbacks, such as Rabbit or Horizon.

FORD PINTO
Test Model Specifications

Body type	2-door	Rear hiproom	39.4 in.
Overall length	178.6 in.	Engine type	V6
Overall width	69.7 in.	Net hp @ rpm	102 @ 4400
Overall height	52.1 in.	Net torque @ rpm	138 @ 3200
Wheelbase	94.8 in.	Displacement	171 cu. in.
Turn diameter	30.7 ft.	Compression ratio	8.7:1
Tire size	A78-13B	Carburetion	2 bbl.
Curb weight	2634 lbs.	Transmission	Automatic
Cargo space	57.2 cu. ft.	Axle ratio	3.08:1
Front headroom	37.7 in.	Acceleration 0-60 mph	15.6 sec.
Front legroom	40.2 in.	Brake stop 60-0 mph	165 ft.
Front hiproom	51.6 in.	Fuel tank capacity	14 gal.
Rear headroom	38.8 in.	EPA city economy rating	18 mpg.
Rear legroom	29.5 in.		

Plymouth Volaré

Volaré is built on the only remaining station wagon body sold by Chrysler Corporation. Plymouth shares the wagon body with Dodge's Aspen and Diplomat and Chrysler's Town & Country. None of the other lines, including Horizon at the small end and Newport/St. Regis at the full-size end, offers a station wagon body. Therefore, what is said about the Volaré also applies to the other Chrysler wagon models.

The Volaré wagon would seem to have all the ingredients of a winner. Its size is right in the middle of the market, a combination of compact and intermediate. It offers a ride that is closer to that of a full-size wagon than to that of a compact, and its straightforward power train and chassis promise troublefree operation. It may be a little dated in concept when compared with Fairmont and Malibu, but the basic ingredients that make up a good station wagon are still offered.

Unfortunately, the reality does not live up to the promise. Volaré has a history of poor quality and frequent breakdowns. Reports from owners in-

Plymouth Volaré

dicate widespread discontent with the whole Volaré line, including the station wagon. This is aside from any safety recalls the company has been forced by the government to perform.

Plymouth offers a dress-up package for the wagon that includes a "Sport" theme. It has little to do with the basic functioning of the vehicle, but instead is focused on cosmetics. It includes special black-out grille, air dam, dual-color paint stripes, padded steering wheel and more.

Volaré has a 225 cubic-inch slant-six engine that has proven dependable for more than a decade at Chrysler. It is slightly small for station wagon use, but is acceptable for those buyers interested primarily in fuel economy. The optional 318 cubic-inch V8 is another Chrysler workhorse. It is better suited to station wagon use than the 225, and is the recommended engine in the Volaré, although its fuel economy is a couple miles per gallon less than that of the Six. The top-performance 360 cubic-inch V8 is recommended only for heavy-duty service, or when a trailer is to be towed.

We tested a Volaré wagon equipped with a 318 cubic-inch V8. Fuel economy averaged 20 miles per gallon in combined city-highway driving, which is slightly better that what Chevrolet offers in a similar size engine and two miles per gallon better than the Ford Fairmont V8 wagon.

Volaré is a two-seat, four-door wagon that offers all the convenience and storage features of its competition. Its hatch-type rear door is superior to the split type offered in the GM mid-size wagons because it opens easily and quickly with one motion. The hatch is also a more rugged design than the separate glass-gate layout of the Malibu and other GM wagons.

Volaré's rear seat is easy to convert into floor area. The seat back pulls forward after one latch is opened. The latch can be reached from either rear door, which is very convenient.

Chrysler plans to build the Volaré wagon for another two years before its smaller, lighter replacement hits the streets. For now, Volaré fills a wide range of needs in the Chrysler lineup, and if the buyer gets a good one, Volaré will stand up against any competitor and offer at least equal value. Though we tend to favor the Fairmont wagon in this class, we also feel that Volaré can be an excellent alternate choice.

PLYMOUTH VOLARÉ
Test Model Specifications

Body type 4-door	Rear hiproom ....57 in.
Overall length ....201.2 in.	Engine type V8
Overall width ....72.8 in.	Net hp @ rpm ....140 @ 4000
Overall height ....55.7 in.	Net torque @ rpm ...245 @ 1600
Wheelbase............112.7 in.	Displacement ....318 cu. in.
Turn diameter ....40.7 ft.	Compression ratio 8.5:1
Tire size ER78-14	Carburetion.............2 bbl.
Curb weight ....3423 lbs.	Transmission ....Automatic
Cargo space ....73.1 cu. ft.	Axle ratio 2.71:1
Front headroom ....39.2 in.	Acceleration 0-60 mph ..14.5 sec.
Front legroom ....42.5 in.	Brake stop 60-0 mph ......178 ft.
Front hiproom ....57.2.	Fuel tank capacity ......19.5 gal.
Rear headroom ....38.7 in.	EPA city economy rating ..16 mpg.
Rear legroom ....36.6 in.	

Imported Automobiles

BMW 320i

BMW's 320i looks like a conventional two-door sedan; it also rides and behaves in a very civilized manner in most traffic. But it's a true sports car as well. Handling is superb, acceleration is excellent for a four-cylinder engine, performance at high speeds is superior, and the car offers an exceptional sense of control. It is also priced in the $10,000 range.

Power is supplied by one of the smoothest-running overhead-cam Fours available. The engine develops a solid 110 horsepower, which seems just right for the 320i's 2600-pound body. Fuel economy is good too, though this is no economy car. In city driving you can get almost 20 miles per gallon, highway driving will deliver as much as 28 mpg.

Interior dimensions are tight, but there is sufficient room for four adults to ride without inordinate squeezing. The front bucket seats are comfortable and provide highly functional side support and firm bottom rests. Due to the height of the front seats, the driver has an excellent view all around. This is in vivid contrast to the position of passengers in low-slung sports cars.

One big reason for not investing in a BMW is the cost of maintenance and repairs. German cars are notorious for their repair bills, and the BMW line is no exception. Expect to pay a couple of thousand dollars for fender repair and painting. Maintenance charges are similarly high. If you are a do-it-yourselfer, though, you can live with the BMW on a small budget. Its simplicity of design is a home mechanic's dream come true.

Noise levels inside the passenger compartment

BMW 320i

are relatively low, thanks to the careful construction of the body and seals. At 30 miles an hour the 320i is noticeably quieter than either the Mazda RX-7 or the Porsche 924 and about equal to domestic sporty cars. At higher speeds, though, the roar of the exhaust takes over and noise rises to a level that is about average for sports cars of this price.

The 320i's sedan body provides good trunk space. In fact, CONSUMER GUIDE Magazine found the trunk size and layout about the best you can get in the sports-car class.

It's a gem of a car that costs a lot to buy and own, but one that is well worth the price in terms of quality, handling, and general driving fun. Buyers will note that the price of this car does not include such items as power steering, electric windows, electric seats, or automatic transmission (available at about $450 extra). But we think the BMW 320i, with its straightforward mechanical setup, is just the ticket for the person who wants a sports car but needs the practicality of a four-passenger sedan.

BMW 320i
Test Model Specifications

Body type	2-door	Rear hiproom	50 in.
Overall length	177.5 in.	Engine type	4 in-line
Overall width	63.4 in.	Net hp @ rpm	110 @ 5800
Overall height	54.3 in.	Net torque @ rpm	112 @ 3750
Wheelbase	100.9 in.	Displacement	121.3 cu. in.
Turn diameter	N/A	Compression ratio	8.1:1
Tire size	185/70SR13	Carburetion	Fuel injected
Curb weight	2650 lbs.	Transmission	4-speed
Cargo space	16.2 cu. ft.		Manual
Front headroom	36 in.	Axle ratio	3.64.1
Front legroom	46 in.	Acceleration 0-60 mph	12.2 sec.
Front hiproom	42 in.	Brake stop 60-0 mph	140 ft.
Rear headroom	33 in.	Fuel tank capacity	15.9 gal.
Rear legroom	39 in.	EPA city economy rating	19 mpg.

Datsun 210

Datsun has replaced the popular B-210 series with the completely new 210 series. This new 210 line has the same engine and transmission as the old B-210 series, but these are the only carry overs.

Included in the 210 line are a four-door wagon, a two-door hatchback, a two-door sedan and a four-door sedan. All are powered by the same rather puny 1397cc four-cylinder engine. A 1488cc engine is available, but only as an option in the wagon version equipped with automatic transmission.

The most noticeable feature of the new 210s is that they are slightly longer and wider than their predecessors. The larger dimensions, combined with the carefully designed interior, give the 210 a big-car feel.

The CONSUMER GUIDE Magazine test car was the 210 four-door wagon. Built on a wheelbase of 92.1 inches, the wagon has a total length of just over 167 inches. The standard 1397cc engine, coupled with the standard four-speed manual transmission, leaves the car very underpowered. Our 0 to 60 acceleration tests took almost 19 seconds. Once cruising speeds were reached, the engine whined like a small top and lacked response, even when called upon for simple passing maneuvers. The Environmental Protection Agency rates the fuel economy of this model at 31 miles per gallon for combined city and highway driving. The optional five-speed transmission boosts the EPA rating slightly, and the fifth gear should certainly help reduce the high-rpm whine of the four-speed.

Datsun offers an optional 1488cc engine, but it is available only on wagons equipped with automatic transmissions. We would like to see Datsun make the 1488cc engine available on the wagons with manual transmissions, as well as on the automatic. We feel that our test model was so underpowered that it bordered on being hazardous in regular freeway traffic.

The 210's front suspension is a strut type, as was the B-210's, but none of the components are interchangeable with the older series. In the rear, the 210 uses a four-link coil spring suspension system that contributes to the car's superior riding comfort and good wheel traction. Only in high-speed cornering tests could we get the rear wheels to skip and finally break contact with the pavement. In all but high-speed maneuvers, the steering and cornering control gives the driver a feeling of confidence. And, the suspension system of the 210 absorbs road bumps and engine vibration for a very smooth and quiet ride.

When all four wheels were locked in panic brake tests, the car stopped straight and true. We did, however, find the braking capabilities disappointing. At 60 mph, it took the wagon more than 175 feet to come to a complete stop. It is immediately obvious that the brake system designers assumed that the car would always be loaded with passengers and cargo. Driving solo, the rear wheels locked and skidded whenever we depressed the pedal hard. Loaded with suitcases, luggage and four adult passengers, this rear-wheel locking diminished substantially, and we were able to bring the car to a halt in less than 160 feet. But wagons are seldom driven fully loaded.

A lot of trim and safety and convenience equipment is standard on all the 210 series cars. Extra-cost options are relatively few: air conditioning, radio, electric clock, five-speed transmission and automatic transmission. As the lowest-priced car in the 1979 Datsun lineup, the 210 series gives you a lot for your money. If a low purchase price and good fuel economy are your priorities, the 210 series deserves consideration.

DATSUN 210
Test Model Specifications

Body type	4-door	Rear hiproom	50.5 in.
Overall length	167.3 in.	Engine type	4-cylinder OHV
Overall width	62.2 in.	Net hp @ rpm	80 @ 6000
Overall height	52.6 in.	Net torque @ rpm	83 @ 3600
Wheelbase	92.1 in.	Displacement	1397 cc
Turn diameter	32.8 ft.	Compression ratio	8.5:1
Tire size	6.15x13	Carburetion	2 bbl.
Curb weight	2050 lbs.	Transmission	4-speed
Cargo space	29.4 cu. ft.*		Manual
Front headroom	36.5 in.	Axle ratio	3.70:1
Front legroom	40 in.	Acceleration 0-60 mph	18.8 sec.
Front hiproom	51 in.	Brake stop 60-0 mph	175 ft.
Rear headroom	36.5 in.	Fuel tank capacity	13.2 gal.
Rear legroom	32 in.	EPA city economy rating	27 mpg.

*with rear seat folded down

Datsun 280-ZX

The 280-ZX is not the same sports car that Z-car lovers are used to. Its emphasis is on luxury rather than performance. The car is still quickly identified as a Z-car, but styling changes have been made. It has cleaner and sleeker lines than previous Z-cars, but it also lacks their crisp, exciting styling. However, in all fairness to the design engineers, the larger side windows of the new 280-ZX do afford better all-around visibility, and the deeper cargo area does increase the luggage-carrying capacity by three cubic feet.

The Z-car's engine is the standard six-cylinder 2753cc fuel-injected power plant with a rating of 135 horsepower at 5200 rpm. In acceleration tests, our 280-ZX clocked 9.2 seconds from 0 to 60 miles an hour. Mileage averaged 21 mpg in combined city and highway driving. Equipped with the five-speed manual transmission, shifting is a little stiff and lacks positive track-type performance.

The car has been given the same basic suspension as the Datsun 810 series, which we feel is a step down from the suspension system previously used. Equipped with this suspension, the 280-ZX seems fat and heavy. Gone is the nimble quickness that helped make the Z series so popular with sports-car enthusiasts. Our test car understeered noticeably and had an overall slower steering response than earlier Z-cars, though the ZX has power assist steering. However, the new front suspension does give a smoother ride than any other Z-car we have driven. On smooth pavement, the ride is like floating on a cushion of air. Luxury seekers will say that this is for the better, while sports car enthusiasts will say the car lacks road feel.

Interior appointments have a completely new design, directed toward the luxury-car buyer. The reclining bucket seats are no wider than on previous models, but driver and passenger have a lot more shoulder and elbow room. Each seat adjusts forward, backward and for rake. In addition, the driver can change the seat cushion angle and lumbar support with a lever. Our test car was equipped

Datsun 280-ZX

with the Grand Luxury package, which includes all-cloth upholstery and thick nylon carpeting. Virtually every convenience from air conditioning to cruise control is standard on the GL package.

Another new system on the ZX is the central warning system. It automatically runs through a computerized checklist while the vehicle is being started. Included in the check list are the headlamps, taillamps, brake lights, washer system, battery and coolant levels. If everything is in working order, the computer displays a big "OK." If any red warning lights appear, the driver can easily determine which system has malfunctioned by manually depressing the warning system button.

Although Datsun's new 280-ZX is a fine automobile, it will take some getting used to, especially by those who appreciated the performance and handling of Z-cars of the past.

DATSUN 280 ZX
Test Model Specifications

Body type	2-seater	Rear hiproom	—
Overall length	174.0 in.	Engine type	6-cylinder
Overall width	66.5 in.	Net hp @ rpm	135 @ 5200
Overall height	51.0 in.	Net torque @ rpm	144 @ 4400
Wheelbase	91.3 in.	Displacement	2753 cc/168 cu. in.
Turn diameter	32.2 ft.	Compression ratio	8.3:1
Tire size	195/70HR14	Carburetion	Fuel injected
Curb weight	2825 lbs.	Transmission	5-speed
Cargo space	19.8 cu. ft.		Manual
Front headroom	36.0 in.	Axle ratio	3.36:1
Front legroom	50 in.	Acceleration 0-60 mph	9.2 sec.
Front hiproom	48 in.	Brake stop 60-0 mph	160 ft.
Rear headroom	—	Fuel tank capacity	21.1 gal.
Rear legroom	—	EPA city economy rating	18 mpg.

Datsun 810

In 1978, sales of the Datsun 810 series jumped dramatically. It's difficult to determine exactly why, but it's plain that many buyers liked the luxury appointments offered in this top-of-the-line passenger car series. The 810s gave drivers the feeling of plushness at an affordable price.

For 1979, the entire 810 series has been restyled to resemble more expensive European touring cars. This redesigning includes a squared-off hood and rear end, dual rectangular headlamps, a new grille and styled taillights. In addition, a new two-door hardtop model with the standard five-speed transmission has joined the four-door sedan and five-door wagon.

All the cars in the 810 series are once again

powered by the six-cylinder fuel-injected 2400cc engine. This is the same engine that was used in the popular 240-Z series. Overall performance of this power plant was proven in the Z-car series, although it lacks low-end power when installed in the larger and heavier 810 sedan. Equipped with the optional automatic transmission, the 810 starts off slow and lumbers down the roadway in an attempt to gain momentum. It took us just over 15 seconds to reach 60 miles an hour from a dead stop. But once the vehicle reached cruising speed, the engine hummed along without even breathing hard. Passing power is adequate because the over-drive of the transmission cuts in to slingshot the sedan past slower moving vehicles. At peak torque, the six-cylinder power plant is rated to deliver an acceptable 120 horsepower at 5200 rpm.

One area in which the 810 does a superb job of imitating the European touring cars is ride and handling. With the windows rolled up the 810 rides almost as quietly as a Mercedes-Benz. Insulation abounds to block out road noise, and the front and rear suspension systems do an admirable job of absorbing bumps and rough spots in the roadway. Steering is nimble and very responsive in both high-speed and low-speed maneuvers, and handling is sure. In fact, the handling of our test car, with conventional front-mounted engine and rear-wheel drive, was comparable to that of a $20,000 BMW.

The 810's power-assisted front disc brakes brought us to a dead stop from 60 miles an hour within 152 feet. Panic stops were also impressive; there was no significant nose dip.

Visibility is good throughout the 810, even though the rear pillars are a little large. The only blind spot we found was over the driver's left shoulder; it was caused by the relatively large driver's headrest. For added visibility, the 810 sedan comes standard with two side-door mirrors that are electrically adjustable from the inside.

Seating comfort for both front and rear passengers is very good. Legroom should cause no complaints, from even tall passengers. When we moved the front seats back to the farthest point on the track, there was still sufficient legroom for rear-seat passengers.

A long list of equipment that would cost at least a thousand dollars extra on any other car is included as standard on the 810. Some of the niceties include AM/FM stereo with four speakers, fully reclining bucket seats; a central sensor system that monitors water and washer fluid levels, battery, headlamps, taillights, and stoplights; quartz clock; tilt steering wheel; power antenna; carpeting; remote trunk and fuel filler releases; and six-way adjustable driver's seat for maximum comfort and visibility. Air-conditioning and an automatic transmission are the only two major options the buyer can purchase as extras.

DATSUN 810
Test Model Specifications

Body type 4-door	Rear hiproom ....49.2 in.
Overall length ....183.9 in.	Engine type ......6-cylinder OHC
Overall width ....64.8 in.	Net hp @ rpm ....120 @ 5200
Overall height ....54.9 in.	Net torque @ rpm ....170 @ 2500
Wheelbase............104.3 in.	Displacement ....2393 cc
Turn diameter ....40.0 ft.	Compression ratio 8.9:1
Tire size 185/70SR-14	Carburetion ....Fuel injected
Curb weight ....2845 lbs.	Transmission ....Automatic
Cargo space ....15.8 cu. ft.	Axle ratio 3.89:1
Front headroom ....38.5 in.	Acceleration 0-60 mph ..15.4 sec.
Front legroom ....40.8 in.	Brake stop 60-0 mph ......152 ft.
Front hiproom ....51.2 in.	Fuel tank capacity ....14.5 gal.
Rear headroom ....37.7 in.	EPA city economy rating ..20 mpg.
Rear legroom ....36 in.	

Dodge Colt
Plymouth Arrow

It first glance, Dodge Colt and Plymouth Arrow look identical. Actually, they are the same car, differing only in trim and option packages.

The Arrow has kept the same basic body design since its introduction in 1976. Carry-over models such as the larger and more luxurious Sapporo also enter 1979 with only the fewest of modifications. Once again, the Plymouth Arrow is offered in fastback body styling with a rear hatch. Three basic series carried over from 1978 are the base Arrow, Arrow GS and Arrow GT. In addition, a new version appears this year: the Fire Arrow.

The new Fire Arrow is the car we selected to test. Like all '79 Arrows it sports a new grille, rectangular headlamps, a larger bumper and larger rear window. In addition, the Fire Arrow comes with the larger 2600cc four-cylinder engine as standard. All other Arrows come standard with the smaller 1600cc engine.

Equipped with the large engine and four-speed manual transmission, the Fire Arrow can perform very well. Our test car ran from 0 to 60 miles an hour in about 11 seconds. It's no slouch in the fuel economy category, either. Our city-highway combined average was 23 miles per gallon. All acceleration tests were smooth and even, as the engine quickly reached maximum rpm in each gear to enable smooth shifting.

The ride of all Arrows in the lineup has been improved, by a new, wider rear track and improved suspension system. The track is now 2¾ inches wider than it was last year and gives the car a greatly improved road feel. Last year, we rated the ride of the Arrow mediocre. This year, thanks to these improvements, the Arrow is more than competitive with many of the smaller imports. High-speed cornering is flat and even. The Arrow responds quickly to the slightest steering commands. Power front disc and rear drum brakes are standard. They provide efficient stopping power during slow, controlled stops and panic stop maneuvers.

The standard interior includes reclining bucket seats, carpeting, tilt steering wheel and numerous other niceties. The dashboard design is appealing and practical. However, headroom throughout the car is minimal, and there's little legroom in the rear. If you're much over six feet tall you will find that your head rubs against the headliner no matter which seat you use. This is a result of the sweeping roofline and the height of the seats. Adjusting the incline of the bucket seat further back can help, but some people may find this seating position uncomfortable. And with just over 28 inches of usable legroom in the rear, rear occupants can have a double problem.

Visibility to the rear has been improved this year by the addition of more glass in the rear door. Few blind spots were noticed in our tests. Over-the-hood visibility on the drivers' side is good, but it's sometimes difficult to look over the right front fender to judge exact distances.

Minor engine work by the owner should present no big problems: everything from spark plugs to carburetor and air filter can be reached easily for service.

We have our doubts as to the future of the Arrow. Since front-wheel drive appears to be the design of the future, the newly introduced Plymouth Champ may be a signal that the Arrow's time is indeed running out. Rumor has it that by 1980 Sapporo will be the last of the Arrow family, and it too may go by the wayside by model year 1981.

PLYMOUTH ARROW
Test Model Specifications

Body type	2-door	Rear hiproom	50.8 in.
Overall length	169.5 in.	Engine type	4-cylinder in-line
Overall width	63.4 in.	Net hp @ rpm	105 @ 5000
Overall height	51 in.	Net torque @ rpm	139 @ 2500
Wheelbase	92.2 in.	Displacement	155.9 cu. in.
Turn diameter	32.3 ft.	Compression ratio	8.2:1
Tire size	165 SR13	Carburetion	2 bbl.
Curb weight	2568 lbs.	Transmission	4-speed
Cargo space	27 cu. ft.*		Manual
Front headroom	36.8 in.	Axle ratio	3.9:1
Front legroom	41.7 in.	Acceleration 0-60 mph	11 sec.
Front hiproom	50.8 in.	Brake stop 60-0 mph	152 ft.
Rear headroom	34.4 in.	Fuel tank capacity	13 gal.
Rear legroom	28.0 in.	EPA city economy rating	21 mpg.

*with rear seats folded down

Dodge Colt FF/ Plymouth Champ

Chrysler Corporation's new Dodge Colt Hatch-back FF and Plymouth Champ are basically the same car. Both of these Chrysler imports are small, front-wheel-drive economy cars. The styling is boxy, and the wheelbase is only 90.5 inches. However, the doors are almost as wide as any car we have tested, so entrance to and exit from the vehicle is easy, even for those more than six feet tall; and the large expanses of glass make you feel like you're riding in an open car.

The power plant of our Colt FF test car was a four-cylinder 1600cc MCA Jet engine, mounted transversely. This engine responds nicely, giving a 0 to 60 miles per hour acceleration time of 12 seconds. For an economy car that delivers about 35 miles per gallon in combined city and highway driving, this is good performance.

One of the more interesting features of the Colt FF is its unique transmission: it has two sticks. At

Plymouth Champ

first glance, it looks like the car has an eight-speed transmission. In truth, the car is equipped with a standard four-speed that has a twin-output ratio — one about 25 percent lower than the other. The second lever lets you select either a "power" or "economy" mode. In the economy mode, about 77 percent of the power is used and transferred through the transmission. In the power mode, that figure increases to 100 percent. Mastering the twin-stick operation takes practice, and the system seems to be more of a gimmick than a practical feature. Chrysler engineers say that the two ratio modes were developed to decrease overall fuel consumption. But CONSUMER GUIDE Magazine's staff believes the same results could have been obtained through the addition of nothing more complicated than a five-speed manual transmission. Rumor has it that Mitsubishi (makers of the car) knew that a five-speed Volkswagen Rabbit was soon to be on the scene and decided to opt for more speeds to make the Colt FF unique.

The Colt FF has a soft ride, like that usually found on larger cars. Credit for this is due to the front suspension's MacPherson struts, coil springs and link stabilizer bar. In the rear, the independent suspension also uses coil springs. The rack-and-pinion steering is light, responsive, and provides good road feel. The steering ratio, however—almost four full turns lock-to-lock—is a bit sloppy at slow speeds. But the car performs well at higher speeds.

Braking with the front disc and rear drum brakes was disappointing. During a controlled stop from 60 mph, the car needed more than 195 feet of stopping room. While this figure is well within safety standards, it is too much for a little car weighing under 2000 pounds.

The Colt FF's interior comfort and attention to detail are right up there with the best of the cars in its class. Appointments are laid out to be both attractive and practical. The front and rear seats are designed for comfort and support and provide fairly good legroom. Sound-deadening insulation limits interior noise to a very low level. This adds to the feeling that you're in a larger, higher-priced automobile.

DODGE COLT FF/PLYMOUTH CHAMP
Test Model Specifications

Body type	2-door	Rear hiproom	51.6 in.
Overall length	156.8 in.	Engine type	4-cylinder in-line
Overall width	62.4 in.	Net hp @ rpm	80 @ 5200
Overall height	50.5 in.	Net torque @ rpm	87 @ 3000
Wheelbase	90.5 in.	Displacement	87.5 cu. in.
Turn diameter	29 ft.	Compression ratio	8.5:1
Tire size	175/HR13	Carburetion	2 bbl.
Curb weight	1956 lbs.	Transmission	4x2-speed
Cargo space	22.9 cu. ft.*		Manual
Front headroom	36.7 in.	Axle ratio	3.47:1
Front legroom	40.5 in.	Acceleration 0-60 mph	12 sec.
Front hiproom	51.6 in.	Brake stop 60-0 mph	195 ft.
Rear headroom	36.0 in.	Fuel tank capacity	15.3 gal.
Rear legroom	51.6 in.	EPA city economy rating	32 mpg.

*with rear seat folded down

Fiat Brava

In 1978, Fiat's most popular model on the American market was the Super Brava. This car slides into 1979 minus the "Super" and loaded with new features to entice compact-car buyers. Offering an uncommonly plush interior for its size and price, the 1979 Brava is available as a two-door coupe, a four-door sedan and a four-door station wagon.

The standard power train on all three 1979 models is a 1995cc engine with a five-speed manual transmission. A three-speed automatic transmission is optional. Our test four-door sedan was equipped with the standard components. It delivered average fuel economy (23 miles per gallon) and above average performance. In acceleration tests, our Brava sprinted from 0 to 60 miles an hour in 13.3 seconds. The engine was quick to respond and provided adequate bursts of speed when needed for passing. One item we question, though, is the use of a five-speed transmission in the Brava. We found no use for the overdrive gear except for highway use, and even then we felt the fourth gear was acceptable.

The Fiat Brava handles like a true sports car. The standard rack-and-pinion steering system breezed through all our cornering tests. And the strut coil-spring suspension maintained total control and a flat, even ride. Road bumps are felt, but no more than in other cars of Brava's size and weight. When taken through a series of emergency stops, Brava responded excellently, providing ample braking power.

Inside, the 1979 Brava is surprisingly rich looking. The instrument panel is well designed, offering complete vital engine information in three gauge clusters. The padded dash and center console provide plenty of storage space for small items. Seating up front is a bit cramped in legroom; but hip room and headroom are ample. The rear seats have adequate overhead space, but they too are wanting in legroom. A definite plus in the 1979 Brava is its excellent driver visibility. We found no blind spots, front or rear. The large windows, combined with the short hood and trunk, made for a wide-open viewing area.

Brava's solid body design contributes to an ex-

Fiat Brava

tremely quiet ride. With the windows up, no wind whistle enters the passenger compartment, although engine whine manages to seep in at high speeds. The trunk provides 14 cubic feet of cargo space, but its depth sometimes makes it awkward to lift heavy cargo in and out.

As is the case with many foreign cars, servicing Brava can become an expensive venture. Parts are more expensive than those of domestic models and are harder to obtain. Also, service centers that work on Fiats are not as numerous as one would like. But Fiat seems aware of these problems and is taking steps to make available a stock of replacement parts and knowledgeable personnel to install them.

For 1979 Fiat offers a number of improvements on their Brava model. In addition to the 1995cc engine made standard this year, Brava offers a number of options that include power steering, a manual sunroof, a choice of velour or leather-grain vinyl upholstery and a padded two-spoke steering wheel.

FIAT BRAVA
Test Model Specifications

Body type	4-door	Engine type	4 in-line
Overall length	172.4 in.	Net hp @ rpm	80 @ 5000
Overall width	65.0 in.	Net torque @ rpm	104.3 @ 3000
Overall height	54.4 in.	Displacement	1995 cc/
Wheelbase	98.0 in.		121.74 cu. in.
Turn diameter	33.8 ft.	Compression ratio	8.1:1
Tire size	165/SR70-13	Carburetion	2 bbl.
Curb weight	2500 lbs.	Transmission	5-speed
Cargo space	14 cu. ft.		Manual
Front headroom	35.0 in.	Axle ratio	3.58:1
Front legroom	45.0 in.	Acceleration 0-60 mph	13.3 sec.
Front hiproom	48.0 in.	Brake stop 60-0 mph	125 ft.
Rear headroom	33.0 in.	Fuel tank capacity	12.2 gal.
Rear legroom	29.0 in.	EPA city economy rating	23 mpg.
Rear hiproom	56.0 in.		

Ford Fiesta

The German-manufactured Ford Fiesta reflects only minor changes as it enters 1979. These changes are so slight that buying a leftover 1978 model at a lower price is a good deal.

All the good and bad features of the 1978 Fiesta have been carried over, as Ford engineers busy themselves in readying a domestic-made Fiesta-like automobile for introduction in either 1980 or early 1981. In spite of this, the little car is still a relatively good automotive buy. Overall fuel economy averaged about 36 miles per gallon in our test. And the spunky 1600cc engine is hard to find fault with. From 0 to 50 miles an hour the Fiesta turned in a respectable time of 10.4 seconds. It is, however, somewhat noisy as the power plant winds out to high rpm. This can be annoying if you are trying to listen to the radio or to carry on a conversation.

Another carry over problem with the Fiesta is its tendency to skip-steer during fast cornering—a common problem with front-wheel-drive cars. When accelerating quickly from low speeds while cornering, the car's driving wheels bounce, grab, break free, grab and bounce again. As CONSUMER

Ford Fiesta

GUIDE Magazine has pointed out in previous tests, the problem could be taken care of by adding a limited slip unit to the differential or by stiffening the basic suspension. While the problem isn't serious, it is annoying.

In normal driving the handling and ride comfort both get excellent ratings. Unless you are a performance driver, the Fiesta should handle very nicely in the city and on the open road. The basic suspension, except when it skip-steers, is good and provides a very smooth ride, even on a rough gravel road.

Basic interior appointments on the standard Fiesta will be a great disappointment to the gimmick- and convenience-oriented buyer. Tachometer, speedometer, fuel gauge and temperature gauge are the only instruments that come with the standard package. Items like air conditioning, radios, carpets and varied cloth interiors are optional. Ventilation through two tiny vents is almost nonexistent. The basic driver and passenger seats are comfort-designed for American builds and offer needed lower back support for longer excursions. Legroom for all the occupants, both in front and in back, is adequate when you consider the car's total dimensions. Long-legged people can't stretch out in complete comfort while riding in the back seat of the Fiesta, but for most the room is adequate because of the way the rear seat is set far back between the wheel wells.

For the do-it-yourself mechanic, the Fiesta is a wise choice. Most do-it-yourselfers will have no trouble working on this car. In addition to plenty of room inside the engine compartment, Ford's owners manual is written with the backyard auto mechanic in mind. Parts and service availability for the Fiesta has always been good.

Overall, the Fiesta is a good car—a gas-conscious and spirited automobile. The main reason that improvements haven't been made this year is simple. Ford is being pressed by government regulations to develop a domestic Fiesta-type auto in order to gain higher Environmental Protection Agency fleet ratings. Foreign imports can no longer be used by Ford to lower the company's fleet average. If it weren't for this, Ford would probably improve and continue to offer the Fiesta for a long time.

FORD FIESTA
Test Model Specifications

Body type	2-door	Rear hiproom	41.2 in.
Overall length	147.1 in.	Engine type	4-cylinder
Overall width	61.2 in.	Net hp @ rpm	66 @ 5000
Overall height	52.3 in.	Net torque @ rpm	82 @ 3200
Wheelbase	90.0 in.	Displacement	97.6 cu. in.
Turn diameter	30.2 ft.	Compression ratio	8.5:1
Tire size	145/SR-12	Carburetion	2 bbl.
Curb weight	1776 lbs.	Transmission	4 speed
Cargo space	29 cu. ft.*		Manual
Front headroom	37.6 in.	Axle ratio	3.58:1
Front legroom	40.1 in.	Acceleration 0-60 mph	10.4 sec.
Front hiproom	50.3 in.	Brake stop 60-0 mph	138 ft.
Rear headroom	36.8 in.	Fuel tank capacity	10 gal.
Rear legroom	34.6 in.	EPA city economy rating	28 mpg.

*with rear seat folded down

Honda Accord

Honda has introduced a four-door Accord for 1979. Previous Accord models were all two-doors. The four-door Accord is built on the same chassis as the two-door models (93.7-inch wheelbase) but is 8.7 inches longer overall. All Accords for 1979, including the four-door, have a 1751cc overhead-cam four-cylinder engine. Through 1978, all Accords came with a smaller 1588cc four-cylinder power plant, which was a major source of buyer complaints. The smaller engine gave Accord generally sluggish performance. Equipped with the larger power plant, the new Accord is somewhat speedier: it can accelerate from 0 to 60 miles an hour in just under 15 seconds. In addition to increased output, the engine is vastly smoother and quieter at all speeds.

With a curb weight of about 2200 pounds, the four-door version is 95 pounds heavier than the base Accord. But it's a mere five pounds heavier than the luxury-laden LX model. The new power plant gave the car a very stable ride and overall good road feel. However, Accord's rear tended to skip when we put the car through a series of high-speed corners. We wouldn't exactly call it fish-tailing, but it was close. The problem seemed less noticeable when there were passengers in the rear seats and when the cargo area was loaded.

Overall, Accord's ride is very smooth and quiet. The car's exterior design and proper placement of generous amounts of insulation give the interior an uncanny silence—even at highway speeds. The basic suspension system absorbs many small road bumps. It smooths out lane changes and small dips, and eliminates the transfer of noisy thumps into the passenger area.

Fuel economy is also very good—a combined average during our tests of 32 miles per gallon. Using the five-speed manual transmission, with which our test car was equipped, we feel that even better fuel mielage could be attained by making maximum use of the fifth gear.

Since this is the first notchback design introduced by Honda, evaluation of the trunk is important. Although the four-door version has a flat trunk for storage, it is not as deep as you might expect. This is because the spare tire is stowed below the floorboard and eats up a lot of the usable depth. There are also two small storage bins on the sides of the trunk for small items. As in all Accords, there is a remote trunk release inside the car on the driver's side.

Overall visibility is good on the Accord, due to the relatively short hood and rear trunk area. The only blind spot we found was over the driver's left shoulder; the comfortable headrest of the high-back seat gets in the way of rear vision.

Interior appointments on the new Accord are very similar to the LX package, minus a few luxuries. The sedan does not have Michelin tires, AM/FM radio with tape player, or air conditioning as standard equipment. It does, however, offer cloth-trim seats, carpeting throughout, tilt steering wheel, maintenance reminder system, and electric clock. Other features include an electronic warning system that covers everything from doors ajar to stoplight failure, a low-fuel warning indicator, remote-control rear door locks, rear seat heater ducts, and front side window defrosters.

With the addition of this year's more powerful engine, the CONSUMER GUIDE Magazine test staff believes the four-door Accord is a good choice for the economy-car buyer.

HONDA ACCORD
Test Model Specifications

Body type 4-door	Rear hiproom . . . . 51.3 in.
Overall length . . . . 173.4 in.	Engine type . . . . . . 4-cylinder OHV
Overall width . . . . 63.8 in.	Net hp @ rpm . . . . 72 @ 4500
Overall height . . . . 53.3 in.	Net torque @ rpm . . . . . 94 @ 3000
Wheelbase . . . . 93.7 in.	Displacement . . . . 107 cu. in.
Turn diameter . . . . 33.7 ft.	Compression ratio 8.01:1
Tire size 165-SR13	Carburetion . . . . 3 bbl.
Curb weight . . . . 2203 lbs.	Transmission 5-speed
Cargo space . . . . N/A	Manual
Front headroom . . . . 38.0 in.	Axle ratio 4.38:1
Front legroom . . . . 40.0 in.	Acceleration 0-60 mph . . 14.9 sec.
Front hiproom . . . . 51.9 in.	Brake stop 60-0 mph . . . . . 152 ft.
Rear headroom . . . . 36.6 in.	Fuel tank capacity . . . . . 13.2 gal.
Rear legroom . . . . 33.5 in.	EPA city economy rating . . 26 mpg.

Honda Civic CVCC

Since its introduction during the 1973 fuel crisis, the Honda Civic has reached fourth place in total import sales in the United States. One of the main reasons for the Civic CVCC's continued acceptance is that it is one of the new generation of automobiles that feature front-wheel drive and transverse-mounted engines.

The CONSUMER GUIDE test vehicle was the sporty three-door hatchback, equipped with a five-speed manual transmission. In addition to the three-door hatchback, the Civic line also includes a two-door sedan and a four-door wagon. Both the wagon and sedan come with a standard four-speed manual transmission; the two-speed Hondamatic is optional. Civic's standard power plant this year is the 1488cc Four, the same as it was last year. Rumors had it that the 1979 Civics would get a larger engine, as the Honda Accord line did. But this did not turn out to be the case. The added horsepower would not have been a good idea anyway, because it would have decreased fuel economy, which is Civic's greatest attribute.

Our combined mileage was about 38 mpg. Considering that this economy car can also accelerate from 0 to 60 miles an hour in 15 seconds, the Civic has to represent one of the best combinations of performance and fuel economy in the small-car field. In addition, Civic's Stratified Charge system eliminates the need for unleaded gasoline. Able to operate efficiently on everything from regular to premium, the Stratified Charge system actually has two combustion chambers in each cylinder. One is a primary and the other a pre-chamber. The spark plug fires a rich mixture, which in turn ignites a lean mixture.

Handling this front-wheel-drive car differs very little from handling a conventional rear-wheel-drive model. We did, however, have to grip the steering wheel tightly when taking off from a stop in any direction but straight ahead. This characteristic is called torque steer, and it is a common problem with front-wheel-drive cars. From a stop, if you turn the wheels and pour on the power, the engine tries to pull the wheels back into a straight-ahead position. But this problem disappears once the car begins to move. On the plus side, the handling characteristics and traction provided by front-wheel-drive are superb. Civic holds the road and has good stability, even in snow. Power-assisted front disc brakes make stopping the Civic easy, even under controlled panic maneuvers. While there was no noticeable brake fade after a panic stop, the odor of overheated brakes was very noticeable. The odor indicated that the brakes were doing their job—but also that they were wearing.

Basic interior appointments are functional; there are no plush frills. Quality control appears good and all driver controls and gauges are easily reached and easily read. Seating comfort, though, is not very good, due to the car's small size. Front seating is adequate for averaged-size drivers, but anyone over six feet is almost guaranteed a hemmed-in feeling. Since a reasonably comfortable seating position in the front is possible only when the seat is pushed as far back on the track as it will go, back-seat legroom is virtually nonexistent.

There aren't any blind spots in the Civic, because of the car's small dimensions and large glass areas. Interior noise, however, becomes apparent at about 35 miles an hour and increases to a nuisance at freeway speeds. Wind whistle through the ventilation ducts is the culprit, whether the vents are open or closed.

CONSUMER GUIDE Magazine considers the Honda Civic CVCC a good buy for persons looking for excellent fuel economy. But if you are very tall, you should try this car on for size before you consider it seriously.

HONDA CIVIC CVCC
Test Model Specifications

Body type	2-door	Engine type	4-cylinder OHC
Overall length	148.6 in.	Net hp @ rpm	63 @ 5000
Overall width	59.3 in.	Net torque @ rpm	77 @ 3000
Overall height	52.4 in.	Displacement	1488 cc/
Wheelbase	86.6 in.		90.8 cu. in.
Turn diameter	31 ft.	Compression ratio	7.92:1
Tire size	155/SR12	Carburetion	3 bbl.
Curb weight	1790 lbs.	Transmission	5-speed
Cargo space	25.0 cu. ft.*		Manual
Front headroom	37.2 in.	Axle ratio	3.875:1
Front legroom	38.4 in.	Acceleration 0-60 mph	15 sec.
Front hiproom	50.1 in.	Brake stop 60-0 mph	147 ft.
Rear headroom	36.2 in.	Fuel tank capacity	10.6 gal.
Rear legroom	24.8 in.	EPA city economy rating	28 mpg.
Rear hiproom	42.7 in.		

*with rear seat folded down

Mazda GLC

That is newsworthy for 1979 is that Mazda has listened to the American buyer and finally boosted the horsepower of the entire GLC line. In addition, a longer, four-door hatchback station wagon now joins the line's three-door and five-door hatchbacks. The four-door GLC wagon is built on the same 91-inch wheelbase chassis as the other models, but the new wagon is nearly nine inches longer overall.

Like all GLCs for 1979, the wagon features a 1415cc four-cylinder power plant, in contrast to last year's 1272cc engine. The new engine results in a 25 percent increase in basic horsepower and an 18 percent increase in usable torque. While the smaller engine was rated at 52 horsepower, the new engines are rated to deliver 65 horsepower. The new engine is also a lot smoother and quicker when winding to maximum rpm. However, it is not a great deal quieter than the old engine at high rpm and is at least as noisy as the engine it is replacing.

The standard transmission on all the GLCs is a four-speed manual, but the CONSUMER GUIDE Magazine test GLC wagon came with the optional five-speed manual transmission. One of the fine features of the GLC transmissions is their ease in shifting. While virtually all imports have synchromesh transmissions, the Mazda design seems to offer the smoothest shifting. Last year's GLC provided a combined city-highway average of 39 miles per gallon. But the larger engine of this year's model has caused that figure to drop to 35 mpg (with the five-speed).

Traditionally, the Mazda GLC cars have been among the smaller of the subcompact imports and have offered limited interior room. The wagon, however, feels much more roomy, and there is adequate legroom for both front and rear passengers. The interior is built for practicality with vinyl seats, carpeting, and only a few instruments on the plain dashboard. It certainly cannot be called luxurious, even though our test car featured the Deluxe package; but it is well planned and well laid out. Getting in and out is easy, thanks to the large doors and good ground height.

Front-to-rear weight distribution on the wagon is good, thanks to a sophisticated suspension system that incorporates a live axle and leaf springs. To many, this suspension system might seem like just an easy way to stretch a sedan into a wagon. But that isn't the case. The chassis and body of the GLC wagon are actually reinforced to give extra load capacity. A coil spring suspension system is standard on the three-door and five-door GLCs.

Handling is not the GLC wagon's best feature.

Slalom steering brings out a great deal of under-steer. While taking hard corners, as the front tires break traction before the rear tires. When loaded with passengers and/or cargo, this problem is reduced but not eliminated.

Convenience and versatility are two of the main features the new Mazda GLC wagon has in its favor. The large rear cargo hatch swings up and away from the car, allowing easy access for bulky loads. In addition, the wagon has no lip on the rear hatch, so loading is much easier. The main part of the cargo has a useable space over 60 inches long, without the rear seats folded forward.

The Mazda GLC is a basic economy wagon with nothing about it to make it outstanding in its class. CONSUMER GUIDE Magazine's test staff feels that it's adequate as a family runabout if you have a Mazda dealership nearby. Mazda's chain of service facilities, although growing, is not large, and this should be considered when making a buying decision.

MAZDA GLC
Test Model Specifications

Body type	4-door	Engine type	4-cylinder OHC
Overall length	163.2 in.	Net hp @ rpm	65 @ 5000
Overall width	63.2 in.	Net torque @ rpm	76 @ 3000
Overall height	56.1 in.	Displacement	1415 cc/
Wheelbase	91.1 in.		86.4 cu. in.
Turn diameter	28.10 ft.	Compression ratio	9.0:1
Tire size	155SR/13	Carburetion	2 bbl.
Curb weight	2120 lbs.	Transmission	5 speed
Cargo space	29.2 cu. ft.*		Manual
Front headroom	39 in.	Axle ratio	3.727.1
Front legroom	42 in.	Acceleration 0-60 mph	13.7 sec.
Front hiproom	51.6 in.	Brake stop 60-0 mph	148 ft.
Rear headroom	38.5 in.	Fuel tank capacity	11.9 gal.
Rear legroom	33 in.	EPA city economy rating	28 mpg.
Rear hiproom	51.6 in.		

*with seats in upright position

Mazda RX-7

Back in 1970, Mazda introduced the first rotary-engine production car in America. At first, it was well accepted. But in a few years the rotary engine lost favor with the American car-buying public because of its poor service record and very low fuel economy. It looked like the engine would soon disappear from the U.S. automotive scene.

In 1978, Mazda unveiled a new rotary car that became an overnight success in the U.S. The car was the RX-7. The RX-7 has proved that a rotary car can provide high performance and good fuel economy. This Mazda accelerates from 0 to 60 miles an hour in 8.7 seconds and can deliver a combined city and highway fuel economy average of 21 miles per gallon.

Low, sleek and fast, the RX-7 is built on a wheelbase of 95 inches and has an overall length of 169 inches. Two models of the RX-7 will once again be offered in 1979. The base car is called the "S," the top-of-the-line version is called the "GS." For both, standard equipment includes AM/FM stereo radio with power antenna, radial tires rated for high speeds, tachometer, reclining bucket seats, carpeting, front anti-roll bar and quartz clock. The "S" model comes standard with a four-speed manual transmission; the "GS" version has a five-speed. Air-conditioning is optional for both versions, and an automatic transmission is a "GS" model option.

The CONSUMER GUIDE Magazine test vehicle was the sporty GS, equipped with a five-speed manual transmission and the 1146cc (70 cubic-inch) rotary engine. The engine weighs only 333 pounds, but develops 100 horsepower at 6000 rpm. Top-end speed is rated at 120 mph, but our tests proved that figure to be a little skimpy. The speedometer reads out to 130 mph. We crossed that figure easily, and still had power to spare.

The rotary's configuration and compact size enable it to be placed low in the car's chassis. This low center of gravity, combined with a wide track and superior suspension system, provides excellent road hugging characteristics—even at high speeds. Winding roads that normally throw driver and passenger from side to side were taken almost flat in our RX-7. Up front, the suspension is made up of independent struts and coil springs. In the rear are a live axle and coil springs with four trailing arms for added stability.

Power-assisted front disc brakes and drums in the rear provided sure stops. Brake fade was minimal after repeating numerous panic stops, and the car's attitude remained straight throughout.

Seating room for the driver and passenger is more than adequate. Seats are fully adjustable, and are mounted on a long track to provide comfortable legroom for tall drivers. The reclining bucket seats are contoured to fit the physical build of most Americans while not being cramped or confining.

Forward visibility is good, because the hood slopes down at a sharp angle. Visibility to the sides is acceptable, but the driver encounters a blind spot when attempting to look to the rear. This is caused by the car's high-backed bucket seats.

The RX-7 is not practical as a family car, but then neither are Porsches or Corvettes. The Mazda was designed as an affordable sports car that offers good fuel economy. Overall, the Mazda RX-7 is an unexcelled combination of styling, luxury, performance and comfort. Its base price of about $7200 makes it one of the best automobile values today.

MAZDA RX-7
Test Model Specifications

Body type	2-seater	Engine type	Rotary, 2 rotors in-line
Overall length	169 in.	Net hp @ rpm	100 @ 6000
Overall width	66 in.	Net torque @ rpm	105 @ 4000
Overall height	50 in.	Displacement	1146 cc/
Wheelbase	95 in.		70 cu. in.
Turn diameter	31 ft.	Compression ratio	9.4:1
Tire size	185/70HR-13	Carburetion	4 bbl.
Curb weight	2385 lbs.	Transmission	5-speed
Cargo space	17 cu. ft.		Manual
Front headroom	33 in.	Axle ratio	3.9:1
Front legroom	N/A	Acceleration 0-60 mph	8.7 sec.
Front hiproom	54 in.	Brake stop 60-0 mph	147 ft.
Rear headroom	—	Fuel tank capacity	14.5 gal.
Rear legroom	—	EPA city economy rating	17 mpg.
Rear hiproom	—		

Renault LeCar

Renault's Le Car for 1979 is a virtual carry over, changed from the '78 only in exterior colors.

Renault's confidence in this little import is well-founded. For drivers who care more about economy and engineering than size and luxury, Le Car is an excellent value. Its tiny four-cylinder engine and four-speed manual transmission are rated by the Environmental Protection Agency to deliver 31 miles per gallon in combined city-highway driving. Our test Le Car stretched its fuel average to 34 mpg in a combination of city and highway road situations. This very good gas mileage was matched by LeCar's performance.

Le Car's acceleration is surprising. Although the engine displaces less than 79 cubic inches, the car runs from 0 to 60 miles an hour in under 14 seconds.

As one of the earliest proponents of front-wheel drive, Renault has had some 20 years to fine-tune this feature on their automobiles. Le Car's steering was somewhat stiffer than that which CONSUMER GUIDE Magazine test drivers were used to, but responded quickly while maintaining a stable ride. Cornering was excellent, although our test car tended to lean in tight turns. Throughout extensive emergency maneuvering tests our Le Car maintained good control. Brake tests proved excellent; we detected no fade after repeated hard stops.

Le Car's ride, like that of small cars, has a tendency toward roughness, but this is somewhat smoothed by Renault's installation of double-acting hydraulic shocks on the front and rear. And independent suspension, incorporating unequal control arms and torsion bar springs, adds to a good ride.

Renault Le Car

Because Le Car has front-wheel drive, interior room in the forward area of the passenger compartment is good. Its high roofline makes for excellent headroom throughout, but rear-seat legroom is cramped. Both front bucket seats lift up and lean forward, however, allowing for easy access to the back seat. The dashboard has a somewhat stark appearance; instrumentation is limited to the bare essentials. With rear seats folded down, Le Car offers 31.5 cubic feet of cargo space, an excellent figure when compared with many of its competitors.

Le Car's interior noise levels are nothing to boast about, especially in the cloth sunroof model. Engine whine is extreme at high speeds and there's a lot of wind noise. Visibility is excellent. Due to Le Car's short hood, large windows and overall small dimensions, there are no blind spots to hinder the driver.

Overall, we like Le Car. It is economical and relatively comfortable to drive, and its performance is good.

RENAULT LE CAR
Test Model Specifications

Body type	2-door	Rear hiproom	49.0 in.
Overall length	141.5 in.	Engine type	4 in-line
Overall width	60.0 in.	Net hp @ rpm	60 @ 6000
Overall height	55.0 in.	Net torque @ rpm	70 @ 3500
Wheelbase	95.8 in.	Displacement	78.66 cu. in.
Turn diameter	32.0 ft.	Compression ratio	9.5:1
Tire size	145-13	Carburetion	2 bbl.
Curb weight	1819 lbs.	Transmission	4-speed
Cargo space	31.5 cu. ft.		Manual
Front headroom	37.0 in.	Axle ratio	3.625:1
Front legroom	39.1 in.	Acceleration 0-60 mph	13.7 sec.
Front hiproom	41.0 in.	Brake stop 60-0 mph	165 ft.
Rear headroom	36.2 in.	Fuel tank capacity	10 gal.
Rear legroom	33.2 in.	EPA city economy rating	26 mpg.

Subaru
4WD Wagon

Without a doubt, one of the most unusual vehicles on the road today is the Subaru four-wheel-drive wagon. Subaru's civilized appearance and gutsy off-road capability set it apart from all other production model autos.

All models in the 1979 Subaru lineup share the same 1600cc engine. And although the four-wheel-drive wagon is almost 300 pounds heavier than any other Subaru model, the engine provided it with adequate power. The impressive feature of the Subaru engine is that it's not burdened by a catalytic converter and/or other power-robbing pollution-control equipment. The engine in the four-wheel-drive wagon tested by CONSUMER GUIDE Magazine, and in all other Subaru cars, features the SEEC-T system. This stands for Subaru Exhaust Emission Control Technique. The SEEC-T system double-burns the fuel, so few pollutants are emitted out the exhaust. Also, the Subaru lineup this year will once again be able to run quite efficiently on leaded or unleaded regular gasoline.

The normal driving mode for our test wagon was front-wheel drive. Our acceleration tests showed that speed is not one of the wagon's strong points—acceleration from 0 to 60 miles an hour took 21 seconds. Subaru's conventional front-drive cars can make the same run in under 16 seconds. But when we switched from two-wheel drive into four-wheel drive for a hill-climbing excursion, the engine proved it was a good match for the wagon, providing the power to pull the wagon to the top of the steep incline.

The CONSUMER GUIDE Magazine test staff was especially impressed with the ease with which the four-wheel drive can be engaged. There is no need to stop and get out to lock the hubs or engage the rear axle. In fact, you don't even have to slow down. The wagon can be swiftly switched from its road-holding front-wheel mode to the even more tenacious four-wheel drive mode at any speed up to 50 mph by the flicking of a lever inside the vehicle.

Driving in the front-drive mode, we found the overall road feel exceptional. The wagon's front-wheel-drive system is superior to many others we have tested. It gives the car excellent tracking, a stable ride and a solid feel. The engine continued to perform very well in passing and accelerated cornering maneuvers. While the car is slow pulling away from the line, once it revs up to cruising speed it is as nimble and as responsive as cars equipped with larger engines.

Subaru's specifications reveal that the wagon's power-assisted front disc brakes are smaller than those of cars of comparable size. But despite their smaller size, the brakes held up and stopped the wagon in a short 139 feet from a speed of 60 mph. After four repeated attempts, we could detect no brake fade.

All the wagon's window pillars are small. This allows good visibility. Last year, Subaru lowered the front hood. This move increased visibility and decreased wind resistance.

The only 1979 Subaru model to get any styling changes is the four-wheel-drive wagon. To make it more attractive and practical, Subaru has upgraded the carpeting used throughout the passenger and cargo area and has redesigned the front seats for added comfort and more lower back support. Also, the dashboard instrument panel was redesigned. Now the driver can check the panel with a quick glance instead of having to take his eyes completely away from the road.

SUBARU 4WD
Test Model Specifications

Body type 4-door	Engine type 4-cylinder
Overall length .... 158.5 in.	Net hp @ rpm .... 65 @ 5200
Overall width .... 61.0 in.	Net torque @ rpm ..... 80 @ 2400
Overall height .... 56.7 in.	Displacement .... 1595 cc/
Wheelbase .... 96.5 in.	97.0 cu. in.
Turn diameter .... 30.3 ft.	Compression ratio 8.5:1
Tire size 155 SR-13	Carburetion .... 2 bbl.
Curb weight .... 2265 lbs.	Transmission 4-speed
Cargo space .... 34.6 cu. ft.*	Manual
Front headroom .... 35 in.	Axle ratio 4.1:1
Front legroom .... 43.5 in.	Acceleration 0-60 mph .... 21 sec.
Front hiproom .... 40 in.	Brake stop 60-0 mph ...... 139 ft.
Rear headroom .... 33 in.	Fuel tank capacity .... 12 gal.
Rear legroom .... 36 in.	EPA city economy rating .. 25 mpg.
Rear hiproom .... 49 in.	

*with rear seat folded down

Toyota Celica

The fully redesigned Toyota Celica of 1978 will continue into 1979 with only slight seat improvements and a little extra interior room. The new body style has been so successful that Toyota has on its drawing boards plans for a longer-wheelbase, six-cylinder version. The planned model will have a 103.5-inch wheelbase, compared with the 98.4-inch wheelbase of existing Celicas.

But until the introduction of the six-cylinder power-er plant—expected to be on the market by mid-1979—all Celicas come equipped with a 2200cc, four-cylinder engine. We felt that this small 133.6 cubic-inch engine fell quite short in the performance department. Our test Celica liftback with five-speed manual transmission trudged from 0 to 60 miles an hour in a mediocre 16 seconds. And the car had even more difficulty gathering the power boost needed to perform passing maneuvers comfortably. In normal city driving this sluggishness isn't noticeable, but the Celica is definitely lacking when you need an extra burst of power. As far as fuel efficiency goes, the Celica averages approximately 18 miles per gallon in city driving.

On the road the 1979 Celica handles extremely well, despite the power shortage. Its low, sleek lines enable it to literally slice through wind resistance at high speeds, although our test car had a tendency to float in its lane when speed exceeded 60 mph. Cornering is a pleasure; the Celica is quick to answer the slightest steering command, with no apparent free play in the steering mechanism. The power-assisted front disc/rear drum brake system was adequate during normal test situations. In emergency braking maneuvers, our Celica stopped within a reasonably short distance.

An above average suspension system, combined with snug, contoured seats provides the Celica with a smooth, comfortable ride. The inches added to the interior haven't made a difference in the driver and passenger roominess, though. Hip room in all seats is adequate, but headroom and legroom leave much to be desired. With an optional sunroof, headroom is further reduced. Legroom in the rear seats is extremely tight, and the front seats offer little more. Also, the steering wheel is large and tends to bump against the driver's legs in some seat positions. Overall, the Celica is a bit cramped, offering some well-shaped bucket seats but not much room around them. In our liftback model,

Toyota Celica

cargo space was about average. The car featured split rear bucket seats that folded down individually to open up 25.4 cubic feet of cargo space.

Outside noise filtering into the cab is minimal except at high speeds, when wind whistle becomes apparent. The 2200cc engine has a nice hum to it, and what seeps into the passenger compartment is neither unpleasant nor distracting. What is surprising about the 1979 Celica is its high degree of driver visibility. The hood is short and low, and the stainless steel side roof pillars are wide, but are positioned so that they present almost no obstructions to the view.

Under the hood the 1979 Celica is crowded, especially when equipped with power steering and air conditioning. But some careful thought went into the engine compartment design. The accessory pumps and motors are situated on the right side of the engine while the spark plugs and distributor are easily accessible on the left side. This is a bonus for the do-it-yourself mechanic.

TOYOTA CELICA
Test Model Specifications

Body type	2-door	Rear hiproom	47 in.
Overall length	173.6 in.	Engine type	4-cylinder in-line
Overall width	64.6 in.	Net hp @ rpm	90 @ 4800
Overall height	50.8 in.	Net torque @ rpm	122 @ 2400
Wheelbase	98.4 in.	Displacement	133.6 cu. in.
Turn diameter	32.8 ft.	Compression ratio	8.4:1
Tire size	185/70SR-14	Carburetion	2 bbl.
Curb weight	2530 lbs.	Transmission	5-speed Manual
Cargo space	.25.4		
Front headroom	37.0 in.	Axle ratio	3.70:1
Front legroom	41.2 in.	Acceleration 0-60 mph	16 sec.
Front hiproom	51 in.	Brake stop 60-0 mph	171 ft.
Rear headroom	37.0 in.	Fuel tank capacity	16.1 gal.
Rear legroom	31.5 in.	EPA city economy rating	18 mpg.

*with rear seat folded down

Toyota Corolla

Except for a slightly larger base engine, the extensive Toyota Corolla line is unchanged for 1979. The Corolla is offered in seven variations of the same body style that has been around for six years or so, and in four newer, larger models: the SR-5 Sport Coupe and Liftback, and the Deluxe Sport Coupe and Deluxe Liftback. Toyota is now testing two new front-wheel-drive cars, called the Tarcel 30-C and the Corsa 30-B — a sport coupe and a sedan. It is possible that these cars will also be included in the Corolla lineup by the end of 1979.

The mini-compact trend today is toward front-engine, front-wheel-drive setups that allow for great interior room and passenger comfort. This area is where our front-engine, rear-wheel-drive, Corolla SR-5 Sport Coupe suffered. Only by running the bucket seats all the way back on their rails could comfortable front legroom be attained. Headroom is tight in front and extremely poor in the rear, especially in the sloped-roof sport coupe

Toyota Corolla

and liftback models. Comparing the roominess of the larger, newer Corollas to those with the older body style, we found the smaller cars to feel roomier—even though on paper their dimensions were smaller.

The instrument panel on our test SR-5 Sport Coupe was well laid out, offering a complete set of easy-to-see gauges. Front and rear visibility is excellent, and the passenger compartment is sealed adequately against outside noises.

As in many economy cars, cargo space in our Sport Coupe was poor. The car offers a mere 6.2 cubic feet of trunk space. But since the back seats are almost useless for anyone but children, shopping bags and luggage can be stored in the rear passenger area.

The 1600cc engine powers the Corolla extremely well. Our car ran from 0 to 60 miles an hour in 15 seconds; freeway speeds and passing maneuvers were accomplished with ease. All the while we maintained a fuel economy average of 33 to 34 miles per gallon. The standard five-speed manual transmission reduces engine wear, increases gas mileage, and seems to perform better than the optional automatic transmission. A fault in the five-speed, though, is the procedure for shifting into reverse. It requires pulling up on the stick and shifting down toward the fourth gear position.

Considering the Corolla's size and excellent sticker price, its ride and handling are very good. Road bumps are apparent and the steering is a bit stiff, but the Corolla can still claim ride superiority over many of its competitors. The power-assisted front disc and rear drum brakes stopped our test model from 60 mph in 160 feet. After a series of repeated emergency stops, we could detect no apparent brake fade. The car did lose traction when performing some simulated panic maneuvers.

One definite plus for the Toyota Corolla is easy maintenance. The car was built with simplicity in mind, and that idea is reflected by the engine compartment layout. All necessary engine components are easily accessible, and replacement parts are readily available. This, combined with the fact that Toyota has set up a very large service network, makes Corolla a car whose servicing needs should not be a problem.

TOYOTA COROLLA
Test Model Specifications

Body type	2-door	Rear hiproom	N/A
Overall length	168.3 in.	Engine type	4 in-line
Overall width	63.6 in.	Net hp @ rpm	73 @ 5400
Overall height	50.6 in.	Net torque @ rpm	83 @ 3800
Wheelbase	93.3 in.	Displacement	1600 cc
Turn diameter	31.3 ft.	Compression ratio	9.0:1
Tire size	175/70SR-13	Carburetion	2 bbl.
Curb weight	2290 lbs.	Transmission	5-speed
Cargo space	6.2 cu. ft.		Manual
Front headroom	36.7 in.	Axle ratio	3.91:1
Front legroom	42.1 in.	Acceleration 0-60 mph	15 sec.
Front hiproom	N/A	Brake stop 60-0 mph	160 ft.
Rear headroom	36.9 in.	Fuel tank capacity	13.2 gal.
Rear legroom	29.1 in.	EPA city economy rating	24 mpg.

Volkswagen Rabbit

The 1979 gas-powered Volkswagen Rabbits sold in America hop off an assembly line in Pennsylvania. These domestic Rabbits differ from the German-made models in the shape of their headlights and little else.

Rabbit's reputation for quick acceleration is still intact, because the 1979 model uses the traditional Rabbit power plant—a 1457cc four-cylinder fuel-injected engine. CONSUMER GUIDE Magazine's acceleration tests showed the car could move from 0 to 60 miles an hour in just under 12 seconds, while retaining very good fuel mileage figures. Our combined average for city and highway driving was 35 miles per gallon.

Rabbit is a front-wheel-drive automobile. A common complaint about front-wheel-drive cars is that they have a tendency to torque steer. From a stop, if the wheels are turned when you accelerate, the engine tends to fight the driver and tug the wheels back into a straight position. Rabbit does not do this. Through all phases of tight turning accelera-tion, Rabbit enables the driver to move the steering wheel easily, and guide the car almost effortlessly. Our test staff believes that the car's rack-and-pinion steering, coupled with front and rear independent suspension, is the reason for its remarkable handling capabilities. At cruising speeds, steering is tight and responsive. In low-speed maneuvers, Rabbit is a little loose and sloppy due to a high steering ratio—almost a full four turns lock-to-lock. This makes parallel parking a bit laborious.

Our Rabbit was the top-of-the-line version, equipped with the luxury appointments called the "L" package. These include carpeting, greater amounts of insulation, trip odometer, AM/FM radio and power-assisted brakes. All of the domestic Rabbits in the series have been dressed up for 1979. Even the base version now sports wider tires, carpeting instead of rubber mats, trim along the trunk, scuff pads on the doors with provisions for stereo speakers, self-adjusting brakes, padded headliner and comfortable three-point safety belts. The "C" option package is the next step up from the base Rabbit. Its two main features are standard power brakes and AM radio. There are six optional packages, or treatments, that can be ordered with either "C" or "L" version cars. These packages give the buyer freedom to choose exactly what he or she needs, and allow VW to keep the prices of the base models to a minimum.

Equipped with power-assisted brakes—discs up front and drum-types in the rear, our car came skidding to a halt from 60 mph in as little as 149 feet. Brake fade was minimal.

Interior appointments on the "L" series Rabbit are nice, but not luxurious. The dashboard is woodgrain applique that looks like an inexpensive add-on. All controls can be reached easily. The instrumentation is highly visible during the daytime, but at night the lighting system on the Rabbit's dashboard is too weak to clearly light the controls.

Overall visibility from the Rabbit is excellent, thanks to the large windows and a short hood that slopes downward so the forward view of the road, especially over the right front quarter panel, is unobstructed.

The Rabbit's front seats are far superior to its back seat. The front seats can be adjusted easily for taller passengers. However, with front seats adjusted to their rearward limits, rear passengers are forced to ride sidesaddle.

Usable cargo capacity of Rabbit is in line with other cars of its size: about 22 cubic feet. Rabbit is a very good car, but its price has increased dramatically since it was introduced. CONSUMER GUIDE Magazine's tests this year and our experience with this car in the past shows that this car is economical and fun to drive. Its good resale value may be of some consolation when you gaze at a new models' window sticker.

VOLKSWAGEN RABBIT
Test Model Specifications

Body type	2-door	Engine type	4-cylinder
Overall length	155.3 in.	Net hp @ rpm	71 @ 5800
Overall width	63.4 in.	Net torque @ rpm	73 @ 3500
Overall height	55.5 in.	Displacement	1457 cc/
Wheelbase	94.4 in.		88.9 cu. in.
Turn diameter	31.2 ft.	Compression ratio	8.0:1
Tire size	145/13	Carburetion	Fuel injected
Curb weight	1870 lbs.	Transmission	5-speed
Cargo space	22.6 cu. ft.*		Manual
Front headroom	37 in.	Axle ratio	3.90.1
Front legroom	42 in.	Acceleration 0-60 mph	11.8 sec.
Front hiproom	48 in.	Brake stop 60-0 mph	149 ft.
Rear headroom	34 in.	Fuel tank capacity	10.9 gal.
Rear legroom	36.5 in.	EPA city economy rating	26 mpg.
Rear hiproom	50 in.		

*with rear seat folded down

Volkswagen Scirocco

Last year, Volkswagen used the same engine in both Scirocco and Rabbit. For 1979, however, Scirocco has been given an engine of its own, a 1588cc Four that is more than seven horsepower stronger than the engine used in last year's Scirocco. As a result, acceleration has improved slightly. Our test car this year accelerated from 0 to 60 miles an hour in 10.3 seconds, which is over a second faster than what last year's Scirocco was capable of.

Equipped with the new, optional five-speed manual transmission, our Scirocco attained a combined city-highway fuel rating of 33 miles per gallon.

Scirocco's only other substantial change for '79 is the addition of self-adjusting power disc and drum brakes. Overall stopping power is about the

Volkswagen Scirocco

same as it was in '78, but brake fade has been virtually eliminated. In our tests, Scirocco stopped straight even when all four wheels were locked. From 60 mph, Scirocco came to a halt in as little as 151 feet.

The overall handling of the Scirocco remains unchanged from last year. However, with the increase of horsepower, the car has a tendency to skip-steer around corners, especially at low speeds and when starting from a complete stop. That is, the front wheels grab, break free, grab, and break free again. This is a problem with most front-wheel-drive cars.

Driver visibility in Scirocco is excellent. The rear roof pillars are small and don't interfere with safe lane changing. However, we did not like the single front windshield wiper. In our tests, the wiper did not do a thorough job until we reached highway speed. At lower speeds, the wiper skipped and streaked; at times it partially obscured our view of the roadway. Once driving speed increased, and wind pressure held the wiper down more snugly, this problem disappeared. We urge that anyone owning a Scirocco install an accessory called a wiper sail.

Interior appointments on the new Scirocco remain about the same as they were in previous years. Standard equipment includes reclining seats that are adjustable for height, a quartz clock, a tachometer, rear window defogger, headlight flasher, steel-belted radial racing tires and an oil temperature gauge. All dashboard instruments can be seen easily day and night.

Interior comfort is adequate in every category except legroom. Legroom is poor for both front and rear passengers. Rear legroom is rated by Volkswagen at 30 inches. However, we doubt that people of even average height will find the rear seat comfortable — even with the front seat all the way forward.

In all, CONSUMER GUIDE Magazine rates the Volkswagen Scirocco very high. It offers fun and economy in a very attractive package. Scirocco's serviceability is excellent: repairs are facilitated by the roominess of the engine compartment and a service manual that is as complete as any we have seen.

VOLKSWAGEN SCIROCCO
Test Model Specifications

Body type	2-door	Engine type	4-cylinder in-line OHC
Overall length	155.7 in.	Net hp @ rpm	78 @ 5500
Overall width	63.9 in.	Net torque @ rpm	84 @ 3200
Overall height	51.5 in.	Displacement	1588 cc/
Wheelbase	94.5 in.		97.0 cu. in.
Turn diameter	31.2 ft.	Compression ratio	8.0:1
Tire size	175/70SR13	Carburetion	Fuel injected
Curb weight	2015 lbs.	Transmission	5-speed
Cargo space	19.1 cu. ft.*		Manual
Front headroom	35 in.	Axle ratio	4.17:1
Front legroom	38.8 in.	Acceleration 0-60 mph	10.3 sec.
Front hiproom	42 in.	Brake stop 60-0 mph	151 ft.
Rear headroom	31.2 in.	Fuel tank capacity	10.9 gal.
Rear legroom	30 in.	EPA city economy rating	25 mpg.
Rear hiproom	50 in.		

*with rear seat folded down

Road Test Rating Charts

The charts below summarize the reports on all the cars CONSUMER GUIDE Magazine tested this year. The charts are designed to enable you to quickly compare the scores of one car with those of all the others.

The numbers in the charts—1 to 5, with 5 being the highest possible score—correspond to the terms poor, fair, good, very good and excellent. Therefore, a car that receives a score of 5 in any category is considered excellent in that area in comparison to all the other models tested. As you look at the charts, it is important that you remember this: the numbers refer to our test cars only; they do not reflect our opinion about any other automobile.

After we've rated the test model in all of the categories shown below, we total up the points. This can give you some idea of our test car's value in relation to all the other models tested. Naturally, a score of 45 points for two cars does not mean that those two cars are identical. One might deliver excellent mileage but handle poorly; the other might excel in handling but gobble gas.

The cars that scored highest of all in our tests have been designated CONSUMER GUIDE Magazine's Best Buys. These Best Buy cars can be found easily in the chart because their names and numbers are printed in bold type.

An explanation of our test criteria is in order. Here is what we mean by the categories shown in the charts.

Fuel economy: A rating of the number of miles per gallon a car delivered in our tests; the higher the mileage, the higher the score.

Power: A measurement of a car's acceleration from 0 to 60 miles an hour and its ability to accelerate at all other speeds.

Ride: A judgment of the car's behavior as it moves over pavement and rough roads, as it travels straight and as it takes corners.

Steering: The amount of road "feel" and other information conveyed to the driver versus unwanted vibration; the effort required from the driver to make the car go where wanted; the precision of the steering mechanism.

Handling: The reaction of the direction of the car in relation to the control of the steering wheel on smooth and rough roads, in turns and in emergency-type maneuvers.

Braking: Performance of the car's braking system in bringing the car to a halt from 60 mph and in "panic" maneuvers.

Front seat and rear seat room and comfort: The combination of headroom, legroom, hip room and knee room, plus seat construction (padding, contours, etc.) that affect the comfort of the driver and passengers.

Serviceability: The ease of maintenance by relatively unskilled persons, such as the car's owner; the opportunity for do-it-yourself service.

Visibility: A judgment of how much is seen of the roadway from inside the car as a result of the design of the car's body, windows and seats.

Quietness: A measurement of noise heard inside the car, including engine noise, wind whistle, and other ambient sounds; the lower the noise, the higher the score.

Cargo capacity: The volume of the car's trunk, or the rear cargo area of a hatchback model with its rear seat in the down position. (Of course, cars that do not have trunks or rear seats cannot be scored in this area.)

Road Test Rating Chart—Domestic Coupes and Sedans

MODEL	FUEL ECONOMY	POWER	RIDE	STEERING	HANDLING	BRAKING	ROOM & COMFORT FRONT SEAT	ROOM & COMFORT REAR SEAT	SERVICEABILITY	VISIBILITY	QUIETNESS	CARGO CAPACITY	TOTAL POINTS
AMC Concord	2	3	3	2	3	4	3	2	4	3	2	2	33
AMC Pacer	2	2	3	3	3	3	3	1	4	5	2	5*	36
AMC Spirit	2	4	3	2	3	5	3	1	4	3	1	5*	36
Buick Century	2	5	4	5	5	2	4	4	5	3	4	4	47
Buick LeSabre	2	3	5	4	4	2	5	5	4	4	4	4	46
Buick Regal	3	5	4	4	4	4	4	3	4	3	2	4	44
Buick Riviera	2	5	5	5	5	3	5	4	3	3	4	3	47
Buick Skyhawk	3	3	2	4	3	2	3	1	3	3	2	4*	33

Model														
Cadillac Coupe de Ville	1	5	5	4	3	3	5	5	3	3	4	5	4	47
Cadillac Eldorado	2	4	5	5	5	2	5	4	3	3	5	3	3	46
Cadillac Seville	4	2	4	5	4	5	5	4	3	3	3	3	2	46
Chevrolet Camaro	2	4	3	4	5	1	4	1	3	1	4	4	1	33
Chevrolet Caprice	2	4	5	4	4	5	4	4	2	3	5	4	4	46
Chevrolet Chevette	5	2	2	3	4	1	3	3	3	5	2	2	4*	37
Chevrolet Corvette	2	5	3	5	5	3	3	—	3	2	3	3	1	35
Chevrolet Malibu	3	2	3	4	3	3	3	3	3	4	3	3	3	37
Chevrolet Monte Carlo	2	4	4	3	3	3	4	3	3	3	4	4	4	40
Chevrolet Monza	2	3	3	3	3	2	3	1	2	3	2	2	1	28
Chrysler Cordoba	1	5	4	3	3	3	4	3	3	4	4	4	3	40
Chrysler LeBaron	2	5	4	3	3	5	4	3	3	4	4	4	3	43
Chrysler Newport	1	5	5	3	3	4	5	5	3	4	2	5	3	45
Dodge Aspen	3	3	4	3	3	5	4	3	4	4	3	3	3	43
Dodge Diplomat	2	5	4	3	3	4	4	3	3	4	2	2	3	40
Dodge Magnum XE	1	3	4	3	3	2	3	2	3	2	3	3	4	33

*Hatchback model, with rear seat folded down

Road Test Rating Chart—Domestic Coupes and Sedans

MODEL	FUEL ECONOMY	POWER	RIDE	STEERING	HANDLING	BRAKING	FRONT SEAT ROOM & COMFORT	REAR SEAT ROOM & COMFORT	SERVICEABILITY	VISIBILITY	QUIETNESS	CARGO CAPACITY	TOTAL POINTS
Dodge Omni	5	3	3	4	5	5	4	3	4	5	3	5*	49
Dodge St. Regis	1	5	5	3	3	4	4	4	3	4	2	5	43
Ford Fairmont	3	3	3	4	4	4	3	3	4	5	3	4	43
Ford Granada	2	3	3	2	2	3	3	3	3	3	3	3	33
Ford LTD	1	5	5	3	4	5	5	4	1	3	5	4	45
Ford LTD II	1	5	4	2	1	4	3	3	2	2	5	3	35
Ford Mustang	2	5	2	4	5	5	3	1	2	2	2	1	34
Ford Pinto	4	4	2	3	3	5	2	1	5	2	1	4	36

Model													Total
Ford Thunderbird	1	5	4	2	2	2	3	3	2	2	5	3	37
Lincoln Continental	1	5	5	3	2	5	5	5	1	3	5	5	42
Lincoln Mark V	1	3	3	2	2	3	5	3	1	2	5	4	34
Lincoln Versailles	1	4	3	2	3	3	3	2	1	3	5	3	33
Mercury Bobcat	4	1	2	3	3	4	2	1	5	2	1	4	32
Mercury Capri	4	5	2	4	5	3	3	1	3	2	2	5*	39
Mercury Cougar	1	3	5	2	1	3	4	3	2	2	5	3	34
Mercury Cougar XR-7	1	5	4	2	2	3	4	3	2	2	5	3	36
Mercury Marquis	2	4	5	4	4	3	5	4	1	3	4	5	44
Mercury Monarch	2	3	3	2	3	5	4	3	3	4	3	3	38
Mercury Zephyr	3	3	3	4	4	5	3	3	4	5	3	4	44
Oldsmobile Cutlass	4	1	3	3	2	3	4	4	3	3	1	4	35
Oldsmobile Cutlass Supreme	3	2	4	5	3	4	3	3	4	4	4	4	43
Oldsmobile Delta 88	4	4	4	3	5	5	5	4	3	3	3	5	49
Oldsmobile Starfire	2	4	3	4	5	3	3	1	2	3	3	4*	37
Oldsmobile Toronado	2	4	5	5	5	2	5	4	4	3	5	3	47

*Hatchback model, with rear seat folded down

Road Test Rating Chart—Domestic Coupes and Sedans

MODEL	FUEL ECONOMY	POWER	RIDE	STEERING	HANDLING	BRAKING	ROOM & COMFORT FRONT SEAT	ROOM & COMFORT REAR SEAT	SERVICEABILITY	VISIBILITY	QUIETNESS	CARGO CAPACITY	TOTAL POINTS
Plymouth Horizon TC3	5	3	3	4	5	5	4	2	3	4	3	5*	46
Plymouth Volare	3	3	4	3	3	5	4	3	4	4	2	3	41
Pontiac Bonneville	2	4	4	4	4	2	4	4	2	3	4	4	41
Pontiac Firebird	1	5	3	4	5	1	3	1	2	1	4	1	31
Pontiac Grand Am	2	4	4	3	4	3	3	2	2	4	3	4	38
Pontiac Grand Prix	2	4	4	4	3	3	4	3	3	3	3	4	40
Pontiac Sunbird	4	2	2	4	3	2	3	1	3	3	3	4*	34

Road Test Rating Chart—Domestic Wagons

AMC Concord	2	4	3	3	3	4	3	2	4	2	2	4	36
AMC Pacer	2	3	3	4	4	4	4	2	3	4	4	4	40
Chevrolet Caprice	1	4	5	4	5	4	5	4	1	3	4	5	**45**
Chevrolet Malibu	2	5	5	4	5	4	4	3	2	3	3	5	**45**
Chevrolet Monza	4	3	2	4	4	4	3	1	4	3	1	4	37
Chrysler Town & Country	2	5	4	3	3	3	4	3	3	3	2	5	40
Ford Fairmont	2	4	3	4	4	5	4	3	4	4	3	5	**45**
Ford LTD Country Squire	2	4	5	4	4	4	5	4	1	3	4	5	**45**
Ford Pinto	3	3	2	3	3	2	2	1	3	2	1	4	29
Plymouth Volare	2	4	4	3	3	2	4	3	3	3	1	5	37

Road Test Rating Chart—Imported Automobiles

BMW 320i	3	5	2	5	5	5	4	3	4	5	3	3	**47**
Datsun 210 Wagon	5	2	4	4	4	3	3	3	4	5	2	5	44
Datsun 280 ZX	3	5	4	3	4	4	4	—	5	3	4	4*	43
Datsun 810	3	3	5	5	5	5	4	4	5	3	4	3	**49**

*Hatchback model, with rear seat folded down

Road Test Rating Chart—Imported Automobiles

MODEL	FUEL ECONOMY	POWER	RIDE	STEERING	HANDLING	BRAKING	FRONT SEAT ROOM & COMFORT	REAR SEAT ROOM & COMFORT	SERVICEABILITY	VISIBILITY	QUIETNESS	CARGO CAPACITY	TOTAL POINTS
Dodge Colt FF Plymouth Champ	5	4	4	3	4	1	4	3	4	5	3	5*	45
Fiat Brava	4	3	3	4	4	5	3	3	3	5	2	3	42
Ford Fiesta	5	3	4	3	3	5	4	3	5	4	1	4*	44
Honda Accord	5	4	4	5	3	5	4	2	5	4	5	2	48
Honda Civic CVCC	5	4	2	4	5	5	3	1	5	5	1	4*	44
Mazda GLC	5	3	3	3	2	5	3	3	5	5	1	5*	43
Mazda RX-7	2	5	4	5	5	5	4	—	4	3	3	4	44
Plymouth Arrow	4	5	4	4	4	5	3	2	4	3	2	5*	45

Road Test Rating Chart—Imported Automobiles

MODEL	FUEL ECONOMY	POWER	RIDE	STEERING	HANDLING	BRAKING	FRONT SEAT ROOM & COMFORT	REAR SEAT ROOM & COMFORT	SERVICEABILITY	VISIBILITY	QUIETNESS	CARGO CAPACITY	TOTAL POINTS
Renault Le Car	5	3	3	4	3	4	3	2	3	4	2	5*	41
Subaru 4WD Wagon	5	2	3	4	5	5	3	3	4	3	3	5	45
Toyota Celica	3	2	3	4	3	3	2	1	4	4	3	3	35
Toyota Corrola	4	3	3	3	4	4	2	1	4	4	2	1	35
Volkswagon Rabbit	5	5	3	4	4	5	3	2	5	5	3	5*	49
VW Scirocco	5	5	4	4	4	5	3	1	5	5	3	4*	48

*Hatchback model, with rear seat folded down

1979 Auto Prices

CONSUMER GUIDE Magazine recommends that you take the following steps before you visit a car dealer's showroom:

1. Determine what type of car you need. The size of your family, your cargo and towing requirements, and the mileage ratings can help you pick an automobile of the size that is best for you.

2. Make a list of the equipment you want. The listings below can tell you which items are standard and which ones are extra-cost options.

3. Check the car prices here, adding the low price of the basic model, the cost of the options, freight charges and taxes.

4. Now you can bargain with the dealer. If he can come within about $50 of your calculated price, he is offering you a good buy.

There is another way to obtain information on car prices. You can use one of the computerized estimating services. For a fee, these companies furnish computer printouts of the dealer's car and option costs. This provides you with an excellent bargaining tool, because you will know how much the dealer will have to pay for the car you choose. Several of these firms will arrange for you to buy the car at their computerized price and pick it up at a dealership near you.

For more information, you can contact:

Computerized Car Costs Co.
P.O. Box 2090
Eleven Mile Road — Lahser Station
Southfield, MI 48034
(800) 521-7007
      or
Nationwide Auto & Truck Brokers, Inc.
17517 W. Ten Mile Rd.
Southfield, MI 48075
(800) 521-7257

American Motors Corporation

AMC AMX

	Retail Price	Dealer Cost	Low Price
AMX			
2-Door Liftback	$ 5899	$ 5187	$ 5537

STANDARD EQUIPMENT (included in above prices)

AMX: Safety and protection equipment plus 258 CID 6-cylinder engine, 4-speed manual transmission w/floor shifter, heavy duty front disc brakes, extra quiet insulation package, dual horn, power liftback release, rally-tuned suspension system, ER60-14 white letter radial tires (4), space saver spare, front armrests, lighter, carpet, center console w/armrest, oil pressure gauge, ammeter, electric clock, tachometer, inside hood release, day/night mirror, vinyl bucket front seats, leather wrapped steering wheel, AMX flame decal, black exterior trim, front air dam, fender flares, rear deck spoiler, dual black remote control mirrors, turbocast II aluminum wheels.

AMX ACCESSORIES

304 CID, V-8 Engine.	$ 250	$ 208	$ 211
California Emission System & Testing	78	65	66
Altitude Driveability Package	NC	NC	NC
Automatic Transmission.	296	246	249
Twin Grip Differential.	63	52	53
Power Steering (Reg. V-8 w/air cond.)	152	126	128

Prices are accurate at time of printing; subject to manufacturer's change.

	Retail Price	Dealer Cost	Low Price
Power Brakes	$ 70	$ 58	$ 59
Air Conditioning System	513	426	431
Air Conditioning Package	722	599	605
Heavy Duty Battery	18	15	16
Cold Climate Group	96	80	81
Heavy Duty Cooling System	39	32	33
Convenience Group	75	62	63
Cruise Control	104	86	87
Rear Defroster	89	74	75
Locking Gas Cap	8	7	8
Tinted Glass	57	47	48
Light Group	35	29	30
Power Door Locks	72	60	61
Moon Roof	178	148	150
Protection Group	27	22	23
Protective Inner Coating	100	83	84
Scuff Moldings	31	26	27
Radio Equipment			
AM	84	70	71
AM/FM Stereo	236	196	198
AM/FM Stereo/CB 40 Ch.	314	261	264
Rear Speaker	24	20	21
Fabric Bucket Seats	NC	NC	NC
Tilt Steering Wheel	72	60	61

AMC CONCORD

CONCORD

	Retail Price	Dealer Cost	Low Price
2-Door Hatchback	$ 4149	$ 3655	$ 3905
2-Door Sedan	4049	3568	3818
4-Door Sedan	4149	3655	3905
4-Door Wagon	4349	3830	4080

CONCORD D/L

2-Door Hatchback	4448	3917	4167
2-Door Sedan	4348	3830	4080
4-Door Sedan	4448	3917	4167
4-Door Wagon	4648	4092	4392

CONCORD LIMITED

2-Door Sedan	5348	4705	5005
4-Door Sedan	5448	4792	5092
4-Door Wagon	5648	4967	5267

STANDARD EQUIPMENT (included in above prices)

Concord: Safety and protection equipment, 6-cylinder 232 CID engine, 4-speed manual transmission w/floor shifter, front disc brakes, single horn, D78-14 blackwall non-
Prices are accurate at time of printing; subject to manufacturer's change.

belted tires (4), stowaway spare tire, front and rear armrests (front only on hatchback), lighter, carpet (including cargo area on hatchback and wagon), inside hood release, bench seats, folding rear seat on hatchback and wagon, rear bumper guards, moldings — drip, wheellip, hood front edge, windshield surround, rear window surround, rocker panel, flipper rear quarter window on hatchback, scuff body side molding, wheel covers.

Concord D/L: Concord equipment plus individual reclining seats, custom door panels, day/night mirror, custom steering wheel, cargo area skid strips, electric clock, trunk carpet, landau vinyl roof (ex. wagon), opera quarter windows (2-dr. sedan), striping, front bumper guards, wagon woodgrain side panels, color-keyed wheel covers, whitewall tires, dual horns, additional sound insulation.

Concord Limited: Concord and Concord D/L equipment plus premium seat trim, premium door trim, upgraded carpet, luxury woodgrain steering wheel, styled wheel covers, P195/75R-14 whitewall glass belted radial tires, power steering, power door locks, AM radio, tilt steering wheel, convenience group, visibility group, light group, protection group.

CONCORD ACCESSORIES

	Retail Price	Dealer Cost	Low Price
Engines			
258 CID, 6-Cyl.	$ 130	$ 108	$ 110
304 CID, V-8 Cyl.	250	208	211
California Emission System & Factory Testing	78	65	66
High Altitude Emission Package.	NC	NC	NC
Transmissions			
4-Speed Manual, Floor Shift	STD	STD	STD
Automatic, Column Shift	323	268	271
Twin-Grip Differential.	63	52	53
Power Steering (std.-D/L)	158	131	133
Front Power Disc Brakes	70	58	59
Power Door Locks			
2-Doors.	72	60	61
4-Doors.	104	86	87
Convenience Grp.	75	62	63
Radio Equipment			
AM (std. LTD)	89	70	71
AM/FM Stereo			
Limited.	152	127	129
Others	236	196	198
AM/FM Stereo W/CB			
Limited.	230	191	193
Others	314	261	264
Rear Speaker.	24	20	21
Air Conditioning System	513	426	431
Air Conditioning Package W/A/C System,			
Tinted Glass & Power Steering.	731	607	614
Tinted Glass, All Windows.	60	50	51
Electronic Cruise Control	104	86	87
Tilt Steering Wheel (std. Ltd)	72	60	61

Prices are accurate at time of printing; subject to manufacturer's change.

AMC Concord

AMC Pacer

AMC Spirit

	Retail Price	Dealer Cost	Low Price
Digital Electric Clock	$ 40	$ 33	$ 34
Visibility Group	62	52	53
Left Remote-Control Mirror	17	14	15
Light Group	49	41	42
Dual Horns	13	11	12
Hidden Compartment	33	27	28
Electric Rear Window Defroster	89	74	75
Roof Rack, Wagon	90	75	76
Moon Roof	178	148	150
Luxury Steering Wheel	29	24	25
Extra-Quiet Insulation Package	48	40	41
Protective Inner Coating	100	83	84
Protection Group	87	72	73
Front Bumper Guards	21	17	18
Locking Gas Cap	8	7	8
Heavy-Duty Engine Cooling System	39	32	33
70-AMP Heavy-Duty Battery	18	15	16
Maximum Cooling Syst.			
W/V-8 Eng. w/o Air Cond.	59	49	50
W/V-8 Eng. & Air Cond.	20	17	18
Cold Climate Group			
W/o Air Cond. or Rear Defroster	96	80	81
W/Air Cond. or Rear Defroster	38	32	33
Handling Pkg. (NA w/4-cyl.-eng.)	30	25	26

AMC PACER

PACER D/L
Hatchback	$ 4699	$ 4137	$ 4437
Wagon	4849	4268	4568

PACER LIMITED
Hatchback	5699	5012	5312
Wagon	5849	5143	5493

STANDARD EQUIPMENT (included in above prices)

Pacer D/L: Safety and protection equipment plus 258 CID 6-cyl. engine, 4-speed manual transmission, disc front brakes, quiet insulation package, dual horn, P195/75R-14 whitewall glass belted radial tires, lighter, electric clock, carpet, day/night mirror, fold-down rear seat, front individual reclining seats, bumper guards, wheel covers.

Pacer Limited: D/L equipment plus premium seat trim, center armrest, upgrade carpet, premium door trim, luxury woodgrain steering wheel, styled wheel covers, power steering, power windows, power door locks, AM radio, tilt steering wheel, convenience group, visibility group, light group, protection group.

PACER ACCESSORIES

304 CID V-8 Engine	$250	$208	$211

Prices are accurate at time of printing; subject to manufacturer's change.

	Retail Price	Dealer Cost	Low Price
Transmissions			
Automatic, Column Shift.	$ 323	$ 268	$ 271
Automatic, Floor Shift	348	289	292
Calif. Emission System.	78	65	66
Vinyl Roof (NA Wagon).	124	103	105
Power Assists			
Steering (std. Ltd.)	158	131	133
Brakes	70	58	59
Door Locks	72	60	61
Windows & Door Locks.	194	161	163
Air Conditioner System.	513	426	431
Air Conditioner Pkg..	734	609	616
Auxiliary Auto. Trans. Oil Cooler	36	30	31
Heavy-Duty Battery	18	15	16
Cold Climate Grp.			
W/o Air Cond. or Rear Defroster.	96	80	81
W/Air Cond. or Rear Defroster	38	32	33
Convenience Grp. (std. Ltd.).	75	62	63
Heavy-Duty Cooling System.	31	26	27
Cruise Control	104	86	87
Rear Window Defroster	89	74	75
Locking Gas Cap	8	7	8
Gauge Pkg.	129	107	109
Tinted Glass	63	52	54
Hidden Compartment	37	31	32
Light Group (std. Ltd.).	39	32	33
Left Remote Mirror.	17	14	15
Moon Roof.	178	148	150
Protection Group (std. Ltd.)	55	46	47
Protective Inner Coating	100	83	84
Radio Equipment			
AM (std. Ltd.)	84	70	71
AM/FM Stereo			
D/L.	236	196	198
Limited	152	126	128
AM/FM Stereo w/Stereo Tape			
D/L.	353	293	296
Limited.	269	223	226
AM/FM Stereo w/CB			
D/L.	314	261	264
Limited.	230	191	193
Rear Speaker.	24	20	21
Roof Rack	62	52	53
Heavy-Duty Shock Absorbers.	14	12	13
Leather-Wrapped Steering Wheel			
D/L.	49	41	42
Limited.	20	17	18
Luxury Woodgrain Steering Wheel (std. Ltd.)	29	24	25
Tilt Steering Wheel.	72	60	61
Visibility Group	50	42	43

Prices are accurate at time of printing; subject to manufacturer's change.

	Retail Price	Dealer Cost	Low Price
Door Vent Windows	$ 36	$ 30	$ 31
Rear Window Washer/Wiper	62	52	53
Woodgrain Side Panels, Wagon	117	97	98

AMC SPIRIT

SPIRIT (43 STATES)

	Retail Price	Dealer Cost	Low Price
2-Dr. Liftback	$3999	$3524	$3824
2-Dr. Sedan	3899	3437	3637

SPIRIT (AZ, CA, ID, NV, OR, UT, WA)

2-Dr. Liftback	3879	3419	3619
2-Dr. Sedan	3779	3332	3532

SPIRIT D/L (43 STATES)

2-Dr. Liftback	4199	3699	3949
2-Dr. Sedan	4099	3612	3862

SPIRIT D/L (AZ, CA, ID, NV, OR, UT, WA)

2-Dr. Liftback	4079	3594	3844
2-Dr. Sedan	3979	3507	3757

SPIRIT LIMITED (43 STATES)

2-Dr. Liftback	5199	4574	4874
2-Dr. Sedan	5099	4487	4787

SPIRIT LIMITED (AZ, CA, ID, NV, OR, UT, WA)

2-Dr. Liftback	5079	4469	4769
2-Dr. Sedan	4979	4382	4682

STANDARD EQUIPMENT (included in above prices)

Spirit: Safety and protection equipment plus 121 CID 4-cyl. engine, 4-speed manual transmission, front disc brakes, C78-14 blackwall unbelted tires, single horn, front ashtray w/light, lighter, carpet, vinyl front bucket seats, vinyl spare tire cover, rear bumper guards, wheel covers.

Spirit D/L: Spirit equipment plus whitewall tires, extra quiet insulation, dual horns, custom seats, custom door panels w/map pockets, luxury woodgrain steering wheel, day/night mirror, electric clock, carpeted spare tire cover, styled wheel covers, front bumper guards.

Spirit Limited: Spirit and Spirit D/L equipment plus P195/75R-14 whitewall glass belted radial tires, power steering, power door locks, power liftback release, AM radio, tilt steering wheel, convenience group, visibility group, light group, center console w/armrest, protection group, premium seats and door trim, upgrade carpet.

SPIRIT ACCESSORIES

Engines

232 CID 6-cyl.	$ 50	$ 42	$ 43

Prices are accurate at time of printing; subject to manufacturer's change.

	Retail Price	Dealer Cost	Low Price
258 CID 6-cyl.	$ 130	$ 108	$ 110
304 CID V-8.	250	208	211
Transmissions			
3-Speed Manual (credit).	(50)	(42)	(42)
Automatic, Column Shift.	296	246	249
Automatic, Floor Shift	321	266	269
Calif. Emission Syst.	78	65	66
Power Assists			
Steering (std. Ltd.)	152	126	128
Brakes	70	58	59
Door Locks (std. Ltd.)	72	60	61
Liftback Release (std. Ltd.).	30	25	26
Air Conditioning System	513	426	431
Air Conditioning Pkg.	722	599	605
Air Deflector, Wagon.	26	22	23
Heavy-Duty Battery	18	15	16
Electric Clock, Spirit	40	33	34
Cold Climate Grp.			
w/o Air Cond. or Rear Defroster	96	80	81
w/Air Cond. or Rear Defroster	38	32	33
Convenience Group (std. Ltd.).	75	62	63
Heavy-Duty Cooling System.	31	26	27
Cruise Control	104	86	87
Rear Window Defroster	89	74	75
Locking Gas Cap	8	7	8
Gauge Pkg.			
W/o GT Pkg.	104	86	87
W/GT Pkg..	52	43	44
Tinted Glass	57	47	48
GT Package			
D/L.	450	383	387
Limited.	200	170	172
GT Rally-Tuned Suspension Pkg.	99	82	83
Dual Horns, Spirit	13	11	12
Light Group (std. Ltd.)			
Spirit	45	37	38
Spirit D/L	35	29	30
Left Remote Mirror.	17	14	15
Moon Roof.	178	148	150
Protection Group	55	46	47
Protective Inner Coating	100	83	84
Radio Equipment			
AM (std. Ltd.)	84	70	71
AM/FM Stereo			
Limited.	152	126	128
Others	236	196	198
AM/FM Stereo w/CB			
Limited.	230	191	193
Others	314	261	264

Prices are accurate at time of printing; subject to manufacturer's change.

	Retail Price	Dealer Cost	Low Price
Rear Speaker	$ 24	$ 20	$ 21
Roof Rack, Sedan	62	52	53
Leather-Wrapped Steering Wheel			
Limited	20	17	18
Others	49	41	42
Luxury Woodgrain Steering Wheel	29	24	25
Tilt Steering Wheel (std. Ltd.)	72	60	61
Tachometer	52	43	44
Visibility Group (std. Ltd.)			
Spirit	62	52	53
Spirit D/L	50	42	43

Chrysler Corporation

Chrysler

CHRYSLER CORDOBA

CORDOBA

	Retail Price	Dealer Cost	Low Price
2-Door Specialty Hardtop, V8	$ 5995	$ 5039	$ 5339

STANDARD EQUIPMENT (included in above prices)

Cordoba: Safety and protection equipment plus 318 cubic-inch 2-bbl. V8 engine, power steering, power front disc brakes, automatic transmission, electronic lean burn system, front and rear bumper guards, hood medallion, inside hood release, velour cloth-and-vinyl bench seat with center armrest, color-keyed shag pile carpeting, luxury wheel covers and steering wheel, glove box lock, cigarette lighter, BSW glass-belted radial tires.

CORDOBA ACCESSORIES

	Retail Price	Dealer Cost	Low Price
Engines			
NA w/Calif. Emission Syst.			
360 CID V-8 2-bbl.	$ 191	$ 145	$ 147
360 CID V-8 4-bbl.	420	319	323
Calif. Emission Syst. Req.			
318 CID V-8 4-bbl.	61	46	47

Prices are accurate at time of printing; subject to manufacturer's change.

	Retail Price	Dealer Cost	Low Price
360 CID V-8 4-bbl.	$251	$191	$193
360 CID HD V-8 4-bbl.	420	319	323
Vinyl Roofs			
Landau	132	100	102
"Crown" Landau, W/o Basic Group	823	626	633
"Crown" Landau, W/Basic Group	691	526	532
Vinyl Side Molding	45	34	35
Tape Stripes			
Body Side	47	36	37
Deck Lid	24	18	19
Interior Trims			
Vinyl Bench Seat W/Center Folding Arm Rest	32	25	26
Velour & Vinyl 60/40 Bench Seat W/Center Arm Rest & Passenger Recliner	147	111	113
Leather Bucket Seats W/Center Seat Cushion W/Folding Center Arm Rest, Dual Recliners	283	215	218
Light Pkg.	29	22	23
Basic Group			
W/318 CID Eng.	1089	828	837
W/360 CID Eng.	1125	855	864
Heavy Duty Package	150	114	116
Special Appearance Pkg.	527	401	406
Two-Tone Paint Pkg.	158	120	122
Air Conditioning	584	443	448
Sure Grip Differential Axle	67	51	52
500 AMP Long Life Battery	35	26	27
Protective Rub Strips, Front & Rear	37	28	29
Electronic Digital Clock	56	43	44
Console	60	46	47
Rear Window Defroster, Electric	98	74	75
Emission Control System & Testing	87	66	67
Locking Gas Cap	7	6	7
Tinted Glass			
All Windows	73	55	56
Windshield Only	47	35	36
Cornering Lights	51	38	39
Accessory Floor Mats	25	19	20
Illuminated Vanity Mirror	50	39	40
Remote Control Mirrors			
Left, Chrome	19	14	15
Left & Right, Chrome			
W/o Basic Group	54	41	42
W/Basic Group	35	27	28
Dual Sport Styled, Chrome			
W/o Basic Group	67	51	52
W/Basic Group	48	36	37
Dual Sport Styled, Painted			
W/o Basic Group	67	51	52
W/Basic Group	48	36	37

Prices are accurate at time of printing; subject to manufacturer's change.

	Retail Price	Dealer Cost	Low Price
Door Edge Protectors	$ 13	$ 10	$ 11
Pedal Dress-Up	10	8	9
Power Assists			
Power Bench/Bucket or 60/40 Split Bench Seat, Left	167	127	129
Power Windows	137	104	106
Power Door Locks	89	68	69
Power Deck Lid Release	26	20	21
Radios & Speakers			
AM..	87	66	67
AM W/40 Channel CB Transceiver			
W/o Basic Group	373	284	287
W/Basic Group	287	218	221
AM/FM			
W/o Basic Group........................	167	127	129
W/Basic Group	80	61	62
W/8 Track Stereo Tape, 2 Front & 2 Rear Speakers			
W/o Basic Group	252	192	194
W/Basic Group	166	126	128
AM/FM Stereo, 2 Front & 2 Rear Speakers			
W/o Basic Group........................	240	183	185
W/Basic Group	154	117	119
AM/FM Stereo W/40 Channel CB Transceiver & Power Tri-Band Antenna, 2 Front & 2 Rear Speakers			
W/o Basic Group	527	400	405
W/Basic Group	440	334	338
AM/FM Stereo W/8 Track Stereo Tape, 2 Front & 2 Rear Speakers			
W/o Basic Group	343	261	264
W/W Basic Group........................	256	195	197
AM/FM Stereo W/Search Tune, 2 Front & 2 Rear Speakers			
W/o Basic Group	368	279	282
W/Basic Group	281	213	216
Rear Speaker, Single	26	20	21
Power Antenna..............................	48	37	38
Seat Belts, Dlx.	20	15	16
Automatic Speed Control.	107	81	82
Steering Wheels			
Tilt...	77	59	60
Leather Covered 2 Spoke....................	40	30	31
Leather Covered, 3 Spoke	40	30	31
Sun Roof, Power Operated....................	546	415	420
"T" Bar Roof.................................	675	513	519
Suspension			
Heavy Duty Shock Absorbers................	8	6	7
Heavy Duty Suspension	28	21	22
Roadability Pkg.	29	22	23

Prices are accurate at time of printing; subject to manufacturer's change.

	Retail Price	Dealer Cost	Low Price
Tachometer	$73	$56	$57
Trunk Dress-Up	47	36	37
Undercoating W/Hood Silencer Pad	36	27	28
Deluxe Windshield Wipers	40	30	31

CHRYSLER LE BARON

LE BARON

	Retail Price	Dealer Cost	Low Price
2-Door	$5024	$4223	$4523
4-Door	5122	4305	4605
Town & Country Wagon	5955	5005	5305

LE BARON SALON

2-Door	5261	4422	4722
4-Door	5489	4614	4914

LE BARON MEDALLION

2-Door	5735	4820	5120
4-Door	5963	5012	5312

STANDARD EQUIPMENT (included in above prices)

LeBaron: Safety and protection equipment plus 225 cubic-inch 2-bbl. 6 cylinder engine, 4-speed manual transmission, power steering, power front disc brakes, isolated suspension system, electronic ignition, electronic voltage regulator, BSW glass-belted radial tires, space-saving spare tire, cloth-and-vinyl bench seat.

LeBaron Medallion adds body side tape accent stripes, remote control left outside mirror, velour cloth 60/40 split bench seat with passenger recliner and center armrest, rear seat fold-down center armrest (4-door), shag carpeting, map/courtesy light under panel courtesy light, deluxe wheel covers.

Town & Country Wagon adds liftgate counter-balanced gas pressure cylinders, simulated-wood body side and liftgate surround moldings, liftgate-open warning light, covered carpeted lockable stowage bins, vinyl bench seat with center armrest.

LE BARON ACCESSORIES

Engines			
318 CID 8 Cyl. 2-BBL	$235	$179	$181
360 CID 8 Cyl. 2-BBL	426	324	328
360 CID 8 Cyl. 4-BBL, Heavy Duty	655	498	503
360 CID 8 Cyl. 4-BBL	487	370	374
360 CID 8 Cyl. 4-BBL, Heavy Duty	655	498	503
318 CID 8 Cyl. 4-BBL	296	225	228
Vinyl Roofs			
Full (std. Medallion)	165	125	127
Landau	148	112	114
Vinyl Body Side Molding	45	34	35

Prices are accurate at time of printing; subject to manufacturer's change.

Interior Trim	Retail Price	Dealer Cost	Low Price
Bench Seat, Vinyl, Split Back W/Center Arm Rest	$ 68	$ 51	$ 52
Leather 60/40 Split Bench Seat			
Le Baron Medallion	283	215	218
Town & Country Wagon	430	327	331
Cloth 60/40 Split Bench Seat, Town & Country			
Wagon	175	133	135
Torqueflite Transmission	193	147	149
Light Package			
Ex. Medallion	84	63	64
Medallion	72	55	56
Deluxe Wiper/Washer Pkg.	47	36	37
Basic Group			
Le Baron 2-Door Coupe	1385	1053	1064
Le Baron 4-Door Sedan	1237	940	950
Salon 2-Door	1319	1003	1014
Salon 4-Dr., T&C Wagon	1172	890	899
Le Baron Medallion 2-Door Coupe	1278	971	981
Le Baron Medallion 4-Door Sedan	1130	859	868
Heavy Duty Package	170	129	131
Deluxe Insulation Pkg.			
Le Baron & Salon 2-Door Coupe & 4-Door Sedan			
W/o Basic Group	93	70	71
Le Baron & Salon 2-Door Coupe & 4-Door Sedan			
W/Basic Group	57	43	44
Town & Country Wagon W/o Basic Group	46	35	36
Town & County Wagon W/Basic Group	10	7	8
Le Baron Medallion 2-Door Coupe & 4-Door			
Sedan W/o Basic Group	34	26	27
Le Baron Medallion 2-Door Coupe & 4-Door			
Sedan W/Basic Group	10	7	8
Air Conditioning	584	444	449
Suregrip Differential Axle	67	51	52
500 AMP Long Life Battery	35	26	27
Front Bumper Guards	24	18	19
Electronic Digital Clock	56	43	44
Rear Window Defroster, Electric	98	74	75
Emission Control System & Testing	87	66	67
Locking Gas Cap	7	6	7
Tinted Glass, All Windows	73	55	56
Cornering Lights	51	38	39
Accessory Floor Mats	25	19	20
Mirrors			
Day/Night, Le Baron	12	9	10
Illuminated Vanity Mirror	50	38	39
Remote Control, Left, Chrome	19	14	15
Remote Control, Right, Chrome	35	27	28
Remote Control, Left & Right, Chrome W/o Basic			
Group	54	41	42
W/Basic Group	35	27	28

Prices are accurate at time of printing; subject to manufacturer's change.

Moldings	Retail Price	Dealer Cost	Low Price
Door Edge Protectors			
2-Door Models	$ 13	$ 10	$ 11
4-Door Models	22	17	18
Pedal Dress-Up	10	7	8
Power Assists			
Power Bench Seat or 60/40 Split Bench Seat, Left	167	127	129
Power Windows			
2-Door Models	137	104	106
4-Door Models	194	147	149
Power Door Locks			
2-Door Models	89	68	69
4-Door Models	124	94	95
Power Deck Lid/Tailgate Release			
All Models Except Wagons	25	19	20
Wagons	25	19	20
Radio & Speakers			
AM	87	66	67
AM W/40 Channel CB Transceiver			
W/o Basic Group	373	284	287
W/Basic Group	287	218	221
AM/FM			
W/o Basic Group	167	127	129
W/Basic Group	80	61	62
AM/FM Stereo, 2 Front & 2 Rear Speakers			
W/o Basic Group	240	183	185
W/Basic Group	154	117	119
AM/FM Stereo W/40 Channel CB Transceiver, 2 Front & 2 Rear Speakers			
W/o Basic Group	527	400	405
W/Basic Group	440	334	338
AM/FM Stereo W/8 Track Stereo Tape, 2 Front & 2 Rear Speakers			
W/o Basic Group	343	261	264
W/Basic Group	256	195	197
AM/FM Stereo W/Electronic Search Tune, 2 Front & 2 Rear Speakers			
W/o Basic Group	368	279	282
W/Basic Group	281	213	216
Rear Speakers Single Radio	26	20	21
Power Antenna	48	37	38
Seat Belts, Dlx	20	15	16
Automatic Speed Control	107	81	82
Station Wagon Items			
Air Deflectors	30	23	24
Luggage Rack	94	71	72
Steering Wheels			
Luxury	20	15	16
Tilt	77	59	60
Leather Covered, 2-Spoke	60	45	46

Prices are accurate at time of printing; subject to manufacturer's change.

	Retail Price	Dealer Cost	Low Price
Leather Covered, 3-Spoke	$ 60	$ 45	$ 46
Sun Roof, Power Operated Glass	827	628	635
"T" Bar Roof...........................	675	513	519
Heavy Duty Suspension...................	28	21	22
Undercoating W/Hood Silencer Pad			
Medallion...........................	25	19	20
Others	36	27	28

CHRYSLER NEWPORT / NEW YORKER

NEWPORT

	Retail	Dealer	Low
4-Door Hardtop.........................	$ 6089	$ 4936	$ 5236

NEW YORKER

4-Door Hardtop.........................	8631	6823	7323

STANDARD EQUIPMENT (included in above prices)

Newport: Safety and protection equipment plus 225 cubic-inch 6-cyl. engine, automatic transmission, power steering, power front disc brakes, splitback cloth-and-vinyl bench seat with center armrest, color-keyed loop-pile carpeting, inside hood release, front and rear bumper guards, dual horns, trip odometer, deluxe wheel covers, BSW radial-ply tires.

New Yorker Brougham: Safety and protection equipment plus 360 cubic-inch 2-bbl. V8 engine, automatic transmission, power steering, power front disc brakes, velour 50/50 divided bench seat with passenger recliner and fold-down dual center armrest, power windows, shag carpeting, color-keyed door handle and mirror appliques, stand-up hood ornament, concealed headlamps, front and rear bumper guards, exterior accent stripes, inside hood release, deluxe washer/wiper package, luxury steering wheel, light package, trip odometer, deluxe wheel covers, electronic digital clock, WSW steel belted radial tires.

NEWPORT / NEW YORKER ACCESSORIES

Engines	Retail	Dealer	Low
NA w/Calif. Emission Syst.			
318 CID V-8 2-bbl., Newport	$ 239	$ 179	$ 181
360 CID V-8 2-bbl. (std. New Yorker)	432	324	328
360 CID V-8 4-bbl. (HD Pkg. Reg.)			
Newport............................	664	498	503
New Yorker..........................	232	174	176
Calif. Emission Syst. Reg.			
318 CID V-8 4-bbl. (NA New Yorker)......	300	225	228
360 CID V-8 4-bbl.			
Newport............................	493	370	374
New Yorker..........................	61	46	47

Prices are accurate at time of printing; subject to manufacturer's change.

	Retail Price	Dealer Cost	Low Price
360 CID V-8 4-bbl. (HD Pkg. Reg.)			
Newport.............................	$ 664	$ 498	$ 503
New Yorker..........................	232	174	176
Vinyl Roof (NA New Yorker)	152	114	116
Fifth Ave. Edition Pkg.			
W/o Basic Group	1500	1125	1137
W/Basic Group	1307	981	991
Vinyl Side Molding......................	51	38	39
Bodyside Tape Upper Stripe	72	54	55
Interior Trim			
Vinyl Bench Seat W/Center Arm Rest	33	25	26
Cloth 60/40 Bench Seat W/Individual Arm Rest, & Passenger Recliner	149	111	113
Vinyl 60/40 Bench Seat W/Front Individual Arm Rests, Rear Integral Center Arm Rest, & Passenger Recliner......................	181	136	138
Leather 60/40 Bench W/Front Individual Arm Rests, Rear Integral Center Arm Rest, & Passenger Recliner......................	287	215	218
Light Pkg.			
Newport.............................	96	72	73
New Yorker..........................	91	68	69
Deluxe Wiper/Washer Pkg.	41	31	32
Basic Group			
Newport.............................	1176	882	891
New Yorker..........................	1098	824	833
Heavy Duty Pkg........................	152	114	116
Air Conditioners			
Manual Control.......................	628	471	476
Automatic Temperature Control			
W/o Basic Group	673	505	511
W/Basic Group.......................	45	34	35
Sure Grip Differential	72	54	55
500 AMP Long Life Battery	35	26	27
Electronic Digital Clock	57	43	44
Rear Window Electric Defroster	105	79	80
Emission Control System & Testing...........	88	66	67
Locking Gas Cap.......................	9	7	8
Cornering Lights.......................	51	38	39
Accessory Floor Mats	26	20	21
Mirrors			
Illuminated Vanity Mirror	50	38	39
Remote Control, Left....................	20	15	16
Remote Control, Right...................	24	18	19
Remote Control Left & Right			
W/o Basic Group	44	33	34
W/Basic Group.......................	24	18	19
Moldings			
Door Edge Protectors	23	17	18
Pedal Dress-Up........................	10	8	9

Prices are accurate at time of printing; subject to manufacturer's change.

Chrysler Cordoba

Chrysler Newport

Chrysler New Yorker

	Retail Price	Dealer Cost	Low Price
Power Assists			
Power Bench or 60/40 Seat, Left 6-Way......	$170	$128	$130
Windows..................................	212	159	161
Door Locks..............................	126	94	95
Deck Lid Release	35	26	27
Radios			
AM....................................	106	80	81
AM W/CB Transceiver			
W/o Basic Group......................	396	297	300
W/Basic Group, Newport...............	290	218	221
W/Basic Grp., New Yorker.............	214	161	163
AM/FM W/o Basic Group................	182	136	138
W/Basic Group (std. New Ykr.).........	76	57	58
AM/FM Stereo			
W/o Basic Group	253	190	192
W/Basic Grp., Newport................	147	110	112
W/Basic Grp., New Yorker.............	71	53	54
AM/FM Stereo W/CB Transceiver & 2 Front, 2 Rear Speakers			
W/o Basic Group	543	407	412
W/Basic Group, Newport...............	437	328	332
W/Basic Grp., New Yorker.............	361	271	274
AM/FM Stereo W/8 Track Tape & 2 Front, 2 Rear Speakers			
W/o Basic Group	360	270	273
W/Basic Group, Newport...............	254	191	193
W/Basic Grp., New Yorker.............	179	134	136
AM/FM Stereo W/Electronic Search Tune, & 2 Front, 2 Rear Speakers			
W/o Basic Group	372	279	282
W/Basic Group, Newport...............	266	200	203
W/Basic Grp., New Yorker.............	191	143	145
Rear Speaker, Single.....................	28	21	22
Power Antenna	50	38	39
Seat Belts, Dlx..........................	21	16	17
Automatic Speed Control	112	84	85
Steering Wheels			
Tilt			
Newport..........................	79	59	60
New Yorker........................	60	45	46
Luxury	20	15	16
Power Sunroof	993	745	753
Suspension			
Heavy Duty Shock Absorbers.............	8	6	7
Heavy Duty Suspension..................	28	21	22
Open Road Handling Pkg.			
Newport..............................	216	162	164
New Yorker............................	194	145	147
Trunk Dress-Up Newport	67	50	51
Undercoating W/Hood Silencer Pad	30	23	24

Prices are accurate at-time of printing; subject to manufacturer's change.

Dodge Magnum

Dodge Omni

Dodge St. Regis

Dodge

DODGE ASPEN

ASPEN	Retail Price	Dealer Cost	Low Price
2-Door Sport Coupe	$3968	$3493	$3693
4-Door Sedan	4069	3582	3832
2-Seat Wagon	4445	3913	4163

STANDARD EQUIPMENT (included in above prices)

Aspen Sedan: Safety and protection equipment plus 225 cubic-inch 1-bbl. 6-cylinder engine, 3-speed manual transmission W/floor shift, bright windshield and head lamp surround moldings, bright roof drip-rail moldings, hubcaps, BSW polyester tires, front ashtray, coat hooks, directional signals, color-keyed passenger compartment carpeting, trunk mat, hazard warning flashers, heater/defroster, single horn, instrument panel safety padding, lane-change features in turn-signal switch, headlight switch and wiper switch lights, brake system warning lights, backup lights, dome light, parking brake warning light, side market lights, interior light switch, inside rearview mirror, manual left outside chrome mirror, 2-way manual front seat adjustment, unibelt passenger restraint system, 2-spoke padded steering wheel W/soft horn button, and 2-speed windshield wipers.
Aspen Coupe adds bright quarter window moldings.
Aspen Wagon adds BSW glass-belted tires, liftgate and fold-down second seat, heavy-duty suspension and liftgate ajar warning system (less trunk mat).

ASPEN ACCESSORIES

Engines			
225 CID 6-Cyl. 2 bbl.	$ 43	$ 35	$ 36
318 CID 8-Cyl. 2 bbl.	216	179	181
360 CID 8-Cyl. 4 bbl. H.D.			
Except Wagons	600	498	503
Wagons	575	477	482
318 CID 8-Cyl. 4 bbl.	271	225	228
Transmissions			
Automatic	319	265	268
4-Spd. Manual	149	124	126
Vinyl Roof			
Full	95	79	80
Halo — Includes Belt Mounting W/o Decor Group, Custom Exterior Pkg., or Special Edition Exterior Pkg.	111	93	94

Prices are accurate at time of printing; subject to manufacturer's change.

CONSUMER GUIDE

	Retail Price	Dealer Cost	Low Price
W/R/T Decor Group, Custom Exterior Pkg., or Special Edition Exterior Pkg.............	$ 95	$ 79	$ 80
Landau..............................	174	144	146
Vinyl Body Side Molding — Black	41	34	35
Interior Trim			
Bucket Seat — Vinyl W/Cent. Cushion & C.A.R.	107	89	90
Light Pkg.	46	38	39
Basic Group			
Cpe. W/o Any Sunrise Pkg................	712	591	597
Cpe. W/Sunrise Coupe Pkg..............	667	554	560
Cpe. W/oSunrise Cpe. Pkg. & Sunrise Decor Pkg.	626	520	526
Sedan & Wagon	712	591	597
Sunrise Coupe Pkg.			
W/Qtr. Window Louvers.................	60	50	51
W/o Qtr. Window Louvers	30	25	26
Sport Package, Wagon.................	630	523	529
Sunrise Decor Pkg.....................	90	75	76
Handling & Performance Pkg., Cpe............	218	181	183
R/T Package, Cpe.	651	540	546
Protection Group			
2-Door Sport Coupe	30	25	26
Other Models	38	32	33
Heavy Duty Pkg.........................	157	130	132
Deluxe Insulation Pkg.			
W/o Basic Group or Custom Int. Pkg.	50	41	42
W/Basic Group or Custom Int. Pkg..........	39	33	34
Custom Int. Pkg. W/ Bench Seat, Vinyl			
W/o Basic Group	191	159	161
W/Basic Group	181	150	152
Custom Int. Pkg. W/Bench Seat, Cloth & Vinyl			
W/o Basic Group	162	134	136
W/Basic Group	151	126	128
Custom Int. Pkg. W/ 60/40 Bench Seat, Vinyl & Center Cushion,			
W/Folding Arm Rest W/o Basic Group	196	163	165
W/Basic Group.........................	186	154	156
Ex. Wagons:			
Special Ed. Int. Pkg. W/Bucket Seat, Vinyl & Center Cushion W/Folding Arm Rest,			
W/o Basic Group	402	334	338
W/Basic Group.........................	375	311	315
Special Ed. Int. Pkg. W/60/40 Split Bench Seat, Vinyl W/C.A.R. & Passenger Recliner,			
W/o Basic Group	442	367	371
W/Basic Group.........................	415	344	348
Special Ed. Int. Pkg. W/60/40 Split Bench Seat, Cloth W/C.A.R. & Passenger Recliner,			
W/o Basic Group	499	414	419
W/Basic Group	471	391	395

Prices are accurate at time of printing; subject to manufacturer's change.

Wagons:	Retail Price	Dealer Cost	Low Price
Special Ed. Int. Pkg. W/Bucket Seat, Vinyl & Center Cushion			
W/Folding Arm Rest, W/o Basic Group.......	$ 286	$ 237	$ 240
W/Basic Group..................	275	228	231
Special Ed. Int. Pkg. W/60/40 Split Bench Seat, Cloth & Vinyl W/C.A.R. & Passenger Recl.			
W/o Basic Group................	326	270	273
W/Basic Group..................	315	262	265
Custom Exterior Pkg.			
2-Door Sport Coupe & 4-Door Sedan	75	62	63
2-Seat Wagon	89	74	75
Special Ed. Ext. Pkg.			
2-Door Sport Coupe	134	111	113
4-Door Sedan	165	137	139
Special Ed. Wagon Woodgrain Group..........	232	192	194
Two-Tone Paint Pkg..................	142	118	120
Two-Tone Decor Pkg.			
Coupe	65	54	55
Sedan	96	80	81
Wagon	78	65	66
Air Conditioning	507	421	426
Arm Rest Rear W/Ash Tray	12	10	11
Optional Axle Ratio..................	18	15	16
Sure Grip Differential Axle	61	51	52
500 Amp — Long Life Battery	32	26	27
Bumper Protection			
Bumper Guards-Front & Rear	43	36	37
Protective Rub Strips-Front & Rear	34	28	29
Cigarette Lighter....................	7	5	6
Electronic Digital Clock	51	43	44
Console	55	46	47
Rear Window Defogger			
Blower Type	52	43	44
Electrically Heated	90	74	75
California Emission System...............	79	66	67
Locking Gas Cap....................	7	6	7
Tinted Glass			
All Windows	61	50	51
Windshield Only	43	35	36
Inside Hood Release	13	11	12
Dual Horns......................	9	7	8
Glove Box Lock	5	4	5
Accessory Floor Mats	23	19	20
Mirrors			
Day/Night — Inside..................	11	9	10
Remote Control — Left — Chrome	17	14	15
Remote Control Left & Right — Chrome			
W/o Basic Group	49	41	42
W/Basic Group	32	27	28

Prices are accurate at time of printing; subject to manufacturer's change.

	Retail Price	Dealer Cost	Low Price
Remote Control — Left & Right — Chrome, Dual Sport Styled			
W/o Basic Group	$ 61	$ 51	$ 52
W/Basic Group........................	44	36	37
Remote Control — Left & Right — Painted, Dual Sport Styled			
W/o Basic Group	61	51	52
W/Basic Group........................	44	36	37
Moldings			
Belt..................................	16	14	15
Upper Door Frame	31	26	27
Wheel Lip............................	22	18	19
Pedal Dress-Up........................	9	8	9
Power Assists			
Power Steering........................	156	129	131
Power Disc Brakes — Front.............	72	60	61
Power Seat — Left W/Bucket or 60/40 Split Bench Seat............................	153	127	129
Power Door Locks			
2-Door Models	76	63	64
4-Door Models	106	88	89
Power Windows			
2-Door Models	120	100	102
4-Door Models	169	141	143
Radios & Speakers			
AM...................................	79	66	67
AM W/40 Channel CB Trans.			
W/o Basic Group	342	284	287
W/Basic Group.......................	262	218	221
AM/FM			
W/o Basic Group	153	127	129
W/o Basic Group	73	61	62
AM W/8 Track Stereo Tape W/2 Front, 2 Rear Speakers			
W/o Basic Group	231	192	194
W/Basic Group.......................	152	126	128
AM/FM Stereo W/2 Front, 2 Rear Speakers			
W/o Basic Group	220	183	185
W/Basic Group.......................	141	117	119
AM/FM Stereo W/40 Channel CB Trans.			
W/o Basic Group	482	400	405
W/Basic Group.......................	403	334	338
AM/FM Stereo W/8 Track Stereo Tape W/2 Front, 2 Rear Speaker			
W/o Basic Group	314	261	264
W/Basic Group.......................	235	195	197
Single Rear Speaker	24	20	21
Seat Belts	18	15	16
Automatic Speed Control	98	81	82

Prices are accurate at time of printing; subject to manufacturer's change.

	Retail Price	Dealer Cost	Low Price
Station Wagon Items			
Air Deflectors..........................	$ 28	$ 23	$ 24
Car Compartment Carpet & Storage Bin......	53	44	45
Luggage Rack..........................	86	71	72
Pwr. Tailgate Release	23	19	20
Steering Wheels			
Luxury..............................	31	26	27
"Tuff"...............................	39	32	33
Tilt	71	59	60
Heavy-Duty Suspension...................	25	21	22
"T" Bar Roof..........................	600	498	503
Trunk Dress-Up	43	36	37
Undercoating W/Hood Silencer Pad	33	27	28
W/Basic Group Custom Int. Pkg., Special Ed.			
Pkg. & Deluxe Insulation Pkg............	23	19	20
Deluxe Windshield Wipers.................	36	30	31

DODGE DIPLOMAT

DIPLOMAT

2-Door Coupe	$ 4901	$ 4120	$ 4420
4-Door Sedan..........................	4999	4202	4502

DIPLOMAT SALON

2-Door	5138	4319	4619
4-Door	5366	4510	4810
Wagon	5769	4849	5149

DIPLOMAT MEDALLION

2-Door Coupe	5612	4717	5017
4-Door Sedan..........................	5840	4908	5208

STANDARD EQUIPMENT (included in above prices)

Diplomat: Safety and protection equipment plus 225 cubic-inch 1-bbl. Super Six-cylinder engine, 4-speed manual transmission, power steering, power front disc/rear drum brakes, stand-up hood ornament, chrome-plated grille, bright-framed dual rectangular headlamps, integrated bumper styling, dual protective front bumper rub strips, rear bumper guards and rub strip, bright roof drip moldings (2-doors), bright quarter-window moldings (2-doors), bright upper door frame moldings (4-doors and wagons), wide body sill moldings, sill molding extensions on lower front fender and rear quarter panel, bright belt moldings, lower deck panel stripe (4-doors), wraparound taillamps, backup lamps, space saving spare tire, BSW fiberglass-belted radial-ply tires, under-hood silencer pad, cloth-and-vinyl bench seat, door-pull straps, one-piece cloth-covered headliner, sun visors (2-doors), rich woodtone trim on instrument cluster and glove box door, glove box door lock, windshield header-mounted reading lamps (2-doors) and color-keyed carpeting.

Diplomat Salon: Diplomat equipment plus dual horns, full vinyl roof (4-door), day/night mirror, wheel covers, upgrade trim.

Prices are accurate at time of printing; subject to manufacturer's change.

Salon Wagon: Diplomat equipment plus teakwood bodyside and liftgate applique W/bodyside gold accent stripe, all-vinyl split-back bench seat W/fold-down center armrest, carpeting and steel skid strips on cargo floor, covered lockable storage bins (less sill molding extensions and space saving spare tire).

Diplomat Medallion: Diplomat & Salon equipment plus premium wheel covers, dual chrome quarter-window stripes and body side accent (2-doors), tape stripes, left-hand remote-control outside mirror, 60/40 front cloth split-bench seats W/reclining passenger seat and fold-down center armrest, fold-down rear armrest (4-doors), courtesy lights, upper assist handles (4-doors), central pillar assist handles (2-doors), rear pillar vanity lamps (4-doors), map reading lamp, trunk dress-up package and color-keyed carpeting.

DIPLOMAT ACCESSORIES

	Retail Price	Dealer Cost	Low Price
Engines			
318 CID 8-Cyl. 2-bbl.	$ 236	$ 179	$ 181
360 CID 8-Cyl. 2-bbl.	426	324	328
360 CID 8-Cyl. 4-bbl.	487	370	374
318 CID 8-Cyl. 4-bbl.	296	225	228
360 CID 8-Cyl. 4-bbl., Heavy Duty	655	498	503
Torque Flite Transmission.	193	147	149
Vinyl Roof-Full.	165	125	127
Vinyl Roof-Landau	148	112	114
Vinyl Body Side Molding	45	34	35
Hood Tape Stripe.	24	18	19
Interior Trim			
Vinyl Bench Seat, Split Back W/Center Arm Rest, Diplomat			
2-Door Coupe & 4-Door Sedan Models Only . . .	67	51	52
Leather 60/40 Split Bench W/C.A.R. & Passenger Recliner,			
Diplomat Medallion Models Only.	283	215	218
Leather 60/40 Split Bench W/C.A.R. & Passenger Recliner,			
Diplomat 2-Seat Wagon Only.	430	327	331
Cloth 60/40 Split Bench W/C.A.R. & Passenger Recliner,			
Diplomat 2-Seat Wagon Only.	175	133	135
Light Package			
Ex. Medallion	84	63	64
Diplomat Medallion Models Only.	72	55	56
Deluxe Wiper/Washer Package	47	36	37
Basic Group			
Diplomat 2-Door Coupe	1385	1053	1064
Diplomat 4-Door Sedan	1238	940	950
Diplomat Salon Cpe.	1319	1003	1014
Diplomat Salon Sdn., Wagon.	1172	890	899
Diplomat Medallion 2-Door Coupe	1278	971	981
Diplomat Medallion 4-Door Sedan	1130	859	868
Heavy Duty Package.	170	129	131
Deluxe Insulation Package			
Diplomat & Salon 2-Door Coupe & 4-Door Sedan			
W/o Basic Group	93	71	72
W/Basic Group	57	43	44

Prices are accurate at time of printing; subject to manufacturer's change.

	Retail Price	Dealer Cost	Low Price
2-Seat Wagon			
W/o Basic Group	$ 46	$ 35	$ 36
W/Basic Group	10	7	8
Diplomat Medallion 2-Door Coupe & 4-Door Sedan			
W/o Basic Group	34	26	27
W/Basic Group	10	7	8
Air Conditioning	584	444	449
Suregrip Differential Axle	67	51	52
500 AMP Long Life Battery	35	26	27
Front Bumper Guards	24	18	19
Electronic Digital Clock	56	43	44
Rear Window Electrically Heated Defroster	98	74	75
California Emission Control System	87	66	67
Locking Gas Cap	7	6	7
Tinted Glass, All Windows	73	55	56
Cornering Lights	51	38	39
Accessory Floor Mats	25	19	20
Mirrors			
Day/Night	12	9	10
Illuminated Vanity Mirror	48	38	39
Remote Control, Left, Chrome	19	14	15
Remote Control, Right, Chrome	35	27	28
Remote Control, Left & Right, Chrome			
W/o Basic Group	54	41	42
W/Basic Group	35	27	28
Door Edge Protectors			
2-Door Models	13	10	11
4-Door Models	22	17	18
Pedal Dress-Up	10	8	9
Power Bench Seat or 60/40 Split Bench Seat, Left	167	127	129
Power Windows			
2-Door Models	137	104	106
4-Door Models	194	147	109
Power Door Locks			
2-Door Models	89	68	69
4-Door Models	124	94	95
Power Deck Lid/Tailgate Release			
Models Except Wagons	25	19	20
Wagons Only	25	19	20
Radio Equipment			
AM	87	66	67
AM W/40 Channel CB Trans.			
W/o Basic Group	373	284	287
W/Basic Group	287	218	221
AM/FM			
W/o Basic Group	167	127	129
W/Basic Group	80	61	62
AM/FM Stereo W/2 Front & 2 Rear Speakers			
W/o Basic Group	240	183	185

Prices are accurate at time of printing; subject to manufacturer's change.

	Retail Price	Dealer Cost	Low Price
W/Basic Group	$ 153	$ 117	$ 119
AM/FM Stereo W/40 Channel CB Tran. W/2 Front & 2 Rear Speakers			
W/o Basic Group	527	400	405
W/Basic Group	440	334	338
AM/FM Stereo W/8 Track Stereo Tape W/2 Front & 2 Rear Speakers			
W/o Basic Group	343	261	264
W/Basic Group	256	195	197
AM/FM Stereo W/Electronic Search Tune, W/2 Front & 2 Rear Speakers			
W/o Basic Group	368	279	282
W/Basic Group	281	213	216
Single Rear Speakers	26	20	21
Power Antenna.........................	48	37	38
Color-Keyed Seat Belts	20	15	16
Automatic Speed Control.................	107	81	82
Air Deflectors, Station Wagon Only	30	23	24
Luggage Rack, Station Wagon Only..........	94	71	72
Steering Wheels			
Luxury	20	15	16
Tilt................................	77	59	60
Leather Covered, 2-Spoke	60	45	46
Leather Covered, 3-Spoke	60	45	46
Power Operated Sunroof, Glass	827	628	635
"T" Bar Roof...........................	675	513	519
Heavy-Duty Suspension	28	21	22
Undercoating...........................	36	27	28

DODGE MAGNUM XE

MAGNUM XE

	Retail Price	Dealer Cost	Low Price
2-Door Specialty Hardtop	$ 5709	$ 4798	$ 5098

STANDARD EQUIPMENT (included in above prices)

Magnum XE: Safety and protection equipment plus 318 cubic-inch 2-bbl. V8 engine, power front disc/rear drum brakes, TorqueFlite automatic transmission W/selector lever quadrant light, power steering, front and rear ashtrays, bumper guards, cigarette lighter, cleaner air system, coat hooks, directional signals, color-keyed shag carpeting, vinyl trunk mat, glove box lock, hazard warning flashers, heater/defroster, inside hood release, dual horns, dual rectangular headlamps, instrument panel W/simulated wood-tone trim, instrument panel safety padding, lane-change signal in turn signals, illuminated headlight W/wiper switch, brake system warning lights, backup lights, dome light, parking brake warning light, park/turn and side marker lights, interior light switch, day/night mirror, manual left outside chrome mirror, 2-way manual front seat adjustment, unibelt passenger restraint system, deluxe 2-spoke steering wheel, space saving spare tire, upper-level ventilation, deluxe wheel covers, 2-speed electric windshield wiper/washers and BSW glass-belted radial-ply tires.

Prices are accurate at time of printing; subject to manufacturer's change.

MAGNUM XE ACCESSORIES

	Retail Price	Dealer Cost	Low Price
Engines			
360 CID 8-Cyl. 2 2-bbl. — E.L.B.	$ 191	$145	$147
360 CID 8-Cyl. 4-bbl.	251	191	193
318 CID 8-Cyl. 4-bbl.	61	46	47
360 CID 8-Cyl. 4-bbl. H.D.	420	319	323
Light Package	29	22	23
Basic Group			
W/ 318 CID Eng.	1018	774	782
W/ 360 CID Eng.	1054	801	810
Heavy Duty Pkg.	150	114	116
Two-Tone Paint Pkg.			
W/o Basic Grp.	221	168	170
W/Basic Grp.	203	154	156
Roadability Pkg.	29	22	23
Gran Touring Pkg.			
W/o Basic Grp., W/360 Eng.	579	440	445
W/o Basic Grp., W/318 Eng.	601	457	462
W/Basic Grp. & 360 Eng.	528	401	406
W/Basic Grp. & 318 Eng.	550	418	423
Air Conditioning	584	443	448
Auto. Temp. Air Cond.			
W/o Basic Grp.	628	477	482
W/Basic Grp.	44	34	35
Sure Grip Differential Axle	67	51	52
500 Amp Long Life Battery	35	26	27
Front & Rear Protective Rub Strips	37	28	29
Electronic Digital Clock	56	43	44
Console			
W/o Velour & Vinyl Bucket Seats or Leather Trim			
Bucket Seats	103	78	79
W/Velour & Vinyl Bucket Seats or Leather Trim			
Bucket Seats	60	46	47
Ctr. Front Cushion W/Folding Arm Rest	43	33	34
Electric Rear Window Defroster	98	74	75
Emission Control System	87	66	67
Locking Gas Cap	7	6	7
Tinted Glass			
All Windows	73	55	56
Windshield Only	47	35	36
Accessory Floor Mats	25	19	20
Illuminated Vanity Mirror	50	38	39
Remote Control Mirrors			
Left Chrome.	19	14	15
Left & Right Chrome			
W/o Basic Group	54	41	42
W/Basic Group	35	27	28
Dual Sport Styled — Chrome or Painted			
W/o Basic Group	66	51	52

Prices are accurate at time of printing; subject to manufacturer's change.

	Retail Price	Dealer Cost	Low Price
W/Basic Group	$ 48	$ 36	$ 37
Moldings			
Door Edge Protector	13	10	11
Wheel Lip Flares	102	78	79
Pedal Dress-Up	10	8	9
Power Assists			
Pwr. Bucket or 60/40 Split Bench Seat-Left....	167	127	129
Pwr. Windows	137	104	106
Pwr. Door Locks	89	68	69
Pwr. Deck Lid Release	26	20	21
Radio			
AM	87	66	67
AM W/40 Ch. CB Trans.			
W/o Basic Group	373	284	287
W/Basic Group	287	218	221
AM/FM			
W/o Basic Group	167	127	129
W/Basic Group	80	61	62
AM W/8 Track Stereo Tape & Front & 2 Rear Spkrs.			
W/o Basic Group	252	192	194
W/Basic Group	166	126	128
AM/FM Stereo W/2 Front & 2 Rear Spkrs.			
W/o Basic Group	240	183	185
W/Basic Group	154	117	119
AM/FM Stereo W/40 Ch. CB Trans., 2 Front & 2 Rear Spkrs.			
W/o Basic Group	527	400	405
W/Basic Group	440	334	338
AM/FM Stereo W/8 Track Stereo Tape, 2 Front & 2 Rear Spkrs.			
W/o Basic Group	343	261	264
W/Basic Group	256	195	197
AM/FM Stereo W/Search Tune, 2 Front & 2 Rear Spkrs.			
W/o Basic Group	368	279	282
W/Basic Group	281	213	216
Single Rear Speaker	26	20	21
Power Antenna	48	37	38
Seat Belts, Dlx.	20	15	16
Automatic Speed Control	107	81	82
Steering Wheels			
Luxury	20	15	16
Tilt	77	59	60
Leather Covered—2- or 3-Spoke	60	45	46
Power Operated Sun Roof	546	415	420
"T" Bar Roof	675	513	519
Suspension			
Heavy Duty Shock Absorber	8	6	7

Prices are accurate at time of printing; subject to manufacturer's change.

	Retail Price	Dealer Cost	Low Price
Heavy Duty Suspension............	$ 28	$ 21	$ 22
Tachometer..................	72	56	57
Trunk Dress-Up	47	36	37
Fender Mounted Turn Signals ...	16	12	13
Undercoating W/Hood Silence Pad.	36	27	28
Deluxe Windshield Wipers.......	40	30	31
Landau Vinyl Roof..............	132	100	102
Vinyl Side Molding.............	45	34	35
Tape Stripe			
Wheel Lip............	24	18	19
Hood & Deck	47	36	37
Body Side	47	36	37

DODGE OMNI

OMNI

	Retail Price	Dealer Cost	Low Price
2+2 Hatchback (024)	$4482	$4012	$4312
4-Door Hatchback	4122	3690	3940

STANDARD EQUIPMENT (included in above prices)

Omni: Safety and protection equipment plus 1.7 litre 4-cyl. 2-bbl. engine, 4-speed manual transmission, disc front brakes, AM radio (AM/FM on 2+2), vinyl bodyside molding on 4-Dr., protective bumper rub strips on 4-Dr., glove box lock on 2+2, belt, drip rail, sill and wheel lip moldings on 2+2, wheel trim rings on 2+2, P165/75R-13 whitewall glass belted radial tires (P155/80R-13 on 4-Dr.).

OMNI ACCESSORIES

	Retail Price	Dealer Cost	Low Price
Automatic Transmission	$319	$265	$268
Vinyl Bodyside Mldg., 2+2	41	34	35
Tape Stripe, 4-Dr.	70	58	59
Interior Trim, Cloth & Vinyl Bucket Seats	22	18	19
Light Pkg.			
2+2	31	26	27
4-Dr..................	46	38	39
Popular Equip. Grp.			
2+2	267	222	225
4-Dr..................	279	231	234
Sport/Classic Two-Tone Paint Pkg.			
2+2	164	136	138
4-Dr..................	114	94	95
Custom Interior Pkg.			
4-Dr. w/Vinyl Buckets.....	79	66	67
4-Dr. w/Cloth & Vinyl Buckets	101	84	85
Premium Int. Pkg.			
2+2 w/Vinyl Buckets.....	146	121	123
2+2 w/Cloth & Vinyl Buckets........	173	144	146

Prices are accurate at time of printing; subject to manufacturer's change.

	Retail Price	Dealer Cost	Low Price
4-Door w/Cloth & Vinyl Buckets..............	$ 270	$ 224	$ 227
Sport Pkg., 2 + 2			
W/o Popular Equip. Grp.....................	340	282	285
W/Popular Equip. Grp......................	278	231	234
Rally Equipment Pkg., 2 + 2			
W/o Sport Pkg.	340	282	285
W/Sport Pkg.............................	177	147	149
W/Spt. Pkg. & Pop. Equip.	177	147	149
W/Spt. Classic Two-Tone Paint	352	292	295
Custom Exterior Pkg., 4-Dr.	74	62	63
Premium Exterior Pkg.			
2 + 2	78	65	66
4-Dr. w/o Two-Tone Paint, Pop. Equip.			
or Tape Stripe	178	148	150
4-Dr. w/Tape Stripe	199	165	167
4-Dr. w/Tape Stripe & Pop. Equip............	158	131	133
4-Dr. w/Two-Tone Paint	163	135	137
4-Dr. w/Two-Tone Paint & Pop. Equip.........	122	101	103
4-Dr. w/Popular Equip. Grp.	137	114	116
Premium Woodgrain Pkg.			
4-Dr. w/o Pop. Equip.....................	331	275	278
4-Dr. w/Pop. Equip.	290	241	244
Air Conditioning............................	507	421	426
Optional Axle Ratio	18	15	16
Maintenance-Free Battery	20	16	17
Bumper Guards, 2 + 2	43	36	37
Bumper Rub Strips, 4-Dr.	34	28	29
Cargo Comp. Dress-Up & Sound Insulation	43	36	37
Front Storage Console	22	18	19
Shift Lever Console	32	26	27
Electric Clock	28	23	24
Calif. Emission Syst.	79	66	67
Locking Gas Cap	7	6	7
Tinted Glass			
All	61	50	51
Windshield Only	43	35	36
Flip-Out Quarter Windows, 2 + 2	54	45	46
Dual Horns	9	7	8
Glove Box Lock, 4-Dr........................	5	4	5
Luggage Rack..............................	86	71	72
Mirrors			
Day/Night	11	9	10
Remote Control Left, 4-Dr.	17	14	15
Remote Control L&R, 4-Dr.			
W/o Pop. Equip. Grp.....................	49	41	42
W/Pop. Equip. Grp.	32	27	28
Sport, Dual Remote, 2 + 2.	61	51	52
Moldings			
Belt, 4-Dr................................	16	14	15

Prices are accurate at time of printing; subject to manufacturer's change.

	Retail Price	Dealer Cost	Low Price
Door Edge			
2+2	$ 12	$ 10	$ 11
4-Dr.	20	17	18
Drip Rail, 4-Dr.	18	15	16
Sill, 4-Dr.	20	17	18
Upper Door Frame, 4-Dr.	31	26	27
Wheel Lip, 4-Dr.	28	23	24
Power Assists			
Brakes	72	60	61
Steering	156	129	131
Rally Instrument Cluster, 2+2	76	63	64
Radio Equipment			
AM/FM, 4-Dr.	73	61	62
AM/FM Stereo			
2+2	67	56	57
4-Dr.	141	117	119
Rear Speaker	24	20	21
Deluxe Seat Belts	31	26	27
Rear Deck Spoiler, 2+2	53	44	45
Luxury Steering Wheel, 4-Dr.	18	15	16
Sun Roof	176	146	148
Heavy-Duty Suspension, 4-Dr.	25	21	22
Sport Suspension, 2+2	41	34	35
Rear Tonneau Cover, 2+2	44	37	38
Undercoating	33	27	28
Rear Window Washer/Wiper, 4-Dr.	62	51	52

DODGE ST. REGIS

ST. REGIS

	Retail	Dealer	Low
4-Door Hardtop	$6216	$5038	$5388

STANDARD EQUIPMENT (included in above prices)

Charger SE: Safety and protection equipment plus 225 CID 2-bbl. 6-cyl. engine, Torque-Flight automatic transmission, power front disc/rear drum brakes, cigarette lighter, heater/defroster, coat hooks, directional signals, color-keyed carpeting, trunk mat, lockable glove box, hazard warning flashers, inside hood release, dual horns, instrument panel W/safety padding and simulated woodtone trim, lane change features in turn signal, headlight switch W/foot operated hi-low beam control, windshield wiper control, brake system warning light, backup lights, parking brake warning light, transmission gear selector lever light, side marker lights and reflectors, fender-mounted turn-signal indicators, day/night inside rearview mirror, driver's side chrome mirror, hood ornament, window and body moldings, keyless door locking system, power steering, unibelt passenger restraint system, deluxe 2-spoke steering wheel, space saving spare tire, deluxe wheel covers, 2-speed electric windshield wipers/washers, tinted glass, deluxe door trim panels, BSW glass-belted radial-ply tires, deluxe sound package and antisway bars.

Prices are accurate at time of printing; subject to manufacturer's change.

ST. REGIS ACCESSORIES

	Retail Price	Dealer Cost	Low Price
Engines			
318 CID V-8 2-bbl.	$ 239	$ 179	$ 181
360 CID 8-Cyl. 2-bbl.	432	324	328
360 CID 8-Cyl. 4-bbl.	664	498	503
318 CID 8-Cyl. 4-bbl.	300	225	228
360 CID 8-Cyl. 4-bbl.	493	370	374
Vinyl Roofs Full —	152	114	116
Vinyl Side Molding	51	38	39
Interior Trims			
Vinyl Split Bench Seats W/Ctr. Cushion, Arm Rest	33	25	26
Light Pkg.	96	72	73
Basic Group	1176	882	891
Heavy Duty Pkg.	152	114	116
Air Conditioning	628	471	476
Auto. Temp. Air Cond.			
W/o Basic Grp.	673	505	511
W/Basic Grp.	45	34	35
Sure Grip Differential Axle	72	54	55
500 Amp Long Life Battery	35	26	27
Electronic Digital Clock	57	43	44
Electric Rear Window Defroster	105	79	80
Emission Control System & Testing	88	66	67
Locking Gas Cap	9	7	8
Accessory Floor Mats	26	20	21
Illuminated Vanity Mirror	50	38	39
Remote Control Mirrors			
Left, Chrome	20	15	16
Left & Right, Chrome			
W/o Basic Group	44	33	34
W/Basic Group	24	18	19
Molding			
Door Edge Protectors	23	17	18
Pedal Dress-Up	10	8	9
Power Assists			
Pwr. Seat — Left	170	128	130
Pwr. Windows	212	159	161
Pwr. Door Locks	126	94	95
Pwr. Deck Lid Release	35	26	27
Radios & Speakers			
AM	106	80	81
AM W/40 Channel CB Trans.			
W/o Basic Group	396	297	300
W/Basic Group	290	218	221
AM/FM			
W/o Basic Group	182	136	138
W/Basic Group	76	57	58
AM/FM Stereo, 2 Front & 2 Rear Spkrs.			
W/o Basic Group	253	190	192
W/Basic Group	147	110	112

Prices are accurate at time of printing; subject to manufacturer's change.

	Retail Price	Dealer Cost	Low Price
AM/FM Stereo W/40 Channel CB Trans., 2 Front & 2 Rear Spkrs.			
W/o Basic Group	$ 543	$ 407	$ 412
W/Basic Group	437	328	332
AM/FM Stereo W/8 Tract Stereo Tape, 2 Front & 2 Rear Speakers			
W/o Basic Group	360	270	273
W/Basic Group	254	191	193
AM/FM Stereo W/Search Tune, 2 Front & 2 Rear Speakers			
W/o Basic Group	372	279	282
W/Basic Group	266	200	203
Single Rear Speaker	28	21	22
Pwr. Antenna	50	38	39
Seat Belts, Dlx.	21	16	17
Automatic Speed Control	112	84	85
Steering Wheels			
Luxury	19	15	16
Tilt	79	59	60
Leather Covered — 2- or 3-Spoke	60	45	46
Power Operated Sun Roof	993	745	753
Suspension			
Heavy Duty Shock Absorbers	8	6	7
Heavy Duty Suspension	28	21	22
Open Road Handling Pkg.	216	162	164
Trunk Dress-Up	67	50	51
Undercoating W/Hood Silencer Pad	30	23	24
Deluxe Windshield Wipers	41	31	32

Plymouth

PLYMOUTH HORIZON

HORIZON

	Retail Price	Dealer Cost	Low Price
2+2 Hatchback (TC3)	$ 4482	$ 4012	$ 4312
4-Door Hatchback	4122	3690	3940

STANDARD EQUIPMENT (included in above prices)

Horizon: Safety and protection equipment plus 1.7 litre 4-cyl. 2-bbl. engine, 4-speed manual transmission, disc front brakes, AM radio (AM/FM on 2+2), vinyl bodyside molding on 4-Dr., protective bumper rub strips on 4-Dr., glove box lock on 2+2, belt, drip rail, sill and wheel lip moldings on 2+2, wheel trim rings on 2+2, P165/75R-13 whitewall glass belted radial tires (P155/80R-13 on 4-Dr.).

Prices are accurate at time of printing; subject to manufacturer's change.

HORIZON ACCESSORIES

	Retail Price	Dealer Cost	Low Price
Automatic Transmission	$319	$265	$268
Vinyl Body Side Mldg., 2 + 2	41	34	35
Tape Stripe, 4-Dr.	70	58	59
Interior Trim, Cloth & Vinyl Bucket Seats	22	18	19
Light Pkg.			
2 + 2	31	26	27
4-Dr..	46	38	39
Popular Equip. Grp.			
2 + 2	267	222	225
4-Dr..	279	231	234
Sport/Classic Two-Tone Paint Pkg.			
2 + 2	164	136	138
4-Dr..	114	94	95
Custom Interior Pkg.			
4-Dr. w/Vinyl Buckets.	79	66	67
4-Dr. w/Cloth & Vinyl Buckets	101	84	85
Premium Int. Pkg.			
2 + 2 w/Vinyl Buckets.	146	121	123
2 + 2 w/Cloth & Vinyl Buckets	173	144	146
4-Door w/Cloth & Vinyl Buckets.	270	224	227
Sport Pkg., 2 + 2			
W/o Popular Equip. Grp..	340	282	285
W/Popular Equip. Grp..	278	231	234
Rally Equipment Pkg., 2 + 2			
W/o Sport Pkg.	340	282	285
W/Sport Pkg..	177	147	149
W/Spt. Pkg. & Pop. Equip.	177	147	149
W/Spt. Classic Two-Tone Paint	352	292	295
Custom Exterior Pkg., 4-Dr.	74	62	63
Premium Exterior Pkg.			
2 + 2	78	65	66
4-Dr. w/o Two-Tone Paint, Pop. Equip.			
or Tape Stripe	178	148	150
4-Dr. w/Tape Stripe	199	165	167
4-Dr. w/Tape Stripe & Pop. Equip..	158	131	133
4-Dr. w/Two-Tone Paint	163	135	137
4-Dr. w/Two-Tone Paint & Pop. Equip..	122	101	103
4-Dr. w/Popular Equip. Grp.	137	114	116
Premium Woodgrain Pkg.			
4-Dr. w/o Pop. Equip..	331	275	278
4-Dr. w/Pop. Equip..	290	241	244
Air Conditioning.	507	421	426
Optional Axle Ratio	18	15	16
Maintenance-Free Battery	20	16	17
Bumper Guards, 2 + 2	43	36	37

Prices are accurate at time of printing; subject to manufacturer's change.

	Retail Price	Dealer Cost	Low Price
Bumper Rub Strips, 4-Dr.	$ 34	$ 28	$ 29
Cargo Comp. Dress-Up & Sound Insulation	43	36	37
Front Storage Console	22	18	19
Shift Lever Console	32	26	27
Electric Clock	28	23	24
Calif. Emission Syst.	79	66	67
Locking Gas Cap	7	6	7
Tinted Glass			
All	61	50	51
Windshield Only	43	35	36
Flip-Out Quarter Windows, 2+2	54	45	46
Dual Horns	9	7	8
Glove Box Lock, 4-Dr.	5	4	5
Luggage Rack	86	71	72
Mirrors			
Day/Night	11	9	10
Remote Control Left, 4-Dr.	17	14	15
Remote Control L&R, 4-Dr.			
W/o Pop. Equip. Grp.	49	41	42
W/Pop. Equip. Grp.	32	27	28
Sport, Dual Remote, 2+2	61	51	52
Moldings			
Belt, 4-Dr.	16	14	15
Door Edge			
2+2	12	10	11
4-Dr.	20	17	18
Drip Rail, 4-Dr.	18	15	16
Sill, 4-Dr.	20	17	18
Upper Door Frame, 4-Dr.	31	26	27
Wheel Lip, 4-Dr.	28	23	24
Power Assists			
Brakes	72	60	61
Steering	156	129	131
Rally Instrument Cluster, 2+2	76	63	64
Radio Equipment			
AM/FM, 4-Dr.	73	61	62
AM/FM Stereo			
2+2	67	56	57
4-Dr.	141	117	119
Rear Speaker	24	20	21
Deluxe Seat Belts	31	26	27
Rear Deck Spoiler, 2+2	53	44	45
Luxury Steering Wheel, 4-Dr.	18	15	16
Sun Roof	176	146	148
Heavy-Duty Suspension, 4-Dr.	25	21	22
Sport Suspension, 2+2	41	34	35
Rear Tonneau Cover, 2+2	44	37	38
Undercoating	33	27	28
Rear Window Washer/Wiper, 4-Dr.	62	51	52

Prices are accurate at time of printing; subject to manufacturer's change.

PLYMOUTH VOLARÉ

VOLARÉ	Retail Price	Dealer Cost	Low Price
2-Door Sport Coupe	$ 3956	$3482	$3732
4-Door Sedan.	4057	3571	3821
2-Seat Wagon.	4433	3902	4152

STANDARD EQUIPMENT (included in above prices)
Volaré: Safety and protection equipment plus 225 cubic-inch 1-bbl. 6-cylinder engine, 3-speed manual transmission, front disc brakes, low-back bench seats with applied head restraints, color-keyed carpeting, electronic ignition, isolated transverse suspension system, electronic voltage regulator, front sway bar. BSW polyester tires.
Volaré Wagon adds 225 cubic-inch 2-bbl. 6-cylinder engine, power front disc brakes, cargo area stowage bins.

VOLARÉ ACCESSORIES

	Retail Price	Dealer Cost	Low Price
Engines			
225 CID 6 Cyl. 2-bbl.	$ 43	$ 35	$ 36
318 CID 8 Cyl. 2-bbl.	216	179	181
360 CID 8 Cyl. 4-bbl.			
W/o Road Runner Pkg. or Heavy Duty Pkg.	600	498	503
W/Road Runner Pkg. or Heavy Duty Pkg.	575	477	482
Wagons.	575	477	482
318 CID 8 Cyl. 4-bbl.	271	225	227
Transmissions			
TorqueFlite	319	265	268
4-Speed Manual Floor Shift O/Drive.	149	124	126
Light Package	46	38	39
Basic Group			
Cpe. w/o Any Duster Pkg.	712	591	597
Cpe. w/Duster Pkg.	667	554	560
Cpe. w/Duster Cpe-Pkg. &			
Decor Pkg.	626	520	526
Sedan & Wagon	712	591	597
Protection Group			
2-Door Sport Coupe Only	30	25	26
Other Models.	38	32	33
Heavy Duty Package.	157	130	132
Deluxe Insulation Package			
W/o Basic Group or Custom Interior Pkg.	50	41	42
W/Basic Group or Custom Interior Pkg.	39	33	34
Custom Interior Package			
Vinyl Bench Seat			
W/o Basic Group	191	159	161
W/Basic Group	181	150	152
Cloth & Vinyl Bench Seat			
W/o Basic Group	162	134	136
W/Basic Group	151	126	128

Prices are accurate at time of printing; subject to manufacturer's change.

	Retail Price	Dealer Cost	Low Price
60/40 Split Bench Seat, Center Cushion W/Folding Arm Rest			
W/o Basic Group	$ 196	$ 163	$ 165
W/Basic Group	186	154	156
Premier Interior Package, coupe			
Vinyl Bucket Seat, Center Cushion W/Folding Arm Rest			
W/o Basic Group	402	334	338
W/Basic Group	375	311	315
Vinyl 60/40 Split Bench Seat W/Passenger Recliner			
W/o Basic Group	442	367	371
W/Basic Group	415	344	348
Cloth 60/40 Split Bench Seat W/Passenger Recliner			
W/o Basic Group	499	414	419
W/Basic Group	471	391	395
Premier Interior Pkg., Wagon			
Vinyl Bucket Seat, Center Cushion W/Folding Arm Rest			
W/o Basic Group	285	237	240
W/Basic Group	275	228	231
Vinyl 60/40 Split Bench Seat W/Passenger Recliner			
W/o Basic Group	326	270	273
W/Basic Group	315	262	265
Custom Exterior Package			
2-Door Sport Coupe & 4-Door Sedan	75	62	63
2-Seat Wagon	89	74	75
Premium Exterior Package			
2-Door Sport Coupe	112	93	94
4-Door Sedan	144	119	121
Premier Wagon Woodgrain Group	232	192	195
Two-Tone Paint Package	142	118	120
Road Runner Package	651	540	546
Duster Decor Group	90	75	76
Duster Coupe Pkg.			
W/Qtr. Window Louvers	60	50	51
W/o Qtr. Window Louvers	30	25	26
Sport Pkg., Wagon	630	523	529
Road Runner Handling & Perf. Pkg.	218	181	183
Air Conditioning	507	421	426
Rear Arm Rest W/Ash Tray	12	10	11
Axle Ratio, Optional	18	15	16
Sure Grip Differential Axle	61	51	52
500 AMP Long Life Battery	32	26	27
Front & Rear Bumper Guards	43	36	37
Front & Rear Protective Rub Strips	34	28	29
Cigarette Lighter	7	5	6
Electronic Digital Clock	51	43	44

Prices are accurate at time of printing; subject to manufacturer's change.

	Retail Price	Dealer Cost	Low Price
Console.................................	$ 55	$ 46	$ 47
Rear Window Defogger	52	43	44
Rear Window Defroster	90	74	75
Emission Control System & Testing	79	66	67
Locking Gas Cap	7	6	7
Glass			
Tinted, All Windows......................	61	50	51
Tinted, Windshield Only	43	35	36
Inside Hood Release........................	13	11	12
Dual Horns	9	7	8
Glove Box Lock	5	4	5
Accessory Floor Mats	23	19	20
Mirrors			
Day/Night, Inside.........................	11	9	10
Remote Control, Left, Chrome	17	14	15
Remote Control, Left & Right, Chrome			
W/o Basic Group	49	41	42
W/Basic Group	32	27	28
Remote Control, Lef & Right, Chrome, Dual Sport Styled			
W/o Basic Group	61	51	52
W/Basic Group	44	36	37
Remote Control, Left & Right, Painted, Dual Sport Styled			
W/o Basic Group	61	51	52
W/Basic Group	44	36	37
Moldings			
Belt	16	14	15
Door Edge Protectors			
2-Door Sport Coupe	12	10	11
4-Door Sedan & 2-Seat Wagon............	20	17	18
Upper Door Frame	31	26	27
Wheel Lip	22	18	19
Pedal Dress-Up	9	8	9
Power Assists			
Power Steering...........................	156	129	131
Power Disc Brakes, Front	72	60	61
Power Seat, Left W/Bucket or 60/40 Split Bench Seat	153	127	129
Power Door Locks			
2-Door Models.........................	76	63	64
4-Door Models.........................	106	88	89
Power Windows			
2-Door Models.........................	120	100	102
4-Door Models.........................	169	141	143
Radio & Speakers			
AM	79	66	67
AM W/40 Channel CB Transceiver			
W/o Basic Group	342	284	287
W/Basic Group	262	218	221

Prices are accurate at time of printing; subject to manufacturer's change.

	Retail Price	Dealer Cost	Low Price
AM/FM			
W/o Basic Group	$153	$127	$129
W/Basic Group	73	61	62
AM W/8 Track Stereo Tape, 2 Front & 2 Rear Speakers			
W/o Basic Group	231	192	194
W/Basic Group	152	126	128
AM/FM Stereo, 2 Front & 2 Rear Speakers			
W/o Basic Group	220	183	185
W/Basic Group	141	117	119
AM/FM Stereo W/40 Channel CB Transceiver 2 Front & 2 Rear Speakers			
W/o Basic Group	482	400	405
W/Basic Group	403	334	338
AM/FM Stereo W/8 Track Stereo Tape, 2 Front & 2 Rear Speakers			
W/o Basic Group	314	261	264
W/Basic Group	235	195	197
Rear Speaker, Single	24	20	21
Seat Belts Dlx.	18	15	16
Automatic Speed Control.	98	81	82
Station Wagon Items			
Air Deflectors	28	23	24
Cargo Compartment Carpet & Stowage Bin	53	44	45
Luggage Rack.	86	71	72
Power Tailgate Release.	23	19	20
Steering Wheels			
Luxury	31	26	27
"Tuff"	39	32	33
Tilt Steering Wheel.	71	59	60
Heavy Duty Suspension	25	21	22
"T" Bar Roof.	600	498	503
Trunk Dress-Up	43	36	37
Undercoating W/Hood Silencer Pad			
W/o Basic Group, Custom Interior Pkg., Premier Interior Pkg., or Deluxe Insulation Pkg.	33	27	28
W/Basic Group, Custom Interior Pkg., Premier Interior Pkg., or Deluxe Insulation Pkg.	23	19	20
Deluxe Windshield Wipers.	36	30	31
Vinyl Roof			
Full	95	79	80
Halo			
W/o Road Runner, Custom Exterior Pkg. or Premium Exterior Pkg.	111	93	94
W/Road Runner, Custom Exterior Pkg. or Premium Exterior Pkg.	95	79	80
Landau.	174	144	146
Vinyl Body Side Molding, Black	41	34	35
Interior Trim			
Vinyl Bucket Seat W/Center Cushion	107	89	90
Vinyl Bench.	30	25	26

Prices are accurate at time of printing; subject to manufacturer's change.

Ford Motor Company

FORD FAIRMONT

	Retail Price	Dealer Cost	Low Price
FAIRMONT			
2-Dr. Sedan	$3710	$3229	$3429
4-Dr. Sedan	3810	3316	3516
Station Wagon	4157	3618	3868
FUTURA			
Coupe	4071	3543	3793

STANDARD EQUIPMENT (included in above prices)

Fairmont: Safety and protection equipment plus 2.3 litre (140 CID) 4-cyl. engine, 4-speed manual transmission, disc front brakes, single note horn, hub caps, carpeting, fold-down rear seat on wagon, B78-14 blackwall bias ply tires (CR78-14 blackwall steel belted radial tires on wagon), carpet.

Futura Coupe: Fairmont equipment plus, unique front-end treatment w/dual rectangular headlights, wrapover roof pillar, cut-pile carpeting, color-keyed seat belts, deluxe steering wheel, luggage compartment light, sound insulation package.

FAIRMONT ACCESSORIES

Engines			
3.3 Litre (200 CID) 6-cyl.	$241	$205	$208
5.0 Litre (302 CID) V-8	524	445	450
Automatic Transmission			
Ex. Wagon (incl. radial tires)	401	341	345
Wagon	307	261	264
Exterior Accent Group	82	70	71
Interior Accent Group			
Sedans	80	68	69
Wagon	84	72	73
Air Conditioner	484	412	417
Heavy-Duty Battery	18	15	16
Lower Bodyside Protection			
w/Ext. Accent Grp.	30	26	27
Others	42	36	37
Front License Bracket	NC	NC	NC
Power Brakes	70	59	60
Deluxe Bumper Group	57	48	49

Prices are accurate at time of printing; subject to manufacturer's change.

	Retail Price	Dealer Cost	Low Price
Rear Bumper Guards......................	$ 20	$ 17	$ 18
Electric Clock...........................	20	17	18
Convenience Group.......................			
Futura Coupe	33	28	29
Others	65	55	56
Power Decklid Release	22	18	19
Exterior Decor Group	223	189	191
Interior Decor Group.....................			
Futura Coupe w/Sports Grp.	170	144	146
Wagon w/Squire Option................	195	166	168
Wagon w/o Squire Option	280	238	241
Sedans...............................	311	264	267
Mud/Stone Deflectors	23	19	20
Rear Window Defogger	51	43	44
Electric Rear Window Defroster	90	77	78

Prices are accurate at time of printing; subject to manufacturer's change.

Ford Fairmont

Ford Fairmont

	Retail Price	Dealer Cost	Low Price
Calif. Emission System	$ 76	$ 65	$ 66
High Altitude Emission System	33	28	29
ES Option	329	280	283
Floor Shift	31	27	28
Futura Sports Group	102	87	88
Ghia Option			
Futura Coupe	207	176	178
Others	498	423	428
Tinted Glass	59	50	51
Instrumentation Group	77	66	67
Light Group			
2-Drs. w/Open Air Roof	27	23	24
4-Dr. Sedan w/Open Air Roof	31	27	28
2-Drs. w/o Open Air Roof, Wagon	39	33	34
4-Dr. Sedan w/o Open Air Roof	43	37	38
Power Door Locks			
2-Doors	73	62	63
4-Doors	101	86	87
Luggage Rack, Wagon	76	65	66
Dual Mirrors			
Futura Coupe, Squire Wag., Others w/Ext. Grp.	37	32	33
Others	43	37	38
Bodyside Molding	39	33	34
Rocker Panel Molding	25	22	23
Wide Bodyside Molding	41	35	36
Metallic Glow Paint	48	41	42
Tu-Tone Paint	51	43	44
Special Tu-Tone Paint			
w/Ext. Decor Grp. or Ghia Opt.	51	43	44
Futura Coupe	89	76	77
w/Ext. Accent Group	176	150	152
Others	207	176	178
Protection Appearance Group			
2-Drs. w/Front License Bracket	40	34	35
4-Drs. w/Front License Bracket	47	40	41
2-Drs. w/F&R License Bracket	36	31	32
4-Drs. w/F&R License Bracket	43	37	38
Radio Equipment			
AM	72	61	62
AM w/8-Track Tape	192	163	165
AM/FM	120	102	104
AM/FM Stereo	176	150	152
AM/FM Stereo w/Cassette or 8-Track	243	207	210
Radio Flexibility Option	93	79	80
Premium Sound System	67	57	58
Full or Half Vinyl Roof	90	77	78
Open Air Flip-up Roof	199	169	171
Bench Seat (Credit)	(72)	(61)	(61)

Prices are accurate at time of printing; subject to manufacturer's change.

	Retail Price	Dealer Cost	Low Price
Power Seat..............................	$ 94	$ 80	$ 81
Bucket Seat............................	72	61	62
Speed Control			
w/Int. Decor Grp., ES Opt. or Tilt Steering ...	104	88	89
Others..............................	116	98	99
Squire Option, Wagon....................	399	339	343
Power Steering.........................	149	127	129
Sport Steering Wheel....................	39	33	34
Tilt Steering Wheel			
w/Int. Decor Grp. or ES Opt.............	69	58	59
Others..............................	81	69	70
Lockable Stowage Box, Wagon............	20	17	18
Accent Stripe..........................	28	24	25
Handling Suspension.....................	41	35	36
Trim			
Cloth & Vinyl Bench (Base level)........	20	17	18
Cloth & Vinyl Seat (Accent level).......	42	36	37
Vinyl Seat...........................	24	20	21
Vent Louvers...........................	35	30	31
Deluxe Wheel Covers....................	37	32	33
Bright Window Frames...................	18	15	16
Power Windows			
2-Doors.............................	116	98	99
4-Doors.............................	163	138	140
Manual Front Vent Windows...............	48	41	42
Interval Wipers.........................	35	30	31
Rear Window Wiper/Washer...............	63	53	54

FORD GRANADA

GRANADA

	Retail Price	Dealer Cost	Low Price
2-Dr. Sedan	$4342	$3693	$3943
4-Dr. Sedan...........................	4445	3780	4030
2-Dr. Ghia Sedan.......................	4728	4020	4320
4-Dr. Ghia Sedan.......................	4830	4107	4407
2-Dr. ESS Sedan.......................	4888	4157	4457
4-Dr. ESS Sedan.......................	4990	4244	4544

STANDARD EQUIPMENT (included in above prices)

Granada: Safety and protection equipment plus 4.1 litre (250 CID) 6-cyl. engine, 4-speed manual transmission w/floor shifter, disc front brakes, DR78-14 blackwall steel belted radial tires, single note horn, turn-signal-mounted washer/wiper control, carpet, wheel covers, lighter, flight bench seat.

Granada Ghia: Granada equipment plus ER78-14 blackwall steel belted radial tires, deluxe sound package, dual note horn, remote control left mirror, color-keyed wheel covers, seat-back map pockets, carpeted lower door panels, carpeted trunk, day/night mirror.

Granada ESS: Granada equipment plus FR78-14 blackwall steel belted radial tires, *Prices are accurate at time of printing; subject to manufacturer's change.*

deluxe sound package, wide wheellip molding, deluxe bumper group, black exterior treatments, color-keyed wheel covers, dual color-keyed mirrors, bucket seats, upgraded carpet, deluxe belts, luggage compartment trim, day/night mirror.

GRANADA ACCESSORIES

	Retail Price	Dealer Cost	Low Price
5.0 Litre (302 CID) V-8 Engine	$ 283	$ 241	$ 244
Automatic Transmission	307	261	264
Automatic Temp. Air Conditioner	555	472	477
Manual Control Air Conditioner	514	437	442
Heavy-Duty Battery	18	15	16
Deluxe Belts	19	16	17
Lower Bodyside Protection	30	26	27
Front License Bracket	NC	NC	NC
Power Brakes	70	59	60
Deluxe Bumper Group	78	67	68
Digital Clock	47	40	41
Cold Weather Group			
w/Air Cond. & Rear Defroster	30	26	27
Others	60	51	52
Console	99	84	85
Convenience Group, w/Floor Shift			
2-Dr. w/o Bucket Seats, 4-Dr.	54	46	47
2-Dr. w/Bucket Seats	86	73	74
2-Dr. Ghia & ESS w/Bucket Seats	66	56	57
Other Ghia or ESS	35	30	31
Convenience Group, w/o Floor Shift			
2-Dr. w/o Buckets, 4-Dr.	63	53	54
2-Dr. w/Buckets	94	80	81
2-Dr. Ghia & ESS w/Bucket Seats	75	64	65
Other Ghia or ESS	43	37	38
Interior Decor Group	211	179	181
Remote Control Decklid Release	22	18	19
Mud/Stone Deflectors	23	19	20
Rear Window Defogger	51	43	44
Electric Rear Window Defroster	90	77	78
Calif. Emission System	76	65	66
High Altitude Emission System	33	28	29
Floor Shift	31	27	28
Tinted Glass	64	54	55
Heavy-Duty Group			
w/Air Cond. & Elec. Rear Defroster	18	15	16
w/Air Cond.	48	41	42
Others	60	51	52
Illuminated Entry System	52	44	45
Cornering Lamps	43	37	38
Light Group			
Base 4-Dr. Sedan	46	39	40
Others	41	35	36

Prices are accurate at time of printing; subject to manufacturer's change.

	Retail Price	Dealer Cost	Low Price
Power Door Locks			
2-Doors	$ 78	$ 67	$ 68
4-Doors	110	93	94
Dual Sport Mirrors			
Base Granada.	63	53	54
Ghia.	46	39	40
Right Illuminated Visor Vanity Mirror.	36	31	32
Bodyside Accent Molding.	43	37	38
Vinyl Insert Bodyside Molding.	39	33	34
Rocker Panel Molding.	25	22	23
Moonroof, Power.	899	764	772
Metallic Glow Paint	48	41	42
Tu-Tone Paint/Tape Option	163	138	140
Protection Group, w/Front License Bracket			
2-Dr. Granada or ESS.	40	34	35
4-Dr. Granada or ESS.	47	40	41
Ghia.	28	24	25
Protection Group, w/o Front License Bracket			
2-Dr. Granada or ESS.	36	31	32
4-Dr. Granada or ESS.	43	37	38
Ghia.	24	20	21
Radio Equipment			
AM.	72	61	62
AM w/Stereo 8-Track.	192	163	165
AM/FM.	135	115	117
AM/FM Stereo.	176	150	152
AM/FM Stereo w/8-Track Tape.	243	207	210
AM/FM Stereo Search	319	271	274
CB.	270	229	232
AM/FM Stereo w/Cassette Tape	243	207	210
AM/FM Stereo w/Quadrasonic 8-Track	365	310	319
Radio Flexibility Option.	93	79	80
Full Vinyl Roof.	106	90	91
Half Vinyl Roof.	106	90	91
4-Way Manual Driver's Seat	34	29	30
4-Way Power Seat.	94	80	81
Speed Control			
Base Granada.	116	98	99
Ghia or ESS.	104	88	89
Power Steering	155	132	134
Tilt Steering Wheel	69	58	59
Bodyside/Decklid Stripes	36	31	32
Heavy-Duty Suspension	20	17	18
Trim			
Cloth & Vinyl Flight Bench Seat	54	46	47
Leather Seat.	271	230	233
Visibility Group			
Granada w/Visor Vanity & Sport Mirrors	11	9	10
Granada w/Sport Mirrors.	16	13	14
Granada w/Visor Vanity Mirror	65	55	56

Prices are accurate at time of printing; subject to manufacturer's change.

CONSUMER GUIDE

	Retail Price	Dealer Cost	Low Price
Granada ex. above	$ 70	$ 59	$ 60
Ghia w/Sport Mirrors, ESS	5	4	5
Ghia w/Visor Vanity Mirror	37	32	33
Ghia ex. above	42	36	37
Deluxe Wheel Covers, Base Granada	41	35	36
Wire Wheel Covers			
Base Granada.	108	92	93
Ghia or ESS.	67	57	58
Cast Aluminum Wheels (4)			
Base Granada.	289	246	249
Ghia or ESS.	248	211	214
Styled Steel Wheels w/Trim Rings (4)			
Base Granada.	124	105	107
Ghia or ESS.	83	71	72
Power Windows			
2-Doors	120	102	104
4-Doors	171	145	147

FORD LTD

FORD LTD

2-Dr. Sedan.	$ 5813	$ 4653	$ 4953
4-Dr. Sedan.	5913	4733	5033
FORD LTD LANDAU			
2-Dr. Sedan.	6349	5082	5432
4-Dr. Sedan.	6474	5181	5531
LTD STATION WAGONS			
LTD Wagon.	6122	4900	5200
LTD Country Squire.	6615	5295	5645

STANDARD EQUIPMENT (included in above prices)

LTD: Safety and protection equipment plus 5.0 litre (302 CID) V-8 engine, automatic transmission, power steering, power brakes, FR78-14 blackwall steel belted radial tires (GR78-14 on wagon), steering column-mounted wiper/washer and headlight dimmer controls, inflatable spare tire, carpeting, single note horn, LTD sound package.
LTD Landau: LTD equipment plus unique grille w/dual rectangular headlights, electric clock, deluxe door trim panels, upgraded sound package, deluxe belts.

FORD LTD ACCESSORIES

5.8 Litre (351 CID) V-8 Engine	$ 263	$ 205	$ 208
Auto. Temp. Air Conditioner	642	501	507
Manual Control Air Conditioner	597	466	471
Optional Axle Ratio	18	14	15
Heavy-Duty Battery	21	16	17
Deluxe Belts	24	18	19
Lower Bodyside Protection			
Country Squire.	46	36	37

Prices are accurate at time of printing; subject to manufacturer's change.

	Retail Price	Dealer Cost	Low Price
Others	$ 33	$ 26	$ 27
Front License Bracket	NC	NC	NC
Front or Rear Bumper Guards	26	21	22
Bumper Rub Strips	54	42	43
Electric Clock, LTD	24	18	19
Electronic Digital Clock			
LTD Landau, Country Squire	32	25	26
Others	55	43	44
Convenience Group			
Landau w/Int. Lux. Grp.	68	53	54
Country Squire w/Int. Lux. Grp.	83	65	66
LTD Sedans	84	66	67
LTD Wagons	99	77	78
Rear Window Defogger	57	44	45
Electric Rear Window Defroster	100	78	79
Calif. Emission System	83	65	66
High Altitude Emission System	36	28	29
Exterior Accent Group			
LTD Wag. w/Tu-Tone Paint/Tape	29	23	24
LTD Wagon ex. above	61	47	48
LTD Sedans w/Tu-Tone Paint/Tape	34	27	28
LTD Sedans ex. above	66	51	52
Tinted Glass	83	65	66
Dual Note Horn	9	7	8
Illuminated Entry System	57	44	45
Interior Luxury Group			
LTD Landau	705	550	556
Country Squire	758	591	597
Cornering Lamps	49	38	39
Light Group			
LTD Landau, Country Squire	32	25	26
LTD 2-Door	36	28	29
LTD 4-Door & Wagon	41	32	33
Power Lock Group			
2-Drs. w/Convenience Grp.	87	68	69
2-Drs. w/o Convenience Grp.	112	87	88
4-Drs. or Wags. w/Conv. Grp.	121	94	95
4-Dr. Sedans w/o Conv. Grp.	146	114	116
Wagons w/o Cong. Grp.	161	125	127
Deluxe Luggage Rack	113	88	89
Luggage Compartment Trim			
Landau or Others w/Ext. Acc. Grp.	41	32	33
Others	46	36	37
Illuminated Visor Vanity Mirror			
W/Convenience Group	36	28	29
Others	41	32	33
Left Remote Control Mirror	18	14	15
Dual Remote Control Mirrors			
Landau, Country Squire	37	29	30

Prices are accurate at time of printing; subject to manufacturer's change.

	Retail Price	Dealer Cost	Low Price
Others	$ 55	$ 43	$ 44
Rocker Panel Molding......................	29	23	24
Vinyl Insert Bodyside Molding...............	43	34	35
Metallic Glow Paint	64	50	51
Tu-Tone Paint/Tape Treatment			
LTD Sedans & Wagon....................	118	92	93
LTD Landau, Country Squire..............	86	67	68
Protection Group			
2-Drs. w/o Front License Bracket............	46	36	37
4-Drs. w/o Front License Bracket............	51	40	41
2-Drs. w/Front License Bracket	50	39	40
4-Drs. w/Front License Bracket	55	43	44
Radio Equipment			
AM	79	62	63
AM/FM	132	103	105
AM/FM Stereo	192	150	152
AM/FM Stereo w/Cassette or 8-Track	266	207	210
AM/FM Stereo Search w/Quadrasonic Tape......	432	337	341
CB	295	230	233
Premium Sound System			
w/Stereo Search Radio	158	123	125
W/AM/FM Stereo Radios.................	74	57	58
Dual Rear Speakers	46	36	37
Power Antenna........................	47	37	38
Radio Flexibility Option	105	82	83
Full or Half Vinyl Roof	143	112	114
Flight Bench Seat.........................	99	77	78
Power Seat, Single Control	164	128	130
Power Seats, Dual Control	329	257	260
Seat Recliner, Dual Flight Bench	58	45	46
Split Bench Seats w/Man. Pass. Recliner			
LTD Sedans, Wagons	233	182	184
LTD Landau...........................	187	146	148
Dual Facing Rear Seats			
LTD Wagon w/o Light Grp..................	149	116	118
Country Squire or LTD Wag. w/Light Grp........	145	113	115
Air Adjustable Shock Absorbers	54	42	43
Deluxe Sound Pkg.........................	55	43	44
Luxury Sound Pkg.........................	42	33	34
Speed Control			
W/Int. Luxury Grp.......................	113	88	89
Others	126	99	100
Tilt Steering Wheel.........................	76	60	61
Handling Suspension.......................	42	33	34
Heavy-Duty Suspension	22	17	18
Conventional Spare Tire	13	10	11
Trailer Towing Package			
Wagons..............................	161	125	127
Sedans	192	150	152

Prices are accurate at time of printing; subject to manufacturer's change.

	Retail Price	Dealer Cost	Low Price
Trim			
Duraweave Vinyl Seat	$ 53	$ 41	$ 42
All-Vinyl Seat	26	21	22
Luxury Wheel Covers	64	50	51
Wire Wheel Covers	145	113	115
Power Windows			
2-Doors	137	107	109
Others	203	158	160

FORD LTD II

	Retail Price	Dealer Cost	Low Price
LTD II S			
2-Door Hardtop	$ 5198	$ 4317	$ 4617
4-Door Hardtop	5298	4400	4700
LTD II			
2-Door Hardtop	5445	4522	4822
4-Door Hardtop	5569	4625	4925
LTD II BROUGHAM			
2-Door Hardtop	5780	4800	5100
4-Door Hardtop	5905	4904	5204

STANDARD EQUIPMENT (included in above prices)

LTD II S: Safety and protection equipment plus 5.0 litre (302 CID) V-8 engine, automatic transmission, power steering, power brakes, flight bench seat, HR78-14 blackwall steel belted radial tires, single note horn, base level sound package, hub caps, carpet, lighter, trunk mat, day/night mirror.

LTD II: LTD II S equipment plus, rocker panel and wheellip molding, upgraded sound package, stand-up hood ornament, high level door trim, opera windows (2-door).

LTD II Brougham: LTD II equipment plus deluxe sound package, dual note horn, deluxe steering wheel, high level seat trim, deluxe belts, split bench seat, carpeted lower door panels, wheel covers, electric covers, electric clock, upgrade carpet.

LTD II ACCESSORIES

	Retail Price	Dealer Cost	Low Price
5.8 Litre (351 CID) V-8 Engine	$ 263	$ 205	$ 208
Automatic Temp Air Conditioner	607	473	478
Manual Control Air Conditioner	562	438	443
Traction-Lok Rear Axle	64	50	51
Heavy-Duty Battery	20	15	16
Deluxe Belts	22	17	18
Lower Bodyside Protection			
W/Rocker Panel Moldings	33	26	27
Others	46	36	37
Front License Bracket	NC	NC	NC
Deluxe Bumper Group	63	49	50
Day/Date Clock			
LTD II Brougham	22	17	18
Others	45	35	36

Prices are accurate at time of printing; subject to manufacturer's change.

	Retail Price	Dealer Cost	Low Price
Convenience Group			
2-Drs. w/Bucket Seats & Floor Shift............	$146	$114	$116
Other 2-Drs.	155	121	123
4-Doors.............................	120	93	94
Mud/Stone Deflectors......................	25	20	21
Electric Rear Window Defroster	99	77	78
Calif. Emission System.....................	83	65	66
High Altitude Emission System	36	28	29
Extended Range Fuel Tank...................	33	26	27
Tinted Glass	70	54	55
Dual Note Horn	9	7	8
Illuminated Entry System	57	44	45
Sports Instrumentation Group			
Brougham w/Conv. Grp....................	121	94	95
Others w/Conv. Grp.....................	143	112	114
Brougham w/o Conv. Grp..................	129	101	103
Others w/o Conv. Grp.	151	118	120
Cornering Lamps	49	38	39
Light Group			
2-Doors.............................	51	40	41
4-Doors.............................	57	44	45
Power Lock Group			
2-Doors.............................	111	86	87
4-Doors.............................	143	112	114
Illuminated Visor Vanity Mirror			
W/Conv. Grp..........................	34	27	28
Others	39	31	32
Left Remote Control Mirror	18	14	15
Dual Sport Mirrors			
W/Conv. Grp..........................	9	7	8
W/o Conv. Grp.	68	53	54
Bodyside Molding	42	33	34
Rocker Panel Molding......................	29	23	24
Wide Bodyside Molding			
LTD II..............................	42	33	34
LTD II S	71	55	56
Metallic Glow Paint	64	50	51
Tu-Tone Paint Treatment....................	82	64	65
Protection Group			
2-Drs. w/o Front License Bracket.............	49	38	39
2-Drs. w/Front License Bracket	53	41	42
4-Drs. w/o Front License Bracket.............	57	44	45
4-Drs. w/Front License Bracket	61	47	48
Radio Equipment			
AM	79	62	63
AM/FM	132	103	105
AM/FM Stereo	192	150	152
AM/FM Stereo Search.....................	349	272	275
AM/FM Stereo w/Cassette or 8-Track Tape	266	207	210
AM/FM Stereo w/Quadrasonic 8-Track	399	311	315
CB	295	230	233

Prices are accurate at time of printing; subject to manufacturer's change.

	Retail Price	Dealer Cost	Low Price
Dual Rear Speakers	$ 46	$ 36	$ 37
Radio Flexibility Option	105	82	83
Full or Half Vinyl Roof	116	90	91
Bucket Seats w/Console			
LTD II 2-Dr.	211	164	165
Brougham 2-Dr.	37	29	30
Power Seat, 6-way	163	127	129
Speed Control			
W/Sports Instrumentation Grp.	113	88	89
Others	126	99	100
Sports Appearance Package			
LTD II S 2-Dr.	449	350	354
LTD II 2-Dr.	301	235	238
Sports Touring Package			
LTD II S 2-Dr.	526	411	416
LTD II 2-Dr.	379	296	299
Tilt Steering Wheel.	75	59	60
Heavy Duty Suspension	41	32	33
Trim			
All-Vinyl Seat.	26	21	22
Cloth & Vinyl	26	21	22
Deluxe Wheel Covers	45	35	36
Luxury Wheel Covers			
Brougham.	66	51	52
Others	111	86	87
Opera Windows	54	42	43
Power Windows			
2-Doors.	132	103	105
4-Doors.	187	146	148

FORD MUSTANG

MUSTANG

	Retail Price	Dealer Cost	Low Price
2-Dr. Sedan.	$ 4071	$ 3543	$ 3793
3-Dr. Sedan.	4436	3861	4111
2-Dr. Ghia.	4642	4040	4340
3-Dr. Ghia.	4824	4198	4498

STANDARD EQUIPMENT (included in above prices)

Mustang: Safety and protection equipment plus 2.3 litre (140 CID) 4-cyl. engine, 4-speed manual transmission, disc front brakes, B78-13 blackwall bias ply tires, dual rectangular headlights, full instrumentation w/tachometer, steering column-mounted wiper/washer control and turn signal/horn/headlamp dimmer control, day/night mirror, lighter, high-back bucket seats, deluxe carpeting, carpeted lower door panels, deluxe steering wheel (2-door), sport steering wheel (3-door), fold-down rear seat (3-door), windshield drip, side and rear window moldings, wheel covers (2-door), sport wheels (4) (3-door).

Mustang Ghia: Mustang equipment plus low-back bucket seats, deluxe belts, luxury carpeting, Ghia door trim, sport steering wheel, light group, passenger-assist grab handle, right visor vanity mirror, Ghia sound package, carpeted trunk (2-dr.) belt and
Prices are accurate at time of printing; subject to manufacturer's change.

rocker panel moldings, pin stripes, turbine wheel covers, BR78-14 blackwall steel belted radial tires.

MUSTANG ACCESSORIES

	Retail Price	Dealer Cost	Low Price
Engines			
2.8 Litre 6-cyl.	$ 273	$ 232	$ 235
2.3 Litre 4-cyl Turbocharged	542	461	466
5.0 Litre (302 CID) V-8 (NC w/. Cobra Pkg.).	514	437	442
Automatic Transmission	307	261	264
Exterior Accent Group	72	61	62
Interior Accent Group			
2-Dr. Mustang	120	102	104
3-Dr. Mustang	108	92	93
Air Conditioner	484	412	417
Heavy-Duty Battery	18	15	16
Deluxe Belts (std. Ghia)	20	17	18
Lower Bodyside Protection	30	26	27
Front License Bracket.	NC	NC	NC
Power Brakes	70	59	60
Cobra Package.	1173	997	1007
Cobra Hood Graphics	78	67	68
Console.	140	119	121
Mud/Stone Deflectors.	23	19	20
Electric Rear Window Defroster	84	72	73
Calif. Emission System.	76	65	66
High Altitude System	33	28	29
Sport Tuned Exhaust	34	29	30
Tinted Glass	59	50	51
Light Group			
w/o Open Air Roof	37	32	33
w/Open Air Roof.	25	22	23
Power Lock Group	99	84	85
Left Remote Control Mirror	18	15	16
Dual Remote Mirrors	52	44	45
Bodyside Molding	39	33	34
Rocker Panel Molding.	24	20	21
Wide Bodyside Molding	66	56	57
Metallic Glow Paint	41	35	36
Tu-Tone Paint	78	67	68
Protection Group			
w/Front License Bracket	36	31	32
w/o Front License Bracket.	33	28	29
Radio Equipment			
AM	72	61	62
AM w/Digital Clock.	119	101	103
AM/FM	120	102	104
AM/FM Stereo	176	150	152
AM/FM Stereo w/Cassette or 8-Track Tape.	243	207	209

Prices are accurate at time of printing; subject to manufacturer's change.

	Retail Price	Dealer Cost	Low Price
Premium Sound System	$ 67	$ 57	$ 58
Dual Rear Speakers	42	36	37
Radio Flexibility Option	90	77	78
Open Air Roof	199	169	171
Vinyl Roof	102	87	88
4-Way Manual Driver's Seat	35	30	31
Speed Control			
2-Drs. w/o Sport Option	116	98	99
Others	108	88	89
Sport Option	175	149	151
Power Steering	141	120	122
Leather Wrapped Sport Steering Wheel			
2-Drs. w/o Sport Option	53	45	46
Others	41	35	36
Tilt Steering Wheel			
2-Drs. w/o Sport Option	81	69	70
Others	69	58	59
Handling Suspension	33	28	29
Trim			
Cloth Seat	20	17	18
Cloth Seat (Accent)	29	25	26
Cloth Seat (Ghia)	42	36	37
Leather Seat	282	240	243
Turbine Wheel Covers			
3-Dr. Sedan or w/Sport Option	10	8	9
Other	39	33	34
Forged Aluminum Metric Wheels			
3-Dr. Sedan or w/Sport Option	269	228	231
Ghias	259	220	223
Others	298	253	256
Interval Wipers	35	30	31
Rear Window Wiper/Washer	63	53	54
TRX 190/65R 390 Blackwall Michelin Tires			
Mustang	241	205	207
Ghia	117	99	100

FORD PINTO

PINTO

	Retail Price	Dealer Cost	Low Price
Pony Sedan	$ 3199	$ 2880	$ 3080
Sedan	3629	3158	3358
Runabout	3744	3259	3459
Station Wagon	4028	3505	3755
Squire Station Wagon	4343	3780	4030

STANDARD EQUIPMENT (included in above prices)

Pinto Pony: Safety and protection equipment plus 2.3 litre (140 CID) 4-cyl. engine, 4-speed manual transmission with floor mounted shifter, disc front brakes, A78-13 blackwall bias ply tires, hub caps, high back bucket seats, carpeting.
Prices are accurate at time of printing; subject to manufacturer's change.

Pinto Sedan, Runabout, Wagon: Pony equipment plus AM radio, BR78-13 blackwall radial tires, fold-down rear seat on runabout and wagon, flipper rear side windows on wagon.

Pinto Squire Wagon: Wagon equipment plus woodgrain bodyside and rear paneling, interior decor group W/low-back bucket seats, wheel covers, load floor carpet.

PINTO ACCESSORIES

	Retail Price	Dealer Cost	Low Price
2.8 Litre 6-cyl. 2-bbl. Engine	$273	$232	$235
Automatic Transmission	307	261	264
Accent Group			
W/Convenience Group	5	4	5
W/o Convenience Group	40	34	35
Air Conditioning	484	412	417
Optional Axle Ratio	13	11	12
Heavy-Duty Battery	18	15	16
Lower Bodyside Protection	30	26	27
Front License Bracket	NC	NC	NC
Power Brakes	70	59	60
Deluxe Bumper Group	52	44	45
Cargo Area Cover	28	24	25
Load Floor Carpet	24	20	21
Convenience Group			
Squire Wagon	24	20	21
Wagon	61	52	53
Others	108	92	93
Cruising Package			
Runabout w/4-cyl. Eng., Man. Trans. & Int. Decor Grp.	343	292	295
Runabout w/Auto. Trans. & Int. Decor Grp.	330	281	284
Runabout w/4-cyl. Eng., Man. Trans. w/o Int. Decor Grp.	367	312	316
Runabout w/Auto. Trans. W/o Int. Decor Grp.	354	301	305
Wagon w/Int. Decor Grp.	542	461	466
Wagon W/o Int. Decor Grp.	566	481	486
Cruising Pkg. Tape Delete (credit)	(55)	(47)	(47)
Exterior Decor Group			
Sedan, Runabout	40	34	35
Wagon	20	17	18
Interior Decor Group			
Sedan W/Convenience Group	137	117	119
Sedan W/o Convenience Group	175	149	151
Runabout, Wagon W/Convenience Group	170	144	146
Runabout, Wagon W/o Convenience Group	207	176	178
Mud/Stone Deflectors	23	19	20
Electric Rear Window Defroster	84	72	73
All Glass Rear Door, Runabout	25	22	23
Calif. Emission System	69	58	59
High Altitude Emission System	33	28	29

Prices are accurate at time of printing; subject to manufacturer's change.

	Retail Price	Dealer Cost	Low Price
Tinted Glass	$ 59	$ 50	$ 51
Light Group			
w/Flip-Up Roof	25	22	23
W/o Flip-Up Roof	37	32	33
Roof Luggage Rack	63	53	54
Dual Sport Mirrors	52	44	45
Bodyside Molding	39	33	34
Premium Bodyside Molding			
Pony	48	41	42
Others W/o Exterior Decor Grp	10	8	9
Metallic Glow Paint	41	35	36
Pinto ESS			
Sedan	236	201	204
Runabout	261	222	225
Protection Group			
W/Front License Bracket	36	31	32
W/o Front License Bracket	33	28	29
Radio Equipment			
AM, Pony	65	55	56
AM Delete, Others (credit)	(65)	(55)	(55)
AM w/Digital Clock			
W/Pony	119	101	103
Others	47	40	41
AM W/8-Track Tape			
Pony	192	163	165
Others	119	101	103
AM/FM			
Pony	120	102	104
Others	48	41	42
AM/FM Stereo			
Pony	161	137	139
Others	89	76	77
AM/FM Stereo w/Cassette Tape			
Pony	222	188	190
Others	157	133	135
Radio Flexibility Option	90	77	78
Flip-Up Roof	199	169	171
Four-Way Manual Driver's Seat	35	30	31
Sports Package			
Sedan & Runabout W/4-cyl. Eng. & Man. Trans.	110	93	94
Others	96	82	83
Power Steering	141	120	122
Tape Stripe	76	65	66
Tu-Tone Paint/Tape Treatment	76	65	66
Wire Wheel Covers	99	84	85
Aluminum Forged or Lacy Spoke Wheels (4)			
W/Cruising Pkg.	217	184	186
W/Pinto ESS.	235	200	203
Others	289	246	249

Prices are accurate at time of printing; subject to manufacturer's change.

	Retail Price	Dealer Cost	Low Price
Aluminum White Painted Forged (4)			
W/Cruising Pkg.	$ 235	$ 200	$ 203
W/Pinto ESS	253	215	218
Others	307	261	264
Styled Steel Wheels W/Trim Rings (4)	54	46	47

FORD THUNDERBIRD

THUNDERBIRD

	Retail Price	Dealer Cost	Low Price
2-Dr. Hardtop	$ 5877	$ 4880	$ 5180
Town Landau	8866	7096	7596
Heritage	10687	8552	9552

STANDARD EQUIPMENT (included in above prices)

Thunderbird: Safety and protection equipment plus 5.0 litre (302 CID) V-8 engine, automatic transmission, power steering, GR78-15 blackwall steel belted radial tires, dual note horn, wheel covers, 10-oz. color-keyed carpet, lighter, electric clock, opera windows, trunk mat, AM radio, Flight-bench seat.

Town Landau: Thunderbird equipment plus air conditioning, brushed-aluminum roof wrapover applique, color-keyed hood ornament, cast aluminum wheels, accent paint, wide vinyl-insert bodyside moldings, 6-way power driver's seat, power windows, power door locks, AM/FM stereo-search radio, interior luxury group, 18-oz. cut-pile carpet, day/date clock, luxury sound package, HR78-15 whitewall steel belted radial tires.

Heritage: Town Landau equipment plus split bench seat w/velour cloth, 36-oz. cut-pile carpet, leather-wrapped steering wheel, sports-instrumentation panel w/tachometer, left illuminated visor vanity mirror, color-keyed trunk carpet, molded decklid liner, padded vinyl roof.

THUNDERBIRD ACCESSORIES

	Retail Price	Dealer Cost	Low Price
5.8 Litre (351 CID) V-8 Engine	$ 263	$ 205	$ 208
Auto-Temp. Air Conditioner			
Thunderbird	607	473	478
Landau, Heritage	45	35	36
Manual Control Air Cond., Thunderbird	562	438	443
Heavy-Duty Battery	20	15	16
Deluxe Belts	22	17	18
Lower Bodyside Protection			
W/Rocker Panel Molding	33	26	27
Others	46	36	37
Front License Bracket	NC	NC	NC
Bumper Rub Strips	37	29	30
Day/Date Clock	24	18	19
Convenience Group			
W/Bucket Seats & Floor Shift	108	84	85
Others	117	91	92
Exterior Decor Group			
W/Conv. Grp. or Int. Lux. Grp.	346	270	273
Others	405	316	320

Prices are accurate at time of printing; subject to manufacturer's change.

CONSUMER GUIDE

	Retail Price	Dealer Cost	Low Price
Interior Decor Group	$322	$251	$254
Sports Decor Group			
W/Conv. Grp. or Int. Lux. Grp..	459	358	362
Others	518	404	409
Mud/Stone Deflectors.	25	20	21
Electric Rear Window Defroster	99	77	78
Calif. Emission System.	83	65	66
High Altitude Emission System	36	28	29
Extended Range Fuel Tank.	33	26	27
Tinted Glass	70	54	55
Illuminated Entry System	57	44	45
Sports Instrumentation Group			
Town Landau or w/Int. Lux. Grp..	87	68	69
W/Convenience Grp..	121	94	95
Others	129	101	103
Cornering Lamps.	49	38	39
Light Group.	51	40	41
Power Lock Group	111	86	87
Luggage Compartment Trim.	43	34	35
Interior Luxury Group.	816	636	643
Luxury Sound Insulation Pkg.	30	24	25
Right Illuminated Visor Vanity Mirror			
W/Interior Decor Grp..	34	27	28
Others	39	31	32
Left Remote Mirror.	18	14	15
Dual Sport Mirrors			
W/Conv. Grp. or Int. Lux. Grp..	9	7	8
Others	68	53	54
Moonroof, Power	691	539	545
Metallic Glow Paint	64	50	51
Tu-Tone Paint Treatment.	82	64	65
Protection Group			
W/Front License Bracket.	53	41	42
Others	49	38	39
Radio Equipment			
AM Delete (credit)	(79)	(62)	(62)
AM/FM	53	41	42
AM/FM Stereo	113	88	89
AM/FM Stereo w/8-Track Tape.	187	146	148
AM/FM Stereo Search	270	210	213
AM/FM Stereo w/Cassette Tape			
Thunderbird	187	146	148
Town Landau & Heritage (credit)	(83)	(65)	(65)
AM/FM Stereo w/Quadrasonic Tape			
Thunderbird	320	249	252
Town Landau & Heritage.	50	39	40
CB	295	230	233
Dual Rear Speakers	46	36	37
Power Antenna	47	37	38

Prices are accurate at time of printing; subject to manufacturer's change.

	Retail Price	Dealer Cost	Low Price
Radio Flexibility Option..................	$ 105	$ 82	$ 83
Two-Piece Vinyl Roof	132	103	105
Seat Belt Warning Chime	22	17	18
Power Seat, 6-way	163	127	129
Bucket Seats w/Console			
W/Int. Decor Grp........................	37	29	30
Others	211	164	166
Auto. Seatback Release.....................	36	28	29
Speed Control			
Town Landau or w/Spts. Inst.			
Grp. or Int. Lux. Grp.	113	88	89
Others	126	99	100
Tilt Steering Wheel........................	75	59	60
Heavy-Duty Suspension	22	17	18
Trim			
All-Vinyl Seat..........................	26	21	22
Ultra-Soft Leather			
Heritage	243	190	192
Others	309	241	244
T-Roof Convertible Option..................	747	583	589
Wire Wheel Covers	118	92	93
Power Windows	132	103	105

Lincoln

LINCOLN CONTINENTAL

LINCOLN CONTINENTAL

	Retail Price	Dealer Cost	Low Price
Coupe..................................	$ 10985	$ 8462	$ 9562
Sedan..................................	11200	8628	9628

STANDARD EQUIPMENT (included in above prices)

Lincoln Continental: Safety and protection equipment plus 6.6 litre (400 CID) engine, automatic transmission, power brakes, power steering, power windows, automatic temperature control air conditioning, tinted glass, AM/FM radio w/power antenna, Cartier signed digital clock, whitewall steel belted radial tires, remote control left mirror, cornering lights, luxury wheel covers.

CONTINENTAL ACCESSORIES

	Retail Price	Dealer Cost	Low Price
Appearance Protection Group			
Coupe w/Rear License Frame...............	$ 80	$ 62	$ 63

Prices are accurate at time of printing; subject to manufacturer's change.

	Retail Price	Dealer Cost	Low Price
Coupe w/Front & Rear License Frame.	$ 84	$ 65	$ 66
Sedan w/Rear License Frame.	87	67	68
Sedan w/Front & Rear License Frame	91	70	71
Higher Ratio Axle	23	17	18
Traction-Lok Rear Axle	71	54	55
Heavy-Duty Battery	21	16	17
Front License Bracket.	NC	NC	NC
Four-Wheel Disc Brakes	525	405	410
Defroster Group.	121	93	94
Rear Window Defroster	101	78	79
Garage Door Opener	92	71	72
Headlamp Convenience Group	140	108	110
Illuminated Entry System	65	50	51
Interior Light Group			
W/o Power Moonroof	135	104	106
W/Power Moonroof.	115	88	89
Coach Lights	67	51	52
Map/Dome Light	20	15	16
Lincoln Continental Collector's Series			
Leather Trim	16148	12438	13938
Luxury Cloth Trim	15936	12274	13774
Right Remote Control Mirror	39	30	31
Narrow Vinyl Insert Molding	51	39	40
Premium Bodyside Molding	136	105	107
Moonroof			
Fixed Glass	1088	838	847
Power Glass Panel			
w/Collector Series	555	427	432
W/Town Car/Coupe	1088	838	847
W/Williamsburg Edition	1068	822	831
All Others	1088	838	847
Moondust Paint	201	155	157
Custom Paint Stripes	56	43	44
Power Lock Convenience Group			
Coupe.	120	92	93
Sedan	155	119	121
Lower Bodyside Protection	35	27	28
Radio Equipment			
AM/FM Stereo	144	111	113
AM/FM Stereo w/Stereo Tape			
Ex. w/Collectors Series.	203	156	158
W/Collectors Series (credit)	(204)	(157)	(157)
AM/FM Stereo Search w/Quadrasonic			
Tape.	407	313	317
40 Ch. CB w/Power Antenna	321	247	250
Coach Roof			
W/Town Car/Coupe	285	220	223
W/Williamsburg Edition	352	271	274
Others	580	247	252

Prices are accurate at time of printing; subject to manufacturer's change.

	Retail Price	Dealer Cost	Low Price
Vinyl Roof	$ 228	$ 176	$ 178
Power Seat, 6-way	159	122	124
Power Seat, 6-way w/Recliner	251	193	195
Twin Comfort Power Seat w/Pass. Recliner	580	447	452
Speed Control	140	108	110
Tilt Steering Wheel	81	63	64
Illuminated Outside Thermometer	28	22	23
Town Car Option	1527	1176	1188
Town Coupe Option	1527	1176	1188
Town Car/Coupe Velour Seats, Leather Delete (credit)	(212)	(163)	(163)
Trailer Towing Pkg.	72	54	55
Leather Interior Trim	312	240	243
Wire Wheel Covers	247	190	192
Aluminum Wheels (4)	373	287	290
Turbine Spoke Wheels (4)	373	287	290
Williamsburg Edition Leather w/Vinyl Twin Comfort Seats	1829	1409	1424
Valleao Velour w/Twin Comfort Seats	1617	1245	1258
Interval Wipers	39	30	31

CONTINENTAL MARK V

CONTINENTAL MARK V	$13,067	$10,065	$11,565

STANDARD EQUIPMENT (included in above prices)

Continental Mark V: Safety and protection equipment plus 6.6 litre (400 CID) engine, automatic transmission, four-wheel power disc brakes, power steering, power windows, automatic temperature control air conditioning, twin comfort lounge seats, six-way power driver's seat, AM/FM radio W/power antenna, whitewall steel belted radial tires, tinted glass, inflatable spare tire, remote control left mirror, cornering lights, premium bodyside moldings, luxury wheel covers.

Mark V Collector's Series: Has in addition AM/FM stereo search radio with quadrasonic tape, appearance protection group, carpeted trunk, color-keyed turbine spoke aluminum wheels, defroster group, garage door opener, headlamp convenience group, illuminated entry system, interior light group, interval wipers, miles-to-empty fuel indicator, passenger recliner, power lock convenience group, power lumbar driver seat, power vent windows, remote control right mirror, rocker panel molding, 6-way/6-way power bucket seats W/console or 6-way/6-way power leather twin comfort seat w/passenger recliner, special keys, umbrella, speed control, tilt steering wheel, tool kit, leather bound owner's manual, unique landau vinyl top W/coach lamps and unique paint stripes.

MARK V ACCESSORIES

	Retail Price	Dealer Cost	Low Price
Mark V Collector's Series			
W/Bucket Seats	$21,326	$16,424	$18,424
W/Twin Comfort	20,926	16,116	18,116

Prices are accurate at time of printing; subject to manufacturer's change.

	Retail Price	Dealer Cost	Low Price
Appearance Protection Group			
W/Rear License Frame	$ 80	$ 62	$ 63
W/o Rear License Frame	84	65	66
High Axle Ratio	23	17	18
Traction-Lok Rear Axle	71	54	55
Sure-Track Brakes	313	241	244
Defroster Group	121	93	94
Rear Window Defroster (Avail. & req. N.Y. state)	101	78	79
Miles-To-Empty Fuel Indicator	133	103	105
Garage Door Opener	92	71	72
Headlamp Convenience Group	140	108	110
Illuminated Entry System	65	50	51
Interior Light Group			
W/Power Moonroof	115	88	89
W/o Power Moonroof	135	104	106
Map/Dome Light	20	15	16
Mark V Designer Series			
Bill Blass Model W/Carriage Roof	2775	2137	2159
Bill Blass Model W/Full Vinyl Roof	1809	1393	1407
Cartier Model W/Leather & Vinyl Int.	1945	1498	1512
Cartier Model W/Velour Cloth Int.	1945	1498	1512
Givenchy Model	2145	1652	1669
Pucci Model	1525	1175	1187
Mark V Luxury Groups			
Champagne Group: W/Moondust Paint	843	649	656
W/o Moondust Paint	743	572	578
Cordovan Group: W/Moondust Paint	843	649	656
W/o Moondust Paint	743	572	578
Crystal Blue Group	743	572	578
Dove Grey Group: W/Moondust Paint	843	649	656
W/o Moondust Paint	743	572	578
Gold/Cream Group: W/Moondust Paint	843	649	656
W/o Moondust Paint	743	572	578
Red/Rose Group: W/Moondust Paint	843	649	656
W/o Moondust Paint	743	572	578
Turquoise Group: W/Moondust Paint	843	649	656
W/o Moondust Paint	743	572	578
Wedgewood Blue Group: W/Moondust Paint	843	649	656
W/o Moondust Paint	743	572	578
White Group: W/Moondust Paint	843	649	656
W/o Moondust Paint	743	572	578
Remote Control Right Mirror	39	30	40
Rocker Panel Molding	31	24	25
Moonroof	1088	838	847
Moondust Paint	201	155	157
Custom Paint Stripes	56	43	44
Power Lock Convenience Group	120	92	93
Lower Bodyside Protection	35	27	28
Radio Equipment			
AM/FM Stereo	144	111	113

Prices are accurate at time of printing; subject to manufacturer's change.

	Retail Price	Dealer Cost	Low Price
AM/FM Stereo w/8-Track Tape................	$203	$156	$158
AM/FM Stereo w/Cassette Tape			
All ex. Collector's Series.................	203	156	158
Collector's Series (credit)................	(204)	(157)	(157)
AM/FM Stereo Search W/Quadrasonic			
8-Track Tape........................	407	313	317
CB	321	247	250
Vinyl Roofs			
Carriage	1201	925	935
Full	236	182	184
Landau	513	395	399
Power Lumbar Seat	113	87	88
Power Passenger Seat, 6-way..............	159	122	124
Reclining Passenger Seat	91	70	71
Speed Control	140	108	110
Tilt Steering Wheel.......................	81	63	64
Illuminated Outside Thermometer	28	22	23
Trailer Towing Package			
W/Traction-Lok Axle or Sure-Track Brakes	84	65	66
Others	107	82	83
Leather Interior Trim	333	257	260
Wire Wheel Covers	247	190	192
Aluminum Wheels (4)......................	373	287	290
Turbine Spoke Wheels (4)..................	373	287	290
Power Vent Window	95	73	74
Interval Wipers	39	30	31

LINCOLN VERSAILLES

VERSAILLES

	Retail	Dealer	Low
Sedan.................................	$12939	$9967	$10967

STANDARD EQUIPMENT (included in above prices)

Lincoln Versailles: Safety and protection equipment plus 5.0 litre (302 CID) V-8 engine, automatic transmission, four-wheel power disc brakes, power steering, power windows, automatic temperature control air conditioning, four-way power seat, AM/FM stereo search radio W/quadrasonic tape and power antenna, wide whitewall steel belted radial tires, forged aluminum wheels, digital clock, tinted glass, illuminated entry system, dual lighted vanity mirrors, flight bench seats, leather wrapped steering wheel, coach lamps, cornering lights, carpeted trunk, remote control mirrors, speed control.

VERSAILLES ACCESSORIES

Appearance Protection Group			
W/Rear License Frames	$87	$67	$68
W/Front & Rear License Frames..............	91	70	71
Defroster Group............................	121	93	94
Garage Door Opener........................	92	71	72

Prices are accurate at time of printing; subject to manufacturer's change.

	Retail Price	Dealer Cost	Low Price
Front License Plate Bracket....................	$ NC	$ NC	$ NC
Premium Bodyside Molding	77	60	61
Protective Bodyside Molding..................	51	39	40
Moonroof	1088	838	847
Dual Shade Paint..........................	63	48	49
Power Lock Group	155	119	120
Lower Bodyside Protection	35	27	28
Radio Equipment			
AM/FM Stereo w/Cassette Tape (credit)	(168)	(129)	(129)
AM/FM Stereo w/8-Track Tape (credit).........	(168)	(129)	(129)
CB....................................	321	247	250
Vinyl Roof			
Coach.................................	NC	NC	NC
Full	NC	NC	NC
Reclining Bucket Seat Group.................	491	378	382
Floor Mounted Shifter (Bucket seats req.)	36	28	29
Tilt Steering Wheel........................	81	63	64
Illuminated Outside Thermometer	28	22	23
Leather & Vinyl Interior Trim.................	312	240	243
Wire Wheel Covers	NC	NC	NC

Mercury

MERCURY BOBCAT

BOBCAT
Runabout	$3797	$3305	$3505
Wagon	4099	3568	3818
Villager Wagon........................	4212	3666	3916

STANDARD EQUIPMENT (included in above prices)

Bobcat: Safety and protection equipment plus 2.3 litre 4-cyl. engine, 4-speed manual transmission, BR78-13 blackwall steel belted radial tires, AM radio, styled steel wheels w/bright trim rings, tinted glass, front bucket seats, fold down rear seat, carpeting, belt and window molding, cargo light on wagons, bumper protection group, electric rear window defroster, wheellip and rocker panel moldings (ex. Villager). Villager wagon also has woodgrain bodyside and rear applique, bright woodgrain surround moldings, load floor carpet.

BOBCAT ACCESSORIES

2.8 Litre V-6 Engine	$273	$232	$235
Automatic Transmission (Req. w/V-6 eng.)........	307	261	264
Interior Accent Group	42	36	37

Prices are accurate at time of printing; subject to manufacturer's change.

	Retail Price	Dealer Cost	Low Price
Air Conditioning............................	$484	$412	$417
Appearance Protection Group			
W/Conv. Grp. w/Rear License Frame	41	35	36
W/Conv. Grp. w/F&R License Frame............	45	38	39
W/o Conv. Grp. w/Rear License Frame	46	39	40
W/o Conv. Grp. w/F&R License Frame	49	42	43
High Axle Ratio	13	11	12
Heavy-Duty Battery	18	15	16
Power Brakes (Req. w/V-6 eng. & w/moonroof)	70	59	60
Load Floor Carpet	24	20	21
Convenience Group			
Runabout	96	82	83
Wagons................................	55	47	48
Mud/Stone Deflector	22	18	19
Glass Rear Door, Runabout...................	25	22	23
Light Group			
Runabout, Wagons.......................	33	28	29
Runabout w/Flip-Up Moonroof...............	20	17	18
Front License Bracket.......................	NC	NC	NC
Luggage Carrier, Wagons.....................	63	53	54
Luggage Compartment Cover	28	24	25
Dual Racing Mirrors			
W/Interior Accent Group	36	31	32
Others	52	44	45
Molding			
Deluxe Bodyside (NA Villager)	51	43	44
Narrow Bodyside........................	41	34	35
Rocker Panel...........................	24	20	21
Moonroof, Runabout........................	199	169	171
Glamour Paint.............................	41	35	36
Lower Bodyside Protection	30	26	27
Radio Equipment			
AM (delete for credit).....................	(72)	(61)	(61)
AM w/Digital Clock.......................	47	40	41
AM/FM	48	41	42
AM/FM Stereo	89	76	77
AM w/Stereo Tape	119	101	103
AM/FM Stereo w/Cassette Tape	157	133	135
Radio Flexibility Option...................	90	77	78
4-Way Driver Bucket Seat (manual).............	35	30	31
Sports Accent Group			
Runabout	247	210	213
Wagons................................	223	189	191
Sports Instrumentation Group	94	80	81
Sports Package Option (NA Villager)	72	61	62
Power Steering.............................	141	120	122
Trim			
Alpine Plaid Seat (Avail. w/dlx. int. trim or Sports accent grp.)	NC	NC	NC

Prices are accurate at time of printing; subject to manufacturer's change.

	Retail Price	Dealer Cost	Low Price
Deluxe Interior			
Runabout, Wagon.....................	$158	$134	$136
Villager Wagon.....................	182	155	157
Kirsten Cloth (base series only)	NC	NC	NC
Deluxe Wheel Covers (replaces styled wheels)...............................	NC	NC	NC
Wire Wheel Covers	33	28	29
Cast Aluminum Wheels (4)	164	139	141
Forged Aluminum Wheels (4)	164	139	141
White Forged Aluminum Wheels (4).............	177	151	153

MERCURY CAPRI

CAPRI

Capri	$4481	$3899	$4149
Capri Ghia...............................	4845	4217	4517

STANDARD EQUIPMENT (included in above prices)

Capri: Safety and protection equipment plus 2.3 litre 4-cyl. engine, 4-speed manual transmission, high back bucket seats, full instrumentation w/tachometer, sport steering wheel, color-keyed front/rear bumper, lighter, carpeting, day/night mirror, remote control left mirror, bodyside molding, liftback third door, B78-13 blackwall bias tires, semi-styled steel wheels.

Capri Ghia: Capri equipment plus deluxe color-keyed mirrors, light group, right remote control mirror, sport wheel covers, upgrade interior trim, BR78-14 blackwall steel belted radial tires.

CAPRI ACCESSORIES

Engines			
2.3 Litre 4-cyl. Turbocharged	$542	$461	$466
2.8 Litre V-6 (Pwr. steering & brakes req.)	273	232	235
5.0 Litre (302 CID) V-8 (Pwr. steering & brakes req.)	514	437	442
Automatic Transmission (NA turbo. eng.)..........	307	261	264
Accent Group (NA Ghia)			
W/Turbo RS Option	42	36	37
Others	108	92	93
Air Conditioning.......................	484	412	417
Appearance Protection Group			
W/Rear License Frame	41	35	36
W/F&R License Frame	45	38	39
Performance Axle Ratio......................	13	11	12
Heavy Duty Battery........................	18	15	16
Deluxe Belts (std. Ghia).....................	20	17	18
Power Brakes	70	59	60
Console.................................	127	108	110
Mud/Stone Deflectors........................	22	18	19
Electric Rear Window Defroster	84	72	73

Prices are accurate at time of printing; subject to manufacturer's change.

	Retail Price	Dealer Cost	Low Price
Sport Tuned Exhaust (V-8 w/auto. trans.)	$ 34	$ 29	$ 30
Tinted Glass	59	50	51
Front License Plate Frame	NC	NC	NC
Light Group			
W/Moonroof	16	13	14
W/o Moonroof	28	24	25
Right Remote Control Mirror (std. Ghia)	30	26	27
Rocker Panel Molding	24	20	21
Moonroof	199	169	171
Glamour Paint	41	35	36
Tu-Tone Paint	48	41	42
Power Door Lock Group	99	84	85
Lower Bodyside Protection	30	26	27
Radio Equipment			
AM	72	61	62
AM w/Digital Clock	119	101	103
AM/FM	120	102	104
AM/FM Stereo	176	150	152
AM/FM Stereo w/Cassette Tape	243	207	210
AM/FM Stereo w/8-Track Tape	243	207	210
Premium Sound System, Amp. & Spkrs.	67	57	58
Radio Flexibility Option	93	79	80
Dual Rear Speakers	43	37	38
RS Option (NA Ghia or Turbo RS)	249	212	215
Turbo RS Option (NA Ghia)	1186	1009	1020
4-way Driver's Seat (manual)	35	30	31
Speed Control	104	88	89
Power Steering	141	120	122
Leather Wrapped Steering Wheel	36	31	32
Tilt Steering Wheel	69	58	59
Radial Sport Suspension	33	28	29
Trim			
Bradford Cloth w/Vinyl (NA Ghia)	20	17	18
Danbury Cloth w/Vinyl (NA Ghia)	20	17	18
Leather/Corinthian Vinyl, Ghia or w/Interior Accent Grp.	283	241	244
Sport Wheel Covers (std. Ghia & RS)	NC	NC	NC
Wire Wheel Covers	64	54	55
Aluminum TRX Wheels (4)	240	204	207
Cast Aluminum Wheels (4)	240	204	207
Styled Steel Wheels w/Trim Rings (4)	65	55	56
Rear Window Washer/Wiper	63	53	54
Interval Wipers	35	30	31
TRX 190/65R X 390 Radial Tires			
Capri w/4-cyl. eng.	241	205	208
Capri Ghia ex. w/V-8 eng.	116	98	99
Capri w/V-6 eng.	219	186	188
Capri w/V-8 eng.	197	168	170
Capri Ghia w/V-8 eng.	51	43	44

Prices are accurate at time of printing; subject to manufacturer's change.

MERCURY COUGAR

	Retail Price	Dealer Cost	Low Price
COUGAR			
2-Door Hardtop	$5379	$4467	$4767
4-Door Hardtop	5524	4587	4887
COUGAR XR-7			
2-Door Hardtop	5994	4978	5278

STANDARD EQUIPMENT (included in above prices)

Cougar: Safety and protection equipment plus 5.0 litre (302 CID) V-8 engine, automatic transmission, power steering, power brakes, HR78-14 blackwall steel belted radial tires, rocker panel and wheellip molding, carpeting, rear bumper guards, hubcaps.

Cougar XR-7: Cougar equipment plus electric clock, padded landau vinyl roof, opera windows with louvers, XR-7 wheel covers, XR-7 handling package, flight bench seat, deluxe sound package, deluxe steering wheel, dual note horn, GR78-15 blackwall steel belted radial tires.

COUGAR ACCESSORIES

	Retail	Dealer	Low
5.8 Litre (351 CID) V-8 Engine (Req. Calif.)	$263	$205	$208
Automatic Air Conditioning	607	461	473
Manual Air Conditioning	562	427	438
Appearance Protection Group			
2-Dr. w/Rear License Frame	66	51	52
2-Dr. w/F&R License Frame	70	54	55
4-Dr. w/Rear License Frame	72	56	57
4-Dr. w/F&R License Frame	76	60	61
Traction-Lok Rear Axle	64	50	51
Heavy-Duty Battery	21	16	17
Deluxe Belts	22	17	18
Brougham Option (NA XR-7)			
2-Door	266	207	210
4-Door	382	298	301
Bumper Protection Group	63	49	50
Seat Belt Warning Chimes, XR-7	22	17	18
Day/Date Clock			
Base Cougar	46	36	37
Cougar w/Brougham Opt., XR-7	22	17	18
Convenience Group			
2-Drs. ex. w/XR-7 Decor Grp. or Racing Mirrors			
Bucket Seats	138	108	110
Others	147	115	117
2-Drs. w/XR-7 Decor Grp. or Racing Mirrors			
Twin Comfort & Bench Seats	93	73	74
Bucket Seats	84	66	67
4-Dr. w/Racing Mirrors	62	48	49
4-Dr. w/o Racing Mirrors	116	90	91
Cougar Brougham Decor Group (Avail. only w/Brougham Option)	221	172	174

Prices are accurate at time of printing; subject to manufacturer's change.

	Retail Price	Dealer Cost	Low Price
Cougar XR-7 Decor Group, XR-7.	$487	$380	$384
Chamois Decor Group, XR-7	625	488	493
Mud/Stone Deflectors.	24	18	19
Electric Rear Window Defroster	99	77	78
Calif. Emission System.	83	65	66
High Altitude Emission System	36	28	29
Extended Range Fuel Tank.	33	26	27
Tinted Glass	70	54	55
Illuminated Entry System	57	44	45
Cornering Lamp.	49	38	39
Light Group.	54	42	43
Luggage Compartment Trim.	42	33	34
Illuminated Visor Vanity Mirror	39	31	32
Left Remote Control Mirror	18	14	15
Dual Racing Mirrors.	64	50	51
Narrow Protective Bodyside Molding	45	35	36
Rocker Panel Molding.	29	23	24
Wide Bodyside Molding, XR-7	58	45	46
Moonroof, Power, XR-7.	789	616	623
Glamour Paint.	64	50	51
Paint Stripes (std. XR-7).	36	28	29
Tu-Tone Paint			
W/Brougham Option.	86	67	68
W/Brougham Decour Opt., XR-7 w/Decor	74	57	58
Base Cougar & XR-7	128	100	102
Power Lock Group			
2-Door	111	86	87
4-Door	143	112	114
Lower Bodyside Protection	33	26	27
Radio Equipment			
AM	79	62	63
AM/FM	132	103	105
AM/FM Stereo	192	150	152
AM/FM Stereo w/Cassette Tape	266	207	210
AM/FM Stereo w/8-Track Tape.	266	207	210
AM/FM Stereo Search.	349	272	275
AM/FM Stereo w/Quadrasonic 8-Track Tape	399	311	315
CB	295	230	233
Power Antenna, XR-7	47	37	38
Dual Rear Speakers	47	37	38
Radio Flexibility Option	105	82	83
Full Vinyl Roof, 4-Door	170	132	134
Landau Vinyl Roof, 2-Door (std. XR-7)	116	90	91
Bucket Seat w/Console			
Base Cougar	259	202	205
Cougar w/Brougham Option, XR-7	184	144	146
W/Brougham Decor	NC	NC	NC
Flight Bench Seat, Base Cougar.	75	59	60
Twin Comfort Seat w/Pass. Recliner.	184	144	146

Prices are accurate at time of printing; subject to manufacturer's change.

	Retail Price	Dealer Cost	Low Price
Power Seat			
6-way Left Bucket, XR-7	$163	$127	$129
6-way Flight Bench.	163	127	129
6-way Twin Comfort, Left	163	127	129
Upgrade Sound Package, XR-7	30	24	25
Speed Control			
W/B'ham. Decor & XR-7 Decor or Spts. Inst. Grp. .	105	82	83
Others	125	98	99
Sports Instrumentation Group			
W/B'ham. Decor or XR-7 Decor	105	82	83
W/Brougham, XR-7 Option	125	98	99
Others	149	116	118
Tilt Steering Wheel	75	59	60
Cross Country Suspension			
Base Cougar	36	28	29
XR-7	22	17	18
Trim			
Leather, XR-7 w/Twin Comfort Seats.	309	241	244
Velour, XR-7 w/Twin Comfort Seats	208	162	164
Vinyl Bench Seat, Base Cougar	30	24	25
Deluxe Wheel Covers, Base Cougar	43	34	35
Luxury Wheel Covers			
Base Cougar	78	61	62
W/Brougham Option	34	27	28
Wire Wheel Covers			
Base Cougar	162	126	128
W/Brougham Option, XR-7	118	92	93
Aluminum Wheels (4)			
Base Cougar	345	269	272
W/Brougham Option, XR-7	301	235	238
W/XR-7 Decor Option	136	106	108
Styled Road Wheels (4), XR-7	166	129	131
Styled Steel Wheels w/Trim Rings (4)			
Base Cougar	163	127	129
W/Brougham Option.	120	93	94
Opera Windows, Base Cougar	54	42	43
Power Windows			
2-Doors.	132	103	105
4-Doors.	187	146	148

MERCURY MARQUIS

	Retail Price	Dealer Cost	Low Price
MARQUIS			
2-Door	$5984	$4789	$5089
4-Door	6079	4865	5165
MARQUIS BROUGHAM			
2-Door.	6643	5317	5667
4-Door	6831	5467	5717

Prices are accurate at time of printing; subject to manufacturer's change.

GRAND MARQUIS	Retail Price	Dealer Cost	Low Price
2-Door	$7321	$5859	$6259
4-Door	7510	6010	6510
STATION WAGONS			
Marquis Wagon	6315	5055	5355
Colony Park Wagon	7100	5683	5933

STANDARD EQUIPMENT (included in above prices)

Marquis: Safety and protection equipment plus 5.0 litre (302 CID) V-8 engine, automatic transmission, power steering, power brakes, FR78-14 steel belted blackwall radial tires, deluxe sound package, rocker panel and wheellip moldings, wheel covers, dual note horn, flight bench seats, carpeting.

Marquis Brougham: Marquis equipment plus color-keyed seat belts, wide lower bodyside molding, power windows, vinyl roof, deluxe wheel covers, analog clock, left remote control mirror, hood/deck lid paint stripes.

Grand Marquis: Marquis and Marquis Brougham equipment plus luxury steering wheel, twin comfort lounge seats, tinted glass, coach lamps, luggage compartment trim, dual beam dome lamp, bodyside paint stripe.

Marquis Wagon: Marquis equipment plus GR78-14 blackwall steel belted radial tires, 3-way tailgate, power rear window, carpeted load floor, heavy-duty frame.

Colony Park Wagon: Marquis and Marquis wagon equipment ex-rocker panel molding, plus power windows, deluxe wheel covers, deluxe seat belts, analog clock, upgraded carpet, left remote control mirror.

MARQUIS ACCESSORIES

5.8 Litre (351 CID) V-8 Engine	$ 263	$205	$208
Automatic Air Conditioning	642	501	507
Manual Air Conditioning	597	466	471
Appearance Protection Group			
2-Dr. w/Rear License Frame	61	47	48
2-Dr. w/F&R License Frame	64	50	51
4-Dr. w/Rear License Frame	67	52	53
4-Dr. w/F&R License Frame	71	55	56
High Ratio Axle	16	12	13
Heavy-Duty Battery	21	16	17
Deluxe Belts, Marquis, Marquis Wagon	24	18	19
Front License Bracket	NC	NC	NC
Front or Rear Bumper Guards	22	17	18
Front & Rear Bumper Rub Strips	41	32	33
Seat Belt Warning Chimes (std. Grand Marquis)	22	17	18
Analog Clock, Marquis, Marquis Wagon	24	18	19
Digital Clock			
Marquis, Marquis Wagon	59	46	47
Others	36	28	29
Convenience Group			
Grand Marquis	78	61	62
Wagons	93	73	74
Others	84	66	67
Electric Rear Window Defroster	100	78	79

Prices are accurate at time of printing; subject to manufacturer's change.

	Retail Price	Dealer Cost	Low Price
Calif. Emission System	$ 83	$ 65	$ 66
High Altitude Emission System	36	28	29
Tinted Glass (std. Grand Marquis)	83	65	66
Grand Marquis Decor Opt., Colony Park	586	457	462
Handling Package	51	40	41
Illuminated Entry System	57	44	45
Cornering Lamps	49	38	39
Manual Load Levelers			
Wagons	53	41	42
Others (incl. LTD frame)	67	52	53
Lock Convenience Group			
w/Convenience Group			
2-Doors	91	71	72
4-Doors & Wagons	120	93	94
w/o Convenience Group			
2-Doors	116	90	91
4-Doors	145	113	115
Wagons	154	120	122
Luggage Carrier, Wagons....................	86	67	68
Luggage Compartment Trim (std. Grand Marq.) ..	45	35	36
Mirrors			
Illuminated Visor Vanity	41	32	33
Left Remote Control, Marquis, Marquis Wagon.	18	14	15
Right Remote Control	38	30	31
Protective Bodyside Molding	45	35	36
Rocker Panel Molding, Colony Park...........	29	23	24
Window Frame Molding			
2-Dr. Marquis........................	34	27	28
4-Dr. Marquis, Marquis Wagon	39	31	32
Glamour Paint	64	50	51
Bodyside Paint Stripes	36	28	29
Hood Paint Stripes	20	15	16
Tu-Tone Paint			
Grand Marquis	99	77	78
Others ex. Colony Park Wagon	129	101	103
Lower Bodyside Protection	33	26	27
Radio Equipment			
AM...............................	79	62	63
AM/FM Stereo.......................	192	150	152
AM/FM Stereo w/Tape.................	266	207	210
AM/FM Stereo w/Cassette Tape	266	207	210
CB...............................	295	230	233
Dual Rear Speakers	47	37	38
Premium Sound Syst., Spkrs. & Amp.	74	57	58
Power Antenna	45	35	36
Radio Flexibility Option	105	82	83
Power Bench Seat (NA Grand Marquis)........	164	128	130
Power 6-Way Driver's Seat (NA Marquis).......	164	128	130
6-Way, 6-Way Power Seats, w/Twin Comf. Seats..	329	257	260

Prices are accurate at time of printing; subject to manufacturer's change.

	Retail Price	Dealer Cost	Low Price
Left & Right Seat Recliners	$ 89	$ 70	$ 71
Dual Rear Facing Seats, Wagons	193	151	153
Twin Comfort Seats, Marquis B'ham, Colony Pk. .	101	79	80
Conventional Spare Tire	13	10	11
Spare Tire Cover.	13	10	11
Speed Control			
Grand Marquis or w/Grand Marquis Decor. . . .	111	86	87
Others	130	102	104
Tilt Steering Wheel	76	60	61
Heavy-Duty Suspension	22	17	18
Trailer Towing Package	146	114	116
Trim			
Cloth-Twin Comfort Seats, Colony Park	42	33	34
Leather-Twin Comfort Seats, Grand Marquis or w/Grand Marquis Opt. .	261	203	206
Polyknit-Flight Bench Seats, Wagons	53	41	42
Vinyl-Flight Bench Seats, Marquis, Marquis Brougham (sta. wagons)	34	27	28
Vinyl-Twin Comfort Seats, All ex. Marquis, Marquis Wagon	34	27	28
Full Vinyl Top, Marquis	143	112	114
Landau Vinyl Top, Marquis 2-Doors.	143	112	114
Visibility Light Group			
Marquis Brougham	33	26	27
Colony Park Wagon.	33	26	27
Grand Marquis	18	14	15
Marquis, Marquis Wagon.	47	37	38
Luxury Wheel Covers			
Marquis, Marquis Wagon.	93	73	74
Others	64	50	51
Wire Wheel Covers			
Marquis, Marquis Wagon.	118	92	93
Others	89	70	71
Power Windows			
2-Door Marquis	137	107	109
4-Door Marquis, Marquis Wagon	203	158	160

MERCURY MONARCH

MONARCH

	Retail Price	Dealer Cost	Low Price
2-Door Sedan.	$ 4412	$ 3752	$ 4002
4-Door Sedan.	4515	3839	4089

STANDARD EQUIPMENT (included in above prices)

MONARCH: Safety and protection equipment plus 4.1 litre (250 CID) 6-cyl. engine, 4-speed manual transmision, DR78-14 steel belted radial tires, front disc brakes, flight bench seat, wheel covers, all vinyl interior, carpeting, belt and window moldings, wheellip and bodyside molding, inflatable spare tire, opera windows (2-door), cigar lighter.

Prices are accurate at time of printing; subject to manufacturer's change.

MONARCH ACCESSORIES

	Retail Price	Dealer Cost	Low Price
5-0 Litre (302 CID) V-8 Engine	$283	$241	$244
Automatic Transmission	307	261	264
Floor-Mounted Auto. Trans. Selector	31	27	28
Automatic Temp. Air Conditioning	555	472	477
Manual Air Conditioning	514	437	442
Appearance Protection Group			
2-Dr. w/Rear License Frame	45	38	39
2-Dr. w/F&R License Frame	48	41	42
4-Dr. w/Rear License Frame	51	43	44
4-Dr. w/F&R License Frame	54	46	47
Ghia w/Rear License Frame	33	28	29
Ghia w/F&R License Frame	36	31	32
Heavy-Duty Battery	19	16	17
Deluxe Belts	20	17	18
Power Brakes	70	59	60
Bumper Protection Group	78	67	68
Digital Clock	45	38	39
Cold Weather Group	57	48	49
Console	84	72	73
Convenience Group w/Floor Shift-4-Speed			
2-Door w/Bucket Seats	86	73	74
All 4-Doors or 2-Dr. w/o Bucket Seats	57	48	49
Ghia or ESS 2-Dr. w/Bucket Seats	65	55	56
Ghia or ESS 4-Drs. or 2-Dr. w/o Buckets	36	31	32
Convenience Group w/o Floor-Shift-4-speed			
2-Door w/Bucket Seats	94	80	81
All 4-Doors or 2-Dr. w/o Bucket Seats	65	55	56
Ghia or ESS 2-Dr. w/Bucket Seats	73	62	63
Ghia or ESS 4-Drs. or 2-Dr. w/o Buckets	45	38	39
Decor Group (NA ESS or Ghia)	211	179	181
Mud/Stone Deflectors	22	18	19
Rear Window Defogger	51	43	44
Electric Rear Window Defroster	90	77	78
ESS Option	524	445	450
Calif. Emission System	76	65	66
High Altitude Emission System	33	28	29
Ghia Option Group	425	361	365
Tinted Glass	64	54	55
Heavy-Duty Group	57	48	49
Illuminated Entry System	52	44	45
Cornering Lamp	45	38	39
Light Group	46	39	40
Front License Bracket	NC	NC	NC
Power Door Locks			
2-Doors	78	67	68
4-Doors	107	91	92

Prices are accurate at time of printing; subject to manufacturer's change.

	Retail Price	Dealer Cost	Low Price
Dual Racing Mirrors			
Ghia...........................	$ 42	$ 36	$ 37
Others	59	50	51
Illuminated Visor Vanity Mirror.............	37	32	33
Protective Bodyside Molding (NA Ghia, ESS)	41	35	36
Rocker Panel Molding......................	24	20	21
Moonroof, Power	849	722	730
Glamour Paint...........................	48	41	.42
Lower Bodyside Protection	30	26	27
Radio Equipment			
AM	72	61	62
AM w/Stereo Tape	192	163	165
AM/FM	135	115	117
AM/FM Stereo	176	150	152
AM/FM Stereo Search	319	271	274
AM/FM Stereo w/Cassette Tape	243	207	210
AM/FM Stereo w/8-Track Tape.............	243	207	210
AM/FM Stereo w/Quadrasonic 8-Track Tape	365	310	314
CB	270	229	232
Radio Flexibility Option	93	79	80
Vinyl Roof			
Full	106	90	91
Landau, 2-Doors only....................	106	90	91
4-Way Manual Adjustable Seat...............	34	29	30
Reclining Bucket Seat Option			
W/Decor Grp., Ghia, ESS options.............	NC	NC	NC
Power Seat			
4-Way Bucket, Driver's...................	94	80	81
4-Way Flight Bench	94	80	81
Speed Control (NA w/Man.Trans.)............	104	88	89
Power Steering...........................	149	127	129
Tilt Steering Wheel........................	69	58	59
Heavy-Duty Suspension	27	23	24
Tone-on-Tone Option	123	104	106
Trim			
Leather, w/Decor Grp., Ghia, ESS w/Buckets....	283	241	244
Rossano Cloth, Base series w/Bench Seats	54	46	47
Willshire Cloth	104	88	89
Electric Trunk Lid Release (NA w/console)........	22	18	19
Visibility Group			
Base Monarch	64	54	55
W/Ghia Option..........................	41	35	36
Base Monarch w/Dual Racing Mirrors	14	12	13
W/ESS & Ghia w/Dual Racing Mirrors	8	7	8
Deluxe Wheel Covers, Base Monarch	40	34	35
Wire Wheel Covers			
Base Monarch	108	92	93
W/ESS Option	69	58	59

Prices are accurate at time of printing; subject to manufacturer's change.

	Retail Price	Dealer Cost	Low Price
Aluminum Wheels (4)			
Base Monarch	$278	$237	$240
W/Ghia Option	170	144	146
W/ESS Option	239	203	206
Styled Steel Wheels w/Trim Rings (4)			
Base Monarch	114	97	98
W/ESS Option	75	64	65
Power Windows			
2-Doors	116	98	99
4-Doors	163	138	140

MERCURY ZEPHYR

ZEPHYR

	Retail Price	Dealer Cost	Low Price
2-Door Sedan	$3870	$3368	$3568
4-Door Sedan	3970	3455	3655
Z-7 Sports Coupe	4122	3587	3837
Station Wagon	4317	3757	4007

STANDARD EQUIPMENT (included in above prices)

Zephyr: Safety and protection equipment plus 2.3 litre 4-cyl. engine, 4-speed manual transmission, disc front brakes, all vinyl trim, carpeting, deluxe wheel covers, body paint stripe, rocker panel and wheellip moldings. Wagon also has cargo area light and carpet, B78-14 blackwall tires (CR78-14 radial tires on wagon)

Zephyr Z-7 Sports Coupe: Zephyr equipment plus interior accent level seat trim, luxury interior option door trim, deluxe belts, bodyside tape stripes, lower bodyside molding, bright window frames.

ZEPHYR ACCESSORIES

	Retail Price	Dealer Cost	Low Price
Engines			
3.3 Litre (200 CID) 6-cyl.	$241	$205	$208
5.0 Litre (302 CID) V-8	524	445	450
Calif. Emission System	76	65	66
High Altitude Emission System	33	28	29
Automatic Transmission			
Ex. Wagon (includes radial tires)	398	339	343
Wagons (NA w/2.3 litre eng.)	307	261	264
Floor Mounted Shifter (Auto. Trans. Reg.)	31	27	28
Accent Group (std. Z-7)			
w/ES Type Option	108	92	93
Others	72	61	62
Air Conditioning	484	412	417
Appearance Protection Group			
2-Dr. w/Rear License Frame	45	39	40
2-Dr. w/F&R License Frame	48	41	42
4-Dr. & Wagon w/Rear License Frame	51	43	44
4-Dr. & Wagon w/F&R License Frame	54	46	47
Heavy-Duty Battery	18	15	16

Prices are accurate at time of printing; subject to manufacturer's change.

CONSUMER GUIDE

	Retail Price	Dealer Cost	Low Price
Power Brakes	$70	$54	$55
Rear Bumper Guards.	20	17	18
Bumper Protection Group	58	49	50
Electric Analog Clock	20	17	18
Convenience Group			
Z-7 Sport Group	31	27	28
Others	51	43	44
Mud/Stone Deflectors	22	18	19
Rear Window Defogger	51	43	44
Electric Rear Window Defroster	90	77	78
ES Type Option	237	202	204
Ghia Option			
Sedans.	428	364	368
Wagon	325	277	280
Z-7 Sport Coupe	211	179	181
Tinted Glass.	59	50	51
Front License Bracket	NC	NC	NC
Light Group			
Ex. Wagon	41	35	36
Wagon	35	30	31
Lighter	6	5	6
Rear Louvers (NA Z-7 or wagon)	35	30	31
Roof Luggage Rack, Wagon	76	65	66
Luxury Exterior Decor	102	87	88
Luxury Interior Option			
Z-7 Sport Coupe	208	177	179
Others	323	274	277
Dual Mirrors, Left Remote.	35	30	31
Deluxe Bodyside Molding, Z-7 Spt. Cpe.	53	45	46
Protective Bodyside Molding	41	35	36
Rocker Panel Molding (std. base models)	24	20	21
Moonroof (NA wagon).	199	169	171
Glamour Paint	48	41	42
Tu-Tone Paint (NA wagon)			
Sedans.	81	69	70
Z-7 Sport Coupe	96	82	83
Power Locks			
2-Doors	78	67	68
4-Doors	107	91	92
Lower Bodyside Protection			
Z-7, Wagon, W/ES, Lux. Ext., Ext.			
Accent Delete or Ghia Option	42	36	37
Others	30	26	27
Radio Equipment			
AM.	72	61	62
AM w/Stereo Tape.	192	163	165
AM/FM.	120	102	104
AM/FM Stereo.	176	150	152
AM/FM Stereo w/8-Track Tape.	243	207	210

Prices are accurate at time of printing; subject to manufacturer's change.

	Retail Price	Dealer Cost	Low Price
AM/FM Stereo w/Cassette Tape	$243	$207	$210
Premium Sound System Speakers	67	57	58
Radio Flexibility Option	93	79	80
Vinyl Roof	90	77	78
Bench Seat (credit) w/4-cyl. & auto. trans.	(72)	(61)	(61)
Bucket Seats (std. w/4-cyl. eng.).	72	61	62
Power Seat, 4-way Bench or Flight Bench	94	80	81
Speed Control (incl. luxury steering wheel)			
w/Ghia, Lux. Int. Opt. or Tilt Wheel	86	73	74
w/ES Type Option.	83	71	72
Others	104	88	89
Sports Instrumentation Group	78	67	68
Power Steering (NA wag. w/4-cyl. eng.).	149	127	129
Sport Steering Wheel.	39	33	34
Tilt Steering Wheel			
w/Ghia or Luxury Interior Opt.	51	43	44
W/ES Type.	48	41	42
Others	69	58	59
Lockable Stowage Compartment, Wagon	20	17	18
Sports Handling Suspension (NA wagon, incl. w/ES)	34	29	30
Trim			
Ardmore Cloth, Bench Seat w/Int. Acc. Grp. or Z-7.	39	33	34
Brodie Cloth. w/Bucket Seats & Int. Acc. Grp. .	39	33	34
Corinthian Vinyl (sta. wagon)	NC	NC	NC
Kirsten Cloth, w/Bench Seat (NA wagon).	20	17	18
Shannon Cloth, Wagon w/Lux. Int. Opt.	NC	NC	NC
Electric Trunk Lid Release	22	18	19
Villager Option, Wagon	195	166	168
Styled Wheel Covers (incl. w/ES)	41	35	36
Wire Wheel Covers			
W/ES Type.	52	44	45
Others	93	79	80
Styled Steel Wheels w/Trim Rings (4)			
W/ES Type.	54	46	47
Others	95	81	82
Aluminum Wheels (4)			
W/ES Type.	237	202	205
Others	278	237	240
Bright Window Frames (NA ES)			
2-Doors	25	22	23
4-Doors	30	26	27
Front Vent Windows (NA Z-7)	41	35	36
Power Windows			
2-Doors	116	98	99
4-Doors	163	138	140
Interval Wipers.	35	30	31
Rear Window Wiper/Washer.	80	68	69

Prices are accurate at time of printing; subject to manufacturer's change.

General Motors Corporation

Buick

BUICK CENTURY

	Retail Price	Dealer Cost	Low Price
CENTURY SPECIAL			
Sedan	$4699	$3901	$4151
Coupe	4599	3818	4068
Station Wagon	5247	4357	4657
CENTURY CUSTOM			
Sedan	4968	4125	4425
Coupe	4843	4021	4321
Station Wagon	5561	4617	4917
CENTURY SPORT COUPE			
Coupe	5151	4277	4577
CENTURY LIMITED			
Sedan	5336	4430	4730

STANDARD EQUIPMENT (included in above prices)

Century Special: Safety and protection equipment plus 3.2 litre (196 CID) V-6 2-bbl. engine [3.8 litre (231 CID) V-6 on wagons], 3-speed manual transmission (automatic on wagons), P185/75R-14 glass belted blackwall radial tires (P195/75R-14 on wagons), disc front brakes (power on wagons), stowaway spare tire, bench front seat, carpeting, steering column headlamp high/low control, inside hood release.

Century Custom: Century Special equipment plus load floor carpet on wagon, rocker panel molding, wheel opening molding, Exterior Molding Package on sedan and wagon, notchback front seat, Front ashtray light, glove box light, under-dash courtesy light.

Century Sport Coupe: Century Special equipment plus sport mirrors, rallye ride & handling suspension, P205/70R-14 blackwall steel belted radial tires, designers' sport wheels.

Century Limited: Century Special and Custom equipment plus belt reveal molding, custom steering wheel, 55/45 notchback split bench seat.

CENTURY ACCESSORIES

Engines
3.8 Litre (231 CID) V-6 2-bbl. (std. wagon)	$40	$31	$32

Prices are accurate at time of printing; subject to manufacturer's change.

	Retail Price	Dealer Cost	Low Price
4.9 Litre (301 CID) V-8 2-bbl.			
Wagons	$195	$152	$154
Coupes & Sedans ex-Sport Coupe	255	199	201
Sport Coupe.......................	235	183	185
4.9 Litre (301 CID) V-8 4-bbl.			
Wagons	255	199	201
Coupes & Sedans ex. Sport Coupe........	316	246	247
Sport Coupe.......................	295	230	233
5.0 Litre (305 CID) V-8 4-bbl.			
Wagons	255	199	201
Coupes & Sedans ex. Sport Coupe........	316	246	247
Sport Coupe.......................	295	230	233
5.7 Litre (350 CID) V-8 4-bbl.			
Wagons	320	250	253
3.8 Litre (231 CID) V-6 Turbocharged			
Coupes & Sedans	470	367	371
Transmissions			
4-speed Manual, Coupes & Sedans	135	105	107
Automatic (std. wagon).................	335	261	264
Air Conditioning......................	562	438	443
Automatic Air Conditioning	653	509	515
Air Deflector, Wagons	30	23	24
Limited Slip Rear Axle	64	50	51
Heavy-Duty Battery.....................	21	16	17
Power Brakes (std. wagon)................	76	59	60
Front & Rear Bumper Guards	45	35	36
Load Area Carpet, Special Wagon	51	40	41
Electric Clock........................	24	19	20
Electric Digital Clock	55	43	44
Console, Custom & Sport Coupe	90	70	71
Convenience Group			
Special Sdn. w/o Dome Reading Lamp.......	47	37	38
Special Sdn. w/Dome Reading Lamp	34	27	28
Special Cpe., Sport Cpe. w/o Dome Reading Lamp, Sunroof or Astroroof.............	35	27	28
Special Cpe., Sport Cpe. w/Dome Reading Lamp, Sunroof or Astroroof	22	17	18
Special Wag. w/o Dome Reading Lamp	58	45	46
Special Wag. w/Dome Reading Lamp	45	35	36
Custom Cpe., Sdn., Limited w/o Dome Reading Lamp, Sunroof or Astroroof.............	19	15	16
Custom Cpe., Sdn., Limited w/Dome Reading Lamp, Sunroof or Astroroof...............	6	5	6
Custom Wag. w/o Dome Reading Lamp	30	23	24
Custom Wag. w/Dome Reading Lamp	17	13	14
Heavy-Duty Cooling			
w/o Air Conditioning..................	58	45	46
w/Air Conditioning	30	23	24
Cruise Master........................	103	80	81

Prices are accurate at time of printing; subject to manufacturer's change.

	Retail Price	Dealer Cost	Low Price
Rear Window Defogger	$ 99	$ 77	$ 78
Power Door Locks			
2-Doors	86	67	68
4-Doors	120	94	95
Calif. Emission System	83	65	66
High Altitude Emission System	15	12	13
Tinted Glass			
All	70	55	56
Windshield Only	50	39	40
Headlamp on Indicator	11	9	10
Trip Odometer Instrumentation	13	10	11
Instrument Gages	27	21	22
Instrument Gages & Fuel Usage Light	57	44	45
Dome Reading Lamp	19	15	16
Front Light Monitors	29	23	24
Luggage Rack, Wagons	90	70	71
Mirrors			
Left Remote (NA Sport Coupe)	18	14	15
Right Remote (NA Sport Coupe)	39	30	31
Sport, Left Remote, Right Manual	45	35	36
Sport, Left & Right Remote			
All ex. Sport Coupe	70	55	56
Sport Coupe	25	20	21
Visor Vanity	10	8	9
Illuminated Right Visor Vanity	46	36	37
Radio Equipment			
AM	86	67	68
AM/FM	163	127	129
AM/FM Stereo	236	184	186
AM w/Stereo Tape	248	193	195
AM/FM Stereo w/Stereo Tape	345	269	272
AM/FM Stereo w/Stereo Cassette Tape	351	274	277
AM/FM Stereo w/CB & Power Antenna	574	448	453
AM/FM Stereo w/Digital Clock & Readout	402	314	318
Rear Speaker	25	20	21
Dual Rear Speakers	50	39	40
Power Antenna, AM/FM			
w/Radio	47	37	38
w/o Radio	76	59	60
Power Antenna, AM/FM/CB			
w/Radio	86	67	68
w/o Radio	115	90	91
Windshield Antenna (incl. w/radio)	29	23	24
Sun Roof, Coupes	529	413	418
Astro Roof, Coupes	729	569	575
Power Seat, Driver's Side	163	127	129
Seat Recliner, Driver or Pass.	62	48	49
Bucket Seats			
Custom	45	35	36

Prices are accurate at time of printing; subject to manufacturer's change.

	Retail Price	Dealer Cost	Low Price
Sport Coupe, Wagon w/Sport Wag. Opt. . . . . . . Notchback Seat	$181	$141	$143
Sport Coupe, Wagon w/Sport Wag. Opt. . . . . . . 55/45 Split Bench Seat	136	106	108
Custom	102	80	81
Sport Coupe, Wagon w/Sport Wag. Opt.	238	186	188
Sport Wagon Option, Special Wag.	473	368	372
Power Steering	163	127	129
Custom Steering Wheel (std. Limited)	10	8	9
Sport Steering Wheel			
All ex. Limited	42	33	34
Limited	32	25	26
Tilt Steering Wheel	75	59	60
Stowage Compartment			
Wagon w/o Limited-Slip Axle	37	29	30
Wagon w/Limited-Slip Axle	42	33	34
Automatic Level Control Suspension	121	94	95
Firm Ride & Handling Suspension	21	16	17
Rallye Ride & Handling Suspension	38	30	31
Electric Tailgate Lock, Wagons	25	20	21
Vinyl Top (NA Wagon)	116	90	91
Trailer Wiring Harness			
5-Wire	22	17	18
7-Wire	35	27	28
Trunk Trim, Custom & Limited	31	24	25
Electric Trunk Release	24	19	20
Turbo Coupe Pkg., Sport Coupe	40	31	32
Power Windows			
2-Doors or Front Doors Only	132	103	105
4-Doors	187	146	148
Controlled Cycle Wipers	38	30	31
Woodgrain Vinyl Applique			
Special Wagon	289	225	228
Custom Wagon	267	208	211

BUICK LE SABRE, ESTATE WAGON, ELECTRA

LE SABRE

	Retail Price	Dealer Cost	Low Price
Sedan	$5780	$4627	$4927
Coupe	5680	4547	4847

LE SABRE LIMITED

Sedan	$6249	$5002	$5302
Coupe	6124	4902	5202

LE SABRE SPORT COUPE

Coupe	6621	5300	5650

ESTATE WAGON

Station Wagon	6714	5374	5724

ELECTRA 225

Sedan	7756	6053	6553
Coupe	7581	5916	6316

Prices are accurate at time of printing; subject to manufacturer's change.

	Retail Price	Dealer Cost	Low Price
ELECTRA LIMITED			
Sedan	$8156	$6365	$6865
Coupe	7981	6228	6728
ELECTRA PARK AVENUE			
Sedan	8598	6710	7210
Coupe	8423	6573	7073

STANDARD EQUIPMENT (included in above prices)

Le Sabre: Safety and protection equipment plus 3.8 litre (231 CID) V-6 2-bbl. engine, automatic transmission, power brakes, power steering, FR78-15 blackwall glass belted radial tires, bench front seat, carpeting, front-door-operated dome light.

LeSabre Limited: Le Sabre equipment plus hood ornament and windsplit molding, wheel opening molding, rocker panel and rear end moldings, custom steering wheel, deluxe wheel covers.

Le Sabre Sport Coupe: Le Sabre equipment plus 3.8 litre (231 CID) V-6 turbocharged engine, GR70-15 blackwall steel belted radial tires, low fuel indicator, hood ornament and windsplit molding, wheel opening molding, sport steering wheel, chromed wheels.

Estate Wagon: Le Sabre equipment plus 5.7 litre (350 CID) V-8 4-bbl. engine, HR78-15 blackwall steel belted radial tires, hood ornament and windsplit molding, wheel opening molding, custom steering wheel, deluxe wheel covers.

Electra 225: Le Sabre equipment plus 5.7 litre (350 CID) V-8 4-bbl. engine, GR78-15 blackwall steel belted radial tires, custom seat belts, remote control left mirror, hood ornament and windsplit molding, window frame scalp molding, wheel opening molding, electric clock, custom steering wheel, deluxe wheel covers, power windows.

Electra Limited: Electra 225 equipment plus dome reading light, wide rocker appearance moldings, front fender and rear quarter lower moldings, litter pocket, 55/45 notchback front seat. Electra Park Avenue: Electra 225 and Limited equipment plus door courtesy and warning lights, custom wheel covers, upgraded trim.

LE SABRE, ESTATE WAGON & ELECTRA ACCESSORIES

Engines			
4.9 litre (301 CID) V-8 2-bbl.			
Le Sabre, Le Sabre Limited	$246	$189	$191
5.7 Litre (350 CID) V-8 4-bbl.			
Le Sabre, Le Sabre Limited	371	286	289
6.6 Litre (403 CID) V-8 4-bbl.			
Estate Wagon, Electras	70	54	55
Air Conditioning	605	466	471
Automatic Air Conditioning	688	530	536
Limited-Slip Rear Axle	68	52	53
Heavy-Duty Battery	21	16	17
Four-Wheel Disc Brakes, Le Sabre Spt. Cpe.	205	158	160
Console, Le Sabre Sport Coupe	94	72	73
Convenience Group:			
w/o Dome Lamp or Digital Radio			
Le Sabre Sedan	99	76	77
Le Sabres ex. Sedan	87	67	68
Estate Wagon	68	52	53
w/Dome Lamp w/o Digital Radio			
Le Sabre Sedan	86	66	67

Prices are accurate at time of printing; subject to manufacturer's change.

	Retail Price	Dealer Cost	Low Price
Le Sabres ex. Sedan	$ 74	$ 57	$ 58
Estate Wagon	55	42	43
w/Dome Lamp & Digital Radio			
Le Sabre Sedan	31	24	25
Le Sabres ex. Sedan.	19	15	16
w/o Dome Lamp w/Digital Radio			
Le Sabre Sedan	44	34	35
Le Sabres ex. Sedan.	32	25	26
Estate Wagon	13	10	11
Heavy-Duty Cooling			
w/o Air Conditioning.	58	45	46
w/Air Conditioning	30	23	24
Cruise Master.	108	83	84
Rear Window Defogger	101	78	79
Power Door Locks			
2-Doors	88	68	69
4-Doors	122	94	95
Automatic Power Door Locks			
2-Door Electras.	146	112	114
4-Door Electras.	175	135	137
Calif. Emission System.	83	64	65
High Altitude Emission System	35	27	28
Engine Block Heater	15	12	13
Estate Wagon Limited Pkg.	1853	1427	1442
Electric Fuel Cap Lock	36	28	29
80-Amp. Generator (w/V-8 eng.)			
w/o Air Cond. or HD Cooling.	46	35	36
w/Air Cond. or HD Cooling	43	33	34
Tinted Glass			
All	84	65	66
Windshield Only (NA Electras)	51	39	40
Four Note Horn	23	18	19
Fuel Usage Light Instrument	30	23	24
Headlamps On Indicator	11	8	9
Low Fuel Indicator (std. Spt. Cpe.).	17	13	14
Speed Alert & Trip Odometer Inst.	23	18	19
Cornering Light.	49	38	39
Dome Reading Light	19	15	16
Door Courtesy & Warning (std. Park Ave.)			
2-Doors	36	28	29
4-Doors	57	44	45
Front Lamp Monitor, All ex. Electras	29	22	23
Front & Rear Lamp Monitor, Electras	62	48	49
Rear Compartment Courtesy, Wagon.	16	12	13
Sunshade Map Light, Electra 225	13	10	11
Luggage Rack, Wagon	140	108	110
Mirrors			
Left Remote (std. Electras)	19	15	16
Right Remote			
All ex. Estate Wagon.	39	30	31

Prices are accurate at time of printing; subject to manufacturer's change.

	Retail Price	Dealer Cost	Low Price
Estate Wagon	$ 34	$ 26	$ 27
Electric control Left & Right, Electras	97	75	76
Electric Control Left & Right w/Left Thermometer, Electras	118	91	92
Remote Left w/Thermometer			
La Sabres, Wagon w/o Limited Pkg.	38	29	30
Electras, Wagon w/Limited Pkg.	21	16	17
Sport, Left & Right Remote			
Le Sabres...............................	70	54	55
Electras	54	42	43
Wagon w/o Limited Pkg...................	65	50	51
Wagon w/Limited Pkg....................	49	38	39
Visor Vanity, Left & Right	10	8	9
Lighted Visor Vanity, Left or Right..........	47	36	37
Radio Equipment			
AM (NA Electras)	99	76	77
AM/FM.................................	174	134	136
AM/FM Stereo...........................	239	184	186
AM w/Stereo Tape.......................	265	204	207
AM/FM Stereo w/Stereo Tape...............	349	269	272
AM/FM Stereo w/Stereo Cassette Tape.......	355	273	276
AM/FM Stereo w/CB & Power Antenna	581	447	452
AM/FM Stereo w/Stereo Tape, CB & Power Antenna, Electras	691	532	538
AM/FM Stereo w/Digital Readouts			
Le Sabres, Estate Wagon.................	402	310	314
Estate Wagon w/Limited Pkg.	347	267	270
Signal Seeking AM/FM Stereo w/Digital Readouts, Electras	447	344	348
Signal Seeking AM/FM Stereo w/Digital Readouts & Stereo Tape	557	429	434
Signal Seeking AM/FM Stereo w/CB, Digital Clock & Pwr. Ant., Electras...............	789	608	615
Signal Seeking AM/FM Stereo w/CB, Digital Clock, Pwr. Ant. & Stereo Tape, Electras	899	692	699
Rear Speaker	26	20	21
Dual Rear Speakers	52	40	41
Power Antenna, AM/FM			
w/o Radio	77	59	60
w/Radio	48	37	38
Power Antenna, AM/FM/CB			
w/o Radio	116	89	90
w/Radio	87	67	68
Windshield Antenna (incl. w/radio)	29	22	23
Astro Roof			
Le Sabres...............................	925	712	720
Electras	998	768	776
Sun Roof			
Le Sabres...............................	725	558	564

Prices are accurate at time of printing; subject to manufacturer's change.

	Retail Price	Dealer Cost	Low Price
Electras	$798	$615	$622
Power Seat, Driver's Side			
La Sabres, Wagon, Electra 225	166	128	130
Electra Limited & Park Ave.	135	104	106
Power Seat, Driver & Passenger			
Le Sabres ex. Base Series, Wagon, Electra 225	332	256	259
Electra Limited & Park Ave.	301	232	235
Manual Seat Back Recliner, Left or Right, Le Sabre			
series Cpe., Sport Coupe	62	48	49
Power Seat Back Recliner, Left or Right, All ex. Le			
Sabre series Sedan	118	91	92
Third Seat, Wagon	194	149	151
Sport Package			
Le Sabre Coupe	160	123	125
Le Sabre Sport Coupe	254	196	198
Custom Steering Wheel, Le Sabre Series	10	8	9
Sport Steering Wheel			
Le Sabre Series	42	32	33
Le Sabre Limited, Estate Wag.	32	25	26
Tilt Steering Wheel	77	59	60
Tilt & Telescope Steering Wheel			
Le Sabre Series	131	101	103
Le Sabre Ltd., Wagon, Electras	121	93	94
Wagon w/Limited Pkg.	44	34	35
Automatic Level Control Suspension	121	93	94
Firm Ride & Handling Suspension	21	16	17
Remote Control Tailgate Lock	34	26	27
Theft Deterrent System (NA Wagon)	135	104	106
Full Vinyl Top			
Le Sabres	145	112	114
Electra Sedans	164	126	128
Full Vinyl Top Heavily Padded, Electras	206	159	161
Landau Vinyl Top, Le Sabre Coupes	155	119	121
Landau Vinyl Top, Heavily Padded, Electra Coupes	200	154	156
Trailer Wiring Harness & Flasher			
5-Wire	22	17	18
7-Wire	35	27	28
Trim			
Custom, Notchback Seat			
Le Sabre Sport Coupe, Estate Wagon	404	311	315
Custom, 55/45 Seat			
Le Sabre Sport Coupe, Estate Wagon	506	390	394
Electra 225, Le Sabre Limited	102	79	80
Trunk Carpeting, Electras	60	46	47
Trunk Trim, Le Sabres	48	37	38
Electric Trunk Release	25	19	20
Power Windows (std. Electras) 2-Doors	138	106	108
4-Doors	205	158	160
Controlled Cycle Wipers	39	30	31
Woodgrain Vinyl Applique, Wagon	293	226	229

Prices are accurate at time of printing; subject to manufacturer's change.

Buick Century

Buick LeSabre

Buick Regal

BUICK REGAL

	Retail Price	Dealer Cost	Low Price
REGAL			
Coupe	$5080	$4218	$4518
REGAL SPORT COUPE			
Coupe	6227	5170	5520
REGAL LIMITED			
Coupe	5477	4547	4847

STANDARD EQUIPMENT (included in above prices)

Regal: Safety and protection equipment plus 3.2 litre (196 CID) V-6 2-bbl. engine, 3-speed manual transmission, P195/75R-14 blackwall steel belted radial tires, deluxe wheel covers, front disc brakes, stowaway spare tire, notchback bench seat, steering column mounted headlight dimmer, bumper protection strips, carpeting, ashtray and glove box lights.

Regal Sport Coupe: Regal equipment plus 3.8 litre (231 CID) turbocharged V-6 engine, automatic transmission, power brakes, power steering, rallye ride & handling suspension, P205/70R-14 blackwall steel belted radial tires.

Regal Limited: Regal equipment plus exterior molding package, 55/45 split bench seat, upgrade trim.

REGAL ACCESSORIES

Engines			
3.8 Litre (231 CID) V-6 2-bbl. (NA Spt. Cpe.) .	$40	$31	$32
4.9 Litre (301 CID) V-8 2-bbl. (NA Spt. Cpe.) .	235	183	185
4.9 Litre (301 CID) V-8 4-bbl. (NA Spt. Cpe.) .	295	230	233
5.0 Litre (305 CID) V-8 4-bbl. (NA Spt. Cpe.) .	295	230	233
Transmissions			
4-Speed Manual (NA Spt. Cpe.).............	135	105	107
Automatic (Std. Sport Coupe)	335	261	264
Air Conditioning	562	438	443
Automatic Air Conditioning	653	509	515
Limited-Slip Rear Axle	64	50	51
Heavy-Duty Battery	21	16	17
Power Brakes (Std. Sport Coupe)	76	59	60
Front & Rear Bumper Guards	45	35	36
Electric Clock...........................	24	19	20
Electric Digital Clock	55	43	44
Console	90	70	71
Convenience Group			
w/o Dome Lamp, Astro Roof or Sun Roof.....	19	15	16
w/Dome Lamp, Astro Roof or Sun Roof	6	5	6
Heavy-Duty Cooling			
w/o Air Conditioning....................	58	45	46
w/Air Conditioning	30	23	24
Cruise Master...........................	103	80	81
Rear Window Defogger	99	77	78
Power Door Locks........................	86	67	68
Calif. Emission System....................	83	65	66
High Altitude Emission System	35	27	28

Prices are accurate at time of printing; subject to manufacturer's change.

	Retail Price	Dealer Cost	Low Price
Engine Block Heater	$ 15	$ 12	$ 13
Tinted Glass			
All	70	55	56
Windshield Only	50	39	40
Headlamps on Indicator	11	9	10
Trip Odometer Instrumentation	13	10	11
Instrument Gages (NA Spt. Cpe.).	27	21	22
Fuel Usage Light & Instrument Gages	57	44	45
Cornering Lights.........................	49	38	39
Dome Reading Light	19	15	16
Front Light Monitor.	29	23	24
Mirrors			
Left Remote Control	18	14	15
Right Remote Control	34	27	28
Sport, Left Remote, Right Manual	40	31	32
Sport, Left & Right Remote	65	51	52
Visor Vanity, Left & Right	10	8	9
Lighted Right Visor Vanity	46	36	37
Radio Equipment			
AM.........................	86	67	68
AM/FM.........................	163	127	129
AM/FM Stereo.........................	236	184	186
AM w/Stereo Tape......................	248	193	195
AM/FM Stereo w/Stereo Tape.............	345	269	272
AM/FM Stereo w/Stereo Cassette Tape	351	274	277
AM/FM Stereo w/CB & Power Antenna	574	448	453
AM/FM Stereo w/Digital Clock & Readout	402	314	318
Rear Speaker	25	20	21
Dual Rear Speakers	50	39	40
Power Antenna, AM/FM			
w/o Radio	76	59	60
w/Radio	47	37	38
Power Antenna, AM/FM/CB			
w/o Radio	115	90	91
w/Radio	86	67	68
Windshield Antenna (incl. w/radio)	29	23	24
Astro Roof	729	569	575
Hatch Roof.........................	655	511	517
Sun Roof	529	413	418
Power Seat, 6-way Driver's Side	163	127	129
Passenger Seat Recliner	62	48	49
Bucket Seats (NA Limited)	45	35	36
55/45 Split Bench Seat (std. Limited).........	102	80	81
55/45 Split Bench Seat w/Limited Trim, Sport Coupe	272	212	215
Sport Coupe Decor Pkg., Sport Coupe	473	369	373
Power Steering (std. Limited)	163	127	129
Sport Steering Wheel.......................	32	25	26
Tilt Steering Wheel......................	75	59	60
Automatic Level Control Suspension	121	94	95

Prices are accurate at time of printing; subject to manufacturer's change.

	Retail Price	Dealer Cost	Low Price
Firm Ride & Handling Suspension............	$ 21	$ 16	$ 17
Rallye Ride & Handling Suspension (std. Spt. Cpe.)	38	30	31
Full Vinyl Top	116	90	91
Landau Vinyl Top			
Regal, Regal Sport Coupe	162	126	128
Limited	146	114	116
Landau Vinyl Top, Heavily Padded			
Regal, Regal Sport Coupe	228	178	180
Limited	178	139	141
Trailer Wiring Harness & Flasher			
5-Wire	22	17	18
7-Wire	35	27	28
Electric Trunk Release	24	19	20
Trunk Trim...........................	31	24	25
Power Windows........................	132	103	105
Controlled Cycle Wipers	38	30	31

BUICK RIVIERA

RIVIERA
	Retail Price	Dealer Cost	Low Price
Coupe	$10112	$7890	$8890
S Type Coupe	10388	8106	9106

STANDARD EQUIPMENT (included in above prices)

Riviera Coupe: Safety and protection equipment plus 5.7 litre (350 CID) V-8 4-bbl. engine, automatic transmission, power brakes, power steering, air conditioning, tinted glass, AM/FM stereo radio, front-wheel drive, power windows.

Riviera S Type Coupe: Riviera Coupe equipment plus 3.8 litre (231 CID) V-6 4-bbl. turbocharged engine, sport suspension, high-effort power steering, sports steering wheel.

RIVIERA ACCESSORIES

Engines			
3.8 Litre (231 CID) V-6 4-bbl. Turbocharged,			
Riviera Coupe (std. S Type)	$110	$85	$86
5.7 Litre (350 CID) V-8 4-bbl., S Type (std.			
Riviera Coupe) (credit)	(110)	(85)	(85)
Automatic Air Conditioning.................	88	68	69
80-Amp. Alternator (W/V-8 eng.)..............	43	33	34
Heavy-Duty Battery	21	16	17
Four-Wheel Disc Brakes....................	205	158	160
Rear Bumper Guards	22	17	18
Heavy-Duty Cooling......................	30	23	24
Cruise Master..........................	108	83	84
Rear Window Defogger	101	78	79
Automatic Electric Door Locks	58	45	46
California Emission System.................	83	64	65
High Altitude Emission System	35	27	28
Engine Block Heater	15	12	13

Prices are accurate at time of printing; subject to manufacturer's change.

	Retail Price	Dealer Cost	Low Price
Electric Fuel Cap Lock	$ 36	$ 28	$ 29
Four Note Horn	23	18	19
Headlamps-on Indicator	11	8	9
Low Fuel Indicator (w/V-8 eng.)	17	13	14
Coach Lamps	85	65	66
Courtesy/Reading Lamp	42	32	33
Fuel Usage Light (w/V-8 eng.)	30	23	24
Illuminated Door Lock & Interior			
Light Control	57	44	45
Front & Rear Light Monitors	62	48	49
Mirrors			
Left Remote Control W/Thermometer (NA S Type)	21	16	17
Electric Control Left & Right (NA S Type)	58	45	46
Electric Control Left & Right w/Left			
Thermometer (NA S Type)	79	61	62
Lighted Visor Vanity, Left or Right	47	36	37
Body Side Molding	59	45	46
Door Guard Molding	14	11	12
Paint			
Designers Accent	193	149	151
Regular Special Color	153	118	120
Firemist Special Color	172	132	134
Radio Equipment			
AM/FM Stereo w/Stereo Tape	110	85	86
AM/FM Stereo w/Stereo Cassette Tape	116	89	90
AM/FM Stereo w/CB & Power Antenna	294	226	229
AM/FM Stereo w/Stereo Tape, CB			
& Power Antenna	404	311	315
AM/FM Stereo Signal Seeking W/Digital			
Readout	182	140	142
AM/FM Stereo Signal Seeking w/Stereo			
Tape & Digital Readout	292	225	228
AM/FM Stereo Signal Seeking w/CB,			
Digital Clock & Readouts & Power Ant.	524	403	408
AM/FM Stereo Signal Seeking w/CB,			
Stereo Tape, Digital Clock & Readouts,			
Power Antenna	634	488	493
Power Antenna, AM/FM/CB	39	30	31
Astro Roof	998	768	776
Sun Roof	798	614	621
Seat Adjusters			
Power Passenger 6-way	166	128	130
Electric Recliner, Left or Right			
Riviera Coupe w/45/55 seats	118	91	92
Manual Recliner, Left or Right			
S Type w/Bucket Seats	62	48	49
Sports Steering Wheel, Riviera Coupe	32	25	26
Tilt Steering Wheel	77	59	60
Tilt & Telescope Steering Wheel,			
Riviera Coupe (NA w/Spts. Wheel)	121	93	94

Prices are accurate at time of printing; subject to manufacturer's change.

	Retail Price	Dealer Cost	Low Price
Body Side Stripe	$ 52	$ 40	$ 41
Firm Ride & Handling Suspension (NA S Type). . . .	21	16	17
Theft Deterrent System.	135	104	106
Full Vinyl Top (incl. coach lamps)	285	219	222
Landau Heavily Padded Vinyl Top (incl. coach lamps)	285	219	222
Trailer Tow Flasher & 5-Wire Harness	22	17	18
Interior Trim			
45/55 Notchback Front Seat, Leather w/Vinyl, Riviera Coupe.	350	270	273
Bucket Seats, Leather, w/Vinyl, S Type	350	270	273
Trunk Carpeting & Trim	25	19	20
Electric Trunk Release	25	19	20
Electric Trunk Lock (Elec. release req.).	60	46	47
Custom Wheel Covers	120	92	93
Three-Speed Wipers w/Low Speed Delay	39	30	31

BUICK SKYHAWK

SKYHAWK S

Hatchback	$4380	$3812	$4162

SKYHAWK

Hatchback	4598	4002	4302

STANDARD EQUIPMENT (included in above prices)

Skyhawk S: Safety and protection equipment plus 3.8 litre (231 CID) V-6 2-bbl. engine, 4-speed manual transmission w/Floor shifter, B78-13 bias-ply blackwall tires, AM radio, disc front brakes, stowaway spare tire, bucket front seats, carpeting.
Skyhawk: Skyhawk S equipment plus Appearance Group, body side stripe, BR78-13 steel belted blackwall radial tires.

SKYHAWK ACCESSORIES

Transmissions			
5-Speed Manual	$175	$145	$147
Automatic.	295	245	248
Acoustic Package	25	21	22
Air Conditioning	496	412	417
Appearance Group, Skyhawk S.	57	47	48
Limited-Slip Rear Axle	60	50	51
Heavy-Duty Battery	18	15	16
Power Brakes.	71	59	60
Electric Clock.	21	17	18
Convenience Group	24	20	21
Heavy-Duty Cooling			
w/o Air Conditioning.	58	48	49
w/Air Conditioning	30	25	26
Rear Defogger.	87	72	73
Calif. Emission System	83	69	70

Prices are accurate at time of printing; subject to manufacturer's change.

	Retail Price	Dealer Cost	Low Price
High Altitude Emission System	$ 35	$ 29	$ 30
Engine Block Heater	15	12	13
Tinted Glass			
All	60	50	51
Windshield Only	50	42	43
Instrument Gages, Clock & Tachometer	73	61	62
Visor Vanity Mirrors	10	8	9
Radio Equipment			
AM/FM	74	61	62
AM/FM Stereo	148	123	125
AM w/Stereo Tape	157	130	132
AM/FM Stereo w/Stereo Tape	250	208	211
Rear Speaker	23	19	20
Astro Roof	641	532	538
Vista Vent Roof	180	149	151
Adjustable Driver's Seat Back	20	17	18
Power Steering	146	121	122
Tilt Steering Wheel	68	56	57

BUICK SKYLARK

	Retail Price	Dealer Cost	Low Price
SKYLARK S			
Coupe	$4082	$3553	$3803
SKYLARK			
Sedan	4308	3749	3999
Coupe	4208	3662	3912
Hatchback Coupe	4357	3792	4042
SKYLARK CUSTOM			
Sedan	4562	3970	4220
Coupe	4462	3883	4133

STANDARD EQUIPMENT (included in the above prices)

Skylark S: Safety and protection equipment plus 3.8 litre (231 CID) V-6 2-bbl. engine, 3-speed manual transmission, E78-14 blackwall bias belted tires, disc front brakes, vinyl bench seat, carpeting, deluxe steering wheel hub caps.
Skylark: Skylark S equipment plus day/night mirror, lighter, stowaway spare tire on hatchback, vinyl or cloth full-foam bench seat, load floor carpet on hatchback.
Skylark Custom: Skylark S and Skylark equipment plus Convenience Group, rocker panel molding, carpeted door trim w/map pocket and reflector, deluxe wheel covers, front-door-operated dome and under-dash courtesy lights, stand-up hood ornament.

SKYLARK ACCESSORIES

	Retail Price	Dealer Cost	Low Price
Engines			
5.0 Litre (305 CID) V-8 2-bbl.	$195	$152	$154
5.7 Litre (350 CID) V-8 4-bbl.	320	250	253
Automatic Transmission	335	261	264
Accessory Package, Skylark S	15	12	13
Acoustic Package			
Skylark S, Skylark	42	33	34
Skylark Custom	28	22	23

Prices are accurate at time of printing; subject to manufacturer's change.

	Retail Price	Dealer Cost	Low Price
Air Conditioning	$529	$413	$418
Limited Slip Rear Axle	64	50	51
Heavy-Duty Battery	21	16	17
Power Brakes	76	59	60
Electric Clock	24	19	20
Carpeted Door Trim (NA 'S')	43	34	35
Console, Skylark	80	62	63
Convenience Group			
Skylark Hatchback	32	25	26
Skylark S, Skylark Coupe	35	27	28
Skylark Sedan	43	34	35
Heavy-Duty Cooling			
w/o Air Conditioning	58	23	24
w/Air Conditioning	30	23	24
Cruise Master	103	80	81
Rear Defogger, Forced Air	55	43	44
Power Door Locks			
2-Doors	111	63	64
4-Doors	110	85	86
Calif. Emission System	83	65	66
High Altitude Emission System	35	27	28
Engine Block Heater	15	12	13
Tinted Glass			
All	64	50	51
Windshield Only	50	39	40
Headlamps On Indicator	11	9	10
Dual Horns	10	8	9
Mirrors			
Left Remote Control	18	14	15
Sport, Left Remote, Right Manual	45	35	36
Radio Equipment			
AM	82	64	65
AM/FM	158	123	125
AM/FM Stereo	236	184	186
AM w/Stereo Tape	244	190	192
AM/FM Stereo w/Stereo Tape	345	269	272
AM/FM Stereo w/Stereo Cassette Tape	345	269	272
Rear Speaker (incl. w/stereo)	25	20	21
Windshield Antenna (incl. w/radio)	29	23	24
Vinyl Bucket Seats, Skylark	90	70	71
Sport Coupe or Sport Sedan (NA 'S')			
w/Stowaway Spare	202	157	159
w/o Stowaway Spare	221	172	174
Power Steering	163	127	129
Sport Steering Wheel	42	33	34
Tilt Steering Wheel	75	59	60
Firm Ride & Handling Suspension	25	20	21
Rallye Ride & Handling Suspension	48	37	38
Stowaway Spare Tire (std. hatchbacks)	19	15	16

Prices are accurate at time of printing; subject to manufacturer's change.

	Retail Price	Dealer Cost	Low Price
Full Vinyl Top			
Skylark S, Skylark	$ 99	$ 81	$ 82
Skylark Custom	104	77	78
Landau Vinyl Top			
Skylark S, Skylark Coupes	195	152	154
Skylark Custom Coupe	190	148	150
Trailer Wiring Harness (5-Wire)	22	17	18
Electric Trunk Release	24	19	20
Power Windows			
2-Doors	126	98	99
4-Doors	178	139	141
Swing-Out Rear Quarter Window, 2-Doors.......	59	46	47
Controlled-Cycle Wipers	38	30	31

Cadillac

CADILLAC DEVILLE, ELDORADO, FLEETWOOD AND SEVILLE

	Retail Price	Dealer Cost	Low Price
DEVILLE			
Coupe de Ville............................	$11139	$8580	$9580
Sedan de Ville...........................	11493	8853	9853
ELDORADO			
Eldorado Coupe	14240	10968	12468
FLEETWOOD			
Fleetwood Brougham	13446	10357	11857
Fleetwood Limousine	20987	16164	17664
Fleetwood Formal Limousine	21735	16740	18240
SEVILLE			
Seville Sedan	15646	12051	13551

STANDARD EQUIPMENT (included in above prices)

De Ville: Safety and protection equipment plus 7.0 litre (425 CID) V-8 engine, automatic transmission, power brakes, power steering, GR78-15 whitewall steel belted radial tires, automatic climate control air conditioning, AM/FM stereo digital display signal seeking radio, cornering lights, lamp monitors, power windows, power antenna, 6-way power seat, tinted glass, wheel covers, remote control left mirror, right visor vanity mirror, automatic parking brake release, stowaway spare tire.

Eldorado Coupe: Safety and protection equipment plus front-wheel drive, 5.7 litre (350 CID) V-8 engine w/fuel injection, automatic transmission, power four-wheel disc brakes, power steering, P205/75R-15 whitewall steel belted radial tires, electronic level control, automatic climate control air conditioning, twilight sentinel, 50/45 dual comfort front seats w/6-way driver's power, side window defoggers, power door locks, power windows, illuminated entry system, controlled cycle wipers, AM/FM stereo radio w/signal seeker & digital display, automatic power antenna, remote control mirrors, electronic trunk release w/power pull-down, cornering lights, lamp monitors, seat belt
Prices are accurate at time of printing; subject to manufacturer's change.

chimes, column-mounted headlamp dimmer, accent striping, tinted glass, auto. parking brake release, right vanity mirror, stowaway spare tire, carpeted trunk.

Fleetwood Brougham: De Ville equipment plus power 4-wheel disc brakes, HR78-15 tires, electronic level control, remote control right mirror, 45/55 dual comfort front seats, opera lamps, controlled cycle wipers.

Fleetwood Limousines: De Ville equipment less 6-way power seat on Formal Limousine, plus HR78-15 8PR tires, electronic level control, remote control right mirror, accent striping, opera lamps.

Seville: Safety and protection equipment plus 5.7 litre (350 CID) V-8 engine w/electronic fuel injection, automatic transmission, power 4-wheel disc brakes, power steering, padded vinyl roof, AM/FM stereo signal seeking radio w/digital display & automatic power antenna, automatic climate control, electronic level control, dual remote control mirrors, illuminated entry system, twilight sentinel, electric trunk release & power lid pull-down, power door locks, power windows, cornering lights, tilt/telescope steering wheel, controlled cycle wipers, lamp monitors, passenger seat recliner, rear seat reading lamps, power seats (6-way driver, 2-way pass.), tinted glass, stowaway spare tire, fuel monitor system, carpeted trunk.

CADILLAC ACCESSORIES

	Retail Price	Dealer Cost	Low Price
5.7 Litre (350 CID) Diesel Engine			
Eldorado & Seville	$287	$221	$224
Accent Striping, Fleetwood B'ham, DeVille	56	43	44
Astroroof			
Painted Roof	1163	896	905
w/Vinyl Roof	998	768	776
Brougham d'Elegance, Brougham			
Cloth	987	760	768
Leather Seating Area	1344	1035	1046
Calif. Fuel Economy Equip., De Villes, B'ham	65	50	51
Cruise Control	137	105	107
Rear Window Defogger	101	78	79
DeVille Cabriolet (Coupe)	384	296	299
DeVille Cabriolet Astroroof (Cpe.)	1522	1172	1184
DeVille Cabriolet Sunroof (Cpe.)	1312	1010	1021
DeVille d'Elegance	725	558	564
DeVille Custom Phaeton	2029	1562	1578
Limited Slip Differential, ex. Eldorado	70	54	55
Automatic Door Locks	121	93	94
Dual Comfort Front Seats, DeVilles	208	160	162
Eldorado Cabriolet	350	270	273
Eldorado Cabriolet Astroroof	1488	1146	1158
Eldorado Cabriolet Sunroof	1278	984	994
Eldorado Biarritz, Leather Seating	2600	2002	2023
Eldorado Biarritz Astroroof, Leather Seat	3738	2878	2906
Eldorado Biarritz Cloth Seat	2250	1733	1751
Eldorado Biarritz Astroroof Cloth Seat	3388	2609	2636
Electronic Fuel Injection (NA limos)	783	603	610
Electronic Level Control, DeVilles	160	123	125
Calif. Emission System	83	64	65
High Altitude Emission Pkg.	35	27	28

Prices are accurate at time of printing; subject to manufacturer's change.

Cadillac Eldorado

Cadillac Fleetwood

Cadillac Seville

	Retail Price	Dealer Cost	Low Price
Engine Block Heater	$ 21	$ 16	$ 17
Fuel Monitor (std. Seville)	31	24	25
80-Amp. Generator	54	42	43
Headlamp Control Guidematic	91	70	71
Illuminated Entry System	62	48	49
Opera Lamps DeVilles, Seville...............	66	51	52
Leather Seating Area			
DeVilles.............................	330	254	257
Other ex. Limos......................	350	270	273
Illuminated Visor Vanity Mirror	52	40	41
Right Remote Mirror, DeVilles	40	31	32
Electric Power Mirrors, DeVilles	130	100	102
Elec. Pwr. Mirrors w/Left Thermometer,			
All ex. DeVilles......................	90	69	70
Firemist Paint	171	132	134
Two-Tone Paint			
Reg. Colors, ex. Limos, Seville	275	212	215
Part. Firemist, ex. Limos, Seville	361	278	281
Standard Radio Plus			
8-Track Tape	195	150	152
8-Track Tape & CB.....................	480	370	374
Cassette Tape........................	225	173	175
Rear Control, 8-Track Tape, Limos	398	306	310
CB...................................	380	293	296
Power Recliner			
Driver's (w/Dual Comfort Seats)	122	94	95
Pass., Incl. Pwr. Adj. (w/Dual Comf. Seats) ..	280	216	219
Seville only	221	170	172
Pass. (w/notch back seat), DeVilles	122	94	95
Padded Vinyl Roof, DeVilles	225	173	175
Seat Adjuster, 6-way Pwr.			
All ex. Limos, Seville	160	123	125
Seville...............................	125	96	97
Seville Elegante	2735	2106	2128
Seville Elegante Sunroof	3663	2821	2850
Tilt & Telescope Steering Wheel	130	100	102
Sunroof			
w/Vinyl Roof..........................	798	614	621
w/Painted Roof........................	953	734	742
Theft Deterrent System	137	105	107
Illuminated Outside Thermometer	28	22	23
Trailering Pkg.			
Brougham, DeVilles	103	79	80
Eldorado, Seville	49	38	39
Trip Computer, Seville	920	708	716
Trumpet Horn (NA Seville)	22	17	18
Power Trunk Lid Release & Pull-Down			
DeVilles, Limos	85	65	66
Twilight Sentinel, DeVilles & Limos..........	56	43	44

Prices are accurate at time of printing; subject to manufacturer's change.

Chevrolet

CAMARO	Retail Price	Dealer Cost	Low Price
Sport Coupe	$4677	$4071	$4371
Rally Sport Coupe	5073	4415	4715
Berlinetta Coupe	5396	4696	4996
Z28 Sport Coupe	6115	5322	5672

STANDARD EQUIPMENT (included in above price)

Camaro Sport Coupe: Safety and protection equipment plus 4.1 litre V-6 1-bbl. engine, 3-speed manual transmission, high energy ignition system, disc front brakes, bucket seats, carpet, FR78-14 steel belted radial blackwall tires, single note horn, power steering.

Rally Sport Coupe: Sport Coupe equipment plus sport mirrors, rear spoiler, sport suspension, rally wheels.

Berlinetta Coupe: Sport Coupe equipment plus electric clock, custom interior, dual horns, special instrumentation group, interior decor/quiet sound group, sport mirrors, custom styled wheels, FR78-14 whitewall steel belted radial tires.

Z28 Sport Coupe: Sport Coupe equipment plus V-8 5.7 litre 4-bbl. engine, 4-speed close-ratio manual transmission, power brakes, electric clock, special instrumentation, sport mirrors, heavy-duty radiator, rear spoiler, stowaway spare tire, sport suspension.

CAMARO ACCESSORIES

Engines			
5 litre V-6 2-bbl.	$235	$183	$185
5.7 litre V-8 4-bbl. (std.-Z-28)	360	281	284
4-Speed Manual Transmission (except Z28)	135	105	107
Automatic Transmission			
Except Z28 Sport Coupe	335	261	264
Z28 Sport Coupe	59	46	47
Air Conditioning			
W/o V-8 Engine	562	439	444
W/V-8 Engine	529	413	418
Performance Rear Axle Ratio	18	14	15
Positraction Rear Axle	64	50	51
Heavy Duty Battery	20	16	17
Deluxe Belts	23	18	19
Power Brakes (std-Z28)	76	59	60
Electric Clock (std-Z28, Berlinetta)	23	18	19
Console	80	62	63
Rear Window Defogger	99	77	78
Power Door Locks	86	67	68
Floor Mats	23	18	19

Prices are accurate at time of printing; subject to manufacturer's change.

Chevrolet Corvette

Chevrolet Monte Carlo

Chevrolet Monza Spyder

	Retail Price	Dealer Cost	Low Price
Tinted Glass	$ 64	$ 50	$ 51
Dual Horns (std. Berlinetta)	9	7	8
Special Instrumentation (std. Z28, Berlinetta)	112	87	88
Interior Decor/Quiet Sound Group (std-Berlinetta)	64	50	51
Auxiliary Lighting			
Sport Coupe w/o Interior Decor/Quiet Sound Grp.	37	29	30
Sport Coupe w/Interior Decor/Quiet Sound Grp. Berlinetta Coupe	31	24	25
Sport Mirrors (Sport Coupe only)	43	34	35
Body Side Moldings	43	34	35
Heavy Duty Radiator (std-Z28)	33	26	27
Radio Equipment			
AM	85	66	67
AM/FM	158	123	125
AM/FM Stereo	232	181	183
AM w/Stereo Tape	248	193	195
AM/FM Stereo w/Stereo Tape	335	261	264
AM/FM Stereo w/Stereo Cassette Tape	341	266	269
AM/FM Citizens Band w/Power Antenna	489	381	385
AM/FM Stereo/Citizens Band w/Power Antenna	570	445	450
AM/FM Stereo w/Digital Clock Display			
W/o Special Instrumentation (except Z28, Berlinetta)	395	308	312
W/Special Instrumentation or Z28, Berlinetta	372	290	293
Rear Speaker	25	20	21
Windshield Antenna (Available only w/o radio)	27	21	22
Power Antenna	47	37	38
Removable Glass Roof Panels	655	511	517
Adjustable Driver's Seat Back	23	18	19
Sport Cloth Bucket Seats	23	18	19
Custom Vinyl Bucket Seats/Custom Interior Trim Sport Coupe	307	239	242
Custom Knit Cloth Bucket Seats/Custom Interior Trim			
Sport Coupe	330	257	260
Berlinetta Coupe	23	18	19
Automatic Speed Control	103	80	81
Rear Spoiler (std. Rally Sport Coupe Z28)	58	45	46
Comfortilt Steering Wheel	75	59	60
Style Trim	73	57	58
Sport Suspension	41	32	33
Vinyl Top	112	87	88
Power Windows	132	103	105
Intermittent Windshield Wiper Equipment	38	30	31

CHEVROLET CAPRICE CLASSIC AND IMPALA

IMPALA

Coupe	$5497	$4400	$4700

Prices are accurate at time of printing; subject to manufacturer's change.

	Retail Price	Dealer Cost	Low Price
Landau Coupe	$5961	$4771	$5071
4-Door Sedan	5597	4480	4780
CAPRICE CLASSIC			
Coupe	5837	4672	4972
Landau Coupe	6234	4990	5290
4-Door Sedan	5962	4772	5072
IMPALA STATION WAGON			
2-Seat	6109	4890	5190
3-Seat	6239	4994	5294
CAPRICE CLASSIC STATION WAGON			
2-Seat	6389	5114	5464
3-Seat	6544	5238	5588

STANDARD EQUIPMENT (included in above prices)

Impala: Safety and protection equipment plus 4.1 litre 6-cylinder 1-bbl. engine, automatic transmission, power brakes, power steering, carpeting, knit cloth bench seat, lighter, FR78-15 Fiberglass belted radial ply blackwall tires. Landau coupe has in addition vinyl top, sport mirrors (left remote, right manual), wheel opening moldings, pin striping.

Caprice Classic: Impala equipment plus electric clock, dual horns, wheel opening molding, quiet sound group, stand-up hood ornaments, carpeted lower door panels.

Impala and Caprice Classic Station Wagons: Impala and Caprice Classic equipment respectively plus V-8 5 litre 2-bbl. engine, vinyl bench seats and interior, HR78-15 steel belted radial ply blackwall tires.

IMPALA AND CAPRICE CLASSIC ACCESSORIES

Engines

	Retail	Dealer	Low
5 Litre V-8 2-bbl. (std wagon)	$235	$181	$183
5.7 Litre V-8 4-bbl. Coupes, Sedans	360	277	280
Wagons	125	96	97
Vinyl Bench Seat, Coupes & Sedans	27	21	22
Knit or Sport Cloth Bench Seat, Wagons	27	21	22
Vinyl 50/50 Seat, Coupes & Sedans	267	206	209
Wagons	240	185	187
Knit Cloth 50/50 Seat, Coupes & Sedans	240	185	187
Wagons	267	206	209
Special Custom Cloth 50/50 Seat, Coupes & Sedans	397	306	310
Four-Season Air Conditioning	605	466	471
Comfortron Air Conditioning	688	530	536
Limited Slip Rear Axle	68	52	53
Performance Rear Axle Ratio	19	15	16
Heavy-Duty Battery	21	16	17
Deluxe Belts, ex. 3-seat Wagons	24	18	19
Deluxe Belts, 3-seat Wagons	27	21	22
Bumper Guards	52	40	41
Bumper Rub Strips	56	43	44
Roof Carrier, Wagons	115	89	90
Digital Electric Clock, Impala	55	42	43

Prices are accurate at time of printing; subject to manufacturer's change.

CONSUMER GUIDE

	Retail Price	Dealer Cost	Low Price
Caprice Classic	$ 31	$ 24	$ 25
Electric Clock, Impala	24	18	19
Rear Defogger			
Electro Clear	101	78	79
Forced Air (ex. Wagons)	57	44	45
Power Door Locks			
Coupes	88	68	69
Sedans, Wagons.	122	94	95
Estate Equipment, Wagons	262	202	204
Floor Covering			
Load Floor, Wagons	75	58	59
Deluxe Cargo Area, Wagons.	107	82	83
Gage Package	54	42	43
63-Amp. Generator.	34	26	27
Tinted Glass	84	65	66
Dual Horns, Impala	10	7	8
Auxiliary Lighting			
Impala Coupe, Sedan, 3-Seat Wagon	38	29	30
Impala 2-Seat Wagon	50	39	40
Caprice Classic Cpe., Sdn., 3-Seat Wag.	35	27	28
Caprice Classic 2-Seat Wagon	47	36	37
Deluxe Luggage Compartment (ex. Wagons)	46	35	36
Mirrors			
Left Remote Control	19	14	15
Left & Right Remote Control	56	43	44
Sport, Left Remote, Right Manual			
All ex. Landau Coupes	44	34	35
Sport, Left & Right Remote			
All ex. Landau Coupes	69	53	54
Landau Coupes	25	19	20
Visor Vanity.	6	4	5
Visor Vanity, Illuminated	41	32	33
Moldings			
Body Side	44	34	35
Door Edge			
Coupes	14	11	12
Sedans, Wagons.	21	16	17
Wheel Opening, Impala.	23	18	19
Quiet Sound Group, Impala.	60	46	47
Heavy-Duty Radiator.	42	32	33
Radio Equipment			
AM.	87	67	68
AM/FM	161	124	126
AM/FM Stereo	236	182	184
AM w/Stereo Tape	265	204	207
AM/FM Stereo w/Stereo Tape.	340	262	265
AM/FM Stereo w/Stereo Cassette Tape	346	266	269
AM/FM w/CB & Power Antenna	503	387	391
AM/FM Stereo w/CB & Pwr. Ant.	578	445	450

Prices are accurate at time of printing; subject to manufacturer's change.

	Retail Price	Dealer Cost	Low Price
AM/FM Stereo w/Digital Clock Display			
Impala	$401	$309	$313
Caprice Classic	377	290	293
Rear Speaker	26	20	21
Dual Front Speakers	22	17	18
Power Antenna	48	37	38
Windshield Antenna (only w/o radio)	28	22	23
Power Seat (50/50 seat required)	166	128	130
Power Sky Roof	625	481	486
Automatic Speed Control	108	83	84
Comfortilt Steering Wheel	77	59	60
Pin Striping (std. Landau)	33	25	26
Heavy-Duty Shock Absorbers	23	17	18
Superlift Rear Shock Absorbers	55	42	43
Sport Suspension (ex. Wagons)	42	32	33
Power Tailgate Lock	40	31	32
Power Trunk Opener	25	19	20
Value Appearance Group	87	67	68
Vinyl Top (ex. Wagons, Landau Coupe)	145	112	114
Power Windows			
Coupes	138	106	108
Sedans, Wagons	205	158	160
Intermittent Wiper System	39	30	31

CHEVROLET CHEVETTE

CHEVETTE — Alaska, Arizona, California, Hawaii, Idaho, Nevada, Oregon, Utah, Washington

	Retail Price	Dealer Cost	Low Price
Scooter Hatchback Coupe	$3299	$2970	$3170
Hatchback Coupe	3676	3199	3399
Hatchback Sedan	3796	3303	3503

CHEVETTE — 41 States

	Retail Price	Dealer Cost	Low Price
Scooter Hatchback Coupe	$3299	$2970	$3170
Hatchback Coupe	3794	3302	3502
Hatchback Sedan	3914	3406	3606

STANDARD EQUIPMENT (included in above prices)
Chevette Scooter: Safety and protection equipment plus 1.6 litre 4-cyl. 2-bbl. engine, 4-speed manual transmission, high energy ignition, rack and pinion steering, disc front brakes, vinyl bucket seats, 155/80-13 fiberglass belted radial blackwall tires.
Chevette except Scooter: Scooter equipment plus deluxe bumpers, cigarette lighter, body side molding, AM radio, whitewall tires, wheel trim rings.

CHEVETTE ACCESSORIES

	Retail Price	Dealer Cost	Low Price
1.6 litre H.O. 4-cyl. Engine	$60	$50	$51
Automatic Transmission	295	245	248
Air Conditioning	496	412	417
Heavy-Duty Battery	19	15	16
Deluxe Belts			
W/Standard Belts	21	17	18

Prices are accurate at time of printing; subject to manufacturer's change.

	Retail Price	Dealer Cost	Low Price
W/Automatic Shoulder Belt system	$ 50	$ 42	$ 43
Automatic Shoulder Belt Convenience Group			
W/o Custom Interior Trim...................	166	137	139
W/Custom Interior Trim	144	120	122
Custom Interior Trim			
Incl. Custom Cloth Bucket Seats	181	150	152
Incl. Custom Vinyl Bucket Seats	160	133	135
Deluxe Appointment Group			
W/o Cust. Int. Trim or Black Int. Trim	137	113	115
W/o Cust. Int. Trim W/Black Int. Trim	116	96	97
W/Cust. Int. Trim w/o Black Int. Trim	115	95	96
W/Cust. Int. Trim W/Black Int. Trim	94	78	79
Power Brakes	71	59	60
Deluxe Bumpers (Scooter)	37	31	32
Deluxe Bumper Guards			
Scooter (incl. Deluxe Bumpers).............	78	65	66
Ex. Scooter	41	34	35
Load Floor Carpet	46	38	39
Roof Carrier	65	54	55
Electric Clock	21	17	18
Rear Window Defogger	87	72	73
Deluxe Exterior	104	86	87
Tinted Glass	60	50	51
Special Instrumentation	67	56	57
Lighter (Scooter)	7	6	7
Auxiliary Lighting			
W/o Automatic Shoulder Belts...............	37	31	32
W/Automatic Shoulder Belts	44	37	38
Day/Night Mirror..........................	10	8	9
Left Remote Sport Mirror	25	21	22
Left Remote & Right Manual Sport Mirrors	40	33	34
Body Side Moldings (Scooter)................	40	33	34
Quiet Sound Group			
W/o Custom Interior Trim..................	47	39	40
W/Custom Interior Trim	35	29	30
Heavy-Duty Radiator.......................	74	61	62
Radio Equipment			
AM (Scooter)............................	74	61	62
AM/FM			
Scooter................................	148	123	125
Ex. Scooter	74	61	62
AM/FM Stereo	148	123	125
Rear Speaker	23	19	20
Sport Cloth Bucket Seats			
W/o Rear Seat	11	9	10
W/Rear Seat	21	17	18
Rear Seat Deletion (credit)	(51)	(42)	(42)
Sport Shifter	30	25	26
Sport Suspension..........................	33	27	28

Prices are accurate at time of printing; subject to manufacturer's change.

	Retail Price	Dealer Cost	Low Price
Comfortilt Steering Wheel	$68	$56	$57
Sport Striping	70	58	59
Intermittent Windshield Wiper System	35	29	30

CHEVROLET CORVETTE

CORVETTE

Coupe.................................	$10220	$7975	$9475

STANDARD EQUIPMENT (included in above prices)
Corvette: Safety and protection equipment plus V-8 5.7 litre 4-bbl. engine, 4-speed manual or automatic transmission (choice), P225/70R-15 steel belted radial ply black-wall tires, power steering, power brakes (disc front), tinted glass, bucket seats, carpet, electric clock, AM/FM radio.

CORVETTE ACCESSORIES

5.7 Litre V-8 Engine, L82	$565	$435	$440
Air Conditioning...........................	635	489	494
Highway Axle Ratio.........................	19	15	16
Heavy-Duty Battery	21	16	17
Trailering Chassis Equipment	98	76	77
Convenience Group	94	73	74
Rear Window Defogger	102	79	80
Sport Mirrors.............................	45	35	36
Radio Equipment			
AM/FM Stereo	90	69	70
AM/FM Stereo w/Stereo Tape..............	228	176	178
AM/FM Stereo w/Stereo Cassette Tape	234	180	182
AM/FM Stereo w/CB & Power Antenna	439	338	342
Power Antenna...........................	52	40	41
Dual Rear Speakers	52	40	41
Removable Glass Roof Panels	365	281	284
Heavy-Duty Shock Absorbers.................	33	25	26
Auto-Speed Control.......................	113	87	88
Tilt-Telescope Steering Wheel	190	146	148
Gymkhana Suspension	49	38	39
Aluminum Wheels	380	293	296
Power Windows	141	109	111
Power Windows & Door Locks	272	209	212

CHEVROLET MALIBU AND MALIBU CLASSIC

MALIBU

Sport Coupe	$4398	$3652	$3902
Sedan...................................	4498	3735	3985

MALIBU CLASSIC

Sport Coupe	4676	3882	4132
Landau Coupe	4915	4081	4381
Sedan...................................	4801	3986	4236

MALIBU STATION WAGON

2-Seat...................................	4745	3940	4190

Prices are accurate at time of printing; subject to manufacturer's change.

MALIBU CLASSIC STATION WAGON	Retail Price	Dealer Cost	Low Price
2-Seat.............................	$4955	$4114	$4414

STANDARD EQUIPMENT (included in above prices)

Malibu: Safety and protection equipment plus 3.3 litre V-6 2-bbl. engine, 3-speed manual transmission, P185/75R-14 fiberglass belted radial ply blackwall tires, knit cloth bench seat, disc front brakes, carpeting, day/night mirror.

Malibu Classic: Malibu equipment plus dual horns, wheel covers. Landau Coupe also has in addition, vinyl top, sport cloth bench seat, pin striping, sport-silver wheel covers.

Malibu And Malibu Classic Station Wagons: Malibu and Malibu Classic sedan equipment respectively plus power brakes, vinyl bench seat and interior trim, P195/75R-14 fiberglass belted radial ply blackwall tires.

MALIBU AND MALIBU CLASSIC ACCESSORIES

Engines			
3.8 Litre V-6 2-bbl., LD5..................	$40	$31	$32
4.4 Litre V-8 2-bbl..	190	148	150
5.0 Litre V-8 4-bbl......................	295	230	233
5.7 Litre V-8 4-bbl., Wagons only............	360	281	284
Transmissions			
4-Speed Manual.......................	135	105	107
Automatic...........................	335	261	264
Vinyl Bench Seat, Coupe & Sedan	26	20	21
Knit Cloth Bench Seat, Wagon.................	26	20	21
Vinyl 50/50 Bench Seat			
Coupe, Sedan	198	154	156
Wagon	172	134	136
Knit Cloth 50/50 Bench Seat			
Coupe, Sedan	172	134	136
Wagon	198	154	156
Vinyl Bucket Seats (except wagon).............	85	66	67
Air Conditioning.......................	562	438	443
Rear Window Air Deflector.................	30	23	24
Limited Slip Rear Axle	65	50	51
Performance Rear Axle Ratio	18	14	15
Heavy-Duty Battery	20	16	17
Power Brakes	76	59	60
Bumper Guards	46	35	36
Bumper Rub Strips......................	41	32	33
Load Floor Carpet, Wagon..................	70	55	56
Roof Carrier	90	70	71
Electric Clock	23	18	19
Console.............................	80	62	63
Rear Window Defogger			
Electro Clear	99	77	78
Forced Air (except Wagons)................	55	43	44
Power Door Locks			
Coupe.............................	86	67	68
Sedan, Wagon	120	94	95

Prices are accurate at time of printing; subject to manufacturer's change.

	Retail Price	Dealer Cost	Low Price
Estate Equipment..................	$258	$201	$204
Gage Package	57	44	45
63-Amp. Generator			
W/o Air Conditioning or Electro Clear..........	33	26	27
W/Air Conditioning or Electro Clear	5	4	5
Tinted Glass	70	55	56
Dual Horns, Malibu series	9	7	8
Instrumentation.....................	125	98	99
Dome Reading Light....................	20	16	17
Auxiliary Lighting			
Malibu Coupe, Sedan.................	50	39	40
Malibu Wagon.....................	56	44	45
Malibu Classic Coupe, Sedan	31	24	25
Malibu Classic Wagon	37	29	30
Deluxe Luggage Compartment (except Wagons).....	43	34	35
Mirrors			
Left Remote Control	18	14	15
Sport, Left Remote, Right Manual...........	43	34	35
Sport, Left & Right Remote	68	53	54
Visor Vanity......................	5	4	5
Visor Vanity, Illuminated	40	31	32
Quiet Sound Group....................	51	40	41
Heavy-Duty Radiator...................	33	26	27
Radio Equipment			
AM...........................	85	66	67
AM/FM.........................	158	123	125
AM/FM Stereo	232	181	183
AM w/Stereo Tape	248	193	195
AM/FM Stereo w/Stereo Tape.............	335	261	264
AM/FM Stereo w/Stereo Cassette Tape	341	266	269
AM/FM w/CB & Power Antenna	489	381	385
AM/FM Stereo w/CB & Pwr. Ant.	570	445	450
AM/FM Stereo w/Digital Clock Display.........	395	308	312
Rear Speaker......................	25	20	21
Dual Front Speakers..................	21	16	17
Power Antenna.....................	47	37	38
Windshield Antenna (only w/o radio)	27	21	22
Cargo Security Package, Wagons	37	29	30
Power Seat	163	127	129
Power Sky Roof, Coupes, Sedans.............	529	413	418
Auto. Speed Control	103	80	81
Power Steering.....................	163	127	129
Comfortilt Steering Wheel................	75	59	60
Pin Striping (std. Landau)	48	37	38
Heavy-Duty Shock Absorbers (ex. Wagons)........	22	17	18
Sport Suspension (ex. Wagons).............	41	32	33
Power Tailgate Window Release.............	25	20	21
Power Trunk Opener...................	24	19	20
Vinyl Top (ex. Wagons) Landau Coupe	116	90	91

Prices are accurate at time of printing; subject to manufacturer's change.

CONSUMER GUIDE

	Retail Price	Dealer Cost	Low Price
Power Windows			
Coupe	$132	$103	$ 105
Sedan, Wagon	187	146	148
Intermittent Wiper System	38	30	31

CHEVROLET MONTE CARLO

MONTE CARLO

	Retail Price	Dealer Cost	Low Price
Sport Coupe	$4995	$4148	$4448
Landau Coupe	5907	4905	5205

STANDARD EQUIPMENT (included in above prices)
Monte Carlo Sport Coupe: Safety and protection equipment plus 3.3 Litre V-6 2-bbl. engine, 3-speed manual transmission, P205/70R-14 steel belted radial ply blackwall tires, cloth bench seat, disc front brakes, carpet, dual horns.
Monte Carlo Landau Coupe: Sport Coupe equipment plus power brakes, power steering, automatic transmission, vinyl top, sport mirrors (left remote, right manual), visor vanity mirror, body sill molding, pin striping, deluxe wheel covers.

MONTE CARLO ACCESSORIES

Engines			
3.8 Litre V-6 2-bbl	$40	$31	$32
4.4 Litre V-8 2-bbl	190	148	150
5.0 Litre V-8 4-bbl	295	230	233
Automatic Transmission, Sport Coupe	335	261	264
Vinyl Bench Seat	26	20	21
Cloth or Vinyl Bucket Seats	85	65	66
Custom Cloth 55/45 Seat	368	287	290
Air Conditioning	562	438	443
Limited Slip Rear Axle	65	50	51
Performance Rear Axle Ratio	18	14	15
Heavy-Duty Battery	20	16	17
Power Brakes (std. Landau)	76	59	60
Console	80	62	63
Rear Defogger, Electro Clear	99	77	78
Power Door Locks	86	67	68
Gage Package	34	27	28
63-Amp. Generator			
W/o Rear Defogger	33	26	27
W/Rear Defogger	5	4	5
Tinted Glass	70	55	56
Special Instrumentation	102	80	81
Dome Reading Light	20	16	17
Auxiliary Lighting	31	24	25
Deluxe Luggage Compartment	43	34	35
Mirrors			
Left Remote	18	14	15
Sport, Left Remote, Right Manual (std. Landau)	43	34	35
Sport Dual Remote			
Sport Coupe	68	53	54

Prices are accurate at time of printing; subject to manufacturer's change.

	Retail Price	Dealer Cost	Low Price
Landau Coupe............................	$ 25	$ 20	$ 21
Visor Vanity (std. Landau).................	5	4	5
Visor Vanity, Illuminated			
Sport Coupe...........................	40	31	32
Landau Coupe.........................	35	27	28
Heavy-Duty Radiator......................	33	26	27
Radio Equipment			
AM...................................	85	66	67
AM/FM...............................	158	123	125
AM/FM Stereo........................	232	181	183
AM w/Stereo Tape.....................	248	193	195
AM/FM Stereo w/Stereo Tape...........	335	261	264
AM/FM Stereo w/Stereo Cassette Tape ...	341	266	269
AM/FM w/CB & Power Antenna	489	381	385
AM/FM Stereo w/CB & Pwr. Ant.	570	445	450
Rear Speaker..........................	25	20	21
Dual Front Speakers....................	21	16	17
Power Antenna........................	47	37	38
Windshield Antenna (only w/o radio).........	27	21	22
Removable Glass Roof panels	655	511	517
Power Seat	163	127	129
Power Sky Roof	529	413	417
Auto. Speed Control	103	80	81
Comfortilt Steering Wheel	75	59	60
Power Steering (std. Landau)	163	127	129
Pin Striping............................	40	31	32
Heavy-Duty Suspension	22	17	18
Vinyl Top (std. Landau)...................	131	102	104
Power Trunk Opener	24	19	20
Power Windows	132	103	105
Intermittent Wiper System................	38	30	31

CHEVROLET MONZA

MONZA

	Retail Price	Dealer Cost	Low Price
Hatchback	$3844	$3345	$3545
Station Wagon	3973	3458	3658
Coupe	3617	3148	3348
Sport Hatchback........................	4291	3734	3984

STANDARD EQUIPMENT (included in above prices)
Monza: Safety and protection equipment plus 2.5 litre 4-cyl. 2-bbl. engine, 4-speed manual transmission with floor mounted shifter, A78-13 whitewall bias ply tires (B78-13 on wagon), stowaway spare tire (ex. wagon), AM radio, bumper guards on wagon, console (ex. coupe), folding rear seat on hatchback, disc front brakes, carpeting, wheel covers, vinyl bucket front seats, tinted glass.
Monza Sport Hatchback: Monza equipment plus custom vinyl interior trim, deluxe wheel covers, body-color door handle inserts, upgrade exterior trim, additional sound insulation.
Prices are accurate at time of printing; subject to manufacturer's change.

MONZA ACCESSORIES

	Retail Price	Dealer Cost	Low Price
Engines			
3.2 Litre V-6 2-bbl........................	$160	$133	$135
3.8 Litre V-6 2-bbl........................	200	166	168
5.0 Litre V-8 2-bbl........................	395	328	332
Transmissions			
5-speed Manual	175	145	147
Automatic..............................	295	245	248
Air Conditioning	496	412	417
Rear Window Air Deflector.................	28	23	24
Performance Rear Axle Ratio	17	14	15
Limited Slip Rear Axle	60	50	51
Heavy-Duty Battery	19	15	16
Power Brakes.............................	71	59	60
Bumper Guards (std. Wagons)	42	34	35
Roof Carrier, Wagon	65	54	55
Digital Clock	49	41	42
Electric Clock.............................	21	17	18
Console, Coupe...........................	75	62	63
Rear Window Defogger	87	72	73
Calif-Emission System			
w/2.5 Litre LS6 Engine..................	150	125	127
w/other Engines	83	69	70
High Altitude Emission System	35	29	30
Special Instrumentation			
w/o Clock or Digital Readout Radio			
All ex. Wagon........................	88	73	74
Wagon	71	59	60
w/Clock or Digital Readout Radio			
All ex. Wagon........................	67	56	57
Wagon	50	42	43
Auxiliary Lighting			
Sport Hatchback......................	20	17	18
Coupe & Hatchback w/o Custom Interior	25	21	22
Coupe & Hatchback w/Custom Interior.......	20	17	18
Wagon w/o Custom Interior...............	37	31	32
Wagon w/Custom Interior	32	27	28
Mirrors			
Day/Night............................	10	8	9
Sport, Left Remote, Right Manual	40	33	34
Quiet Sound Group			
All ex. Sport Hatchback	39	32	33
Sport Hatchback.......................	29	24	25
Heavy Duty Radiator (incl. w/air cond.)	31	25	26
Radio Equipment			
AM...................................	STD	STD	STD
AM/FM................................	74	61	62
AM/FM Stereo..........................	148	123	125
AM w/Stereo Tape......................	159	132	135

Prices are accurate at time of printing; subject to manufacturer's change.

	Retail Price	Dealer Cost	Low Price
AM/FM Stereo w/Stereo Tape..............	$242	$201	$204
AM/FM Stereo w/Stereo Cassette Tape.......	242	201	204
AM/FM Stereo w/Digital Clock & Readouts....	299	248	251
Rear Seat Speaker	23	19	20
Seats/Trim			
Folding Rear, Coupe & Wagon.............	97	81	82
Cloth Buckets..........................	21	17	18
Custom Cloth Buckets			
All ex. Sport Hatchback	21	17	18
Sport Hatchback.......................	180	149	151
Custom Vinyl Buckets (std. Sport)..........	159	132	134
Front & Rear Spoilers.....................	97	81	82
Spyder Appearance Package	231	192	194
Spyder Equipment.......................	164	135	137
Front Stabilizer Bar (incl. w/radial tires)	27	22	23
Power Steering.........................	146	121	123
Tilt Steering Wheel	68	56	57
Sport Strining, Wagon....................	84	70	71
Sun Roof	180	149	151
Sport Suspension (incl. w/Spyder Equip.)	31	26	27
Vinyl Top.............................	156	129	131
Intermittent Wiper System.................	35	29	30

CHEVROLET NOVA

NOVA

	Retail Price	Dealer Cost	Low Price
Hatchback Coupe........................	$4118	$3584	$3834
Coupe.................................	3955	3442	3642
Sedan.................................	4055	3529	3779

NOVA CUSTOM

Coupe.................................	4164	3624	3874
Sedan.................................	4264	3711	3961

STANDARD EQUIPMENT (included in above prices)

Nova: Safety and protection equipment plus 4.1 litre 6-cylinder 1-bbl. engine, 3-speed manual transmission, E78-14 bias belted blackwall tires, stowaway spare on hatchback, vinyl bench seat, disc front brakes, carpet.

Nova Custom: Nova equipment plus custom vinyl bench seat and interior trim, Interior Decor Package.

NOVA ACCESSORIES

Engines			
5 Litre V-8 2-bbl.........................	$235	$183	$185
5.7 Litre V-8 4-bbl.......................	360	281	284
Transmissions			
4-speed Manual	135	105	107
Automatic	335	261	264
Sport Cloth or Custom Sport Cloth Bench Seat	23	18	19
Custom Vinyl Bucket Seats	85	66	67

Prices are accurate at time of printing; subject to manufacturer's change.

	Retail Price	Dealer Cost	Low Price
Air Conditioning			
W/6-cyl. Engine	$562	$438	$443
W/V-8 Engine	529	413	418
Limited Slip Rear Axle	64	50	51
Performance Rear Axle Ratio	18	14	15
Heavy-Duty Battery	20	16	17
Power Brakes	76	59	60
Electric Clock	23	18	19
Console	80	62	63
Rear Window Defogger, Forced Air	55	43	44
Power Door Locks			
Coupes	80	62	63
Sedan	111	87	88
Gage Package	53	41	42
Tinted Glass	64	50	51
Dual Horns	9	7	8
Special Instrumentation	112	87	88
Interior Decor Package (std. Custom series)	31	24	25
Auxiliary Lighting			
Hatchback w/o Int. Decor Pkg.	43	34	35
Hatchback w/Int. Decor Pkg.	31	24	25
Coupe w/o Int. Decor or Custom Interior	43	34	35
Coupe w/Int. Decor or Custom Interior	31	24	25
Sedan w/o Int. Decor or Custom Interior	48	37	38
Sedan w/Int. Decor or Custom Interior	36	28	29
Mirrors			
Inside Day/Night	11	8	9
Left Remote	18	14	15
Sport, Left Remote, Right Manual	43	34	35
Heavy-Duty Radiator	33	26	27
Radio Equipment			
AM	82	64	65
AM/FM	158	123	125
AM/FM Stereo	232	181	183
AM w/Stereo Tape	244	190	192
AM/FM Stereo w/Stereo Tape	335	261	264
AM/FM Stereo w/Stereo Cassette Tape	341	266	269
AM/FM Stereo w/Digital Clock Display	395	308	312
Rear Speaker	25	20	21
Windshield Antenna (only w/o radio)	27	21	22
Rally Equipment	211	165	167
Auto. Speed Control	103	80	81
Power Steering	163	127	129
Comfortilt Steering Wheel	75	59	60
Stowaway Spare Tire (std-Hatchback)	19	16	17
Pin Striping	30	23	24
Heavy-Duty Suspension			
6-cyl. w/o pwr. steering or steel belted radial tires	36	28	29

Prices are accurate at time of printing; subject to manufacturer's change.

	Retail Price	Dealer Cost	Low Price
6-cyl. w/pwr. steering or steel belted radial tires, 8-cyl.	$ 11	$ 9	$ 10
Sport Suspension	45	35	36
Vinyl Top			
Cabriolet	190	148	150
Full	99	77	78
Value Appearance Group	79	62	63
Power Windows			
Coupes	126	98	99
Sedan	178	139	141
Swing-Out Rear Quarter Window	59	46	47
Intermittent Wiper System	38	30	31

Oldsmobile

OLDSMOBILE CUTLASS

	Retail Price	Dealer Cost	Low Price
CUTLASS SALON			
Coupe	$4623	$ 3917	$4167
Sedan	4723	3921	4171
CUTLASS SALON BROUGHAM			
Coupe	4907	4075	4375
Sedan	5032	4178	4478
CUTLASS SUPREME			
Coupe	5063	4204	4504
CUTLASS CALAIS			
Coupe	5491	4559	4859
CUTLASS SUPREME BROUGHAM			
Coupe	5492	4560	4860
CUTLASS CRUISER			
Wagon	4980	4135	4435
CUTLASS CRUISER BROUGHAM			
Wagon	5517	4581	4881

STANDARD EQUIPMENT (included in above prices)

Cutlass Salon: Safety and protection equipment plus 3.8 litre (231 CID) V-6 engine, 3-speed manual transmission, disc front brakes, blackwall glass belted radial tires, carpet, day/night mirror, bench seat, hub caps.

Cutlass Salon Brougham: Salon equipment plus custom sport bench seat, upgraded interior and exterior trim.

Prices are accurate at time of printing; subject to manufacturer's change.

Cutlass Supreme: Salon equipment plus door pull handles, deluxe steering wheel and hub caps.

Cutlass Calais: Salon equipment plus steel belted radial tires, custom sport steering wheel w/padded rim, stand-up hood ornament, special wheel discs, ride and handling suspension, reclining front contour seats.

Cutlass Supreme Brougham: Salon and Supreme equipment plus upgraded sound insulation, loose cushion look front seats, deluxe steering wheel, deluxe wheel covers.

Cutlass Cruiser: Salon equipment plus vinyl bench seats, power brakes.

Cutlass Cruiser Brougham: Cruiser equipment plus automatic transmission, upgraded trim.

CUTLASS ACCESSORIES

	Retail Price	Dealer Cost	Low Price
Engines			
4.8 Litre (260 CID) V-8 2-bbl..............	$140	$109	$111
5.0 Litre (305 CID) V-8 4-bbl...............	255	199	201
5.7 Litre (350 CID) V-8 4-bbl., Wagons only	320	250	253
4.8 Litre (260 CID) V-8 Diesel (NA Wagons).....	735	573	579
5.7 Litre (350 CID) V-8 Diesel, Wagons only	895	698	705
Transmissions			
4-Spd. Manual (NA Supreme B'ham., Wags.)	135	105	107
5-Spd. Manual (NA Supreme B'ham., Wags.)	310	242	245
Automatic (NA B'ham. Wagon)	335	261	264
Four Season Air Conditioning	562	438	443
Tempmatic Air Conditioning	602	470	475
Rear Window Air Deflector, Wagons	30	23	24
High Capacity Alternator......................	49	38	39
Astroroof, Electric Sliding, Coupes.............	729	569	575
Limited Slip Rear Axle	64	50	51
Heavy Duty Battery...........................	21	16	17
High Flow Heater Blower......................	19	15	16
Power Brakes (ex. Wagons)....................	76	59	60
Bumper Guards	45	35	36
Electric Clock	24	19	20
Electric Digital Clock	55	43	44
Console (NA Supreme B'ham., B'ham. Wag.)	80	62	63
Convenience Group			
Cpes. ex. Salon, Supreme	29	23	24
Wagons..................................	47	37	38
Salon & Supreme Coupes...................	41	32	33
Salon Sedan	49	38	39
Salon B'ham. Sedan.......................	36	28	29
Cooling System, Eng. & Trans.			
W/Air Cond...............................	29	23	24
W/o Air Cond.	75	59	60
W/Diesel Eng. & Air Cond., Ex. Wags........	61	48	49
W/Diesel Eng. w/o Air Cond., Ex. Wags.	92	72	73
Wag. w/Diesel Eng. & Air Cond..............	21	16	17

Prices are accurate at time of printing; subject to manufacturer's change.

	Retail Price	Dealer Cost	Low Price
Wag. w/Diesel Eng. w/o Air Cond.	$ 52	$ 41	$ 42
High Capacity Cooling System, Eng.	21	16	17
Cruise Control	103	80	81
Electric Rear Window Defroster	99	77	78
Calif. Emission System.	83	65	66
High Altitude Emission System	35	27	28
Engine Block Heater	15	12	13
Engine Oil Cooler (NA Wags.)	40	31	32
4-4-2 Appearance & Handling Pkg.			
Salon Coupe	276	215	218
Salon Brougham Coupe.	122	95	96
Gauges (NA Calais)	66	51	52
Gauges Incl. Tachometer (NA Calais).	118	92	93
Gauges, Canadian Inst. Cluster	3	2	3
Tinted Glass	70	55	56
Cornering Lamps	49	38	39
Dome/Reading Lamp			
Salon, Supreme, Wags. w/o Conv. Grp.	19	15	16
Salon, Supreme, Wags. w/Conv. Grp.	11	9	10
Others	11	9	10
Lamp Monitor (NA Base Wagon)	62	48	49
Automatic Load Leveling System	120	94	95
Power Door Locks			
2-Drs.	86	67	68
4-Drs.	120	94	95
Locks, Tire Storage, Rear Qtr. Storage			
W/Limited-Slip Axle	47	37	38
W/o Limited-Slip Axle	52	41	42
Luggage Rack, Wagon	90	70	71
Mirrors			
Left Remote Control	18	14	15
Right Remote Control			
All ex. Supreme, Calais, Supreme B'ham.	39	30	31
Calais, Supreme, Supreme B'ham.	34	27	28
Sport			
All ex. Supreme, Calais, Supreme B'ham.	43	34	35
Supreme, Calais, Supreme B'ham.	37	29	30
Sport Remote Control			
All ex. Supreme, Calais, Supreme B'ham.	70	55	56
Supreme, Calais, Supreme B'ham.	64	50	51
Illuminated Visor Vanity			
W/o Conv. Grp.	46	36	37
W/Conv. Grp.	43	34	35
Radio Equipment			
AM	86	67	68
AM/FM	163	127	129
AM/FM Stereo	236	184	186
AM w/Stereo Tape	248	193	195
AM/FM Stereo w/Stereo Tape.	345	269	272

Prices are accurate at time of printing; subject to manufacturer's change.

CONSUMER GUIDE

	Retail Price	Dealer Cost	Low Price
AM/FM Stereo w/Cassette Tape	$351	$274	$277
AM/FM Stereo w/CB & Pwr. Ant.	574	448	453
Radio Accommodation Pkg.	29	23	24
Power Antenna			
W/Radio	47	37	38
W/o Radio	76	59	60
Rear Speaker.	25	20	21
Dual Rear Speakers	50	39	40
Reminder Pkg., Low Fuel, Headlamp-On	38	30	31
Removable Roof Panel, Glass, Cpes. ex. Salon, Salon			
Brougham	655	511	517
Sun Roof, Coupes.	529	413	418
Full Vinyl Roof (NA Wagons).	116	90	91
Landau Vinyl Roof			
Supreme.	194	151	153
Calais, Supreme Brougham.	178	139	141
Contour Bucket Seat			
Salon Coupe & Sedan	90	70	71
Salon B'ham. Cpe. & Sdn., Supreme, B'ham. Wag.	45	35	36
Divided Front Bench Seat			
Salon B'ham. Cpe. & Sdn., Supreme, B'ham. Wag.	102	80	81
Power Seat, 6-Way			
Left Bucket (NA Supreme B'ham., B'ham. Wag.). .	163	127	129
Divided Bench (NA Salon, Calais, Cruiser).	163	127	129
Bench, Salon B'ham., Supreme, B'ham. Wag.	163	127	129
Manual Seat-Back Recliner			
Salon, Salon B'ham., Supreme, B'ham. Wag.	62	48	49
Firm Ride Shock Absorbers	7	5	6
Superlift Rear Shock Absorbers	54	42	43
Power Steering.	163	127	129
Custom Sport Steering Wheel (NA Calais).	39	30	31
Tilt-Away Steering Wheel.	75	59	60
Heavy-Duty Suspension	25	20	21
Rally Suspension			
Cpes. ex. Calais, Sedans.	37	29	30
Power Tailgate Release, Wagons	25	20	21
Trailer Wiring Harness			
5-Wire.	22	17	18
7-Wire.	35	27	28
Trim			
Custom Leather Seating, Supreme B'ham.	264	206	209
Designer			
Salon B'hams., B'ham. Wagon	95	74	75
Supreme Brougham	125	98	99
Trip Odometer (NA Calais)	12	9	10
Trip Odometer Delete (credit)	(12)	(9)	(9)
Power Trunk Lid Release (NA Wagon)	24	19	20
Deluxe Trunk Trim, Supreme, Calais, Supreme			
Brougham.	46	36	37

Prices are accurate at time of printing; subject to manufacturer's change.

	Retail Price	Dealer Cost	Low Price
Power Windows			
2-Drs.	$132	$103	$105
4-Drs.	187	146	148
Pulse Wiper System	38	30	31
Woodgrain Vinyl Bodyside Paneling			
Cruiser w/o Lower Bodyside Molding	261	204	207
Cruiser w/Lower Bodyside Mldg., B'ham. Wag.	243	190	192

OLDSMOBILE DELTA 88, NINETY-EIGHT, TORONADO

	Retail Price	Dealer Cost	Low Price
DELTA 88			
Coupe	$ 5782	$4628	$4928
Sedan	5882	4708	5008
DELTA 88 ROYALE			
Coupe	6029	4826	5126
Sedan	6154	4926	5226
CUSTOM CRUISER			
Wagon	6742	5397	5747
NINETY-EIGHT LUXURY			
Coupe	7492	5847	6247
Sedan	7673	5988	6388
NINETY-EIGHT REGENCY			
Coupe	7875	6146	6646
Sedan	8063	6292	6792
TORONADO BROUGHAM			
Coupe	10112	7890	8890

STANDARD EQUIPMENT (included in above prices)

Delta 88: Safety and protection equipment plus 3.8 litre (231 CID) V-6 engine, automatic transmission, power steering, power brakes, ashtray and dome lights, deluxe steering wheel, bumper impact strips, carpeting, carpeted lower door panels, wheel covers, glass-belted radial tires.

Delta 88 Royale: Delta 88 equipment plus custom sport front bench seat, velour upholstery, glove box lamp, reading/dome lamp, door-pull straps, bodyside moldings.

Custom Cruiser: Delta 88 equipment plus 5.7 litre (350 CID) V-8 engine, 3-way tailgate, velour or vinyl interior.

Ninety-Eight Luxury: Safety and protection equipment plus 5.7 litre (350 CID) V-8 engine, automatic transmission, power steering, power brakes, power windows, 2-way power driver's seat, electric clock, front & rear fold-down center armrests, front ashtray lamp, glove box and courtesy lamps, steel belted radial tires.

Ninety-Eight Regency: Luxury equipment plus loose-cushion look interior, velour upholstery, divided front seat w/dual controls, digital clock, door courtesy lamps, front seat-back pouches.

Toronado: Safety and protection equipment plus 5.7 litre (350 CID) V-8 engine, front-wheel drive, automatic transmission, power steering, power brakes, power windows, four-season air conditioning, automatic level control, side window defrosters, temperature gage and trip odometer, cornering lamps, remote control mirrors, AM/FM stereo radio w/power antenna, 6-way power driver's seat, tinted glass.

Prices are accurate at time of printing; subject to manufacturer's change.

DELTA 88, NINETY-EIGHT
TORONADO ACCESSORIES

	Retail Price	Dealer Cost	Low Price
Engines			
4.3 Litre (260 CID) V-8, Delta 88's ex. Wag...	$140	$108	$110
4.9 Litre (301 CID) V-8, Delta 88's ex. Wag...	195	150	152
5.7 Litre (350 CID) V-8, Delta 88's ex. Wag...	320	246	249
6.6 Litre (403 CID) V-8, Wagon, Ninety-Eights .	70	54	55
5.7 Litre (350 CID) V-8 Diesel			
Delta 88's ex. Wagon	895	689	696
Wagon, Ninety-Eights, Toronado	785	604	611
Four-Season Air Cond. (std. Toronado)	605	466	471
Tempmatic Air Conditioner			
Toronado	45	35	36
Others	650	501	507
High-Capacity Alternator	49	38	39
Astroroof			
Delta 88's ex. Wagon	925	712	720
Ninety-Eight's Toronado	998	768	774
Limited-Slip Rear Axle (NA Toronado)	68	52	53
High-Capacity Battery	21	16	17
4-Wheel Power Disc Brakes, Toronado	205	158	160
Bumper Guards F&R (NA Toronado)	45	35	36
Bumper Guards Rear, Toronado	22	17	18
Rear Bumper Step, Wagon	17	13	14
Electric Clock, Delta 88's	24	18	19
Electric Digital Clock			
Delta 88's	55	42	43
Ninety-Eights	31	24	25
Convenience Group			
Delta 88 Sedan	34	26	27
Delta 88 Coupe	29	22	23
Wagon	23	18	19
Delta 88 Royale Cpe. & Sdn	14	11	12
Ninety-Eight, Toronado	14	11	12
Cooling System			
W/Air Cond	29	22	23
W/o Air Cond	75	58	59
W/Diesel Eng. & Air Cond	21	16	17
W/Diesel Eng. w/o Air Cond	52	40	41
High-Capacity Cooling System, Eng	21	16	17
Cruise Control	108	83	84
Electric Rear Window Defroster	101	77	78
Calif. Emission System	83	64	65
High Altitude Emission System	35	27	28
Engine Block Heater	15	12	13
Fuel Economy Meter (NA Toronado)	30	23	24
Gauges			
Toronado	36	28	29
Others	54	42	43

Prices are accurate at time of printing; subject to manufacturer's change.

	Retail Price	Dealer Cost	Low Price
Gauges, Canadian Instrument Cluster			
Toronado	$ 39	$ 30	$ 31
Others w/Gasoline Eng.	3	2	3
Others w/Diesel Eng.	15	12	13
Tinted Glass (std. Toronado)	84	65	66
Holiday Coupe Option, Delta 88 Cpe..	288	222	225
Illumination Pkg.	57	44	45
Cornering Lamps (std. Toronado)	49	38	39
Courtesy/Warning, Delta 88 Royale	30	23	24
Dome/Reading Lamp			
Delta 88, Wagon.	19	15	16
Others	11	8	9
Dome/Reading Lamp, Sail Mtd., Toronado	42	32	33
Opera Lamps, Ext., Toronado	65	50	51
Reading Lamp, Sail Mtd., Ninety-Eight Sdns.	55	42	43
Lamp Monitors.	62	48	49
Automatic Load Leveling System (std. Toro.)	120	92	93
Power Door Locks			
2-Drs. (std. Toronado)	88	68	69
4-Drs. ex. Wagon	122	94	95
Wagon	159	122	124
Luggage Carrier, Roof, Wagon	140	108	110
Mirrors			
Remote Control Left, Delta 88's.	19	15	16
Remote Control Right			
Delta 88 2-Drs..	34	26	27
Delta 88 4-Drs., Wagon, Ninety-Eights	39	30	31
Remote w/Thermometer (NA Delta 88's)	29	22	23
Power Left & Right			
Ninety-Eights	97	75	76
Toronado	58	45	46
Sport			
Delta 88 2-Drs..	37	28	29
Delta 88 4-Drs., Wagon.	43	33	34
Sport Remote Control			
Delta 88 2-Drs..	64	49	50
Delta 88 4-Drs., Wagon.	70	54	55
Illuminated Visor Vanity			
w/o Conv. Grp.	44	34	35
w/Conv. Grp.	47	36	37
Radio Equipment			
AM (NA Toronado)	99	76	77
AM/FM (NA Toronado)	174	134	136
AM/FM Stereo (NA Toronado)	239	184	186
AM w/Stereo Tape (NA Toronado)	265	204	207
AM/FM Stereo w/Stereo Tape			
Toronado	110	85	86
Others	349	269	272

Prices are accurate at time of printing; subject to manufacturer's change.

	Retail Price	Dealer Cost	Low Price
AM/FM Stereo w/Cassette Tape			
Toronado	$116	$ 89	$ 90
Others	355	273	276
AM/FM Stereo w/Tape w/o Eject			
All ex. Toronado	274	211	214
AM/FM Stereo w/CB & Pwr. Ant.			
Toronado	294	226	229
Others	581	447	452
Power Antenna (NA Toronado)			
W/Radio	48	37	38
W/o Radio	77	59	60
Rear Speaker (NA Toronado)	26	20	21
Dual Rear Speakers (NA Toronado)	52	40	41
Radio Accommodation Pkg. (NA Toronado)	29	22	23
Reminder Pkg.	48	37	38
Sun Roof, Power			
Delta 88's	725	558	564
Others	798	614	621
Full Vinyl Roof			
Delta 88's	145	112	114
Ninety-Eight Sedans	164	126	128
Full Vinyl Roof, Padded (NA Delta 88's)	197	152	154
Landau Vinyl Roof			
Delta 88 Coupes	185	142	144
Ninety-Eight Coupes, Toronado	200	154	156
Divided Front Bench Seat			
Delta 88 Royale, Ninety-Eight Luxury	102	79	80
Wagon	147	113	115
Power Seat, 6-Way	166	128	130
Third Seat, Wagon	193	149	151
Seat-Back Recliner	62	48	49
Firm Ride Shock Absorbers (NA Toronado)	7	5	6
Superlift Rear Shock Absorbers (NA Toronado)	55	42	43
Tilt-Away Steering Wheel	77	59	60
Tilt & Telescope Steering Wheel	121	93	94
Heavy-Duty Suspension			
All ex. Wagon, Toronado	25	19	20
Wagon	10	8	9
Rally Suspension			
Delta 88 Coupe	37	28	29
Toronado	28	22	23
Trailer Wiring Harness			
5-Wire	22	17	18
7-Wire	35	27	28
Custom Leather Trim			
Delta 88 Royale	287	221	224
Ninety-Eight Regency, Toronado	264	203	206
Royal Brougham Trim, Delta 88 Royale	155	119	121
Trip Odometer (NA Toronado)	12	9	10

Prices are accurate at time of printing; subject to manufacturer's change.

	Retail Price	Dealer Cost	Low Price
Power Trunk Release............	$ 25	$ 19	$ 20
Deluxe Trunk Trim, Delta 88's	46	35	36
Twilight Sentinel............	47	36	37
Power Windows			
Delta 88 2-Drs............	138	106	108
Delta 88 4-Drs., Wagon......	205	158	160
Pulse Wiper System..........	39	30	31
Woodgrain Vinyl Bodyside Paneling, Wagon.....	243	187	189

OLDSMOBILE OMEGA

OMEGA

	Retail Price	Dealer Cost	Low Price
Hatchback...........	$4345	$3782	$4032
Coupe............	4181	3639	3889
Sedan............	4281	3726	3976
OMEGA BROUGHAM			
Coupe............	4387	3818	4068
Sedan............	4487	3905	4155

STANDARD EQUIPMENT (included in above prices)

Omega: Safety and protection equipment plus 3.8 litre (231 CID) V-6 engine, 3-speed manual transmission, disc front brakes, bench front seat, carpet, day/night mirror.

OMEGA ACCESSORIES

	Retail Price	Dealer Cost	Low Price
Engines			
5.0 Litre (305 CID) V-8 2-bbl...........	$195	$152	$154
5.7 Litre (350 CID) V-8 4-bbl...........	320	250	253
Transmissions			
4-speed Manual...........	135	105	107
Automatic............	335	261	264
Air Conditioning...........	529	413	418
Limited-Slip Rear Axle...........	64	50	51
Deluxe Belts			
w/Bench Seat...........	21	16	17
w/Bucket Seats...........	20	15	16
Power Brakes...........	76	59	60
Bumper Guards			
w/Omega LS Pkg...........	45	35	36
w/o Omega LS Pkg...........	82	64	65
Bumper Rub Strips...........	37	29	30
Electric Clock...........	24	19	20
Console (NA sedans)...........	80	62	63
Convenience Group			
Hatchback...........	30	23	24
Others...........	31	24	25

Prices are accurate at time of printing; subject to manufacturer's change.

	Retail Price	Dealer Cost	Low Price
High Capacity Cooling System			
w/Air Cond.	$ 30	$ 23	$ 24
w/o Air Cond.	58	45	46
Cruise Control	103	80	81
Rear Window Defogger	55	43	44
Calif. Emission System	83	65	66
High Altitude Emission System	35	27	28
Engine Block Heater	15	12	13
Gages			
w/Conv. Grp.	85	66	67
w/o Conv. Grp.	109	85	86
Tinted Glass	64	50	51
Power Door Locks			
2 Drs.	80	62	63
4-Drs.	111	87	89
Remote Control Left Mirror	18	14	15
Sport Mirrors	43	34	35
Omega LS Pkg., B'ham. Sedan	2078	1619	1636
Omega SX Pkg., Hatchback, Base Cpe.	231	180	182
Paint Scheme, Sedans.	161	126	128
High Capacity Radiator	21	16	17
Radio Equipment			
AM.	82	64	65
AM/FM.	158	123	125
AM/FM Stereo.	236	184	186
AM w/Stereo Tape.	244	190	192
AM/FM Stereo w/Stereo Tape.	345	269	272
Rear Speaker	25	20	21
Radio Accommodation Pkg.	29	23	24
Bucket Seats	90	70	71
Power Steering	163	127	129
Custom Sport Steering Wheel	39	30	31
Tilt-Away Steering Wheel	75	59	60
Rally Suspension	43	34	35
Power Trunk Release.	24	19	20
Full Vinyl Top			
w/o Omega LS Pkg.	99	77	78
w/Omega LS Pkg.	79	62	63
Landau Vinyl Top, Coupes.	190	148	150
Power Windows			
2-Drs.	126	98	99
4-Drs.	178	139	141
Swing-Out Rear Quarter Windows (NA Sdns.)	59	46	47
Pulse Wiper System	38	30	31

OLDSMOBILE STARFIRE

STARFIRE

	Retail Price	Dealer Cost	Low Price
Coupe	$4095	$3564	$3814
SX Coupe	4295	3738	3988

Prices are accurate at time of printing; subject to manufacturer's change.

STANDARD EQUIPMENT (included in above prices)

Starfire: Safety and protection equipment plus 2.5 litre (151 CID) 4-cyl. engine, 4-speed manual transmission, disc front brakes, bucket seats, console, sport mirrors, rally wheels, AM radio, carpet.

STARFIRE ACCESSORIES

	Retail Price	Dealer Cost	Low Price
Engines			
3.8 Litre (231 CID) V-6	$200	$166	$168
5.0 Litre (305 CID) V-8 2-bbl.			
w/o GT Pkg.	395	328	332
w/GT Pkg.	195	162	164
Transmissions			
5-speed Manual	175	145	147
Automatic	295	245	248
Accent Stripe	28	23	24
Air Conditioning.	496	412	417
Limited-Slip Rear Axle	60	50	51
Heavy-Duty Battery	18	15	16
Deluxe Belts	20	16	17
Power Brakes	71	59	60
Bumper Guards	42	35	36
Electric Clock	21	17	18
High Capacity Cooling System			
w/Air Cond.	30	25	26
w/o Air Cond.	58	48	49
Elec. Rear Defroster	87	72	73
Calif. Emission System.	83	69	70
High Altitude Emission System	35	29	30
Engine Block Heater	15	12	13
Firenza Sport Pkg.	375	310	314
Gages	61	51	52
Tinted Glass	60	50	51
GT Package			
Starfire.	577	477	482
Starfire SX	447	370	374
Light Group	15	12	13
Day/Night Mirror	10	8	9
High Capacity Radiator	20	17	18
Radio Equipment			
AM w/Stereo Tape	157	130	132
AM/FM	74	61	62
AM/FM Stereo	148	123	125
AM/FM Stereo w/Stereo Tape.	250	208	211
Rear Speaker	23	19	20
Seat-Back Adjuster, Driver's	20	17	18
Power Steering.	146	121	123
Tilt-Away Steering Wheel.	68	56	57
Sunroof, Removable Glass Panels	180	149	151

Prices are accurate at time of printing; subject to manufacturer's change.

Oldsmobile Cutlass

Oldsmobile Omega

Oldsmobile 98

Pontiac Bonneville

Pontiac Bonneville

Pontiac Sunbird

Pontiac Catalina

Pontiac Firebird

Pontiac Grand Prix

Pontiac

PONTIAC CATALINA AND BONNEVILLE

	Retail Price	Dealer Cost	Low Price
CATALINA			
Coupe	$5690	$4555	$4855
Sedan	5746	4599	4899
Wagon	6273	5022	5322
BONNEVILLE			
Coupe	6205	4967	5167
Sedan	6330	5067	5367
Wagon	6632	5309	5659
BONNEVILLE BROUGHAM			
Coupe	6960	5571	5971
Sedan	7149	5722	6122

STANDARD EQUIPMENT (included in above prices)

Catalina: Safety and protection equipment plus 3.8 litre (231 CID) V-6 2-bbl. engine (4.9 litre, 301 CID, V-8 2-bbl on wagon), automatic transmission, power brakes, power steering, FR78-15 fiberglass belted radial blackwall tires (HR78-15 steel belted on wagon), bench front seat, hubcaps, deluxe cushion steering wheel, column-mounted dimmer switch, carpeting.

Bonneville: Catalina equipment plus 4.9 litre (301 CID) V-8 2-bbl. engine, FR78-15 blackwall steel belted radial tires on coupe and sedan, additional sound insulation, notchback bench seat, deluxe wheel covers.

Bonneville Brougham: Catalina and Bonneville equipment plus power windows, custom seat belts, electric clock, luggage compartment trim, remote control left mirror, visor vanity mirror, windowsill moldings, notchback 60/40 split bench seat w/velour cloth trim, luxury cushion steering wheel.

CATALINA AND BONNEVILLE ACCESSORIES

Engines

4.9 Litre (301 CID) V-8 2-bbl., Catalina ex. Wag...	$195	$150	$152
4.9 Litre (301 CID) V-8 4-bbl.			
Catalina Coupe, Sedan	255	196	198
All others	60	46	47
5.7 Litre (350 CID) V-8 4-bbl.			
Catalina Coupe, Sedan	320	246	249
All others	125	96	97
6.6 Litre (403 CID) V-8 4-bbl., Wagons only	195	150	152

Prices are accurate at time of printing; subject to manufacturer's change.

	Retail Price	Dealer Cost	Low Price
Custom Air Conditioning....................	$605	$466	$471
Automatic Climate Control Air Cond.	688	530	536
63-Amp Alternator, w/o Rear Defroster			
Air Cond. or Cold Weather Group	32	25	26
80-Amp. Alternator			
W/o Air Cond., Rear Defroster or Cold			
Weather Group........................	55	42	43
W/Rear Defroster or Air Cond...............	23	18	19
Limited Slip Rear Axle	67	52	53
Heavy-Duty Battery, w/o Cold Wea. Grp.......	21	16	17
Front or Rear Bumper Guards.................	23	18	19
Rear Bumper Step Pad, Wagon w/o Third Seat......	7	5	6
Load Floor Carpeting, Wagons.................	76	59	60
Load Floor & Sidewall Carpeting			
Wagons w/o Custom Trim	106	82	83
Wagons w/Custom Trim	30	23	24
Digital Clock			
Catalina & Bonneville.....................	55	42	43
Bonneville Brougham	31	24	25
Electric Clock Catalina & Bonneville	24	18	19
Cold Weather Group			
Incl. 63-amp. Alternator			
W/o Rear Defroster or Air Cond.............	68	52	53
W/Rear Defroster or Air Cond..............	36	28	29
Incl. 80-amp. Alternator			
W/o Rear Defroster or Air Cond.............	91	70	71
W/Rear Defroster or Air Cond..............	59	45	46
Cruise Control	108	83	84
Remote Control Deck Lid Release.............	25	19	20
Rear Window Defroster	101	78	79
Power Door Locks			
2-Doors..............................	88	68	69
4-Door Sedans.........................	122	94	95
Wagons (incl. tailgate release)	156	120	122
Calif. Emission Requirements	83	64	65
High Altitude Emission Option.................	35	27	28
Rally Cluster, Clock & Trip Odometer Gages			
Catalina & Bonneville....................	78	60	61
Bonneville Brougham	54	42	43
Rally Cluster, Fuel Economy & Trip			
Odometer Gages........................	85	65	66
Tinted Glass	84	65	66
Rally RTS Handling Pkg.			
Catalina w/o Stowaway Spare	180	139	141
Catalina w/Stowaway Spare	150	116	118
All Others w/o Stowaway Spare	128	97	98
All Others w/Stowaway Spare	109	82	83
Additional Sound Insulation, Catalina	36	28	29
Cornering Lamps	49	38	39

Prices are accurate at time of printing; subject to manufacturer's change.

	Retail Price	Dealer Cost	Low Price
Dome Reading Lamp........................	$ 19	$ 15	$ 16
Door Courtesy Lamps			
2-Doors ex. Catalina......................	34	26	27
4-Doors ex. Catalina......................	56	43	44
Lamp Group			
Catalina Coupe, Bonneville ex. Wagon	15	12	13
Catalina Sedan, Bonneville Wagon............	21	16	17
Catalina Wagon	27	21	22
Bonneville Brougham	8	6	7
Roof Luggage Carrier	115	89	90
Luggage Compartment Trim (std. Brougham)	41	32	33
Mirrors			
Left Remote Control Chrome (std. B'ham)	18	14	15
Sport, Left Remote, Right Manual			
Catalina & Bonneville....................	44	34	35
Bonneville Brougham	26	20	21
Sport, Left & Right Remote			
Catalina & Bonneville....................	71	55	56
Bonneville Brougham	53	41	42
Visor Vanity (std. Brougham)	6	5	6
Illuminated Visor Vanity			
Catalina & Bonneville....................	41	32	33
Bonneville Brougham	35	27	28
Super Cooling Radiator			
W/o Air Cond. or Trailer Grp..............	60	46	47
W/Air Cond. w/o Trailer Grp..............	32	25	26
Radio Equipment			
AM	99	76	77
AM/FM	174	134	136
AM/FM Stereo	239	184	186
Am w/Stereo Tape	265	204	207
AM/FM Stereo w/Stereo Tape................	349	269	272
AM/FM Stereo w/Stereo Cassette Tape	355	273	276
AM/FM w/CB & Power Antenna	507	390	394
AM/FM Stereo w/CB & Pwr. Ant.	581	447	452
AM/FM Stereo w/Digital Clock & Readouts			
Catalina & Bonneville....................	402	310	314
Bonneville Brougham	378	291	294
Power Antenna, AM/FM			
W/o Optional Radio	67	37	38
W/Optional Radio	48	52	53
Power Antenna, AM/FM/CB			
W/o Optional Radio	88	68	69
W/Optional Radio ex. CB	69	53	54
Rear Speaker			
Coupes & Sedans.......................	26	20	21
Wagons..............................	30	23	24
Dual Rear Speakers			
Coupes & Sedans.......................	40	31	32

Prices are accurate at time of printing; subject to manufacturer's change.

	Retail Price	Dealer Cost	Low Price
Wagons..............................	$ 44	$ 34	$ 35
Radio Accommodation Package			
W/o Optional Radio or Pwr. Ant.	29	22	23
W/o Opt. Radio w/Pwr. Ant................	10	8	9
Power Drive Seat, 6-way	166	128	130
Power Driver & Pass. 60/40 Seat (ex. Catalina)	332	256	259
Vinyl Bench Seat, Catalina (std. Wagon)	30	23	24
Notchback 60/40 Seat			
Bonneville (cloth or vinyl)	102	79	80
Bonneville (Chamonix Cloth)	197	152	154
Bucket Seats w/Console, Bonneville Coupe........	157	121	123
Reclining Passenger Seat (ex. Catalina Cpe., Sdn.) ..	62	48	49
Third Seat, Wagons	183	141	143
Superlift Shock Absorbers....................	55	42	43
Custom Sport Steering Wheel			
Catalina & Bonneville......................	77	59	60
Bonneville Brougham.....................	57	44	45
Luxury Cushion Steering Wheel (std. B'ham.)......	20	15	16
Tilt Steering Wheel........................	77	59	60
Glass Sunroof, Power	925	712	720
Steel Sunroof, Power	725	558	564
Automatic Level Control Suspension			
W/o Trailer Group	121	93	94
W/Trailer Group.........................	66	51	52
Firm Ride Suspension.	13	10	11
Power Tailgate Lock Release	24	26	27
Full Vinyl Top (ex. Wagons)	145	112	114
Landau Vinyl Top (Coupes only)	298	229	232
Light Trailer Group			
W/o Air Conditioning	150	116	118
W/Air Conditioning........................	122	94	95
Heavy Trailer Group			
W/o Air Cond. ex Wagons	187	144	146
W/Air Cond. ex. Wagons	159	122	124
Wagons w/o Air Cond..	150	116	118
Wagons w/Air Cond......................	122	94	95
Trailer Light Cable, 5-wire	22	17	18
Trailer Light Cable, 7-wire (w/Trlr. Grp.)	14	11	12
Power Windows (std. Brougham)			
2-Doors................................	138	106	108
4-Doors................................	205	158	160
Controlled Cycle Wipers	39	30	31

PONTIAC FIREBIRD

FIREBIRD

Firebird	$4825	$4199	$4499
Esprit...................................	5193	4520	4820
Formula	6018	5238	5588
Trans Am	6299	5482	5832

Prices are accurate at time of printing; subject to manufacturer's change.

STANDARD EQUIPMENT (included in above prices)

Firebird: Safety and protection equipment plus 3.8 litre V-6 2-bbl. engine, 3-speed manual transmission w/floor shifter, FR78-15 steel belted radial blackwall tires, power steering, disc front brakes, hub caps, carpet, vinyl bucket seats.

Esprit: Firebird equipment plus sport mirrors, rocker panel & roof drip moldings, wheel opening molding, windowsill & hood rear edge moldings, luxury cushion steering wheel, custom vinyl doeskin trim, deluxe wheel covers, additional sound insulation.

Formula: Firebird equipment plus 4.9 litre V-8 2-bbl. engine (5.0 litre in Calif.), 4-speed manual or automatic transmission, console, rally cluster & clock gages, sport mirrors, power brakes, formula steering wheel, rally II wheels & trim rings, 225/70R-15 steel belted radial blackwall tires, RTS handling package, stowaway spare tire.

Trans Am: Firebird and Formula equipment plus 6.6 litre (403 CID) V-8 4-bbl. engine, limited slip differential, tachometer, rear deck spoiler.

FIREBIRD ACCESSORIES

	Retail Price	Dealer Cost	Low Price
Engines			
4.9 Litre (301 CID) V-8 2-bbl. (ex. Calif.)			
Firebird & Esprit	$195	$152	$154
4.9 Litre (301 CID) V-8 4-bbl.			
Firebird & Esprit	280	218	221
Formula	85	66	67
Trans Am (credit)	(165)	(129)	(129)
5.0 Litre (305 CID) V-8 2-bbl. (Calif. only)			
Firebird & Esprit	195	152	154
5.7 Litre (350 CID) V-8 4-bbl.			
Firebird & Esprit	320	250	253
Formula	125	98	99
6.6 Litre (400 CID) T/A V-8 4-bbl.			
Formula	340	265	268
Trans Am	90	70	71
6.6 Litre (403 CID) V-8 4-bbl.			
Formula	250	195	197
Transmissions			
4-Speed Manual, Firebird & Esprit	335	261	264
Automatic, Firebird & Esprit	335	261	264
Air Conditioning	529	413	418
63-Amp. Alternator, W/o Air Cond. or			
Rear Window Defroster	32	25	26
Formula Appearance Package, Formula	92	72	73
Redbird Appearance Package			
Esprit (Incl. velour cloth trim)	491	383	387
Esprit (Incl. vinyl trim)	449	350	354
Special Edition Appearance Package			
Trans Am	674	526	532
Trans Am (Incl. Hatch Roof Panels)	1329	1037	1048
Limited Slip Rear Axle (std. Trans Am)	83	49	50
Heavy Duty Battery	21	16	17

Prices are accurate at time of printing; subject to manufacturer's change.

	Retail Price	Dealer Cost	Low Price
Power Brakes, Firebird & Esprit	$ 76	$ 59	$ 60
Power 4-Wheel Disc Brakes			
Formula & Trans Am w/o Spl. Perf. Pkg.	150	117	119
Electric Clock	24	19	20
Console, Firebird & Esprit.	80	62	63
Cruise Control	103	80	81
Remote Deck Lid Release	24	19	20
Rear Window Defroster	99	77	78
Calif. Emission Requirements	83	65	66
High Altitude Emission Option.	35	27	28
Rally Cluster & Clock Gages	67	52	53
Rally Cluster, Clock & Tachometer Gages			
Firebird & Esprit.	130	101	103
Trans Am	63	49	50
Tinted Glass	64	50	51
Hatch Roof, Glass Panels	655	511	517
Engine Block Heater.	15	12	13
Hood Decal, Trans Am	95	74	75
Additional Sound Insulation	31	24	25
Dome Reading Lamp.	19	15	16
Lamp Group	19	15	16
Power Door Locks	86	67	68
Mirrors			
Sport, Firebird.	43	34	35
Visor Vanity.	6	5	6
Super Cooling Radiator			
W/o Air Conditioning	59	46	47
W/Air Conditioning.	32	25	26
Radio Equipment			
AM.	86	67	68
AM/FM	163	127	129
AM/FM Stereo	236	184	186
AM w/Stereo Tape	248	193	195
AM/FM Stereo w/Stereo Tape.	345	269	272
AM/FM Stereo w/Cassette Stereo Tape	351	274	277
AM/FM w/CB & Power Antenna	492	384	388
AM/FM Stereo w/CB & Pwr. Ant.	574	448	453
AM/FM Stereo w/CB & Pwr. Ant.	402	314	318
AM/FM Stereo w/Digital Clock Display	25	20	21
Rear Speaker.	38	30	31
Power Antenna, AM/FM			
W/o Radio.	66	51	52
W/Radio	47	37	38
Power Antenna, AM/FM/CB			
W/o Radio.	87	68	69
W/Radio ex. CB	68	53	54
Radio Accommodation Package			
W/o Radio	29	23	24
W/o Radio, w/Opt. Pwr. Ant.	10	8	9

Prices are accurate at time of printing; subject to manufacturer's change.

	Retail Price	Dealer Cost	Low Price
Special Performance Package			
Formula	$434	$339	$343
Trans Am w/o Spl. Edn. Pkg.	434	339	343
Trans Am w/Spl. Edn. Pkg.	250	195	197
Rear Deck Spoiler, Firebird, Esprit			
Formula w/o Formula App. Pkg.	57	45	46
Formula Steering Wheel			
Firebird	68	53	54
Esprit w/o RedBird App. Grp.	48	37	38
Luxury Cushion Steering Wheel, Firebird	20	16	17
Tilt Steering Wheel	75	59	60
Vinyl Accent Stripes, Firebird & Esprit	54	42	43
Vinyl Top	116	90	91
Custom Trim Group			
Formula & Trans Am (vinyl trim)	108	84	85
Formula & Trans Am (velour cloth trim)	150	117	119
Esprit (velour cloth trim) w/o RedBird Pkg.	42	33	34
Power Windows (console req.)	132	103	105
Controlled Cycle Wipers	38	30	31

PONTIAC GRAND PRIX

GRAND PRIX

	Retail Price	Dealer Cost	Low Price
Grand Prix	$5113	$4245	$4545
Grand Prix LJ	6192	5141	5491
Grand Prix SJ	6438	5345	5895

STANDARD EQUIPMENT (included in above prices)

Grand Prix: Safety and protection equipment plus 3.8 litre (231 CID) V-6 2-bbl. engine, 3-speed manual transmission w/floor shift, 195/75R-14 blackwall steel belted radial tires, disc front brakes, hubcaps, carpet, deluxe cushion steering wheel, electric clock, notchback front seat.

Grand Prix LJ: Grand Prix equipment plus 4.9 litre (301 CID) V-8 2-bbl. engine, automatic transmission, power brakes, power steering, custom seat belts, additional sound insulation, sport mirrors, pedal trim package, luxury cushion steering wheel, deluxe wheel covers.

Grand Prix SJ: Grand Prix and Grand Prix LJ equipment plus 4.9 litre (301 CID) V-8 4-bbl. engine, rally cluster & trip odometer gages, lamp group, vinyl bucket seats w/console, custom sport steering wheel, upper accent stripes, custom-finned wheel covers.

GRAND PRIX ACCESSORIES

Engines	Retail Price	Dealer Cost	Low Price
3.8 Litre (231 CID) V-6 2-bbl., LJ (credit)	$(195)	$(152)	$(152)
4.9 Litre (301 CID) V-8 2-bbl., Grand Prix	195	152	154
4.9 Litre (301 CID) V-8 4-bbl.			
Grand Prix	255	199	201
Grand Prix LJ	60	47	48
5.0 Litre (305 CID) V-8 4-bbl.			
Grand Prix	255	199	201
Grand Prix LJ	60	47	48

Prices are accurate at time of printing; subject to manufacturer's change.

	Retail Price	Dealer Cost	Low Price
Transmissions			
4-Speed Manual w/Floor Shift			
Grand Prix	$135	$105	$107
Grand Prix LJ & SJ (credit)	(200)	(156)	(156)
Automatic Grand Prix	335	261	264
Custom Air Conditioning	562	438	443
Automatic Climate Control Air Cond.	653	509	515
Heavy-Duty Alternator, w/o Air Cond.,			
Rear Window Defroster or Cold Wea. Grp.	32	25	26
Limited Slip Rear Axle	63	49	50
Heavy-Duty Battery, w/o Cold Wea. Grp.	21	16	17
Power Brakes	76	59	60
Front or Rear Bumper Guards	22	17	18
Digital Clock	31	24	25
Cold Weather Group			
W/o Air Cond. or Rear Defroster	68	53	54
W/Air Cond. or Rear Defroster	36	28	29
Cruise Control	103	80	81
Remote Control Deck Lid Release	24	19	20
Rear Window Defroster	99	77	78
Power Door Locks	86	67	68
Calif. Emission Requirements	83	65	66
High Altitude Emission Option	35	27	28
Rally Cluster & Trip Odometer Gages (std. SJ)	53	41	42
Rally Cluster, Tachometer & Trip Odometer Gages			
Grand Prix, Grand Prix LJ	121	94	95
Grand Prix SJ	68	53	54
Tinted Glass	75	59	60
RTS Rally Handling Pkg. (incl. blackwall tires)	72	56	57
RTS Rally Handling Pkg. (incl. whitewall tires)	116	90	91
RTS Rally Handling Pkg. (incl. white letter tires)	128	100	102
Hatch Roof	655	511	517
Additional Sound Insulation, Grand Prix	31	24	25
Cornering Lamp	49	38	39
Dome Reading Lamp	19	15	16
Door Courtesy Lamps	32	25	26
Lamp Group (std SJ)	23	18	19
Luggage Compartment Trim	41	32	33
Mirrors			
Sport, Left Remote, Grand Prix	23	18	19
Sport, Left Remote, Right Manual, Grand Prix	43	34	35
Sport, Left & Right Remote			
Grand Prix	70	55	56
Grand Prix LJ & SJ	27	21	22
Visor Vanity	6	5	6
Illuminated Visor Vanity	40	31	32
Pedal Trim Package, Grand Prix	8	6	7
Super-Cooling Radiator			
W/o Air Cond. or Trailer Group	59	46	47

Prices are accurate at time of printing; subject to manufacturer's change.

	Retail Price	Dealer Cost	Low Price
W/Air Cond. w/o Trailer Group	$ 32	$ 25	$ 26
Radio Equipment			
AM	86	67	68
AM/FM	163	127	129
AM/FM Stereo	236	184	186
AM w/Stereo Tape	248	193	195
AM/FM Stereo w/Stereo Tape..............	345	269	272
AM/FM Stereo w/Stereo Cassette Tape	351	274	277
AM/FM w/CB & Power Antenna	492	384	388
AM/FM Stereo w/CB & Pwr. Ant.	574	448	453
AM/FM Stereo w/Digital Clock & Readouts	378	295	298
Rear Speaker.................................	25	20	21
Dual Front & Rear Speaker	50	39	40
Power Antenna, AM/FM			
W/o Optional Radio	66	51	52
W/Optional Radio	47	37	38
Power Antenna, AM/FM/CB			
W/o Optional Radio	87	68	69
W/Optional Radio ex. CB	68	53	54
Radio Accommodation Package			
W/o Pwr. Ant. or Optional Radio	29	23	24
W/Pwr. Ant. w/o Optional Radio...........	10	8	9
Power Driver Seat, 6-way	163	127	129
Bucket Seats w/Console			
Vinyl or Cloth, Grand Prix..................	155	121	123
Velour Galante Cloth Trim			
Grand Prix LJ	85	66	67
Grand Prix SJ	55	43	44
Viscount Leather Trim w/Vinyl Bolster			
Grand Prix LJ	349	272	275
Grand Prix SJ	319	249	252
Notchback 60/40 Split Seat (ex. SJ)	102	80	81
Reclining Passenger Seat	62	48	49
Superlift Shock Absorbers (NA Trailer Grp.)	54	42	43
Power Steering, Grand Prix...................	163	127	129
Custom Sport Steering Wheel			
Grand Prix	76	59	60
Grand Prix LJ	56	44	45
Luxury Cushion Steering Wheel, Grand Prix	20	16	17
Tilt Steering Wheel..........................	75	59	60
Glass Sunroof, Power........................	729	569	575
Steel Sunroof, Power	529	413	418
Automatic Level Control Suspension			
W/o Trailer Group	120	94	95
W/Trailer Group..........................	66	51	52
Firm Ride Suspension, w/o Trailer Grp.	13	10	11
Landau Vinyl Top............................	239	186	188
Medium Trailer Group			
W/o Air Conditioning ......~.............	148	115	117

Prices are accurate at time of printing; subject to manufacturer's change.

	Retail Price	Dealer Cost	Low Price
W/Air Conditioning.........................	$121	$ 94	$ 95
Trailer Light Cable, 5-wire, w/o Trailer Grp........	22	17	18
Power Windows	132	103	105
Controlled Cycle Wipers	38	30	31

PONTIAC LeMANS, GRAND LeMANS, GRAND AM

LeMANS
	Retail Price	Dealer Cost	Low Price
Coupe.................................	$4608	$3826	$4076
Sedan.................................	4708	3909	4159
Wagon	5216	4331	4631

GRAND LeMANS
Coupe.................................	4868	4042	4342
Sedan.................................	4993	4145	4445
Wagon	5560	4617	4917

GRAND AM
Coupe.................................	5084	4221	4521
Sedan.................................	5209	4325	4625

STANDARD EQUIPMENT (included in above prices)

LeMans: Safety and protection equipment plus 3.8 litre (231 CID) V-6 2-bbl. engine, 3-speed manual transmission (automatic on wagons), power brakes on wagons, 185/75R-14 blackwall fiberglass belted radial tires (195/75R-14 on wagons), disc front brakes, front bench seat, deluxe steering wheel, carpet, day/night mirror, lighter.

Grand LeMans: LeMans equipment plus dual horns, additional sound insulation, rocker panel moldings, side window reveal molding, windowsill & hood rear edge molding, notchback front seat w/center armrest, luxury cushion steering wheel, carpeted lower door panels.

Grand Am: LeMans equipment plus power steering, 205/70R-14 blackwall steel belted radial tires, Rally RTS Handling Package, dual horns, rocker panel molding, side window reveal molding on sedan, windowsill molding, cloth bench front seat.

LeMANS, GRAND LeMANS, GRAND AM ACCESSORIES

Engines	Retail Price	Dealer Cost	Low Price
4.9 Litre (301 CID) V-8 2-bbl................	$195	$152	$154
4.9 Litre (301 CID) V-8 4-bbl...............	255	199	201
5.0 Litre (305 CID) V-8 4-bbl...............	255	199	201
5.7 Litre (350 CID) V-8 4-bbl. (wagons only)	320	250	253
Transmission			
4-Speed Manual (ex. wagons)	135	105	107
Automatic (std. wagons)...................	335	261	264
Custom Air Conditioning....................	562	438	443
Automatic Climate Control Air Conditioning	653	509	515
Heavy-Duty Alternator......................	32	25	26
Appearance Package (ex. wagons, Grand Am)	166	129	131
Limited Slip Rear Axle	63	49	50
Heavy-Duty Battery (w/o cold weather grp.)	21	16	17
Power Brakes (std. wagons)	76	59	60
Front or Rear Bumper Guards (ex. Grand Am)......	22	17	18

Prices are accurate at time of printing; subject to manufacturer's change.

CONSUMER GUIDE

	Retail Price	Dealer Cost	Low Price
Load Floor Carpet, Wagons w/o Cust. Trim	$ 47	$ 37	$ 38
Digital Clock (w/lamp grp. & air cond. only).	55	43	44
Electric Clock	24	19	20
Cold Weather Group			
W/o Air Cond. or Rear Defroster.	68	53	54
W/Air Cond. or Rear Defroster.	36	28	29
Console (w/lamp grp. & bucket seats)	80	62	63
Cruise Control	103	80	81
Custom Trim Group			
LeMans Wagon w/Notchback Seat	157	122	124
LeMans Wagon w/60/40 Notchback Seat.	259	202	205
LeMans Wagon w/Bucket Seats	232	181	183
Grand LeMans Wagon w/Notchback Seat	145	113	115
Grand LeMans Wagon w/60/40 Notchback Seat. . .	247	193	195
Grand LeMans Wagon w/Bucket Seats	220	172	174
Remote Control Rear Deck Lid Release	24	19	20
Rear Window Deflector	30	23	24
Rear Window Defroster	99	77	78
California Emissions Req.	83	65	66
High Altitude Emissions Opt.	35	27	28
Custom Exterior Group			
LeMans ex. Coupe	98	76	77
LeMans Coupe . . . . :	46	36	37
Rally Cluster & Trip Odometer Gages	53	41	42
Rally Cluster, Tachometer & Trip Odometer Gages. . .	121	94	95
Tinted Glass	70	55	56
Rally RTS Handling Pkg. (Incl. Blackwall Tires)			
Sedans, Coupes (std. Grand Am).	133	104	106
Wagons.	114	89	90
Rally RTS Handling Pkg. (Incl. Whitewall Tires)			
Sedans, Coupes ex. Grand Am	177	139	141
Wagons.	157	122	124
Grand Am	44	34	35
Rally RTS Handling Pkg. (Incl. White Letter Tires)			
Sedans, Coupes ex. Grand Am	189	148	150
Wagons.	170	133	135
Grand Am	56	44	45
Dual Horns, LeMans.	8	6	7
Additional Sound Insulation (std. Grand LeMans). . .	31	24	25
Dome Reading Lamp.	19	15	16
Lamp Group			
LeMans Coupe.	23	18	19
LeMans Sedan.	29	23	24
LeMans Wagon.	36	28	29
Grand LeMans ex. Wagon, Grand Am	23	18	19
Grand LeMans Wagon.	30	23	24
Power Door Locks			
2-Doors.	86	67	68
4-Doors.	120	94	95

Prices are accurate at time of printing; subject to manufacturer's change.

	Retail Price	Dealer Cost	Low Price
Roof Luggage Carrier, Wagons	$ 90	$ 70	$ 71
Luggage Compartment Trim	41	32	33
Luxury Group			
Grand LeMans w/Notchback Seat	148	115	117
Grand Le Mans w/60/40 Notchback Seat	250	195	197
Grand LeMans w/Bucket Seats	153	119	121
Grand Am w/Notchback Seat	246	192	194
Grand Am w/60/40 Notchback Seat	348	271	274
Grand Am w/Bucket Seats	251	196	198
Mirrors			
Left Remote	18	14	15
Sport, Left Remote, Right Manual	43	34	35
Sport, Left & Right Remote	70	55	56
Visor Vanity	6	5	6
Visor Vanity, Illuminated	40	31	32
Super Cooling Radiator			
W/o Air Cond. or Trailer Grp.	59	46	47
W/Air Cond. w/o Trailer Grp.	32	25	26
Radio Equipment			
AM	86	67	68
AM/FM	163	127	129
AM/FM Stereo	236	184	186
AM w/Stereo Tape	248	193	195
AM/FM Stereo w/Stereo Tape	345	269	272
AM/FM Stereo w/Stereo Cassette Tape	351	274	277
AM/FM w/CB & Power Antenna	492	384	388
AM/FM Stereo w/CB & Pwr. Ant.	574	448	453
AM/FM Stereo w/Digital Clock & Readout	402	314	318
Power Antenna, AM/FM			
W/o Optional Radio	66	51	52
W/Optional Radio	47	37	38
Power Antenna, AM/FM/CB			
W/o Optional Radio	87	68	69
W/Optional Radio ex. CB	68	53	54
Rear Speaker			
Sedans, Coupes	25	20	21
Wagons	29	23	24
Dual Front & Rear Speaker (std. w/stereo)			
Sedans, Coupes	50	39	40
Wagons	54	42	43
Radio Accommodation Package			
W/o Pwr. Ant. or Optional Radio	29	23	24
W/Pwr. Ant. w/o Optional Radio.	10	8	9
Power Driver Seat, 6-way	163	127	129
Seats			
Vinyl Bench, LeMans & Grand Am (std. wags.) . . .	30	23	24
Vinyl or Cloth Notchback, Grand Am	98	76	77
Vinyl or Cloth Notchback 60/40			
Grand LeMans	102	80	81

Prices are accurate at time of printing; subject to manufacturer's change.

	Retail Price	Dealer Cost	Low Price
Grand Am	$200	$156	$158
Vinyl or Cloth Buckets			
Grand LeMans	75	59	60
Grand Am	173	135	137
Reclining Passenger	62	48	49
Wagon Security Package			
W/Limited Slip Rear Axle	37	29	30
W/o Limited Slip Rear Axle	42	33	34
Power Steering (std Grand Am)	163	127	129
Superlift Shock Absorbers, w/o Trailer Grp.	54	42	43
Custom Sport Steering Wheel			
LeMans, Grand Am	76	59	60
Grand Le Mans	56	44	45
Luxury Cushion Steering Wheel			
LeMans	20	16	17
Tilt Steering Wheel	75	59	60
Glass Sunroof w/Power, Coupes	729	569	575
Steel Sunroof w/Power, Coupes	529	413	418
Automatic Level Control Suspension			
W/o Trailer Group	120	94	95
W/Trailer Group	66	52	53
Firm Ride Suspension			
W/o Trailer Group	13	10	11
Power Tailgate Lock Release	25	20	21
Vinyl Top			
Full (ex. wagons, Grand Am sedan)	116	90	91
Landau (coupes only)	239	186	188
Medium Trailer Group			
W/o Air Conditioning	148	115	117
W/Air Conditioning	121	94	95
Trailer 5-wire Wiring Harness			
W/o Trailer Group	22	17	18
Power Front Windows	132	103	105
Power Rear Vent Window (ex. coupes)	55	43	44
Controlled Cycle Wipers	38	30	31

PONTIAC PHOENIX

PHOENIX

	Retail Price	Dealer Cost	Low Price
Hatchback	$4239	$3690	$3900
Coupe	4089	3559	3809
Sedan	4189	3646	3896
PHOENIX LJ			
Coupe	4589	3994	4244
Sedan	4689	4081	4381

STANDARD EQUIPMENT (included in above prices)

Phoenix: Safety and protection equipment plus 3.8 litre V-6 engine, 3-speed manual transmission, E78-14 bias belted backwall tire, stowaway spare on hatchback, disc front brakes, hubcaps, cloth or vinyl front bench seat, lighter, carpet.

Prices are accurate at time of printing; subject to manufacturer's change.

Phoenix LJ: Phoenix equipment plus additional sound insulation, deluxe wheel covers, bumper strips and guards, inside day/night mirror, rocker panel molding, side window reveal and wheel opening moldings, notchback front seat w/center armrest, luxury cushion steering wheel.

PHOENIX ACCESSORIES

	Retail Price	Dealer Cost	Low Price
Engines			
5.0 Litre V-8 2-bbl	$195	$152	$154
5.7 Litre V-8 4-bbl	320	250	253
Transmissions			
4-Speed Manual (w/5.0 Litre V-8)	135	105	107
Automatic	335	261	264
Air Conditioning	529	413	418
63-Amp. Alternator, w/o air cond. or Electric Rear Window Defroster	32	25	26
Limited Slip Rear Axle	63	49	50
Heavy-Duty Battery	21	16	17
Power Brakes	76	59	60
Bumper Strips & Front Guards, Phoenix	59	46	47
Bumper Strips & F&R Guards, Phoenix	90	70	71
Load Floor Carpet, Hatchback	26	20	21
Electric Clock (w/o Rally Gages)	24	19	20
Console	80	62	63
Cruise Control	103	80	81
Rear Window Defogger, Forced Air Hatchback	55	43	44
Rear Window Defroster, Electric, All ex. Hatchback	99	77	78
California Emission Requirements	83	65	66
High Altitude Emission Option	35	27	28
Custom Exterior Group			
Phoenix Sedan	97	76	77
Phoenix Hatchback Coupe	91	71	72
Firm Ride Option (w/o Trailer Grp.)	13	10	11
Gages	77	60	61
Tinted Glass	64	50	51
RTS Handling Package, Incl. Whitewall Tires			
W/o Stowaway Spare Tire	214	165	167
W/Stowaway Spare Tire	182	140	142
RTS Handling Package, Incl. White Letter Tires			
W/o Stowaway Spare Tire	230	178	180
W/Stowaway Spare Tire	195	151	153
Engine Block Heater	15	12	13
Dual Horns	8	6	7
Additional Sound Insulation, Phoenix	31	24	25
Lamp Group			
Hatchback	16	12	13
Coupes, Phoenix LJ Sedan	23	18	19
Phoenix Sedan	29	23	24

Prices are accurate at time of printing; subject to manufacturer's change.

	Retail Price	Dealer Cost	Low Price
Mirrors			
Inside Day/Night, Phoenix	$ 9	$ 7	$ 8
Left Remote.	18	14	15
Sport, Left Remote, Right Manual.	43	34	35
Sport, Left & Right Remote	70	55	56
Visor Vanity.	6	5	6
Pedal Trim Package	8	6	7
Power Door Locks			
2-Doors.	80	62	63
4-Doors.	111	87	88
Heavy-Duty Radiator (w/V-8 only)			
W/o Air Cond. or Light Trailer Grp.	59	46	47
W/Air Cond., W/o Light Trailer Grp.	32	25	26
Heavy-Duty Radiator, Cooling System (w/V-6)			
W/o Air Conditioning	59	46	47
W/Air Conditioning.	32	25	26
Radio Equipment			
AM	82	64	65
AM/FM	158	123	125
AM/FM Stereo	236	184	186
Windshield Antenna (w/o radio only)	29	23	24
Rear Speaker.	25	20	21
Vinyl Bench Seat, Phoenix Coupe & Sedan	19	15	16
Notchback Seat, Phoenix Coupe & Sedan	120	94	95
Bucket Seats			
Phoenix Coupe, Sedan	195	152	154
Phoenix LJ	75	59	60
Power Steering.	163	127	129
Vinyl Top			
Full	99	77	78
Landau Padded, Coupes only.	190	148	150
Light Trailer Group (w/V-8 & Auto. Trans.)			
W/o Air Conditioning	72	56	57
W/Air Conditioning.	45	35	36
Power Windows			
2-Doors.	126	98	99
4-Doors.	178	139	141
Swing-Out Rear Quarter Window (NA Sedan).	56	44	45
Controlled Cycle Wipers	38	30	31

PONTIAC SUNBIRD

SUNBIRD

	Retail Price	Dealer Cost	Low Price
Coupe	$3781	$3291	$3491
Sport Coupe	3964	3450	3650
Sport Hatch	4064	3537	3787
Sport Safari Wagon.	4138	3601	3851

STANDARD EQUIPMENT (included in above prices)
Sunbird Coupe: Safety and protection equipment plus 2.5 litre (151 CID) 4-cyl. 2-bbl. engine, 4-speed manual transmission w/floor shifter, disc front brakes, A78-13
Prices are accurate at time of printing; subject to manufacturer's change.

whitewall bias ply tires, stowaway spare tire, AM radio, carpeting, vinyl bucket seats, custom wheel covers, tinted glass.

Sunbird Sport Coupe & Sport Hatch: Coupe equipment plus rocker panel, wheel opening and windowsill moldings, folding rear seat on hatchback, sport mirrors, custom interior trim.

Sunbird Sport Safari Wagon: Coupe equipment except stowaway spare tire, front & rear bumper guards, rocker panel & wheel opening molding, folding rear seat, sport mirrors, B78-13 whitewall bias ply tires.

SUNBIRD ACCESSORIES

	Retail Price	Dealer Cost	Low Price
Engines			
3.8 Litre (231 CID) V-6 2-bbl	$200	$166	$168
5.0 Litre (305 CID) V-8 2-bbl	395	328	332
Transmissions			
5-speed Manual (NA w/V-8 eng.)	175	145	147
Automatic	295	245	248
Air Conditioning	496	412	417
Heavy-Duty Alternator			
V-8 Eng. w/o Air Cond., 4&6-Cyl.			
Eng. Ex. w/Rear Defroster & Air Cond	32	27	28
Appearance Package, Coupes	91	76	77
Limited Slip Rear Axle	59	49	50
Heavy-Duty Battery	18	15	16
Power Brakes (Reg. Wagon w/air cond.)	71	59	60
Bumper Guards (std. Wagon)	42	35	36
Bumper Strips	37	31	32
Electric Clock	21	17	18
Console	77	64	65
Rear Window Deflector, Wagon	28	23	24
Rear Window Defroster	87	72	73
Calif. Emission System			
w/4-cyl. LS6 Eng.	150	125	127
All Other Engines	83	69	70
High Altitude Emission System	35	29	30
Engine Block Heater	14	12	13
Formula Package w/Aluminum Wheels			
Sport Coupe w/Stowaway Spare	557	462	467
Sport Coupe w/Conventional Spare	580	481	486
Sport Hatch w/Stowaway Spare	568	471	476
Sport Hatch w/Conventional Spare	591	491	496
Formula Package w/Rally Wheels			
Sport Coupe w/Stowaway Spare	415	344	348
Sport Coupe w/Conventional Spare	455	378	382
Sport Hatch w/Stowaway Spare	426	354	358
Sport Hatch w/Conventional Spare	466	387	391
Gages	87	72	73
Graphics Package, Sport Hatch	73	61	62
Rally RTS Handling Pkg-w/Blackwall Tires			
Coupes & Hatchback			

Prices are accurate at time of printing; subject to manufacturer's change.

	Retail Price	Dealer Cost	Low Price
w/Stowaway Spare w/o Formula Pkg.........	$125	$102	$104
w/Conventional Spare w/o Formula Pkg.	149	121	123
w/Formula Pkg.	3	3	3
Wagon	128	105	107
Rally RTS Handling Pkg w/Whitewall Tires			
Coupes & Hatchback			
w/Stowaway Spare w/o Formula Pkg.........	161	132	134
w/Conventional Spare w/o Formula Pkg.	194	159	161
w/Stowaway Spare & Formula Pkg.	38	30	31
w/Conventional Spare & Formula Pkg.	50	39	40
Wagon	173	142	144
Rally RTS Handling Pkg. w/White Letter Tires			
Coupes & Hatchback			
w/Stowaway Spare w/o Formula Pkg	174	143	145
w/Conventional Spare w/o Formula Pkg.	210	172	174
w/Stowaway Spare & Formula Pkg.	51	41	42
w/Conventional Spare & Formula Pkg.	66	52	53
Wagon	189	155	157
Additional Sound Insulation, Wagon...........	31	26	27
Lamp Group			
Coupes, Hatchback	4	3	4
Wagon	18	15	16
Roof Luggage Carrier, Wagon...............	65	54	55
Luxury Trim Group, Sport Cpe. & Hatch	190	158	160
Mirrors			
Day/Night (w/o Lux. Trim)	9	7	8
Sport, Left Remote, Right Manual, Coupe.....	40	33	34
Heavy-Duty Radiator (incl. w/air cond.).......	33	27	28
Heavy-Duty Radiator & Cooling System			
w/V-6 Eng. w/o Air Cond.	59	49	50
w/V-6 Eng. & Air Cond..................	26	22	23
Radio Equipment			
AM.................................	STD	STD	STD
AM/FM.............................	74	61	62
AM/FM Stereo........................	148	123	125
AM w/Stereo Tape.....................	157	130	132
AM/FM Stereo w/Stereo Tape..............	242	201	204
Rear Seat Speaker	23	19	20
Folding Rear Seat, Coupes	99	82	83
Rear Deck Spoiler (NA Wagon)..............	50	42	43
Power Steering.......................	146	121	123
Formula Steering Wheel (NA Wagon)			
w/o Luxury Trim Grp....................	43	36	37
w/Luxury Trim Grp.	24	20	21
Luxury Cushion (incl. w/Lux. Trim)...........	19	16	17
Tilt Steering Wheel.....................	68	56	57
Glass Sunroof........................	180	149	151
Landau Vinyl Top, Coupes.................	156	129	131
Controlled Cycle Wipers	35	29	30

Prices are accurate at time of printing; subject to manufacturer's change.

1979 Prices Imports

BMW 320i

2-Door Sedan $9735

DATSUN 210

2-Door Std. Sedan $3899
2-Door Dlxe. Sedan 4449
4-Door Dlxe. Sedan 4589
2-Door Hatchback 4809
5-Door Wagon 4949

DATSUN 280-ZX

2-Seater $9899
2 + 2 11599

DATSUN 810

4-Door Sedan $8129
2-Door Coupe 8279
5-Door Station Wagon 8529

DODGE COLT

2-Door Coupe $3984
4-Door Sedan 4490
Wagon 5591

DODGE COLT HATCHBACK

Base Model $4425
Custom Hatchback 4743
Prices are accurate at time of printing; subject to manufacturer's change.

FIAT BRAVA

2-Door Coupe	$5290
4-Door Sedan	5490
Station Wagon	5790

FORD FIESTA

3-Door Hatchback	$4198

HONDA ACCORD

CVCC

3-Door Sedan 5-Speed	$5799
3-Door Sedan Automatic	5949

LX CVCC

4-Door 5-Speed	6365
4-Door Automatic	6515
3-Door Sedan 5-Speed	6799

HONDA CIVIC CVCC

2-Door Sedan 4-Speed	$3999
2-Door Sedan 4-Speed (NY State)	4029
3-Door Hatchback 4-Speed	4499
3-Door Hatchback Automatic	4649
4-Door Wagon 4-Speed	4759
3-Door Hatchback 5-Speed	4849
4-Door Wagon Automatic	4909

MAZDA GLC

3-Door Hatchback	$3895
3-Door Hatchback Dlxe.	4195
5-Door Wagon	4295
5-Door Hatchback Dlxe.	4395
3-Door Hatchback Sport	4595
5-Door Wagon Dlxe.	4595

MAZDA RX-7

RX-7 S	$6995
RX-7 GS	7695

PLYMOUTH ARROW

2-Door Hatchback	$4647
Arrow GS	5005
Arrow GT	5696

Prices are accurate at time of printing; subject to manufacturer's change.

CONSUMER GUIDE

PLYMOUTH CHAMP

Hatchback $4425
Custom Hatchback 4743

RENAULT LE CAR

Base Model $3895
DIxe. Model 4445

SUBARU 4 X 4 WAGON

Base Model* $5429

TOYOTA CELICA

2-Door Coupe ST 5-Speed $5899
2-Door Coupe GT 5-Speed 6329
Coupe GT Liftback 5-Speed 6559

TOYOTA COROLLA

2-Door Sedan $3748
4-Door Sedan 4253
4-Door Sedan Custom 4533
2-Door Liftback 4928
4-Door Wagon DIxe. 4933
2-Door SR5 Sport Coupe 5248

VOLKSWAGEN BEETLE

Convertible. $6245

*This price is effective as of September 1, 1978.
Prices are accurate at time of printing; subject to manufacturer's change.

Honda Accord

Ford Fiesta

VOLKSWAGEN RABBIT

2-Door Hatchback..$4499
4-Door Hatchback, Custom...5039
2-Door Hatchback, Custom Automatic.................................5194
2-Door Hatchback, Custom Diesel....................................5199
4-Door Hatchback, Dlxe. Automatic..................................5784

VOLKSWAGEN DASHER

2-Door Hatchback..$6650
4-Door Hatchback..6810
2-Door Hatchback Diesel..6950
2-Door Hatchback Automatic...6975
4-Door Wagon...7080

VOLKSWAGEN SCIROCCO

Base Model...$6545
Automatic..6870

Prices are accurate at time of printing; subject to manufacturer's change.